Collecting ART NOUVEAU

Identification and Value Guide

by Don Fredgant

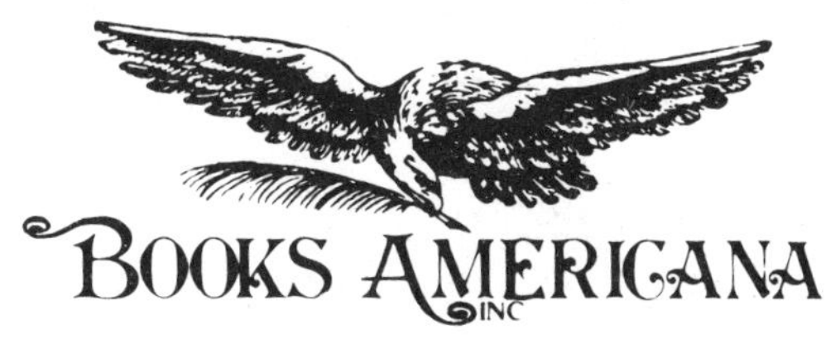

ISBN 0-89689-036-8

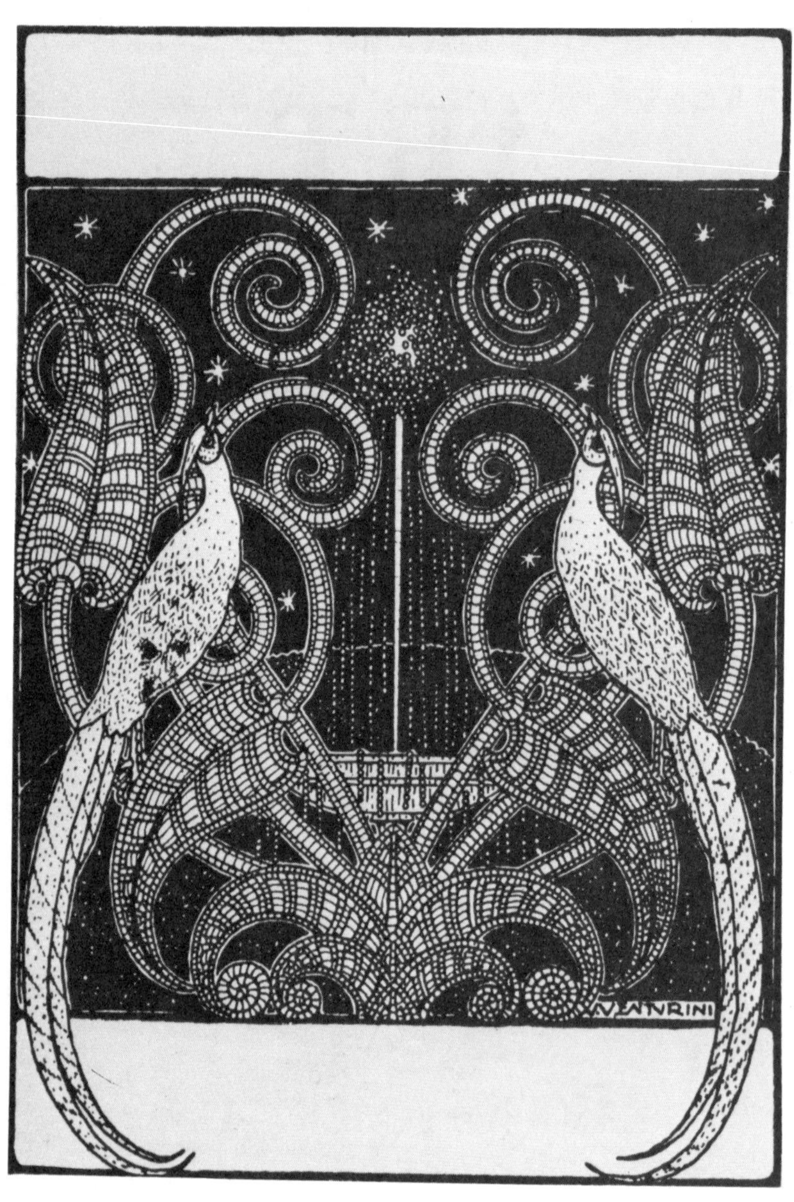

ACKNOWLEDGEMENTS

My thanks go out to the following people and businesses for their assistance in obtaining information and illustrations for this volume: Missy McHugh, of Christie's New York; Cintra Huber, of Phillips New York; Susan Finkelstein, of Morton's Auction Exchange, New Orleans; Chester I. Burnett, Russell, Ohio; Bill McKeown, Quincy, Florida; Phil Leilich, Gainesville, Florida; Joan Davey, of Butterfield's, San Francisco; Phyllis Jacobson, of L'Imagerie, Sherman Oaks, California; Ms. Sandy Verin, Icart Vendor Gallery, Los Angeles; A.T. Merber, Merber Enterprises, Ltd., Washington, D.C.; Maryon Allen, at the time with C.G. Sloan & Company, Washington, D.C., and now "back home" in Alabama; June Greenwald Antiques, Cleveland Heights, Ohio; and the fine Public Relations staff of Sotheby's New York.

Important roles were also played in different ways by others not directly involved in the antiques field: Marilyn Macartney, Lakewood, Ohio; Doris-Ann Matthey (who, disguised as my wife, fights a never-ending battle to pry me away from my typewriter and coffee cup); and publisher Dan Alexander, of Books Americana. My thanks also go to Dover Publications, Inc., of New York City, for permission to reproduce several illustrations from Carol Belanger Grafton's, *Treasury of Art Nouveau Design & Ornament* (New York: Dover Publications, 1980). Finally, my thanks go to Kathleen Kahn, Lakewood, Ohio, for reading the galleys and disagreeing with my interpretations.

TABLE OF CONTENTS

INTRODUCTION

There is no "Art Nouveau" style. Instead, there are a variety of related yet different styles which made up a large portion of the modern art of their day. The day could have been in the 1880s, or it could have been in the days of World War I. It may have been even earlier if we consider some of the mid-19th century precursors of the new art movement; isolated artisans continued crafting in recognizable Art Nouveau styles into the 1920s, and even after that.

The 1960s and 1970s saw a renaissance of one type of Art Nouveau design, the flowing, curvilinear sort associated with some of the French artists of the 1890s. In the secondary market place, Art Nouveau as a collectible field skyrocketed to unprecedented heights. For a while, every major Art Nouveau auction could be counted upon to set new pricing records and news releases from the big New York auction houses emphasized this price escalation.

Today prices are still high — too high, say some collectors (and dealers, too). A couple of auction houses have cautiously asserted that prices may be leveling off in some specialty areas, while at the same time pointing out that, in the competitive arena of the public auction, buyers should be prepared to spend more than ever to acquire the objects of their affections.

You may be talking about Art Nouveau when you mention the "Stile Liberty" in Italy, or the Secessionist style in Austria, or the early work of the Wiener Werkstatte in Germany, or the parallelism of the Glasgow School. You may call it by names such as "English style", or "Art Moderne", or any of several other names (and a few epithets). All remain facets of the Art Nouveau movement.

What I have attempted to do is bring together the many disparate elements and separate interpretations of the Art Nouveau movement into a unified whole. This is a pricing guide, but it is also (and perhaps more importantly) an identification guide. It is a book primarily for collectors and others who have Art Nouveau items they may wish to identify or evaluate.

When I originally conceived this book, I had grandiose hopes of including **every** type of Art Nouveau collectible, **every** type of Art Nouveau influence in **every** conceivable sphere — including such items as Art Nouveau treatments of automobiles, ships, architecture, and the like. From the standpoint of the collector, that would have meant an unwieldy book priced higher than many of the items in it. From the standpoint of the author, it would have meant more headaches than a warehouse full of aspirin could ever alleviate.

Thus, selectivity and subjectivity entered in. Architecture was ruled out almost immediately; unless one is extremely wealthy, one does not "collect" specimens of architecture in the same way one collects, say, ceramics or glassware.

Original paintings were also omitted. Art Nouveau was primarily practiced in the "decorative arts" rather than the "fine arts" (more about that later), and in very few instances can paintings truly be considered Art Nouveau. While many of the Symbolist and pre-Raphaelite painters influenced and participated in decorative arts design, their works of original, "easel art" are not properly considered as Art Nouveau.

Problems were encountered even among some of the more acceptable realms of Art Nouveau decoration. For instance, glass offered the Art Nouveau-inspired artisan a wonderful, colorful, plastic medium in which to forge his "new art". Glass items, especially the vases in French cameo glass, have proven popular with collectors, and many collectors and writers on the subject have chosen to include **all** French cameo glass production under the general heading of "Art Nouveau". In truth, many French cameo glass objects — vases, bowls, or whatever — are more representative of the Art Deco movement of the 20th century, and many others merely reflected historical stylistic tendencies from which artists and artisans tried to extricate themselves.

Even in the work of a single craftsman the problems seemed inherent. In the case of Rene Lalique, for one, we can see a noted practitioner of an accepted Art Nouveau type of design slowly transcend the restrictive nature of Art Nouveau to become a primary Art Deco designer. Not only did Lalique jump from Art Nouveau to Art Deco; he also traveled from his role of being France's premier Art Nouveau designer in jewelry to his new role as France's premier designer in glass. In between were many glass designs in the Art Nouveau modes with which he was most familiar. Not all of Lalique's glass was Art Nouveau, though, nor should it be treated that way.

The subjective judgments regarding which items should be included or excluded were based upon several factors. First, of course, was this writer's conception of Art Nouveau. Second was the information regarding items offered for sale either at auction or by dealers; in all too many cases it was necessary to exclude mention of an item which may have sold, due to the incomplete description the dealer provided. Third were a group of personal biases against overemphasis on certain "big name" designers; as examples, Rookwood Pottery pieces from the United States, and Galle glass from France, could each have been enlarged to several times their present listings if every sale price, every auction listing, every dealer listing for some of these wares had been included. I strove for representative listings in these cases, not all-inclusive listings.

Prices were obtained in a variety of ways, divisible into dealer and auction prices. Dealer prices were obtained from in-person inspection of items offered for sale at shows and in shops. Other dealer prices were derived from dealers who were asked to cooperate by providing descriptions and prices of Art Nouveau items. Still other dealer prices came from collector periodicals, in which dealers advertised the items they had for sale.

Dealer prices present problems, though. In only a couple of cases were dealers willing to provide the ACTUAL SELLING PRICE of items, providing instead their asking prices — and as both collectors and dealers know, there can be great gaps between prices sought and prices brought. The fact that a dealer offers a piece at a given price certainly doesn't mean that the item will actually sell for that price. Yet, when observers view a range of prices for similar objects, they can usually spot the prices which are out-of-line. Most dealer prices listed here should be accepted for what they are: asking prices for merchandise which may be sold later at a lower price.

Auction prices don't have the same element of suspense and mystery about them that some dealer prices have. These are prices actually paid in a (supposedly) free, open marketplace, with knowledgeable bidders competing with one another for given pieces of merchandise. In the cases of items which were auctioned by one of the larger houses which impose a 10% buyer's premium on merchandise purchased through them, that fact is noted by an asterisk (*) preceding the price. (In such a case, if the hammer price for an item was $100, the buyer would actually have to pay $110 to the auction house.)

An interesting paradox presents itself regarding auction prices. Most of the auction action in the Art Nouveau market has taken place at the "Big 3" houses in New York City — Sotheby Parke Bernet, Christie's, and Phillips. On the other hand, New York is not representative of the nation as a whole when pricing; a dealer in Keokuk, Iowa probably won't be able to obtain the same price from local trade in Art Nouveau that a major auction house will (sorry, Keokuk). As a result, I made a conscious effort to obtain prices from other auctioneers as well as those in New York. The houses I chose to work with — Sloan's in Washington, D.C., Morton's in New Orleans and Butterfield's in San Francisco — unfortunately do not hold specialty auctions for Art Nouveau items as the New York houses do. All do have Art Nouveau pieces among their general auction lots.

Readers will note that no estimations of value are given in this book. All prices shown are either auction prices or dealer prices from a specific time period, November 1, 1980 through October 31, 1981. Due to time lags which are inevitable in publishing, this is about as up-to-date as a price guide in book form can get. Since all prices are those for items actually offered or actually sold during only this particular time period, some types of items which are familiar to Art Nouveau enthusiasts may not be represented. If they are sold during the time period used for any future edition, I will try to include them.

And now, for the obligatory disclaimer about price guides. It's become **de rigueur** to include in price guides a statement about a price guide being only a **guide** and not the final word on pricing; about the true guide being what an actual piece, in a specific condition and at a certain place and at a particular time, will bring in the constantly-changing marketplace; about the author and the publisher not being responsible for typographical errors; and about the listings in the guide not being construed as an offer to buy or sell at the prices shown.

Very well. Consider all those statements as made. However, I have enough confidence in my sources and my own work to state unequivocally that the prices listed here are representative of the state of the market for these items at the time the book was compiled.

Both my publisher, Dan Alexander, and I feel you are holding the first edition of a book which will be revised and re-released when necessary. Your comments, hints, suggestions, compliments (**especially** compliments), disparaging remarks, and corrections are eagerly sought. Yes, I'll be happy to answer (even the disparaging remarks) if only you'll provide a self-addressed stamped envelope.

Good luck in collecting or investing.

Don Fredgant
17905 Nottingham Rd.
Cleveland, OH 44119

ART NOUVEAU: ITS PRECURSORS AND INFLUENCES

Art Nouveau was the modern art of its day. "New art" — that's what the French called it, especially after the reorganization of Mr. S. Bing's now-famous Paris shop on the rue de Provence in 1895. The new name was "L'Art Nouveau", specializing in fine works of decorative art from around the world.

The "new art" movement neither started in France nor ended there. It spread throughout Western Europe, hopping the Atlantic rather late in its life to influence design in this country. Like a plant, its tendrils stretched out to influence design in Latin America, Japan, and Russia. Though the movement itself long ago ceased being either cohesive or even very relevant, it is still influential in modern design.

No art movement can create itself from whole cloth; no artists, no matter how much they try, can completely divorce themselves from art's history. Such was the case with the many artists and craftsmen working under what is generically called "Art Nouveau" today. Many factors, many influences, worked on the decorative artists; they in turn melted these disparate elements together, creating a different way of viewing their own art and the realm of decoration.

ACADEMIC ART

The accepted artistic styles of the mid-19th century stressed several factors, especially when applied to the decorative arts. Abstract design and personally expressive art were scorned in favor of realism and naturalistic motifs; allegorical works were standard production of both the academic artists and the commercial factories making decorative art. Symmetrical design was required, both in the decoration of individual elements of a piece as well as in the piece as a whole.

In decorative art, extreme reliance upon classical shapes and classical motifs was the norm. Most importantly, though, there was a perceived difference between "fine art" — painting and sculpture, activities seen as creating works of beauty which had inherent worth — and "decorative art" — all other types of artistic creation, seen in a secondary and even subservient role to fine art whch served only to provide extraneous ornament.

WILLIAM BLAKE

The English poet and engraver/designer whom Charles Lamb called "one of the most extraordinary persons of the age" died a full half-century before Art Nouveau is considered to have started, but his influence was revived after his death. His graphic work was admired by many of the early leaders in the English Arts and Crafts Movement of the late 1800s, and it may be considered as an authentic influence upon the works of Dante Gabriel Rosetti, Arthur Mackmurdo, and others. Blake's mysticism, while not necessarily an influence on other artists, is a recurring theme in the lives of artists from different countries, most notably that of Alphons Mucha. Blake's use of flowing, undulating lines in his book illustrations would be repeated by many other graphic artists into the 20th century.

GOTHIC REVIVAL

One of the many architectural and furniture design trends which helped occupy the 19th century was the Gothic Revival. It was a period of renewed interest in the design elements of the Middle Ages; the revival actually started in the middle of the 18th century and continued, with varying degrees of emphasis, until the late 19th century. It had been during the late Gothic period originally that the double ogee curve, flame-like decorative devices, and ornament reminiscent of flora became prevalent; these curvilinear devices would be adopted by the Art Nouveau artists in the late 19th century.

NEO-ROCOCO ELEMENTS

The Rococo period in art history was predominantly one of the 18th century. It was marked by light, gay ornamentation which stressed pierced shellwork and curved, fancy design elements. Excessively intricate designs, often featured naturalistic floral forms and open, realistic flowers. This was a period of light (as opposed to heavy) design, utilizing nature's full range of colors.

The Rococo style was reborn twice in the 19th century, once in the middle of that century and again in the last quarter. This Neo-Rococo style shared the general attributes of its 18th century predecessor, including greater asymmetrical ornamentation. When found in Neo-Rococo styles, asymmetry remained only as a decorative device, not extending to the general form of the object decorated in this style. Art Nouveau designers would take that asymmetry and extend it to include both form and ornament.

ORIENTALISM

Nineteenth century artists turned increasingly to the lands of the East — both Far East and Middle East — for inspirations. Designs suggestive of Islamic minarets are found in graphic art and commercial container design, as well as in ceramic decoration. Indonesian batik-printed fabrics were brought back to Europe by Dutch traders and colonialists in Java, and the designs they contained were spread over part of Europe to influence other artists.

Most important to the development of Art Nouveau, though, was the introduction of Japanese graphic art. It's instrumental to remember that some of the most influential names in what was to become Art Nouveau — Louis Comfort Tiffany, James MacNeill Whistler, Aubrey Beardsley, Henri de Toulouse-Lautrec, Arthur Liberty — shared an affection for and collecting interest in Japanese art. The trend toward Japonism became fashionable in the late 1800s. Indeed, the Paris shop which would give its name (L'Art Nouveau) to a movement started as a dealer in and importer of Oriental art. Even after expanding its scope the shop retained its stock of Japanese art.

Japanese art avoided the illusional strivings to create a three-dimensional appearance which characterized Western art. The Japanese instead stayed within the constraints of the two-dimensional flat plane effect, utilizing color, linear divisions, spatial contrasts, flat unadorned backgrounds, and asymmetrical composition.

The painter Whistler was probably the chief catalyst in the acceptance of Japanese art in England and, in turn, in other parts of Western Europe. Whistler was a collector (his blue-and-white stoneware from Japan appears in some of his paintings) and appropriated elements of design which, while acceptable by today's standards, were unusual in the second half of the 19th century. European traditional art almost insisted upon a complex, busy background even for portraiture, pulling the viewer's eyes away from the central focus of the work; the Japanese, and Whistler in their footsteps, tended toward uncluttered bare backgrounds.

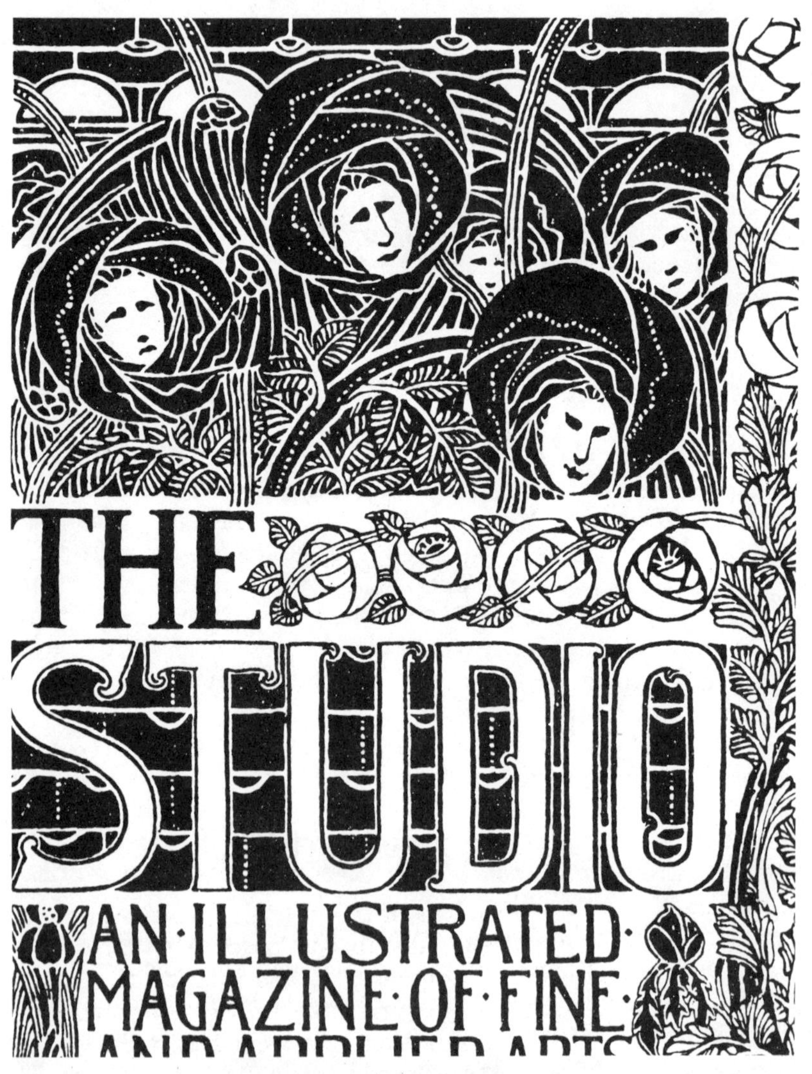

(Carol Belanger Grafton, **Treasury of Art Nouveau Design & Ornament,** used by permission of Dover Publications, Inc.)

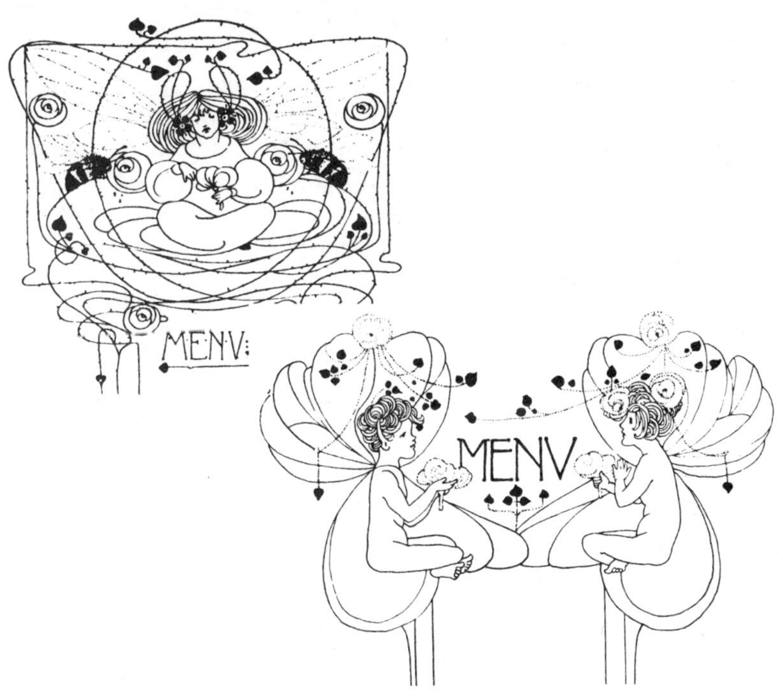

(Carol Belanger Grafton, **Treasury of Art Nouveau Design & Ornament,** used by permission of Dover Publications, Inc.)

CELTIC INFLUENCES

One of the minor influences in the new art was the historic precedent of the Celts, especially in Scotland. Flat-appearing Celtic manuscripts inspired graphic art of the Glasgow School at the turn of the century and, in turn, inspired those who turned to the Glasgow School for inspiration. Most obvious of the Celtic influences was their use of interlaced linearity and spirals springing from coils, adapted by Art Nouveau designers into jewelry, metalwork and graphics.

WILLIAM MORRIS AND THE ARTS AND CRAFTS MOVEMENT

The English essayist, political philosopher, poet, and art critic John Ruskin had great significance for his followers, including William Blake. Beginning with his book on modern painters, the first volume of which was published in 1843, Ruskin set up and knocked down many of the accepted names in painting, like so many straw men placed before him. They had strayed, he felt, from truth and honesty in art; true art was, by definition, honest art, and honesty was insured through an adherence (one might even say a rigid adherence) to nature as the sole source of inspiration.

Among those to carry the Ruskin banner was William Morris, the English poet, painter, multi-talented craftsman, and pamphleteer for Socialist and other causes. To Morris goes great credit for the creation of what has been known as the Arts and Crafts Movement in England, both a forerunner and a contemporary of Art Nouveau. To Morris and others who adopted Ruskin's aims of truth in art, the Gothic age revealed itself as one which was worthy of emulation by creative individuals. Artists in the Middle Ages took pleasure in their work, as all craftsmen should, and they did this in communal organization. Such was to be the model of the various "workshops" which sprang up in England, and the "ateliers" which would flourish in France.

Morris abhored the artificiality of the division between "fine arts" and "decorative arts". To Morris, the talents of creative individuals should be applied to all types of decorations, making decorations works of art. As Walter Crane would say later, the aim of Morris' movement was "turning our artists into craftsmen and our craftsmen into artists". This was to be one of the greatest characteristics of the Art Nouveau movement, too: painters who would become glassmakers, ceramicists who would also work in metal, glassmakers who would design books and furniture and even buildings, all forsaking the older conventions of staying within their established crafts. The synthesis of the arts and artists, while conceived as a theoretical and social issue, had practical consequences in the art world that are still felt.

THE PRE-RAPHAELITES

The Pre-Raphaelites, a late 19th century group of painters, should really be termed the "Neo-Pre-Raphaelites". After all, Raphael, the Italian master, had been active two-and-one-half centuries earlier, so they could scarcely have **preceded** him. Yet they shared with the original Pre-Raphaelites the inspiration of nature and the desire to depict it in truth — although some critics said they did so vulgarly.

A leader in the Pre-Raphaelite Brotherhood, Dante Gabriel Rosetti, was both an admirer of William Blake and an apostle of John Ruskin; Ruskin, in turn, seconded every new work issued by the Pre-Raphaelites, turning his art criticism into a sort of mutual admiration society. From Ruskin, Rosetti took the realm of nature as a subject for his art, finding a rhythmic grace which he transmitted to his graphic designs, if not to his paintings. The Pre-Raphaelites placed increasing emphasis upon the strength of the line, the floral form, and other devices which recurred in Art Nouveau decoration.

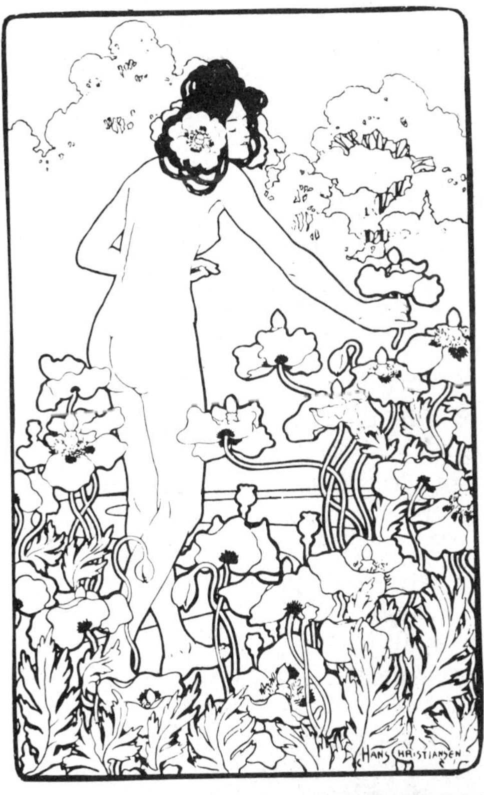

(Carol Belanger Grafton, **Treasury of Art Nouveau Design & Ornament**, used by permission of Dover Publications, Inc.)

SYMBOLISM

Art has gone through many different viewpoints regarding truth versus beauty. Is it more important to be truthful in art, or should the artist create a work of beauty regardless of the distortions of reality it may contain? The best of all possible art worlds, incorporating both views, would be that, through selectivity of subject, it would be possible to create that which is both honest (transmitting the reality of the subject) as well as beautiful. Then, of course, there is always the view of Keats, that "Beauty is truth, truth beauty" — but that's another matter.

In some ways attempts at symbolic meaning in art could be seen as reconciliation between the two divergent opinions on beauty and truth. For the Symbolists, realistic representations were to be avoided. Instead, suggestions of greater meaning were suggested through both form and lines. It was an adaptation of similar trends in both poetry and prose, one which the Art Nouveau adherents would clutch to their bosoms. One of the most common Art Nouveau applications of Symbolism was in the selection of floral subjects; while the neo-rococo stylists invariably concentrated on flowers in full bloom, the Art Nouveau designers made greater use of the bud or the partially opened bloom, with all the promise that each held.

ANTI-ESTABLISHMENT TENDENCIES

There are artists in each new generation who reject the established norms and try to blaze new paths for themselves and others. In the late 19th century the anti-establishment feelings

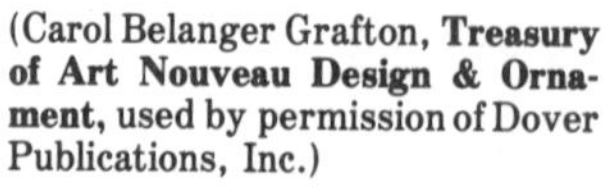

(Carol Belanger Grafton, **Treasury of Art Nouveau Design & Ornament,** used by permission of Dover Publications, Inc.)

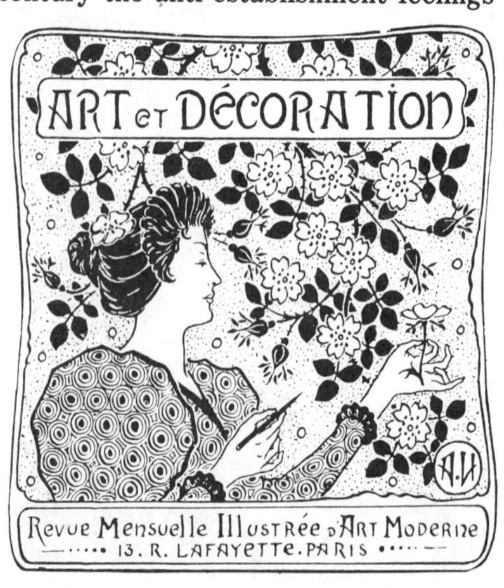

took precedence, eventually manifesting themselves in many ways. The retreat to workshops by the Arts and Crafts artisans was a rejection of the isolated work done by the individual craftsmen. Searching for new forms, including the adaptation of Oriental shapes, was a purposeful rejection of the old and established classical forms. Adventurous research into glazes and glassmaking produced new surface textures — and after all, this was the "new" art. In fact, the new and different, the unusual, the exotic — all were elevated to positions of importance, especially when compared with the classical and academic.

NEO-BAROQUE TENDENCIES

One of the many revivals of previous art eras in the late Victorian years was the resurgence of the baroque period that had been prevalent in the 17th century. Sometimes called elaborate, sometimes called grotesque, it was a period that made use of curved and arched structural members, as well as the principle of "dynamic opposition". Continental practitioners of Art Nouveau occasionally turned to the baroque revival to borrow both ornamental and structural details. Some artists also picked up the baroque mysticism and used it through imaginative use of imagery.

PUTTING IT TOGETHER INTO ART NOUVEAU

Obviously, all these influences were not combined by a single artist into a single piece. Each artist took from his or her past knowledge that which was most useful in achieving the sought-after end. In the chapter on "National Styles and Tendencies" the issue of which influences were used, and where, will be explored more. Suffice it to say now that Art Nouveau was an attempt to formulate a "new art" that was a reaction against and a rejection of historicism in art; to that extent, it was doomed to failure, for it kept reaching into its past for inspirations. To the extent that Art Nouveau combined new outlooks with different combinations of materials, emphasizing the beauty in semi-precious stones, for example, rather than merely precious stones, it carved a path which should be remembered.

NATIONAL STYLES AND TENDENCIES

As the Art Nouveau movement grew in the 1880s, 1890s, and very early 1900s, it grew like an untended plant, sending off tendrils for support in various directions. To a certain extent the new growth anchored itself in various styles according to the nation where it was practiced, as well as the influences that area felt from outside its own geographic sphere.

Some of the Art Nouveau-decorated objects assumed what can now be considered almost a nationalistic character, incorporating the artistic traditions of a particular area or nation. These differences now serve as one means of identification for the sources of some Art Nouveau-inspired decorative art.

A couple of points must be made regarding these national styles. First, in many instances, they were only **tendencies** and not true **styles.** It's possible to note similarities from a given geopolitical area and conclude that these points are representative of a style endemic to that area. However, it must be remembered that **innovation** played a major role in the developing Art Nouveau and, by definition, innovation meant a break with the established norms — even the norms of the new art.

Second, the United States and its Art Nouveau-inspired works present a special problem. In no other major nation which was influenced by Art Nouveau was this new art practiced without a national tradition on which to fall back and incorporate in its art. (More precisely, Americans had not yet incorporated Native American art designs, which would have been truly nationalistic if they had been used.) Inspiration for American artists came from the same areas which had influenced so much of American art: France and England, especially the former. That didn't prevent the United States from developing its own Arts and Crafts Movement, nor did it prevent occasional innovation on the part of American craftsmen.

THE BRITISH ISLES

As has been mentioned earlier, it was from the English that much of the original inspiration for the Art Nouveau movement sprang. Theoreticians like William Blake and John Ruskin helped build a foundation for the new art. Practitioners began early to assimilate some of the theoretical concepts, although most writers have been hesitant (if not downright opposed) to admit these early workers and their products as Art Nouveau. They have been called "Proto-Art Nouveau," indicating that there is some sort of ancestral link between them and the Art Nouveau which was to follow.

As early in the 1860s and 1870s, textiles were being produced in England which incorporated features later found in Art Nouveau: rhythmic, flowing lines, abstract floral designs, and a flat plane effect. Workers such as Edward Burne-Jones designed in this manner and their designs held a certain fascination, although it must be admitted that they were usually symmetrical in their compositions. However, we can see recurrent patterns in which foreground merges with background, the arrangement melds with that which is arranged.

The Arts and Crafts Movement in England served both as a stimulus and an inhibitor to Art Nouveau at various times. (One leader in the Arts and Crafts group, who is credited with some of the earliest British uses of "true" Art Nouveau, would later repudiate the entire Art Nouveau movement.) The renewed interest in graphic arts led to elaborate, artistic book bindings and illustrations. Surprisingly, poster art, also a graphic art, never achieved the same levels of popularity as on the Continent.

English linearity was manifested in a typically reserved British fashion. Little of the extreme "whiplash" lines found in some Continental Art Nouveau was seen in the British Isles (with some notable exceptions), especially after the 1880s. Instead, an increasing trend toward rectilinear (as opposed to curvilinear) shapes was seen. This became particularly prominent in the Glasgow School.

The entire reserved, conservative British atmosphere is visible both in conception and in execution. Much more than the French, for instance, the English emphasized elongated stem and unopened or partially opened flower buds, rather than the fully bloomed flower. The positive value of white space was realized, and in general, surface decorations were relegated to less-important roles than in much of the Continental Art Nouveau production.

The Celtic influence was incorporated, particularly in Scotland. **Entrelac** decoration was utilized in such diverse areas as graphics, jewelry, ironwork, furniture (rarely), and silver and other metal wares.

Yet the primary contribution of the British was in the area of theory. Visiting Continental artists who were exposed to the British techniques and philosophies often took them back to their own countries where they were incorporated (with national changes). Most Western European nations which produced Art Nouveau-inspired works can point to some degree to Britain as a link. So true is this in Italy, in fact, that the firm of Liberty and Company, a London-based firm with Continental outlets, gave its name to the Italian version of Art Nouveau: Stile Liberty.

FRANCE

French decorative art in the late 1800s became almost synonymous with Art Nouveau, especially as it became commercialized. Two separate centers developed in France, one at Paris, the other at Nancy, each with stylistic patterns of its own. In each case an uphill fight was involved to overcome the artistic past.

France as a nation had been a pacesetter in the arts for quite a while. The predominant decorative style of the late 1800s was neo-rococo. This style, emphasizing curvilinear designs, asymmetrical placement of ornament, and a general ostentatious quality, served both as a pathway into as well as an obstacle to French Art Nouveau development.

French Art Nouveau is intimately bound up with neo-rococo design. In both cases floral designs were used extensively; the Art Nouveau practitioners added another dimension by introducing and emphasizing numerous winged insects. Scrollwork, pierced rims on metalwork, and other neo-rococo tendencies continued.

The Nancy designers in the Art Nouveau modes, like their English counterparts, turned partially to the Neo-Gothic styles which had been popular earlier in the century. Combined with the highly detailed rococo penchant for extremism in detail and ornamentation, the Gothic-inspired pieces took on some rather unusual qualities. In some instances, for example, one might find turreted cornices on a piece of furniture overlooking a panel with floral decoration done in detail.

The Oriental influence can't be overlooked in France. Both Nancy designers (indirectly, for the most part) and Paris designers (directly) felt the flat planar effects of Japan's graphics. Decorative wares in glass (some of Galle's) and ceramics (Delacherche, for example, or Chaplet) were adaptations of Japanese forms or designs or both.

It can be successfully argued, perhaps, that French Art Nouveau practitioners never really accomplished what they set out to do, that is, to develop a "new art" form without reference to the artistic past. Maybe the artistic heritage of France was such that it could never hope to be surmounted in a single artistic generation. Some things which had made 19th century French art what it was definitely continued in Art Nouveau: the fundamental assymmetrical decoration of everything from furniture to posters; the use of curving lines adapted from nature; the inspiration of nature as the primary source for design elements; the use of gilding in ornamentation, which was so popular in the neo-rococo tradition and which was continued in Art Nouveau.

Yet the French versions of Art Nouveau were successful, both in theory and in practice. It was the French Art Nouveau designers who gave the world some of the finest of graphic art in posters. French glass craftsmen appropriated some English glassmaking techniques in developing sophisticated (and eventually, highly commercialized) versions of overlay glasses. French ceramicists played with the effects of mineral glazes in producing iridescent finishes, giving a characteristic appearance to their products which was eventually carried to England and America.

HOLLAND

Dutch Art Nouveau, like the French version, was indebted to the English in many respects. Under the unofficial leadership of Gerrit Disselhof and Theodore Nieuwenhuis, both of whom were influenced by the English Arts & Crafts Movement, Art Nouveau in Holland broke away from both English tradition and Continental practice to form a distinctive blend all its own.

The national emphasis on Art Nouveau was at first an attempt to reinterpret the Western European experience of the Middle Ages through reintroduction of Gothic design elements. By the turn of the century the emphasis had shifted to nature, but in an unusual way. English nature-inspired works centered around the flower and plant, French works introduced such naturally-derived elements as the butterfly, dragonfly, and various insects; Dutch Art Nouveau emphasized the curvilinearity inherent in various animals (the whiplashed snakes and jellyfish, for instance) and almost ignored flower forms.

Dutch Art Nouveau, observed quickly, will usually look highly symmetrical. A studied glance at the details will reveal asymmetry there. Like some British works, the Dutch were also fond of repeated designs featuring a single element across an entire work, or across one part of it.

The distinctive Orientalism indigenous to Holland's Art Nouveau came from the Javanese-derived batik designs, brought back from ocean voyages by Dutch adventurers and sailors. These were incorporated especially into Dutch ceramics designs as well as into wallpapers and fabrics.

GERMANY

German Art Nouveau developed into a strange hybrid known as the "Jugendstil", after the German magazine *Jugend.* Where other national tendencies favored curvilinearity and shunned right angles in design, German (and related) designers used arched struts, rectilinear planar surfaces, and embraced right angles in their designs, especially in furniture design. Ornamentation of glassware remained primarily on the surface, rather than being placed within the object; the same was true with German furniture design, its ornament being a part of its overall structure rather than something to be added on extra.

Germany also had its floral stylists, those designers following the lead of Otto Eckmann first at Munich, later as an instructor in Berlin. It was from these two cities that most of the German floral styles emanated; Darmstadt, another German art center, shared more in common with the Viennese Secessionists. But floral motifs, when used, centered on the flower itself, rather than being concerned with vines or stems or leafage. Such floral uses were accompanied by curving lines having a peculiar thickening within the curves.

Much of the German work involved abstractions of nature. Like both the English and Dutch, Jugendstilists often repeated motifs, adapting a scrolled entrelac form to much of their work.

German theoreticians worked both within the universities and craft schools, and through major publications such as *Jugend* and *Pan.* Their influence eventually spread across the Atlantic although a time lag of a decade or so would be necessary for Americans to begin to see the effects of what they were doing. Their furniture was generally unsuccessful within the Art Nouveau styles, being ponderous and bulky and unsuited to most of the design techniques being attempted.

AUSTRIA

Austrian Art Nouveau was centered at Vienna. Its history is the tale of revolution after revolution in attempts to arrive at truly innovative art. In the end, like all the Art Nouveau movements, it failed in what it set out to do, but it accomplished much more in its influences.

The Secessionist styles from Vienna and elsewhere in Austria can be considered the bastard children of the Art Nouveau movements. While Art Nouveau designers across Europe were enthralled with the flowering plant (either in its entirety or in part), Secessionists substituted geometric patterns for floral forms in most cases. When a floral form was used, it was often a rather unusual, highly distinctive one: a tree might have clusters of circles looking somewhat like large apples, much out of scale to the rest of the tree, for instance. The symbolic bud was preferred to any developed portion of a flower.

Most distinctive of the Secessionist patterns was the flame-filled circle, a device which shared similarities with Scottish elements used by Mackmurdo. It was often used alone or in combination with repeated squares; indeed, the checkerboard pattern on much metalwork is sufficient to warrant an attribution to Austria upon cursory examination.

That the Secessionist theories and designs served as one of many influences upon the later Art Deco movement seems obvious. Less obvious, though, are the lines of demarcation between Art Deco and Art Nouveau. Here one can truly be at a loss in describing a piece, which may either be "late Art Nouveau", or "early Art Deco", or both.

AMERICA

It would be easiest to claim that America had no Art Nouveau style, no tendencies all her own. To a certain extent, that would be correct, but it would ignore some of the common trends in Art Nouveau decoration. It is true, though, that America developed no tendency or style which went on to influence any other nation's work.

American Arts and Crafts were derivative of English Arts and Crafts; American ceramics were the heritage of Anglo-Germanic potters, with some new ideas brought in by the French; American glass techniques, especially those pioneered by Tiffany, were copied from earlier efforts in Continental Europe.

What, then, was original? The ways various elements were used. In glassware, for example, Tiffany used leaded stained glass in much the same way it had been used historically in Europe, but he turned the production of his many-colored marvels into a commercially successful endeavor. Other makers of glassware, particularly iridescent glass makers such as Steuben and Durand, brought with them their knowledge of glassmaking from Europe and settled into making commercial copies of the work previously done. Surface decoration in the way of opalescent or iridescent finishes were added to what would otherwise be very ordinary shapes of bowls, vases, sherbet dishes, plates and such.

America's physical and cultural distances from Europe helped delay the arrival of Art Nouveau in a commercial way until it was already on its decline in Europe. As a result, American makers were still manufacturing in styles that were outdated by a decade or more according to European artistic standards. It mattered little, for the manufacturers found buyers. It's doubtful that many ever understood the principles behind the Art Nouveau work they were imitating. Only in the Arts and Crafts movement in the United States, and in the work of a select minority of manufacturers — including Louis Tiffany, of course — can we be sure that their works stemmed from a desire to influence the tastes and artistic traditions of their people.

COLLECTING ART NOUVEAU

There are probably as many different ways to go about collecting Art Nouveau, and about as many reasons, as there are collectors. I will pass no value judgments upon any collector's motivations, for I've had several different motivations in collecting different items. It is possible, though, to note some general things about collecting in general and then apply them to Art Nouveau.

First, experienced dealers and collectors are usually in agreement about one thing: a person should collect what they like and avoid what they don't like. In Art Nouveau, the matter is simple. Those who enjoy Art Nouveau jewelry should collect it, leaving Art Nouveau posters to the poster afficionados. Those who like French cameo glass should collect it and leave the bronze Tiffany desk sets to those who find them appealing. And those who don't like Art Nouveau at all — if such people really exist — shouldn't collect it!

Second, the profit motive is perfectly honorable in building a collection. (After all, one would have to be rather foolish to amass a collection while expecting it to **decrease** in value.) Yet profiting by buying at retail and having to sell at wholesale is extremely difficult to do in any field, and antiques (including Art Nouveau) are no exception. Short-term gains are practically impossible when buying and selling this way, at least on any large scale. The word coming from several major auction houses seems contradictory. Some report a "softening" of demand and prices for much of the better-quality Art Nouveau pieces in mid-to-late 1981; at the same time, at least one house simultaneously claims buyers are still paying record prices. One definite thing we can conclude, though, is that nobody can now get in on the "ground floor" of the Art Nouveau market, so any investment in it better have some built-in personal satisfaction for the buyer; it seems it will be more and more difficult to "buy low and sell high".

Third, the collector who takes the time and effort to educate himself will be in a far better situation when it comes to making buying decisions than the collector who can't be bothered amassing background information. In the Art Nouveau field, collectors can still make exciting discoveries about the origins of their collections, about the firms which made the collectible objects, about the people who were influential in shaping the "new art" movements in Europe and America. In the glass field, for instance, are you willing to accept Julies Traub's thesis, that much of the early glass carrying Galle signatures was actually produced under the direction of Desire Christian at Burgun, Schverer & Company? Only with some background knowledge and a knowledge of the glass involved can you make a reasoned decision.

Fourth, be aware of the old maxim in the antiques market, that "The best quality anything will always continue to rise in value". Be aware, but don't be misled. As a general principle, it probably has a great deal of validity. When one begins to apply it to particular instances and particular objects, surprises may pop up. Part of the problem lies in the definition of "the best." (Too often, uaction houses tend to equate "best" with "most expensive," a tenuous decision at best.) Another part of the problem lies with existing market conditions. Auctioneers freely admitted (in 1980 and 1981) that they had witnessed a "softening" of demand, particularly in what they referred to as the "middle ranges" of prices. Depending upon which house was involved, this may have meant in the $500 to $5,000 range, or in the $5,000 to $20,000 range. In any case, it was neither the top end nor the bottom end of the auction market for the particular auction house. Yet much of the "best" of Art Nouveau regularly falls within these varied ranges; should we buy, thinking that the "best" will always increase in value, or should we hold off, realizing that buyers within this price range are becoming reluctant (if not unable) to part with the necessary funds to make purchases? And if the latter is the case, how long will it last? Such is part of the gamble of investing in antiques. Of course, to the collector interested only in acquiring for personal pleasure, the questions are much less immediate, although they are still valid. There are plenty of objects which have ceased to appreciate in value, but such cessation may be only temporary. Others have actually dropped a bit in price over the last couple of years; fortunately, these are few in number, and how long **that** trend will continue is again conjectural.

Fifth, remember that your collection becomes just as much your signature as a handwritten signature. The collector who accumulates from a particular style or period, of different though similar objects, is recognizable from perusal of that collection. The collector whose collection "tells a story" by showing developmental changes or variations between works of a particular district, nation, or two or more artists, is also recognizable by the signature of the collection. The collection continually in a state of flux due to upgrading processes serves as its own type of signature. Fortunately, it's much easier to change your collecting signature than your handwritten one!

WHERE AND WHEN

Become an Art Nouveau collector and you'll begin spotting Art Nouveau pieces in the most unexpected places. One collector remembers a dining room in France (where she grew up) which was filled with old furniture. She never appreciated it until years later, when she began collecting the same type for her American home — and she only wishes she could have access to her family's furniture, now sold, once again.

Not that every Art Nouveau piece you encounter will be to your taste or fit in with your personal collection. Unless you are an accumulator, it won't. Art Nouveau was the first international artistic/craftsmanship movement to fully enjoy the benefits of mass-production, though, and very few objects now collected are truly "one of a kind." They were often created in huge quantities. (How many now survive is another issue, one which is really more relevant in determining the available "supply" which collectors "demand.")

Due to the age of most Art Nouveau pieces, most non-collectors will recognize that they should have a premium attached to them at, say, a garage sale or flea market solely by virtue of their supposed "antiquity". Non-collectors may not be able to recognize the cryptic signatures on various pieces, the patterns which are in particular demand, the often little-known makers whose products now bring high prices. Come across one of the "better" pieces under such circumstances and you'll likely pick it up for a pittance!

But you're unlikely to come across better pieces quite so easily. For them, you will be forced to turn to three major sources: dealers, auction houses, or other collectors seeking to sell directly to raise money (perhaps to buy something with which to upgrade his or her collection). Each of these sources has its advantages and disadvantages.

DEALERS come in every conceivable size (both personal girth and shop size, as well as sales volume), shape, color, location, and degree of specialization. Antiques generalists carry a little of everything, recognizing that they are appealing to a wide audience with vastly different tastes. Some of what they carry are likely to be in the Art Nouveau styles. Generalist dealers may not be quite "up" on prices for what they are carrying, and some may not even recognize the objects for precisely what they are. In such cases, it's often possible to buy from them at excellent, low prices. (Of course, the dealer who is not "up" on prices may have overpaid originally and be asking too high a price.) The specialist in Art Nouveau, on the other hand, will offer an extensive selection, something like a treasure trove to the searching collector. Being a specialist, this dealer will generally be very aware of current values, making spectacular bargains hard to obtain. However, another benefit of this specialization is that the Art Nouveau specialist will have a broad knowledge base and should make fewer mistakes in attribution and identification than the dealer forced by circumstances to know a little about everything. Even the specialist, though, will usually specialize in only one or two areas of Art Nouveau, so occasional bargains are still possible. (For a listing of just some of the dealers in Art Nouveau across the nation, see the next chapter.)

AUCTIONEERS are nearly as varied as dealers are, and the auction house has been in the process of becoming a greater and greater factor in the antiques marketplace for the past decade or so. There are very few specialist auctioneers — those concentrating on auctioning only a particular type of antiques merchandise — although there are some very interesting specialized auctions. Phillips, Christie's, and Sotheby's (all in New York) hold several such Art Nouveau auctions each year (often teaming that category with Art Deco) and release excellent, scholarly catalogues of the sales. The high quality of their catalogues, and the thorough descriptions of the lots to be sold, make it easy for bidders far removed from the sites of the auctions to participate by mail bidding. Can a bidder come away from such auctions with any true bargains? That question will be answered differently depending upon whom you speak to about it. Major dealers regularly buy from such auctions, later marking their merchandise up for retail sale, so the cautious bidder **can** often buy below current retail prices. On the other hand, it's all too easy to get caught up in bidding and pay too much. Any prospective bidder at an auction should carefully note the "Conditions of Sale" (posted in the gallery or printed in the catalog) and remember that not every defect may be noted in a catalogue description. Then there are the general auctions, held by small auction houses catering to local trade, medium-size houses attracting a regional trade, and also by the major houses which attract national and international bidding. Art Nouveau items are regularly included in such auctions (although the "Big Three" houses usually shunt their better Art Nouveau pieces to their specialized auctions). Since these auctions don't attract the same attention among Art Nouveau collectors that the major specialized auctions do, it's very likely you (the careful bidder) will spot Art Nouveau pieces when attention is not being drawn to them. Such pieces will not show up with great frequency, but when they do, they may be bargains. (See the next chapter for addresses of some of the leading auction houses in the country.)

OTHER COLLECTORS represent an often-untapped source for antiques, and the Art Nouveau field is no exception. Collectors part with their collections (or parts of them) for many different reasons: the need for immediate funds for either antiques or non-antiques expenditures, disenchantment with the collecting speciality, an attempt to upgrade the collection by ridding it of lesser specimens in favor of better ones, a personal dislike for a particular piece or group of pieces within a collection, a shift in emphasis of the collection. In all cases, other collectors, when they can be found, can provide both buying and selling opportunities. Collectors know that, to sell to a dealer, they must expect much less than the object will bring at retail — in some cases, as little as 40 percent to 50 percent of the retail price. Selling the pieces at auction involves a gamble unless a high "reserve" (price below which the item will not be sold) is imposed; even then, the owner has to pay a percentage of the hammer price — generally, between 10 and 30 percent — to the auction house. A sale to you, a collector, at a higher price than dealers would pay, but lower than retail, will benefit both parties. Look at your fellow collectors as competitors, of course, when you both want the same thing, but consider yourselves allies when you can help each other.

But WHEN do you buy? The old and standard thinking was, "Buy now, because they're not making them anymore, and the next one you see will probably be priced higher". If only things were that simple! There once was a time when art collectors could borrow money specifically to purchase a work of art — but at high interest rates, that just means the piece has to be held longer, or the value of it has to rise precipitously, for the collector just to break even. Buy now? Not if the price is too high. Buy now? There's no shortage of many types of Art Nouveau pieces — most are not like one-of-a-kind paintings — so the chances are others will be offered in the future.

Is this a plea to stop buying? NO! It's everything but that. Buy now if you can satisfy yourself that the price is right. Buy now if the piece is in good shape, unmarred by defects. Buy now if you like the piece in question and wish to add it to your collection. Buy now if you are sure the piece is scarce enough that it might not be offered again for quite a while, and you don't want to wait. Buy now if you are sure of the piece's authenticity, workmanship and quality. Buy now if you want to.

But just remember that there is seldom an item that a collector "needs" for his or her collection. We add to our collections because we want to, not because we need to.

Which is better for the collector, to buy five $100 items or one $500 item? No answer is possible, because "better" isn't applicable in this case. The collector with the five $100 pieces can be just as happy as the one with the single $500 piece, or vice versa. In terms of potential for monetary gain, it's **usually** the case that the higher-priced items will continue to climb in value — but that doesn't mean lower-priced items won't climb, too, or even leap-frog in price. But if you, as a collector, are happy with the less-expensive items, add them to your collection and the heck with what anybody else says!

SELLING

The antiques market is unique among retail sectors. In no other endeavor are so many buyers claiming to be sellers! Many collectors have found that it pays off to hold proper licensure, sales tax registration, and other governmental accouterments of a retail business. There are fulltime dealers, part-time dealers, weekend dealers, occasional dealers, and probably other varieties.

One need not be a dealer to sell, however. In the collecting lifetime of many collectors the urge to divest one's self of part of a collection arises. How one sells, and to whom, depends upon a number of factors: how many items are to be sold, the overall value of the items, the type of items, the speed with which the items must be sold, the geographic location of the seller (in this case, the collector) relative to buyers.

One would not expect most part-time dealers to have sufficient working capital to buy a hundred or so major pieces at one time, especially if a great deal of monetary value were involved (although some do). The larger the collection (or part of one) to be disposed of, the better the collector's chances of going to either a major dealer or an auction house. A distinct drawback to the auction method, apparent especially in catalogue sales, is the delay between consignment of the merchandise and the time the money is received by the consignor, a time period which can run up to several months. Some auction houses will actually purchase the items you approach them with, but the collector should not expect to receive nearly the price obtainable through auctioning it outright. In the case of major New York houses (**any** auction house, for that matter), never ship your merchandise to them without their approval in advance.

The use of reserves (which are never revealed to the public ahead of time) is one way to help assure that your collection will not be sold for too low a price. Most auction houses which permit reserves will advise you about what range they feel a reserve should be in for a particular "lot" (item or group of items to be sold for a single price).

Some phases of Art Nouveau seem to overlap the so-called "fine arts". Particularly if one wishes to dispose fine art posters from the Art Nouveau period, or some of the better bronze figures or figural groups, try contacting local art galleries. Some purchase such items or accept them for sale on consignment. You may have to contact several, for galleries often specialize in certain periods or styles and may have no interest in what you have to offer. Just don't give up!

Finally, remember that you can sell to other collectors, but you must first locate them. If you live in an area where there are not many Art Nouveau collectors, or if you wish to appeal to a broad audience of potential buyers, try advertising in national or regional antiques trade papers. *The Antique Trader Weekly* offers wide exposure at reasonable costs.

DEALERS AND AUCTIONEERS

The primary buying sources for most collectors will be, quite naturally, antiques dealers and auction houses. Virtually every antiques dealer in the country (except those who deal only with very early merchandise or "collectibles" of the 20th century) carries some Art Nouveau stock, sometimes unknowingly.

In the same way, most auction houses which conduct auctions of old merchandise auction pieces in the Art Nouveau styles from time to time. Some purchase directly from owners, so that they wind up auctioning merchandise they already own; others are dependent upon what crosses their thresholds, which may or may not include Art Nouveau items. Still others aggressively seek out Art Nouveau items to conduct special auctions.

It would be folly to attempt to list every dealer, every gallery, every auction house in the country who carries Art Nouveau merchandise. Such a list would be impossible to compile and accurately update; it would be outdated before it ever entered print.

As a result, the dealers and auctioneers listed here are those which have lent their assistance in some way to the compilation of this book. This is not meant as a blanket endorsement of each dealer or house listed; rather, it is an indication of the widespread sources from which Art Nouveau can be obtained.

Just a couple of notes are in order. First, because I have listed a particular dealer as specializing in a certain type of Art Nouveau item, that doesn't necessarily mean they won't have other, dissimilar items in their stocks. Second, keep in mind that some of the most interesting buys at auction houses occur at general auctions, when the attention of Art Nouveau-minded crowds isn't focused upon the particular auction.

DEALERS

The Bonfoey Co.
1710 Euclid Avenue
Cleveland, OH 44115
(general line fine prints, posters, art)

Phil Leilich
3911-A Newberry Rd.
Gainesville, FL 32607
(specialist in American art glass)

A. T. Merber
Merber Enterprises, Ltd.
2700 Virginia Ave., N.W.
Washington, D.C. 20037
(specialist in art glass; stocks other Art Nouveau items as well)

Bill & Sara Ruth McKeown
The Commissary
Rt. 2
Quincy, FL 32351
(general line antiques dealers)

Phyllis Jacobson
L'Imagerie
15030 Ventura Blvd.
Sherman Oaks, CA 91403
(specialist in graphic arts, especially Art Nouveau posters)

Sandy Verin
Icart Vendor Gallery
7956 Beverly Blvd.
Los Angeles, CA 90048
(specialist in graphic arts, especially of the Art Nouveau and Art Deco periods)

AUCTION HOUSES

Butterfield's
1244 Sutter St.
San Francisco, CA 94109
(general auction house; no specialty auctions of Art Nouveau, but the styles are well represented in their general auctions and some of their specialty auctions such as silver and jewelry)

Christie's (Christie, Manson & Woods International, Inc.)
502 Park Avenue
New York, NY 10022
(New York branch of a major international auction house; their Art Nouveau specialty auctions and catalogs are well worth the time, money and effort you may take to see them; look for more Art Nouveau in some of their general auctions, too)

Christie's East
219 E. 67th St.
New York, NY 10021
(a branch of a branch of the major London firm; no specialty Art Nouveau auctions, but merchandise from these styles occasionally mixed in with some of their general sales)

Morton's Auction Exchange, Inc.
P. O. Box 30380
643 Magazine St.
New Orleans, LA 70190
(general line of auctioned goods; no specialty Art Nouveau auctions, but many pieces found in their general auctions)

Phillips (Phillips Son & Neale, Inc.)
867 Madison Avenue
New York, NY 10021
(New York branch of a major London-based auction house; offers Art Nouveau through fine specialty auctions as well as through general auctions; catalogs available)

C.G. Sloan & Co., Inc.
715 Thirteenth St., N.W.
Washington, D.C. 20005
(issues fine, thick general catalogs with a disproportionate share of Art Nouveau items included; their organization (or disorganization) means you must read each page to find them)

Sotheby's (Sotheby Parke Bernet Inc.)
1334 York Avenue
New York, NY 10021
(New York branch of the famous London-based auction house, the largest in the world; fine specialty auctions of Art Nouveau, with catalogs; other Art Nouveau items found within other catalogs and at general auctions)

PUBLICATIONS

American Print Review
P. O. Box 6909
Chicago, IL 60680
(Although mainly concerned with fine art prints, this bimonthly magazine includes ads for posters and prints and other graphics, both wanted and for sale)

The Antique Trader Weekly
P. O. Box 1050
Dubuque, IA 52001
(This weekly tabloid is read for its advertisements by collectors and dealers, but it also contains articles of interest; one of the most widely-read publications on antiques in America)

CERAMICS

Ceramics — both the various earthenwares and porcelain — received more than their deserved treatments in Art Nouveau fashions during the late 19th and early 20th centuries. The field is usually divisible into "decorative" ceramics and "useful" (or utilitarian) ceramics; if one can agree with this dichotomy, then it will follow that most Art Nouveau stylings were reserved for the decorative wares — remembering that there was occasional overlap between those pieces which were decorative, those which were useful, and those which were a bit of both.

The decoration of ceramic wares has an ancient heritage, going back thousands of years. Early decorations were usually made an integral part of the bodies of ceramic items through incising or impressing designs. Such techniques were also used in the Art Nouveau decorations, but much more important were several other decorative techniques: painting underglaze designs, applications of unusual glazes for pronounced effects, and moulding.

Painted designs are what make some of the Rookwood and other American art pottery pieces so highly collectible; they were used in Britain and on the Continent, too, but American pieces engender the greatest following here in this country. Skilled painters created what amount to well-executed paintings on a "canvas" of clay, and some collectors today collect those specimens executed by a particular artist — for instance, Matt A. Daly. The designs used tend toward the realistic, often including pastoral scenes or Indian portraits.

The period of Art Nouveau styling was also one of tremendous experimentation in ceramics glazes as well as in glass. (See the chapter on glass for further information regarding the experiments as they applied to glass.) As a result, it's difficult to separate those developments which were natural progressions of increased understandings of ceramic and glaze chemistry from those which were conscious attempts to produce particular effects with glazes. Perhaps the simplest matter is just to conclude that experimentation was part of the spirit of the late 19th century, and those experiments which produced desired effects were repeated in commercial production techniques.

Iridescent glazes were one characteristic "new" decorative technique used to advantage by manufacturers during this period. Clement Massier in France (and other Massiers as well) became widely known for his many iridescent glazes. The work of Massier became directly tied to that of America when a

Massier workman, Jacques Sicard, carried with him to Ohio the formulas for producing special glaze effects with metallic salts. Even Sicard was not the first to introduce iridescent glazes here, for the omnipresent Louis Comfort Tiffany had been producing similar wares in New York for years. Elsewhere in Europe, the Zsolnay works in Hungary found that their red glazed ceramic bodies accepted iridescent glazes well and consequently produced lines of such wares. English Arts and Crafts potteries maintained their individuality well into the 20th century by of eschewing highly decorated products in favor of innovation of both shapes and glazes.

Moulded wares demonstrate some of the most obvious examples of the Art Nouveau styles in ceramics. Like cast bronze figures, many copies of a single model could be made by first manufacturing a mould in which the body would be formed. Here was the direct application of modern production techniques to what were originally objects of art, mass production of what could previously have been only a single creation. Such pieces are illustrated later in the book, ususally in the form of figural vases or other figural pieces. Once formed, of course, the moulded ceramic piece could also receive a special glaze treatment.

Other types of decoration were used, too — applied decorations come readily to mind — but these were the main decorative devices manufacturers used. National tendencies seem to have dictated in many cases exactly what the decoration would be. For instance, the Germanic nations (heart of the Secessionist movements and the Jugendstil) would of necessity have used painting techniques to create the geometric patterns which came to characterize their works. Moulded wares were produced in practically all ceramics centers, with greater numbers being seen today from France than from the British Isles. (Moulded wares were certainly made in England, but apparently few were created in Art Nouveau styles.) America, that great melting pot for ideas from the arts, used all decorative techniques at one time or another in this period, relying more upon painting than upon glazing, and more upon glazing than upon moulding, for the Art Nouveau effects produced.

Art Nouveau ceramics designers took their inspirations for the arts from a variety of sources. That presents a problem in itself, for by definition this was to be the period of the "New Art." Time and again designers would reach back into their classical pasts to resurrect the ghosts of stylings currently out of favor. Orientalism, brought back to Europe in the 18th century and earlier in the 19th century, was the inspiration (in shapes) for works of some of the potters working in France (Auguste Deleherche, for example, or Ernest Chaplet) and England (including some of the major firms which adapted classical Chinese or Japanese shapes to British production). The Dutch, particularly the Rozenberg firm at the turn of the century, used their colonial experience in Indonesia to adapt the batiks of Java to ceramics production. Other workers found merit in Hispano-Moorish traditional vessels, producing new works based upon the classical precedent.

Much of the production during this period was the embodiment of a less-than-perfect understanding of the principles behind Art Nouveau. Classical shapes, derived from the Greek and Roman artistic traditions and thus acceptable to the academics of the day, were given surface treatments out of keeping with their supposed purposes; some designers, failing to recognize the necessity of viewing the object as a "whole" rather than in its parts, "tacked on" decoration which may today seem odd and inharmonious.

In comparison with glass of the same period, Art Nouveau ceramics may seem undervalued — with exceptions. However, when one looks at the prices brought for the ceramics of, for instance, Galle or Tiffany, and compares them to the glass products from the same firms, one must conclude that there is a great disparity. Why? Collector resistance, in some cases, to "break new ground" rather than travel the heavily trod paths already being pursued by other collectors; the recognition that, though the ceramics from these houses are from reputable and major innovators, some of it is really inconsequential and not very meritorious; the inability to distinguish the Art Nouveau products from some of their earlier and later competitors; all may have something to do with it.

At the same time, some of the peculiarly American pieces may be over-priced. (That's not a prediction, just an observation!) It's hard to justify the prices in the several of thousands of dollars for some American ceramics without taking into consideration the army of collectors waiting to buy it. Look for some of the potteries other than Rookwood to begin to climb in price; in some cases, the climb is well underway.

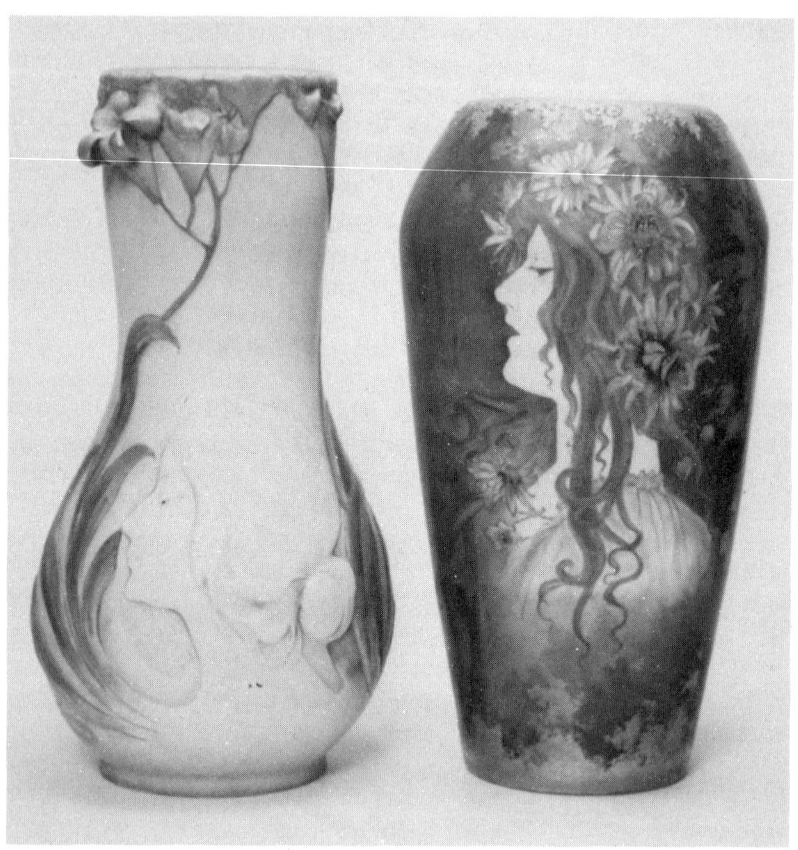

TWO AUSTRIAN "AMPHORA" PORCELAIN PORTRAIT VASES. (Left) impressed marks of Imperial Amphora, Austria, 18"; *$750 A. (Right) impressed "Amphora" and printed mark of Riessner, Stellmacher and Kessel, with artist initial "A," 17¼"H, base repair; *$1,600 A. (Christie's)

ALTENBURG

Chocolate Pot — Pate sur Pate, raised woodland scene of semi-nude maiden, aqua blue pearlized ground; $85 D.

AMERICAN ENCAUSTIC TILING CO.

Plaque — earthenware, modeled with pink glaze, impressed mark, 18"L; *$750 A.

Tile — green, profile, 6 x 6; $42 D.

Tile — blue, three for $35 D.

AMPHORA (Included here are the many different companies incorporating the word "Amphora" as part of their marks, provided they were from the proper part of Austria to be so considered.)

Bowl — top embellished with raised apples/leaves/blossoms/ vines on beige ground; footed, 8" x 5"; $150 D.

Bust — of Cleo de Merode, a Parisian beauty in the Art Nouveau era; green/gold/white, gold headbands, 8½"H; $875 D.

Centerpiece — jeweled with about 20 cabochons; 20"H x 18"W; $850 D.

— nude among water lilies, gold and white; 13"L x 4"H, mint; $650 D.

Ewer — maiden on side, large spout opposite above Bacchus; flesh tones, factory mark on base; $1,500 D.

— bulbous with straight neck, gold flecking, turquoise handle; large gold flower and leaf, small pink/lavender flowers; 10½"H, marked Crown/Teplitz; $120 D.

Figural Group — Arab riding camel, gilt decor, 20" H; *$350 A.

— same, colorful pastel glaze, factory mark and AUSTRIA, 19"H; *$350 A.

Jardiniere — textured surface, hot pink on midnight blue, highly iridescent with inset jewels; $395 D.

Pitcher — multi-stem handle with flower-form top, large embossed leaves, green/gold/iridescent moddling, 15"H; $335 D.

Tray — blue and green with busts of Art Nouveau maidens flanking, 11"L; $450 D.

Urn — 4 female faces in relief with gold highlighting; label of Riessner, Stellmacher & Kessner, base impressed AMPHORA AUSTRIA; 12"H, base repair; *$2,100 A.

Vases (most common of the Amphora production, as they were from most potteries working in the Art Nouveau manner)

— "portrait" type, oviform porcelain with narrow neck and printed mark of the Riessner, Stellmacher & Kessel firm, 5¼"H; *$700 A.

— camelrider astride camel sitting crosslegged and playing lyre, wearing golden burnoose; impressed Imperial mark, 9 x 13; $675 D.

— pair, green and cream with Shell pattern, dark blue jewels, each 9"H; the pair, $475 D.

— iridescent glaze of blue with dark red spots; leaves are shades of green to pink to red with gold stems; interior mottled grey-green to ivory; 8¼"H, 3¼"D at mouth, 4½"D at middle; handled, impressed Amphora mark with Crown and Austria, and impressed numbers; 2 hairline cracks, minor crazing, possible repair; $325 D.

— owl stands on edge looking in, large bird with fish in beak in fine relief on side; cattails and dragonflies in relief, 13"H; $300 D.

— jeweled type, impressed mark of Amphora, Austria, 11"H; *$300 A.

— 4-handled bowl type, Moorish-inspired with heavy enamel poppies; 10 x 9, marked with Turn Teplitz mark and Castle; $295 D.

— reticulated 3-handled, gold iridescent webbing, jeweled; Imperial Crown mark, #3356; $289 D.

— beige/gold ground covered with large opal beads; 2 large gold handles; $289 D.

— jeweled conical form, impressed mark; 11"H; *$280 A.

— iridescent floriform; bulbous base has swirling leaves in relief, 4 stems form handles, top portion an open tulip, some reticulation; subdued colors of grey-greens and blues and pinkish top with gold; impressed mark, 10¼"H x 8"W; $265 D.

— reticulated floriform neck, multicolored; Imperial Crown mark, 10¼"H; $265 D.

— 4-handled bowl form, poppies on Moorish grey ground; 9" x 8"; $265 D.

— bulbous base floriform, molded and blown-out leaves; extending stem handles join to reticulated blossom top, iridescent finish, impressed mark; 10½"H, base 7¾"D; $245 D.

— pink flowers and limbs, 11½"H; pair, $235 D.

— 4-handled cobalt blue body with olive green open handles; 4 medallions of gold flowers and trailed enamel; in 2 are painted medallions; in other 2 are painted Kate Greenaway-type girls; 7"H, neck 3½"D, 7"D handle to handle, widest point of body about 6"D; impressed AMPHORA AUSTRIA; $175 D.

— 2-handled, enameled woman with white crown on one side, white swan opposite, on light brown base; mark of impressed crown, eagle, Amphora, and #11888; 1/8" nick underside one handle; $145 D.

—gold handles, glossy blue/green ground, gold trim, reticulated neck; impressed with crown, Austria Amphora, and #; 12½"H; $125 D.

— baluster form, naturalistically molded twig handles; sunflower decor on body, gold highlights; 14¾"H; *$100 A.

— burnished gold with "candle drippings", applied roses, marked and signed; 6¾"H; $90 D.

— portrait of Gibson-type girl, Teplitz Stellmacher Amphora; $85 D.

— green ground, enameled caped man in knickers, 7"H; $80 D.

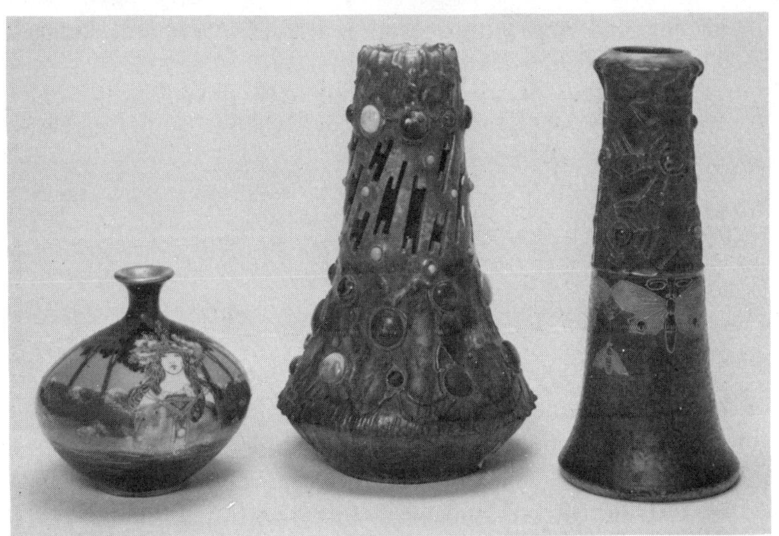

THREE AMPHORA VASES. (Left) portrait porcelain vase by Riessner, Stellmacher & Kessner; *$700 A. (center & right) "jeweled" earthenware vases by Amphora, Austria; respectively, *$300 A and *$280 A. (Christie's)

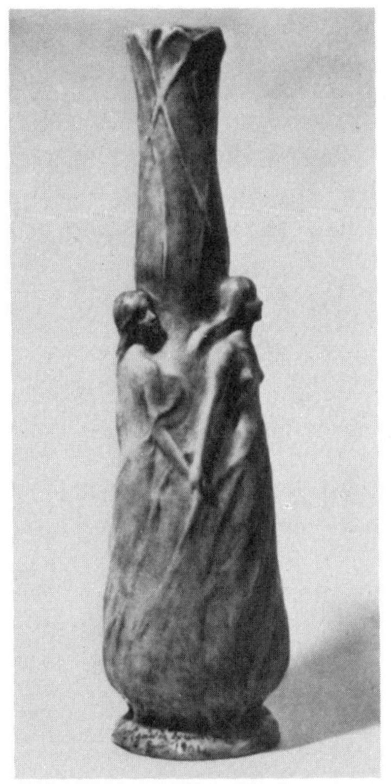

FORSTER FIGURAL VASE, encircled by 3 semi-clad females dissolving into base; buff shading into ginger; impressed mark, and signed "Agniddle Frumerie Paris 1901," 21¾"H; *$550 A. (Phillips)

— cobalt with applied gilt grapes, faint hairline, marked and #d; $65 D.

— beige ground with dark blue and pink floral; 8½"H, initialed RM, Amphora signature; $60 D.

CAMBRIDGE ART POTTERY

Vase — painted by A.V. Lewis, dog on dark brown ground; impressed mark and artist's initials, 9"H; *$680 A.

CORALENE

Vase — floral decor, heavy beading, 2 gold-beaded handles, patent mark; 6½"H; $249 D.

— 2-handled stylized floral green/yellow/orange decor with gold beading; patent mark 1909; 5"H; $190 D.

DALPAYRAT

Vase — hour-glass shape, irregular lining and prunts in black mottled tan glazed surface, painted with artist's signature; 7"H; *$400 A.

— impressed mark, 5"H; *$200 A.

DEDHAM

Bowl Set — 3 bowls in "Swan" pattern, flower center with "frog" in shape of rabbit, each stamped with firm's marks; bowl 5¾"D, flower center 9¼"D; *$500 A.

Creamer & Cups — "Swan" pattern, 5 cups, each marked, 4"H; *$350 A.

Plate — 7 dessert plates, 4 dinner plates, all in "Swan" pattern, each with firm's mark; dessert 6¼"D, dinner 10"D; *$500 A.

— 10 plates, each in "Swan" pattern and stamped with firm's mark, 7½"D; *$300 A.

— "Iris" pattern, art by Maude Davenport, 8"D; $135 D.

DOULTON

Decanter — floral decor on mottled green ground, artist signed; Doulton Lambeth; $55 D.

Vase — 3 jeweled reserves bearing pairs of donkeys, incised with numerous marks and initials in addition to marks of Doulton, Burslem, and artist's initials of Hannah Barlow, date 1884; 10¼"H; *$480 A.

— blues and greys in Nouveau style, impressed E.B. (Ethel Beard, decorator for Doulton, 1890-1930); $75 D.

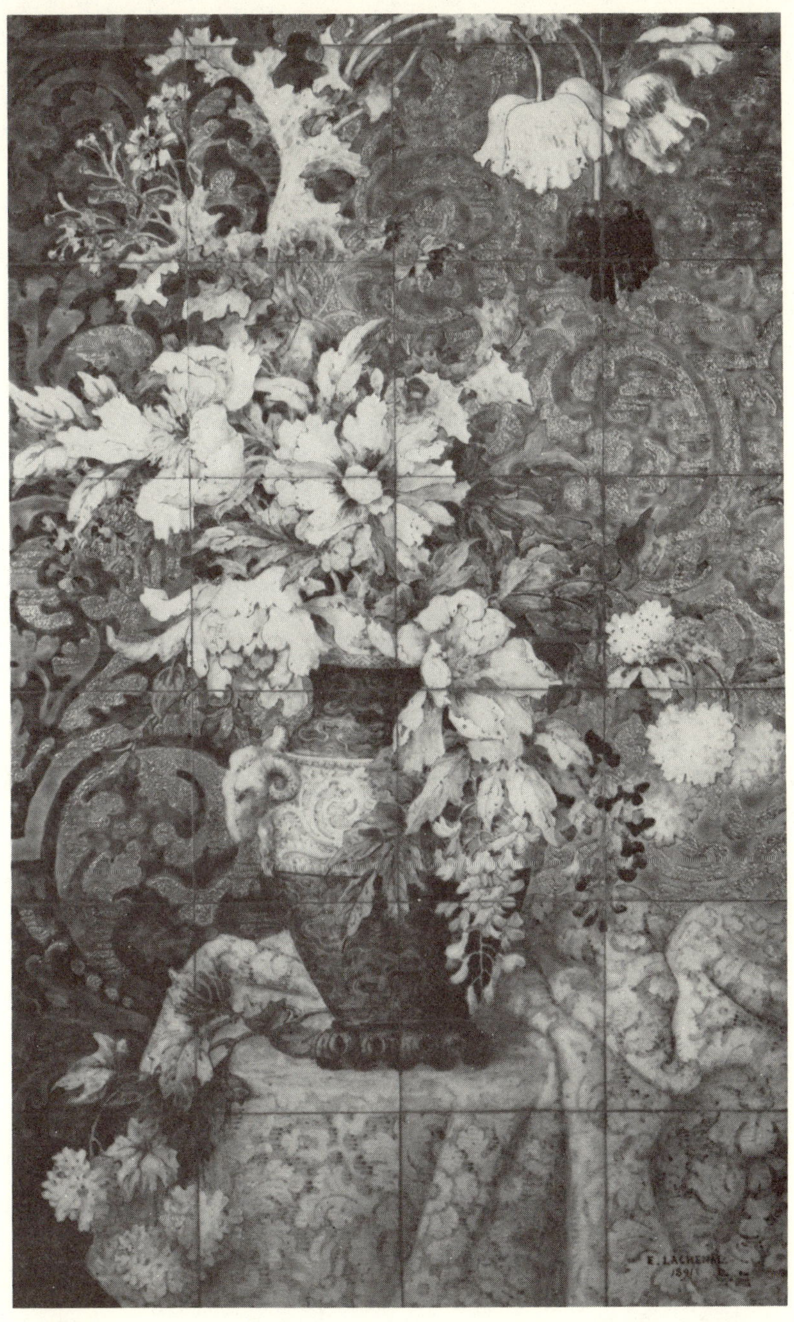

PLAQUE BY E. LACHENAL, Paris, 1891, composed of 28 tiles; *$5,500 A. (Christie's)

ELITE LIMOGES

Chocolate Set — heavy encrusted gold on creamy yellow ground, large blown-out cherry both sides of rim, others extending down body with leaves; handle is branch formation with leaves extending onto body; intricate gold scalloped foot; double Elite mark in red and green; pot 13"H; 6 matching cups and saucers; 13 pieces, $855 D.

FISCHER

Charger — predominant red design outlined in gold, 13"L; $340 D.

Vase — multi-handled, cream ground, gold flowers with green enamel beads, gold glaze; 12½"H; $295 D.

— flattened bulbous (canteen) shape with 2 handles) cream and sanded gold ground for the multi-colored branches/ flowers/leaves; surface completely decorated, 13 1/8"H, 8 3/8"D; $195 D.

FULPER

Bowl — handled, crystal blue/sky blue/brown glaze; stamped mark; 7¾"D; *$110 A.

— aqua rose bowl, roses in relief on front; $80 D.

Vase — blue and lime-green glaze, impressed mark; 13¼"H; *$240 A.

GALLE POTTERY (Not as well known or collected as Galle's glass, this may be one of the more undervalued collectibles on the market.)

Condiment Holder — blue and white reticulated, 10"; $225 D.

Ewer — beetle and locust decor, 8"H; $675 D.

Inkwell — signed, $695 D.

Pitcher — tree-handled, painted in black/gold/blue/silver on white ground, in florals, plants, birds; "E. Galle" painted on, as well as firm's stamp, 13½"H; *$750 A.

Planter — Egyptian Revival influence, different scene each side, blue/black/beige on cream ground; 14½"L x 4½"W x 4"H, couple of glaze chips; $1,200 D.

Vase — spherical en feience parlant piece, inscribed "De ses ailes la nemophile alpetre fait des carolles au plaintine sans elat"; signed and with original label 6¼"H; *$1,200 A.

— bulbous vase with flared rim, misty scene of landscape in browns and ochre, 5½"H; $750 D.

— spherical with crimped rim, 3½"H; *$250 A.

— ovoid with split stepped lip, molded with stylized thistle blossoms covered in foil, overall glaze streaking in mustard/ ochre, lip turquoise blue; molded "Emile/Galle/depose" over thistle blossom, 9"H, chips, c. 1900; *$200 A.

GOUDA (Several firms operated here, generically classified as Gouda potteries.)

Ashtray — Chinese-style decor, 7½"; *$50 A.

Humidor — burnt orange/greens/cobalt/yellow, with Plazuid-Kurba mark; $105 D.

Jar, Cracker — 8"H; $135 D.

Matchbox Holder — Regina mark; $28 D.

Pitcher — stylized floral, 4½"H; $125 D.

Vase — oviform, grey/turquoise/brown geometric design on white ground; painted signature "1043 RUMBA FLORA GOUDA HOLLAND," 8¼"H; *$200 A.

— handled, 12"H, mint condition; $160 D.

— bulbous long-neck form, Art Nouveau floral in high glaze; house and tree mark, 6½"H; $110 D.

— trumpet form, black with primitive sand-brown Phoenix; marked Distel Goedewaagen, Gouda Holland XXX; 10"H; $110 D.

— black and white design, from Schoonhoven; $95 D.

— stick neck, multi-colored; mark of Royal Holland Zuid, 6"H; $72 D.

— bulbous, in greens/mustard/Rhodian/orange/cobalt, 6½"H; $40 D.

— pinched sides, 2¾"H; marked Holland DV; $40 D.

GRUEBY

Tile — earthenware, turtle facing right beneath leaves, stamped mark, painted "K.C.," and paper label; 6 x 6; *$620 A.

— earthenware, knight, 6 x 6; $225 D.

— earthenware, mermaid, 6 x 6; $225 D.

— earthenware, stylized tree, 4 x 4; $175 D.

— earthenware, flower, 4 x 4; $100 D.

— architectural design, green/brown/blue, 4 x 6; $60 D.

— allover brown, 6 x 9; $45 D.

Vase — matte cucumber glaze, impressed mark, 11"H; *$600 A.

— matte cucumber glaze, 5-sided rim, impressed mark, 10¼"H; *$500 A.

— textured cucumber glaze, spherical with large neck, impressed mark, 12¾"H; *$350 A.

— matte blue, bowl vase form, 6½ x 5; $310 D.

— flared spherical form, dark yellow, impressed mark, 5"H; *$250 A.

GUERIN

Vase — baluster form, pale celery-green glaze streaked with ivory and brown over stoneware grey lower body; inscribed "Guerin/62/E," impressed circular mark OGER GUERIN, 12¾"H; *$200 A.

HAVILAND (Many of the Haviland undecorated pieces, or blanks, were supplied to china decorators both amateur and professional throughout Europe and the United States.)

Plate — portrait of red-haired Art Nouveau-tressed lady, surrounded by gold/copper borders, gold flowers, and other decoration; artist signed A.B.L., 9"D; $125 D.

HEREND

Tray — bone-white porcelain with Basketweave raised edge, decorated with 2 birds on bough with insects and butterflies around; blue crown mark plus handpainted Herend, Hungary; 11 x 9¾; $125 D.

— figural shell shaped with dish at each end, full figure of bird perched on tree trunk in center, red/gold border, floral motif each dish, 13½"L; $60 D.

HEUBACH

Vase — Pate-sur-pate 2-handled, lady waving scarf on pale green body, gold interior; $175 D.

E. LACHENAL, PARIS

Plaque, Wall — 28 square tiles depicting vase of bright flowers of freshly-painted high-glazed enamels; ground has applied gold scrolled flowers; signed E. LACHENAL 1891; in excellent wooden frame, 55½ x 31½; *$5,500 A.

Vase — ovoid, turquoise crackle glaze over stoneware, 7"H; tiny glaze nick on top; $75 D.

LASEYNIE

Sugar and Creamer — lustreware with Art Nouveau design, signed by artist Smith, marked "Laseynie PP France," dated 1913; $60 D.

LENOX

Bowl — Belleek, handpainted orange/gold/lavender/green/orange scrolls and florals, and heavy embossed decoration as well; green pallette mark, artist signed, 10"D, 3"H; $150 D.

Pitcher, Cider — Belleek, floral, much gold; $125 D.

LIMOGES

Vase — peacock and vines, 12¾"H; $125 D.

LONHUDA — See WELLER

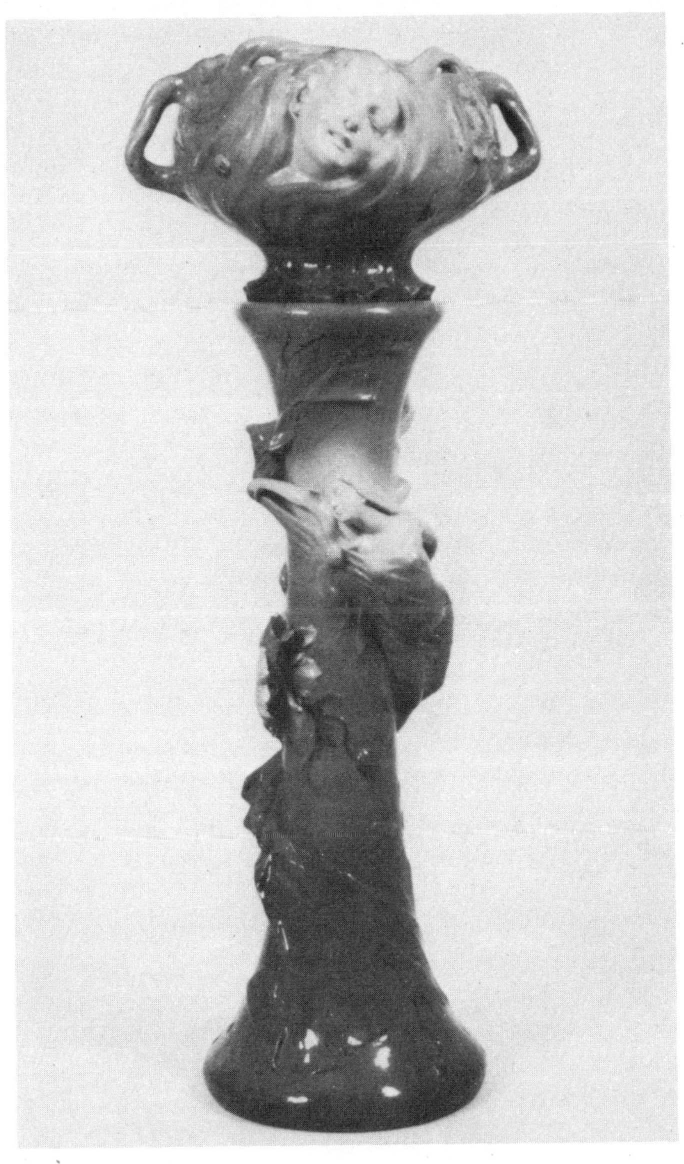

JARDINIERE & STAND, by Delphin Massier; rose/yellow/green glaze, printed DELPHIN MASSIER & CIE/Vallauris (A.M.); 54½H, 24"D over handles; *$4,100 A. (Sotheby's)

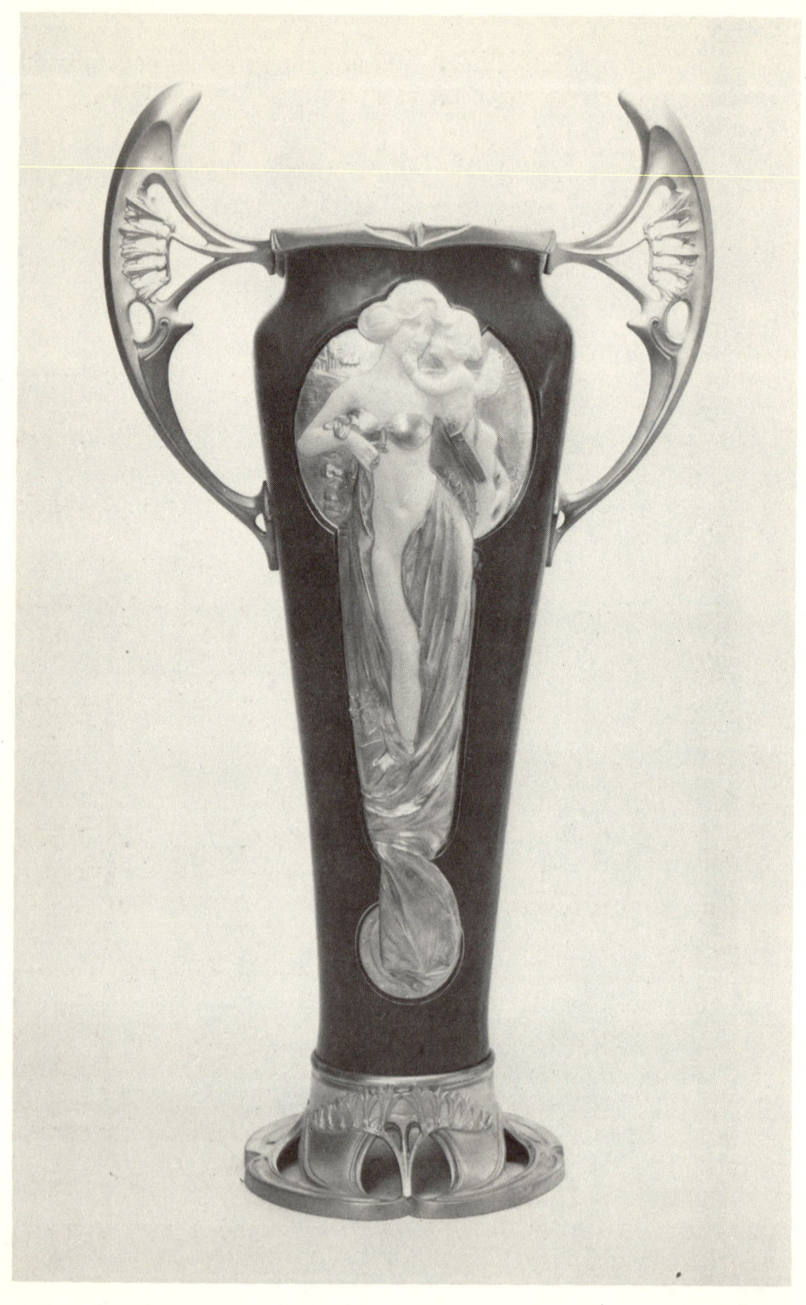

VASE BY CHARLES KERSCHANN, French, early 20th century; porcelain in ormolu mounts; *$4,000 A. (Christie's)

LOSANTI

Tile — painted by Mary Louise McLaughlin, c. 1905, portrait of a woman, inscribed with artist's initials; 3½"; *$300 A.

LOW

Tile — set of 3 measuring 6 x 18; 4 winged cherubs in high relief hold banner proclaiming "Tempus Fugit"; rich brown, excellent condition; $175 D.

— lady with turban, olive glaze, artist signed; $120 D.

— green floral, 6 x 6; $35 D.

MARTIN BROTHERS, ENGLAND

Vase — light ground with aquatic decor, incised mark, dated 1887, 8½"H; *$1,200 A.

— gourd-type, vertical glaze streakings, incised mark and "10-1903," 10"H, minor glaze flake; *$820 A.

— slightly footed, pushed-in rim, floral and plant decor, incised mark, 8¼"H; *$800 A.

— grotesque fish vase, 10"H; $500 D.

— footed, everted rim, dark ground decorated; incised mark and "10-1896," with original paper label, 8½"H; *$420 A.

— incised with firm's marks, 7 1/8"H; *$400 A.

— floral decor around body and with bottle neck also decorated, incised mark of N.W. Martin Brothers, London, 1890; 9½"H; *$300 A.

— bottle form, 6"H; $150 D.

MASSIER (Best-known was Clement Massier, at Golfe-Juane, France, although Jerome and Delphine Massier also worked in ceramics, all mainly in earthenware.)

Centerpiece — marked, 8¼"H; *$260 A.

Ewer — handled, bottle neck, marked, 6¾"H; *$300 A.

Vase— marked, 6¼"H; *$850 A.

— dimpled spherical form, irregular raised patches, in raisin/grey-green/violet glaze; impressed CLEMENT MASSIER GOLF JUAN (A-M); 8"H; *$420 A.

— looped handles rise from near base to neck on this conical piece, 10"H; *$380 A.

— iridescent orange glaze, 5¼"H; $250 D.

— iridescent glaze, 6"H; $222 D.

ALFRED MEAKIN

Butter Pat — Art Nouveau decor; $8 D.

METTLACH

Tea Set — tray 15"D, teapot, creamer, open sugar, all decorated in white with blue and mustard; $800 D.

MOORCROFT

Bowl — embossed Irises all over interior, in dark green and blue; 12½"D x 3½"H; $475 D.

— hemispherical, decorated on interior and exterior with mushrooms in reds/yellows/blues on green ground; signed and inscribed, "Made for Shreve and Company, San Francisco, 1912"; 9¾"D; *$325 A.

— yellow/red/purple Wisteria with green leaves inside and out on cobalt ground; 11"D x 3¼"H, minor nick on inner edge; $165 D.

— yellow/orange flowers on cobalt ground, script signature, 10"D; $135 D.

— Hibiscus blossoms on cobalt ground, paper label, signed England, 9¾"D; $122 D.

— green, with multi-color Iris decor in bowl, 4½"D; $65 D.

— blue-green ground, large flower in center, 4"D x 2"H; $40 D.

Dish — covered type, poppies on cobalt, impressed MOORCROFT MADE IN ENGLAND, 6¾"D; $135 D.

— candy type, green ground, colorful flowers on cover; $65 D.

— cobalt ground, rose & yellow flowers, 9 x 5½"; $35 D.

Jar, Ginger — iridescent orange lustre, no design; covered, marked "Moorcroft Burslem," c. 1913, 8¾"H; x 6¾"D; $115 D.

— iridescent orange, covered, 8¾"H x 6¾"D; $100 D.

— pink Magnolia blossom decoration, 4½"H; $70 D.

Teapot — mushroom decor, 6-cup capacity; $275 D.

Vase — bulbous, cascading purple/yellow/blue Pansies on pale green ground; MacIntyre mark, c. 1887-1915, signed Moorcroft, 7½"H; $425 D.

— 3-handled, fruit pattern at rim top, Pomegranates and other fruit on bulbous bottom, green to cobalt ground; impressed "Moorcroft Burslem England," c. 1916; 6½"H; $375 D.

— bulbous, Pomegranates & Grapes, cobalt ground, script signature, 6"H; $196 D.

— mushroom design, 3½"H; $175 D.

— Pomegranate design, 8¼"H x 4 5/8"D, green mark; $165 D.

— Poppies with green stems on cobalt ground, 6¼"H; $145 D.

— pair, Orchids on cobalt, "Royal" mark, 3½"H; the pair, $145 D.

— Pomegranate design, 9½"H; $125 D.
— Pomegranate design, bulbous body, 6"H; $100 D.
— yellow and red Freesia on cobalt ground, impressed MOORCROFT MADE IN ENGLAND, 5"H; $95 D.
— Pomegranate design on cobalt ground, footed, 6"H, script signature; $85 D.
— bulbous flambe, paper label, 2¾"H; $75 D.
— floral on cobalt ground, script signature, 3¼"H; $68 D.
— bulbous form, colorful flowers on cobalt ground, 5"H; $65 D.
— square shape, Pomegranates on blue ground, impressed MOORCROFT, 3½"H; *$50 A.
— yellow lustre, signed, 9"H, c. 1916; $50 D.

NEWCOMB COLLEGE POTTERY

Bowl — pink floral with trailing vines on blue ground, artist signature "HB" (Henrietta Bailey), 7"D x 2½"H; $425 D.
— standard "NC" mark, 3"H; *$125 A.

Toothpick Holder — deep blue with brown specks, marked "JM-NC"; $175 D.

Vase — modeled with blue pines, matte glaze; paper label, impressed mark and "JH330", 9¼"H; *$1,900 A.
— modeled with blue-green trees on green/yellow ground; impressed mark and "L N," painted FG67; 6¾"H; *$1,600 A.
— blue with moon shining through Spanish Moss-draped trees, decorated by Henrietta Bailey, 6"H; $1,400 D.
— aquamarine Spanish Moss on blue trees; impressed mark and "161 MK21", 8½"H; *$950 A.
— blue with white flowers, by Henrietta Bailey, 6"H; $700 D
— modeled light blue Irises with yellow interior, impressed mark and "JM202," painted "GL83"; 5"H; *$580 A.
— 2-handled, wide mouth, decorated by Sadie Irvine, 4"H; *$280 A.
— mauve leaves on off-white ground; $85 D.

NIPPON

Humidor — sailboat scene top half, beaded geometric lower half; 5½"H x 6"D; $210 D.

NORITAKE

Cup and Saucer — Art Nouveau floral, set of 1 cup and saucer; $7 D.

Dish — lady's powder dish, Nouveau styling; $12 D.

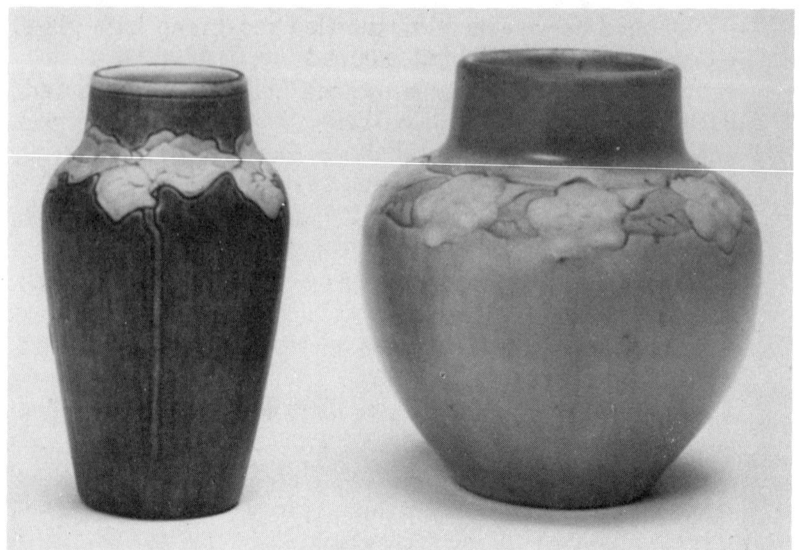

TWO EARTHENWARE VASES FROM NEWCOMB COLLEGE. (Left) modeled white flowers on blue ground, matte glaze, impressed mark & "JM", 5¼"H; *$520 A. (Right) molded pastel green flowers on aquamarine ground, impressed mark & "EJ61," 5½"H; *$550 A. (Christie's)

OHR (The debate may continue as to whether or not George Ohr was a pottery genius or the "Mad Potter of Biloxi," as he was sometimes called. His works were original, even if a bit monotonous when taken as a group; his rise at the same time as the Art Nouveau movement was probably merely coincidental. Still, his work was innovative for its time, expanding the boundaries of what could and should be done with ceramics.)

Boar — figural, indecipherable side inscription, impressed mark, 10"L; *$250 A.

Bowl — green/tan glossy glaze, rim pulled to very thin sawtooth edge, 3"D x 2"H; base incised "George E. Ohr Biloxi"; $235 D.

— mottled green/tan with crimped rim, signed "George E. Ohr, Biloxi," 3"D x 2½"H; $165 D.

Jug — puzzle type, wide mouth, high brown glaze, dated 1889, impressed mark and incised "G.E. Ohr, Biloxi, Miss.", 8"H; *$280 A.

Log Cabin — figural, high olive green glaze, impressed mark, 2¾"H; *$360 A.

Mug — iridescent dark brown, pale orange interior, inscribed horizontal lines; incised "G E Ohr," 3¾"H; *$125 A.

Vase — pink/yellow/green "lava" textured ground, impressed mark, 5"H; *$2,800 A.

— 2 applied curved handles, mottled red/green high glaze, impressed mark, 8¼"H; *$1,800 A.

— 2 applied unusual handles on tall cylinder, mottled red/pink/blue/green high glaze, incised mark, 6¾"H; neck repair; *$1,600 A.

— olive green and fuschia, impressed mark, 8"H; *$800 A.

— metallic gunmetal grey glaze, imprinted mark, pushed in sides, 6"H; *$700 A.

— charcoal grey matte textured finish, pinched neck, impressed mark, 6¼"H; *$400 A.

— 2 applied pair of handles, tan with grey spots, high gloss, 4½"H, impressed mark; *$270 A.

— gunmetal grey matte finish, center grotesquely pulled, scalloped rim, 4¼"D x 4"H; $255 D.

— ribbed, lizard around top, brown glaze, 3 x 3; $250 D.

— textured brown with high glaze, pushed in rim, impressed mark, 4¾"H; *$250 A.

— mottled brown high glaze, pushed in rim, 7¾"H, impressed mark; *$240 A.

— shaped like owl head, grey/green matte glaze, incised mark, 4½"H; glaze chip at rim; *$220 A.

— 2 applied handles, mottled brown high gloss glaze, 6¾"H; *$200 A.

— brown speckled light brown glaze, impressed mark, 4"; *$200 A.

— spherical, blue high gloss, incised mark, 5"H; *$170 A.

— spherical, brown speckled high gloss, impressed mark, 3½"H; *$110 A.

— mottled brown high gloss, impressed mark, 4"H; *$80 A.

OWENS UTOPIAN (The J.B. Owens Pottery Company was one of many Ohio potteries founded in the late 1800s. It ceased production in 1933, and their early Utopian line was one of the quality American-made hand-painted types now available to collectors.)

Ewer — decorated by Steele, 6"H; $175 D.

Jardiniere/Pedestal — matte glaze; $350 D.

Mug — berries and foliage, artist signed; $145 D.

— floral decor, artist signed, 1908; $100 D.

Pitcher — ruffled top, shaded Standard glaze, orange floral decoration; artist signed "S.B.", 4"H; $135 D.

Tankard — Cherries and leaves on brown glaze, 12"H; $200 D.

Vase — pair, swirled, each 14"H, one with Nasturtium, the other with Open Rose; the pair, $350 D.

— half-moon shape, floral decoration by Delores Harvel; $165 D.

— half-moon shape, footed, floral decoration, artist signed; $155 D.

— Pansies on glossy brown glaze, 13"H; $140 D.

— swirled, Nasturtium decoration, 14"H; $135 D.

— swirled, Rose decoration, 14"H; $135 D.

— inverted cone shape, russet Tulip decoration, 11¼"H, incised block mark; $130 D.

PEWABIC POTTERY

Tile — iridescent bronze; $165 D.

— Indian Maiden, iridescent bronze, 6 x 6; $165 D.

Vase — monumental highly iridescent, 15½"H; faint Pewabic circle mark on base; $1,200 D.

— textured blue & pale green ground mottled with gold, impressed mark, 6¼"H; *$500 A.

— bright blue & irregular silver-grey/blue high gloss glaze, wide at shoulders, impressed mark, 5½"H; *$450 A.

— lavender drippings on orange-brown ground, impressed mark, 7¾"H; *$450 A.

— iridescent gold/violet body with pale green neck, original paper label, 6¾"H; *$450 A.

PICKARD (Blanks from a variety of porcelain and other ceramics manufacturers were used by this decorating firm; a common practice was the use of lacy, heavy gold decoration.)

Bottle — perfume type, decorated with yellow Irises, 5"H, signed Beutlich; Pickard's brown mark of 1894-1905 period, plus GDA mark on blank; $145 D.

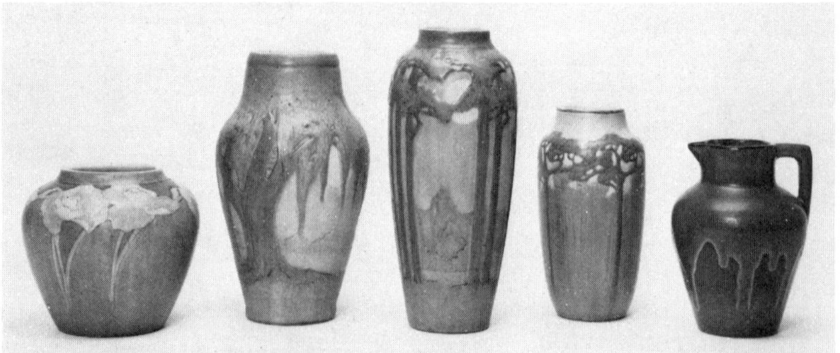

EARTHENWARE PIECES FROM NEWCOMB COLLEGE. (A) vase, modeled light blue Irises with yellow centers, impressed mark & "JM202," with painted GL83, 5"H; *$580 A. (B) vase, aquamarine Spanish moss on trees, impressed mark & "161 MK21," 8½"H; *$950 A. (C) vase, modeled blue pines in matte glaze, impressed mark & "JH 330," with original paper label, 9¼"H; *$1,900 A. (D) vase, modeled blue-green trees on green/yellow ground, impressed mark & "L N," painted "FG67," 6¾"H; *$1,600 A. (E) pitcher, brown & irregular pale green ground, impressed mark & "V G," 5¼"H; *$240 A. (Christie's)

Bowl — open-handled, Strawberries & flowers, decoration and gold trimming inside and out, 11"D, artist signed "Peitler"; $239 D.

— footed and handled salad type, fruit decoration and gold, 11½"D; signed "Vokral," c. 1912; $225 D.

— bird in center sits on branch with background of Autumn leaves, gold border 2¾" wide; bowl 9½"D, artist sig. E. Challinor; $195 D.

— watery scene of golden lily pads, water lilies, water, trees on green ground with gold borders; artist signature "Leach", Limoges blank, 10"D, 1898-1904 period; $175 D.

— gold and silver decorated, signed "Voboy"; $150 D.

— floral and geometric decoration, 10¼"D, artist signed "Eduard"; $130 D.

— low bowl, landscape with pink roses on inner surface of sides, the entire bottom gold with 2 black line borders; 7½"D x 1½"H, signed F. Vobor (for Vobornik); $125 D.

— reddish-orange Poppies, heavy gold bottom and outer rim, artist "L.O.L."; $95 D.

— Horse Chestnuts on Crown Pottery blank, marked "P.C. & M.R., Edgerton," 6"D x 3"H; $95 D.

— yellow/pink Roses, green leaves, shaded green interior, lemon exterior, deep gold scalloped edges; 7½"D, signed "H. Reury," on Limoges blank, 1898; $75 D.

Celery Dish — pheasant game scene, artist signed E. Challinor on T & V Limoges blank, 13"L; $185 D.

Charger — berries/blossoms/leaves, wide scalloped gold border, 12½"D, artist Kiefur, mark 1898-1904; $250 D.

— leaves and floral decoration in bright gold/crimson/ burgundy, some iridescence, on 12½"L blank, signed "Yeschek"; $185 D.

— Raspberries/blossoms/leaves with wide scalloped gold border, 12½"D, artist signed, c. 1900; $185 D.

Creamer — overall decoration of gold/black/orange luster with leaf scrolls of light blue, early circle mark, artist signed "Hessler" on Silesia blank; $60 D.

Creamer & Sugar — blue Tulips on vine, gold jewels, heavy gilding; sugar covered; $175 D.

— red Peony-like flowers, gold handles, artist signed "Vabornik" on fancy T & V Limoges blanks; $125 D.

— gold-etched on R.S. Germany blanks; $50 D.

Cup & Saucer — Violets, with gold, artist signed "Revey"; $48 D.

Dresser Set — oval tray, hair receiver, scent bottle, and pin tray; pink and blue flowers with gold trim; $175 D.

Jug, Syrup — stylized design of large gold Daisies over entire body, also covering wide black band with white daisies and green leaves; with underplate, both pieces artist signed, c. 1911; $115 D.

Mustard, Covered — floral and gold, gold-leaf Ravenswood stamp; $36 D.

Pitcher — hops/wheat/autumn leaves, with high curved handle; 5½ x 7½, artist signed "Lind", c. 1908; $325 D.

— same as above, listed as cider pitcher; $285 D.

— Strawberries on fancy blank, lemonade pitcher; artist signed "Beitler"; $275 D.

— pastel pond scene, brilliant pink water lilies & lazily swimming fish; gold rim & handle; 7"D x 6"H, artist signed "A. Reuvy" and marked "Pickard Handpainted China"; $245 D.

— metallic Grape decoration, artist signed "Hessler," 8¼"H, circle mark; $225 D.

— Currants as decoration on Limoges blank, 4½"H; $195 D.

— conventional floral upper half in silver, golden lower half; artist signed, c. 1908; $180 D.

— thick gold/pink/blue/green oak leaves, signed "H. Reury" on Limoges blank, 8"H, c. 1908; $125 D.

— Art Nouveau gold grapes/leaves on charcoal ground with orange accents; artist initialed, Limoges blank, 4¼"H; $80 D

Plate — frosted scene of palm trees/moon/lake, signed E. Challinor, 8½"D; $135 D.

— Poppies & Daisies, much gold, 8¾"D, artist signed by Schoner" c. 1900; $125 D.

— Pears and Medallions of blossoms, much gold, 8¾"D, artist signed "Schoner", c. 1900; $125 D.

— Carnations, much gold/green, signed "Reau"; $75 D.

Relish — open-handled, gold center with wide band of fruits, 12½"D, artist signed; $89 D.

Salt & Pepper — Art Nouveau gold etching, $12 D.

Tray — oval, decorated with Poppies, artist signed "Gaspar," 12¾"L, c. 1910; $195 D.

— moonlight scenic, signed "C. Marker," 8¾"D; $195 D.

— oblong, metallic Grape pattern, artist signed "Rean" on R.S. Prussia blank, c. 1910; 8½"L; $95 D.

— oblong, open gold handles, floral decor, 14"L, signed "Passony," 1912-1919 period; $85 D.

Vase — 2-handled, yellow Autumn weeping trees by blue river, artist signed on Nippon/Noritake blank, 6¼"H; $365 D.
— scenic, signed E. Challinor, 6½"H; $325 D.
— 2-handled, Poppies decoration, 9¼"H, c. 1910; $295 D.
— 2-handled, moon scene over palms around lake, artist signed, 9"H; $285 D.
— Tulip decoration, artist signed, 12¼"H; $225 D.
— 2-handled, trees around lake at sunset, 7"H; $195 D.
— long-stemmed American Beauty roses on dark green ground, much gold; artist signed "Coufall" on French blank, c. 1910, 13½"H; $195 D.
— 2-handled, sunset landscape of palms around lake, 7"H; $180 D.

PILKINGTON

Vase — bulbous base with cylindrical neck, glazed with 3 fish swimming among algae in lustrous mustard/tomato-red/olive green tones; decorated by Richard Joyce, c. 1910; silver luster mark; 8"H; *$200 A.
— sange de Bouef-type lustreware glaze, Royal Lancastrian, impressed marks, 13"H; *$200 A.

RED WING

Vase — green Art Nouveau styling, 8"H; $29 D.

ROOKWOOD (Easily the most collectible and highest-rated of the American art potteries, many of the early Rookwood products are highly sought and high-priced. Others can occasionally be picked up for a song (well, not quite, but still rather inexpensively). Among the famed ceramicists to decorate for Rookwood were Matt A. Daly and Artus Van Briggle. The Oriental influence upon this firm was both direct and indirect, coming directly from their prolific Japanese decorator, Kataro Shirayamadani, and indirectly from the rage for things Oriental after the 1876 Centennial Exposition. Dating can be accomplished on most Rookwood wares by counting the flame points in their marks (1887-1900), or the use of Roman numerals from 1901. See any of the many references on this fine pottery's products.)

Ewer — "Standard" glaze, painted by Matt A. Daly, 1892; impressed firm mark & "387C" plus artist's initials, 11"H; *$620 A.

Jardiniere — "Standard" glaze, leaves & berries; painted by A.R. Valentien, 1888; 6"H; x 9½"D; $1,200 D.
— "Standard" glaze, floral decoration by Matt A. Daly, 1888; impressed mark, artist's initials, and "407W," 13"H; *$900 A.

— "Standard" glaze with leaves & berries, painted by Leonore Asbury, 1896; 2-handled; 2 small hairlines on rim, glaze scratch; $500 D.

Jug — "Standard" glaze, corn decoration by Irene Bishop, with original stopper, 1900; $950 D.

— "Standard" glaze, scrafiato decoration, painted by Edward P. Cranch, 1891; impressed firm mark, artist's initials, "85W," handled, 6"H; *$700 A.

— "Standard" glaze, painted by Maria Longworth Nichols, 1882; impressed mark, 8½"H; *$650 A.

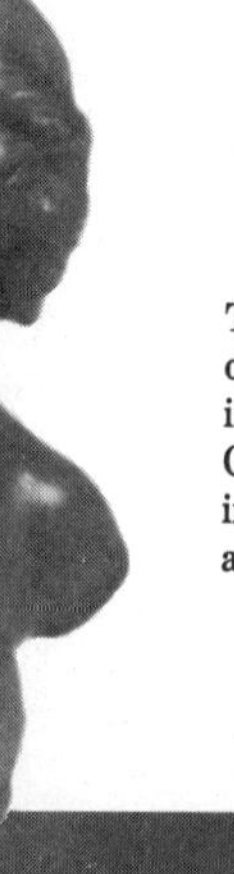

TERRA COTTA BUST by Charles Theodore Perron; pinkish-brown glaze, side inscribed "Ch. Perron," back impressed CH. PERRON/STATUAIRE/PARIS, plus inscribed "56," c. 1900; 28"H, minor restorations; *$500 A. (Sotheby's)

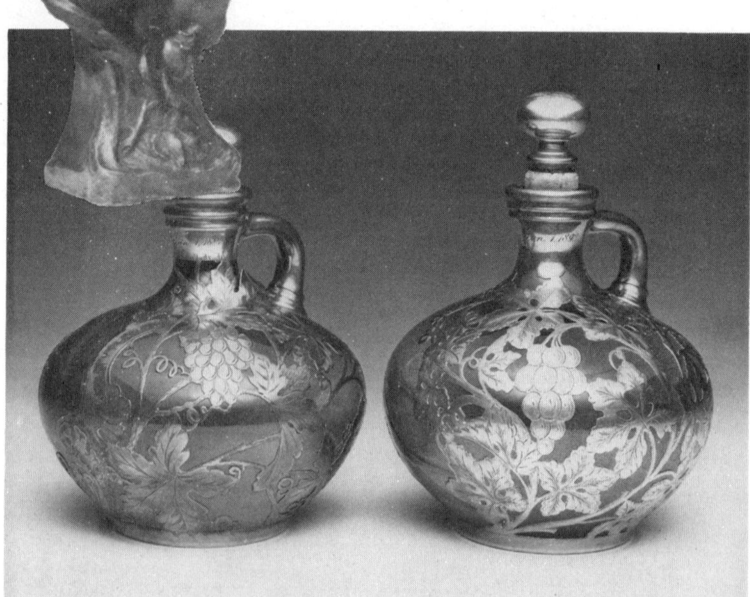

EWERS BY ROOKWOOD, each with silver overlay and decorated with grapes, each inscribed "January 1, 1893," each 7¾"H; (Left) *$1,200 A. (Right) *$1,100A. (C. G. Sloan)

— "Standard" glaze syrup jug, painted by Hattie Horton, 1883; impressed mark, "R61" and artist's initials, 4¾"H; *$250 A.

— "Standard" glaze syrup jug, painted by Albert R. Valentien, 1884; impressed mark, artist's initials & "61R", 4½"H; *$220 A.

— syrup jug decorated by Harriet Wentworth with intaglio flowers; impressed mark, initials, & "S61", 4¾"H; *$200 A.

Mug — "Standard" glaze, painted by O. Geneva Reed, 1889; inscribed "Ben Johnson," impressed mark, 656, initials, 4¾"H; *$2,200 A.

— "Standard" glaze, painted by Edward P. Cranch, 1891; impressed mark, initials, "587W," and 4½"H; *$440 A.

— "Standard" glaze, painted by Edward P. Cranch, 1891; impressed mark, initials, "537 W," & date; 4½"H, hairline rim crack; *$300 A.

— raised snails as decoration, matte green, by M. Mitchell, 1905; $195 D.

— "Standard" glaze, decorated by Albert R. Valentien; impressed "650 S" & artist's initials, 5 7/8"H; *$190 A.

— "red flowers in relief, painted by Albert Pons, 1907; impressed mark, artist's initials, & "587C X," 5"H; *$150 A.

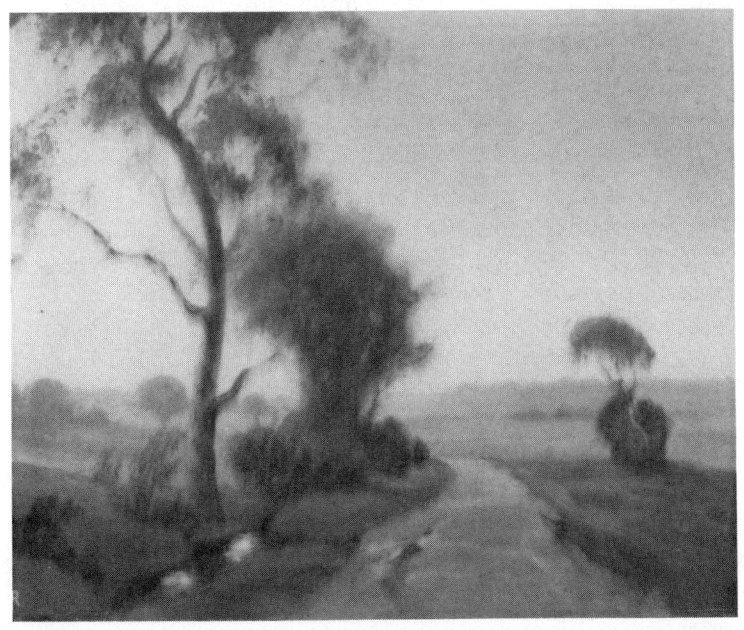

PLAQUE BY ROOKWOOD, earthenware, 1918, framed; *$1,100 A. (Christie's)

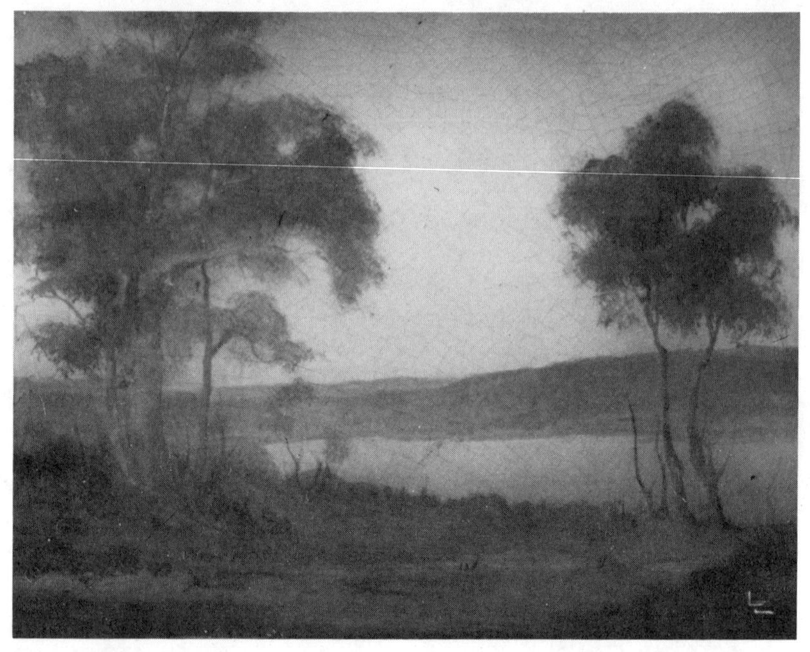

PLAQUE BY ROOKWOOD, earthenware, 1920; *$1,000 A. (Christie's)

Pitcher — "Standard" glaze, painted by Josephine E. Zettel, 1892; impressed mark, artist's initials, & "259C", 6"H; *$1,500 A.

— "Standard" glaze, painted by Kataro Shirayamadani, 1891; impressed mark, artist's signature, & "S934 W", 10½"H; neck and handle repair; *$1,200 A.

— "Standard" glaze on truncated cone form, painted by William P. McDonald, 1893; impressed mark, initials, & "564B W," 10¾"H; *$280 A.

Plaque — "Vellum" glaze, trees & lake in front of distant mountains, painted/signed by Sallie E. Coyne, 1912; framed, impressed mark, 10½"L; *$1,900 A.

— "Vellum" glaze, painted/signed by Lorinda Epply, 1920; impressed mark, 12¼"L; *$1,000 A.

— faience, child in purple blanket wrapped in white bands with blue glossy ground; 14 x 19 oval, signed; $495 D.

Vase — "Standard" glaze, Indian portrait inscribed "BAHBES-KEIT" PONCA, painted by Sturgis Laurence, 1898; impressed mark, initials, & "786D," 8¼"H; *$5,200 A.

— "Standard" glaze, Indian portrait inscribed "ES-SENCE" or "LITTLE SHELL" CHIPPEWA,' painted by Sturgis Laurence, 1898; impressed mark, initials, & "614E," 8"H; *$5,000 A.

— painted by Matt A. Daly, 1895, on blue/tan ground; impressed mark, initials, & "743C 199G," 7"H; *$3,000 A.
— painted by Albert R. Valentien, 1896; white/green Morning Glory vine on smear-glazed powder blue ground; impressed mark, initials, & "162X," 20¾"H; *$2,600 A.
— painted by Arthur P. Conant, 1918, with blue ground; impressed mark, initials, & "999C," 8¾"H; *$2,600 A.
— orange trumpet flowers with silver overlay, decorated by Fred Rothenbusch, 1896; $2,250 D.
— "Standard" glaze, decorated by Artus Van Briggle, 1892; impressed mark, initials & "S1048 W," 16½"H; *$1,800 A.
— "Standard" glaze, painted by Mary Nourse, 1892; impressed mark, initials, & "623W," 5½"H; silver overlay stamped GORHAM MFG. CO. R137; *$1,600 A.
— "Sea Green" glaze, decorated by Matt A. Daly, 1896; impressed mark, initials, & "744C," 8"H; *$1,400 A.
— "Iris" glaze, decorated by Edward Diers, 1902; impressed mark, initials, & "932E," 7½"H; *$1,350 A.
— "Iris" glaze, decorated by Laura E. Lindeman, 1906; impressed mark, initials & "904E W," 6¾"H; *$960 A.
— moss green ground, decorated by Harriet E. Wilcox, 1900; impressed mark, initials & "30 F," 6"H; *$920 A.
— "Iris" glaze, decorated with grapes by Fred Rothenbusch, 1902; impressed mark, initials, & "922C," 8½"H; *$900 A.
— "Iris" glaze, decorated with Cornflowers by Edith Noonan, 1909; impressed mark, initials, & "907F," 7¼"H; *$860 A.
— "Iris" glaze, decorated by Lenore Asbury, 1905; impressed mark, initials, & "905D W," 7¾"H; *$850 A.
— matte glaze, 3-handled, painted by Sallie Toohey, 1904; impressed mark, initials, & "268Z," 7¾"H; *$820 A.
— "Vellum" glaze, painted by Fred Rothenbusch, 1919; impressed mark, initials, & "30 E V," 9"H; *$800 A.
— "Vellum" glaze, painted by Edward Diers, 1921, with naturalistic trees; impressed mark, initials, & "732C V," 7¼"H; *$780 A.
— "Sea Green" glaze, painted by Sallie Toohey, 1899, on flattened spherical form; impressed mark, initials, & "762c," 5½"H; *$700 A.
— "Vellum" glaze, painted by Sara Sax, 1903; impressed mark, initials, & "989C," 8¼"H; *$600 A.
— "Vellum" glaze, lake & tree scene, painted by Edward T. Hurley, 1914; impressed mark, initials, & "1658E," 8"H; *$560 A.

— painted by William P. McDonald on light blue ground (c. 1885?); impressed "141 W" with artist's initials, 11"H; *$550 A.

— "Vellum" glaze, painted by Sallie E. Coyne, 1915; impressed mark, initials, & "2040D V," 9½"H; *$500 A.

— "Vellum" glaze, painted by Lenore Asbury, 1912; impressed mark, initials, & "1658V," 8"H; *$500 A.

— cafe-au-lait ground, painted by Hattie Horton, 1883; impressed mark, initials, & "126 1883," 12"H; *$480 A.

— "Standard" glaze, painted by Lenore Asbury, 1900; impressed mark, initials, & "814A," 9½"H; *$450 A.

— baluster in 6-panel form, underglaze yellow/brown floral on shaded yellow-to-brown ground, high gloss, painted by Elizabeth Neave Lincoln, c. 1899, 8½"H; *$425 A.

— "Standard" glaze, painted by Anna M. Valentien; impressed mark, initials, & "814A X," 9¾"H; *$420 A.

— "Standard" glaze, painted by Edward T. Hurley, 1897; impressed mark, initials, & "753," 6½"H; *$380 A.

— "Standard" glaze, painted by Katherine Hickman, 1895; impressed mark, initials, & "744C," 8"H; *$380 A.

— "Standard" glaze, brown underglaze floral decoration on ground shading from chartreuse to brown, painted by Elizabeth Neave Lincoln, c. 1903; cylinder shape, 9¼"H; *$325 A.

— "Standard" glaze, painted by Clara C. Lindeman, 1906; impressed mark, initials, & "605," 5"H; *$320 A.

— "Standard" glaze, painted by Harriet R. Strafer, 1893; impressed mark, initials, & "642W," 10¼"H; *$300 A.

— "Standard" glaze, painted by Anna M. Valentien, 1891, on spherical body with crimped rim; impressed mark, initials, & "612W," 4¾"H; *$280 A.

— painted by Charles S. Todd, 1922, with stylized scarlet/navy flowers in pink ground; impressed mark, initials, & "2369," 10¾"H; *$280 A.

— painted by Kataro Shirayamadani, 1923, on pastel blue/pink ground; impressed mark, artist's signature, & "1358F X," 6"H; *$280 A.

— painted by Rose Fechheimer, 1904, with blue Irises on burnt orange ground; impressed mark, painted artist's initials, & "67," 5¼"H; *$220 A.

— "Standard" glaze painted by Carrie Steinle, 1907 with floral design; impressed mark, initials, & "950E," 7"H; *$200 A.

— "Standard" glaze, painted by Josephine E. Zettel, 1895; impressed mark, initials, & "605", 5"H; *$170 A.

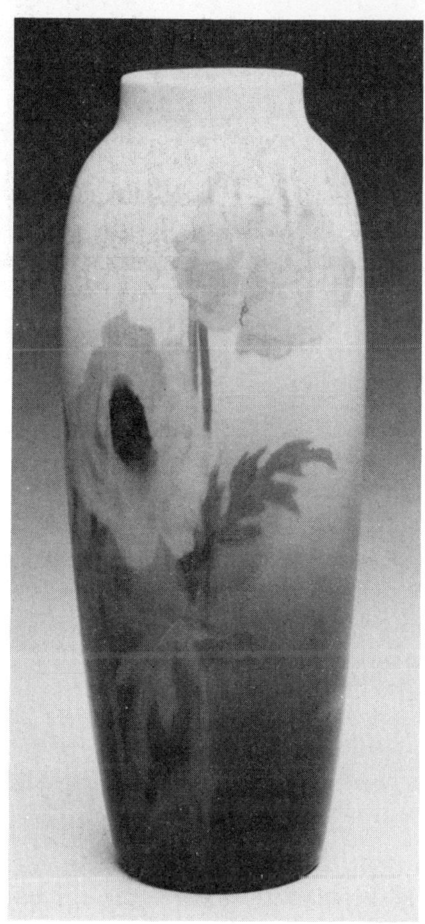

VASE BY ROOKWOOD, pastel shades with Poppy decor, signed "L.A.," 14"H; *$825 A. (C.G. Sloan)

RORSTRAND

Vase — decorated with moonlit forest scene on blue ground, painted marks, 17½"H; *$360 A.

— floral decoration, highly glazed, 4½"H; $135 D.

ROSEVILLE POTTERY (Following the leads of Rookwood, J.B. Owens, Weller and other Ohio potteries, the Roseville Pottery Company entered the art pottery field with their "Rozane" line about 1900, not registering the trademark name until 1904. Following in 1902 was the "Azurean" line, directly competitive with Weller's blue Louwelsa line. The firm was reactive in its lines, responding to what competitors brought out rather than establishing new, different lines for themselves. Their rarely signed "Mara" line was issued in response to Weller's Sicardo line about 1904. Collector interest continues in this firm's products.)

Ewer — Rozane ware, Tiger Lily decor, ornate handle, 7¾"H; $175 D.

Jardiniere — "Persian" line, florals in pink, 2 hairline cracks, large; $75 D.

Mug — Rozane ware, grape motif on brown ground, spreading foot & scrolling handle; 4¾"H; *$80 A.

Vase — baluster form decorated with clusters of olive green/purple grapes, painted & signed by Lily Mitchell; molded mark, 16½"H; *$300 A.

— 2-handled, yellow flowers on brown ground, 11"H; *$225 A.

— 2-handled, Pansies; base flake, 4½"H; $75 D.

ROYAL BONN

Vase — tapestry surface, alternating floral & Rose panels with gilt highlights, 9"H; $235 D.

— green banded, pink/yellow Roses, 5½"H x 6½"D; $125 D.

— multi-colored florals against shaded blues/oranges, Mehlem mark, 10"H; $115 D.

— orange/green/lavender flowers, worn gold handle trim; marked "Mehlem," 12"H; $85 D.

— bulbous body narrows to ¼-inch neck, orangish flower; olive green base shades to cream-colored top, 5"H; $79 D.

— slightly pinched waist, polychrome/gilt floral decoration, 8½"H; *$60 A.

ROYAL COPENHAGEN

Ginger Jar — ovoid with Poppy blossoms/leaves/buds in blue/grey/slate against ground shading from white to pale blue; white domed cover; printed factory mark of triple wave; 1880s, 7"H; *$400 A.

ROYAL CROWN DERBY

Ewer — pair, bulbous bodies decorated in underglaze blue/iron-red enamel with floral motifs washed in gilding; printed ROYAL CROWN DERBY and ENGLAND around crowned monogram in iron-red; early 20th century, 15¾"H; the pair, *$750 A.

ROYAL DUX

Centerpiece — maiden with clam, 10"H; $400 D.

Dresser Piece — lady bordering separate beveled mirror, set into flowered pin tray, 19 x 14; $795 D.

Vase — 2-handled, blown-out Geranium motif, 16"H; $165 D.

ROYAL FLEMISH

Vase — bulbous bottom and slender neck, raised gold sections with medallions of dragon heads, stained glass-type floral background, 12"H; $1,675 D.

ROYAL VIENNA

Pitcher — Oriental influence, floral with gold decoration, 4"H; $95 D.

ROYAL WORCESTER

Cracker Jar — melon-ribbed, decorated with purple Thistles/leaves, Orange blossoms/leaves, plus pink/yellow/lavender flowers; gold claw-foot handle on lid, gold decorated collar (showing some wear); 5½"H x 6"D at widest; $325 D.

Vase — bottle form, gilt/polychrome floral motif on yellow ground, 12"H; *$80 A.

— pair, Highland cattle grazing in foggy landscapes, gilt details; each painted by J. Stinton, 1922; printed crown circle marks in puce, 16"H; pair, *$2,000 A.

ROZENBURG

Vase — cabinet vase, painted with stylized yellow/rust flowering plants by "JVR," printed mark, 4½"H; *$980 A.

— 2-handled angular, with scrolling floral vine in violet/yellow/green tones on mottled green/brick-red ground; painted underglaze marks, 9½"H, minor foot chip; *$425 A.

R.S. GERMANY

Tankard — blown-out flowers, gold/white, 9"H; $200 D.

SCHAFFER & VATER

Hair Receiver — triangular bisque, lady's face & jeweling decoration; $90 D.

Hat Pin Holder — bisque, lady's face in relief front & back, jeweling; $150 D.

Powder Box — Lady's head on cover, dusty pink/green; $75 D.

SEVRES

Urn — Ormolu acorn finial over flattened pear-shape body, decoration of painted Byzantine women surrounded by flowers, with gilt accents; ormolu mounts; signed "Edabonevil," 13"H, pair; *$325 A.

Vase — orange/blue with 3 masks at shoulder, painted by Taxile Doat; firm mark, artist signature, 6¼"H; *$2,000 A.

— grey mottled with blue/green/grey/rust/mauve; 3 grey medallions pendant from neck with white cameo portraits

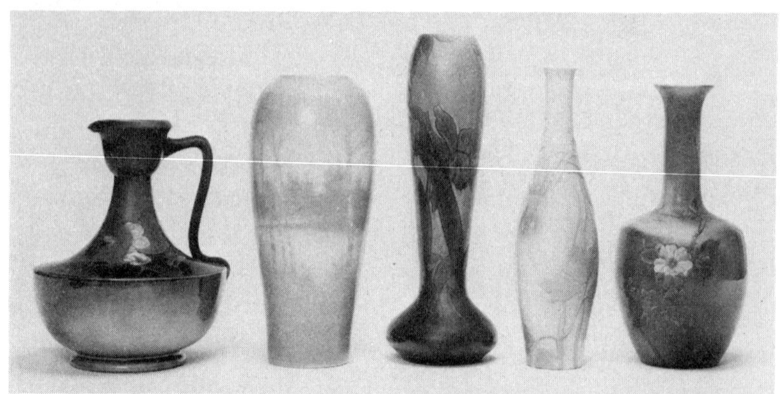

FIVE ROOKWOOD EARTHENWARE PIECES. (A) pitcher, "Standard" glaze, painted by Kataro Shirayamadani, 1891, #S934 W; 10½"H, neck & handle repairs; *$1,200 A. (B) vase, "Vellum" glaze, painted by Edward T. Hurley, 1913, #2033C V; 12¼"H; *$950 A. (C) vase, "Sea Green" glaze, painted by Albert R. Valentien, 1898, #S1431; 14"H; *$4,000 A. (D) vase, "Iris" glaze painted by Matt A. Daly, 1900, #S1658; 12¾"H; *$4,200 A. (E) vase, "Standard" glaze painted by Anna M. Valentien, 1888, #735S W; 12¼"H; *$400 A. (Christie's)

of lizard, frogs, and kangaroo respectively; decorated and signed by Taxile Doat, firm mark, 7¼"H; *$1,900 A.

— covered specimen decorated by Taxile Doat in shades of moss green; firm mark, dated 1901, 8½"H, repair to cover interior; *$1,800 A.

— covered specimen decorated by Taxile Doat in floral designs of green/white; firm mark, 6¾"H; *$1,400 A.

— beige/white decoration with 3 gilt mask medallions, by Taxile Doat, firm mark, dated 1907; *$900 A.

— red/white/blue decoration by Taxile Doat, firm mark, 4½"H; *$620 A.

— puce/green/charcoal decoration by Taxile Doat, firm mark, dated 1905; *$550 A.

— periwinkle shading to inky blue decoration by Taxile Doat, firm mark, dated 1902, 6"H; *$500 A.

— puce/green/white decoration by Taxile Doat, firm mark, 7"H; *$500 A.

— blue/fawn decoration by Taxile Doat, firm mark, dated 1905, 6¼"H; *$460 A.

— pair figural decorated vases with square bronze bases, one lacking a cover, with Art Nouveau-style floral & figural decoration; 13"H; pair, *$350 A.

— thick white crystalline glaze by Taxile Doat, firm mark, 3"H; *$350 A.

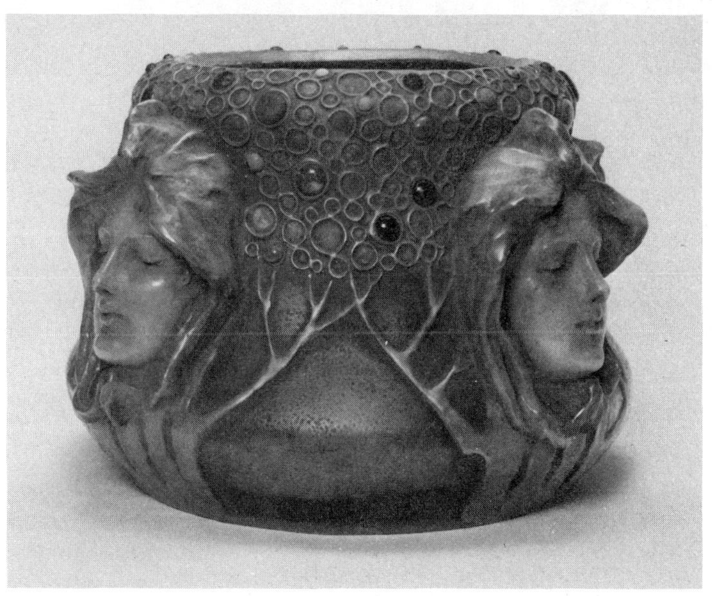

URN BY REISSNER, STELLMACHER & KESSNER, "jeweled" earthenware; *$2,100 A. (Christie's)

TIFFANY (Much less well known than Tiffany's lighting fixtures or glassware, the pottery was not nearly the same success, either aesthetically or financially. In comparison with the Tiffany glass, prices for earthenware are rock bottom, but speculators should remember the old rule, that the best of quality will continue to increase in value — and Tiffany's ceramics just weren't the best!)

Teapot — designed as flower, body with bud-form handle and molded as flowerhead covered with pine/olive green semi-gloss glaze; cover has tendril finial, covered with mottled green semi-gloss glaze; incised "L.C. Tiffany - Favrile Pottery P729," 5¼"H, repair to spout; *$360 A.

Vase — free-form, apple green, with Pears/Apples in relief on ribbed body, 7"H; *$1,150 A.

— multiple leaf molded design, apple-green glaze, 10"H, inscribed "LCT 7"; *$1,000 A.

— molded with birds on branches, semi-gloss glaze, inscribed LCT, 5¼"H; *$880 A.

— ovoid molded sides, green glazed interior, 6"H; *$225 A.

TURN AUSTRIA/TURN VIENNA

Vase — full nude female with draped grown, long hair; girl light blue with gold highlights on vase of brown with gold highlights, 12"H; Turn Austria; $375 D.

— large Art Nouveau flowers in cream/pale blue/maroon outlined in heavy gold on pale pink ground; cobalt/gold trim at top & base; $125 D.

VAN BRIGGLE (Most of the Van Briggle output came after the Art Nouveau styles passed from favor, although some of the earlier patterns are collectible as examples of Art Nouveau.)

Bowl — Dragonfly decoration with matching flower frog; $75 D.
Vase — bulbous base, Art Nouveau decoration, 4½"H; $35 D.

WAHLISS, ERNST

Vase — matte green glaze on earthenware, floral motif; stamped with firm's mark & impressed "9 MADE IN AUSTRIA 4654," 5¼"H; *$800 A.

WALTER, A. (better known in the world of glass)

Vase — turquoise/green scenic trees, signed, 7½"H; $275 D.

WELLER (Sam Weller's pottery grew into a commercial success by adapting the techniques of others to their commercial production. After acquiring W.A. Long's Lonhuda Pottery, Weller continued to produce the equivalent of the Lonhuda line under the name "Louwelsa," a copycat cousin of Rookwood's "Standard" ware. Other Weller lines of particular significance include the "L'Art Nouveau" line and that designed for Weller by Jacques Sicard — "Sicardo." The top wares rank with the best of the commercial pottery products in the country.)

Dish & Flower Frog — lily form, signed; $150 *$150 A.
Ewer — woman & floral decoration, 11"H; $350 D.
— matte finish, 13½"H; $175 D.
— L'Art Nouveau, 13½"H, matte; $175 D.
Jardiniere — Louwelsa line, 10"D x 8½"H, glossy brown with shaded brown flowers; pair, $350 D.
— floral, ivory with brown glaze, 9½"D; $47 D.
Mug — Floretta line, base marked "Weller," Art Nouveau design; $140 D.
— Grape decor on brown ground, looping handle, 5"H; *$100 A.
Tankard — Art Nouveau decoration, 14"H, hairline crack at handle; $110 D.

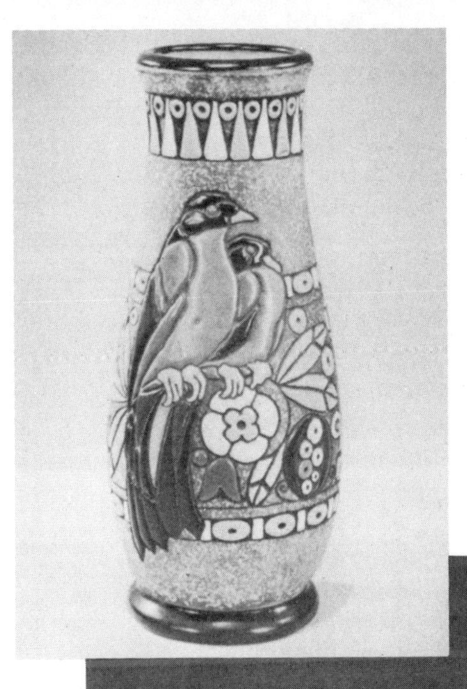

VASE, AMPHORA TYPE from RS & K in abstract motif, c. 1920, 13½"H; *$70 A. (Morton's)

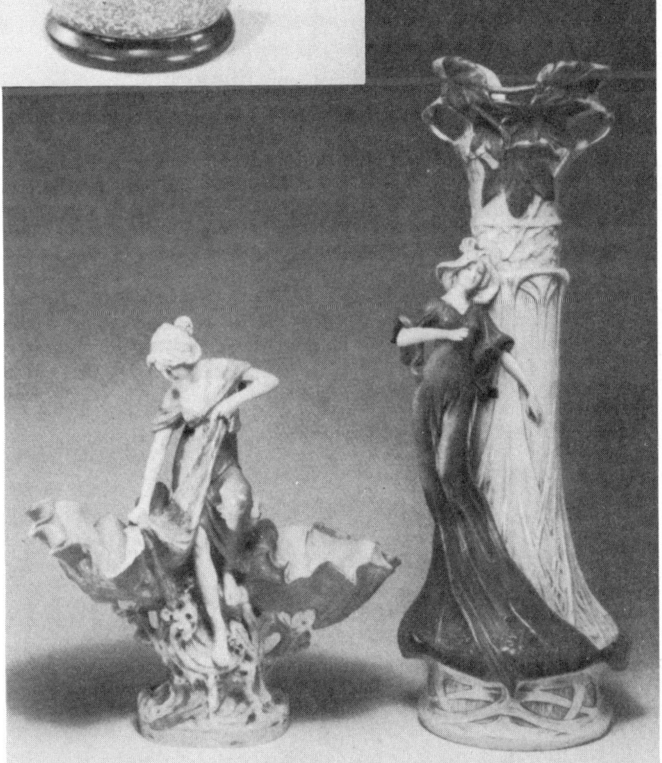

TWO ROYAL DUX CERAMIC PIECES, dating c. 1900, with some restorations. (Left) Figural centerpiece, ochre/mauve/ivory, gilt-heightened, 15¾"H; *$250 A. (Right) Figural vase, olive/ivory/rust tones, gilded, applied factory mark, 26"H; *$350 A. (Sotheby's)

Vase — Indian portrait on brown ground, impressed LOUWELSA WELLER K690; 10½"H; *$1,800 A.

— floral and multi-spotted, 13"H, signed Jacques Sicard for Weller; *$850 A.

— bottle form, iridescent purple to green glaze, 18"H; signed SICARDO, also "Weller"; $800 D.

— deep red metallic glaze with gold/green tall Tulip-style motif; signed "Weller Sicardo" on side, 7½"H; $495 D.

— Thistle pattern, Sicard, 6¼"H; $460 D.

— Sicardo line, 7¼"H x 3¾"D; $350 D.

— 2-handled, artist signed V. Adams, 12¾"H, perfect condition, from Louwelsa Weller line; $325 D.

— Sicardo, floral decoration, 6½"H; *$320 A.

— leaves & flowers painted on blue ground by Timberlake, impressed WELLER, painted firm mark & artist signature, 8¼"H; *$300 A.

— floral motif painted on pink ground, impressed WELLER, painted artist signature, 12¾"H; *$300 A.

— Lily of the Valley motif, white to dark grey shading, signed "Eocean" (one of Weller's many lines), 8"H, $275 D.

— L'Art Nouveau line, matte finish, female decoration, 10"H; $225 D.

— Sicardo, wine color, 6"H; $190 D.

— Louwelsa line, high glaze floral, 6 1/8"H; $170 D.

— Sicardo, iridescent with Lily motif, 3½"H; $145 D.

— L'Art Nouveau line, single stemmed flower, 5½"H; $110 D.

— sgraffito floral motif, 1905, 4"H; $85 D.

— Art Nouveau decoration on Floretta blank, 9½"H; $85 D.

— Lavonia line, Grapes/leaves/vines, 8"H; $40 D.

ZSOLNAY

Bowl — 3 multifloral heart-shaped panels joined by reticulated floral/foliage insets on highly glazed ivory ground, folded handle, 10½"D; $200 D.

— triangular, completely reticulated, all-over raised yellow Poppies & lavender florals, overturned corners forming pockets, castle mark, 12"H; $150 D.

Ewer — rope-twist handle & pierced lip, slip-glazed Rose with overall ochre floral patterns of Near Eastern origin/inspiration, gilt-heightened; underglaze factory mark plus impressed mark, c. 1900, 14½"H; *$300 A.

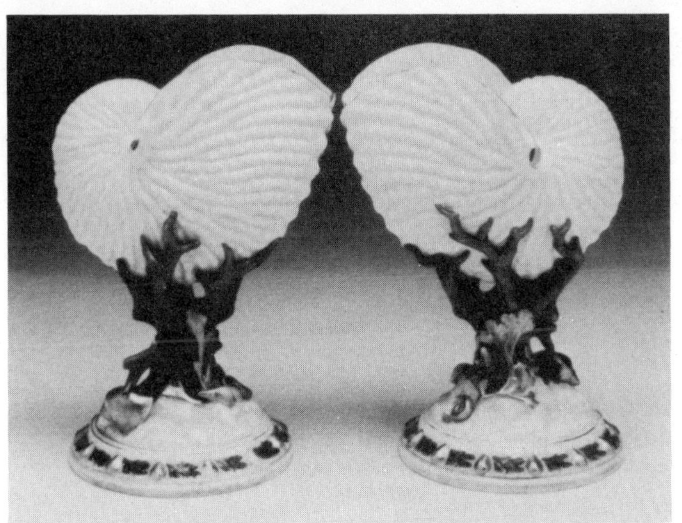

ROYAL WORCESTER COMPOTES, pair, each ribbed shell held aloft by bronzed/gilt coral & seaweed, impressed & printed marks; 8¼"H, some gilding worn; *$500 A. (Sotheby's)

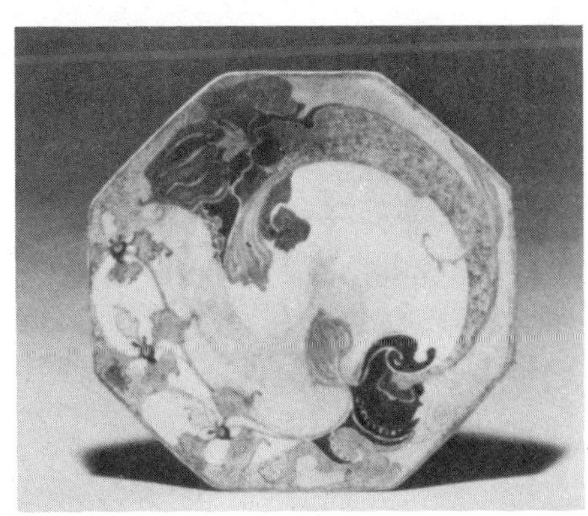

ROZENBURG DER HAAG SAUCER, porcelain; painted with Iris blossoms/leaves in pink/purple/sage green by J. Schellink; full Rozenburg marks, artist monogram; 5¼"D; *$650 A. (Phillips)

Pitcher — Persian-type design, pierced reserves in high relief with cabochon prunts, much gold, colorful florals; steeple castle mark, 8¼"H; $399 D.

— closed top, spout formed as a man in pink, floral decoration, 13"H; $195 D.

Planter — 4 reticulated panels, gold/red/blue/green floral; $125 D.

Tumbler — gold/green iridescent lustre with relief of 4 standing nudes holding cups & vines in vineyard, 6½"H; $85 D.

Vase — floral design and black cats painted on blue ground, impressed marks, 11"H; *$1,000 A.

— green lustre glaze, arboreal form, molded mark, 12½"H; *$800 A.

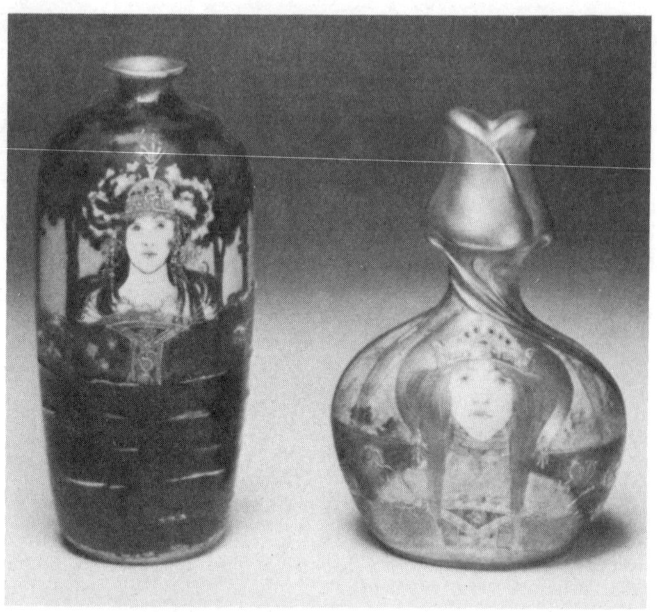

TWO AMPHORA POTTERY VASES, c. 1900, each marked TURN TEPLITZ BOHEMIA/RS &K/MADE IN AUSTRIA. (Left) bust portrait of warrior maiden in blue/olive/brown, gilt-heightened; 6¾"H; *$350 A. (Right) bust of royal maiden before forest, gilt-heightened, 6¼"H; *$700 A. (Sotheby's)

— double-wall base, completely reticulated, cobalt/beige/gold, with steeple mark; $389 D
— lustre-decorated with Middle Eastern designs, with firm's lozenge, 4½"H; *$240 A.
— peacock lustre, marked Zsolnay Pecs, 9½"H; $165 D.
— wide mouth, iridescent, molded with Art Nouveau women, 6½"H; $75 D.

UNSIGNED SPECIMENS (Included here, as a wrap-up for the ceramics section, are both those pieces not attributable to a specific pottery, and those which are attributed to a particular pottery although perhaps not marked.)

Bowl & Pitcher — Satsuma type, unmarked; cream ground with gold, green/gold Chrysanthemums, handle formed as swan's neck; $750 D.

Cups, Demitasse — Art Nouveau-inspired silver overlay cups with undertrays, brown glaze; set of 6, *$210 A.

Figure — bisque nude with arm over shell-shaped bowl forming handle, her lower half swirling to form bowl; flowing hair forms openwork above back, rainbow of colors swirls interior/exterior, elongated leaves form footing, gold beading; unsigned, 9"L x 6½"H x 6¾"W; $195 D.

— Art Nouveau lady seated in evening gown smoking cigar, legs out; marked Czechoslovakia; $37 D.

Hatpin Holder — decorated with 2 ladies beside column of Forget-Me-Nots, marked Paris; $155 D.

Jardiniere — glazed multicolor floral design on yellow-to-brown ground; base marked "HBc," 12"H; *$175 A.

Plaque — St. Theresa at piano with cherubs, 4 1/8" x 6 1/8", in goldtone Art Nouveau frame; $245 D.

Plate — stylized bird, from Austria, 8"D; $28 D.

Platter — cobalt flow blue in Art Nouveau manner, 15½"L; $85 D.

Stein — grey ceramic body with Art Nouveau decor, green trim; pewter lid marked "RG 451W," 6"H; $100 D.

Teapot — heavy floral Art Nouveau silver overlay on blue porcelain body; $135 D.

Tile, Faience — high relief tulips in brown/green/blue; framed; $125 D.

Toothpick Holder — red/green scrolling decor on white ground; $15 D.

Tray — two women's heads molded, unsigned but attributed to R.S. Prussia; $140 D.

Vase — bisque 7"H Art Nouveau woman standing on pearlized interior shell bowl 8¼"D; she holds jug with one hand, other arm resting on flower formation depicting fountain which is also vase; scrolled footing, overall 8¾"H; $160 D.

— full figure, female, bisque; $145 D.

— enamel decorated, signed by Edith Richards & dated 1917; American Arts & Crafts, 13"H; *$125 A.

— molded round body, loop handles, square neck, iridescent purple; 4"H; *$110 A.

— majolica, Iris handles, 12"H; $88 D.

— figural bathing beauty, Art Nouveau styling, marked "Germany #5678"; $65 D.

— bulbous base, flared rim, free-form handles; brown with painted floral motif, 9¼"H, impressed "Germany"; small chip on base; $60 D.

— globular art pottery, glaze shading from blue to green, illegible base signature, 7"H; *$40 A.

— naturalistically modeled in form of trimmed tree trunk, loop handle, 11½"H; *$35 A.

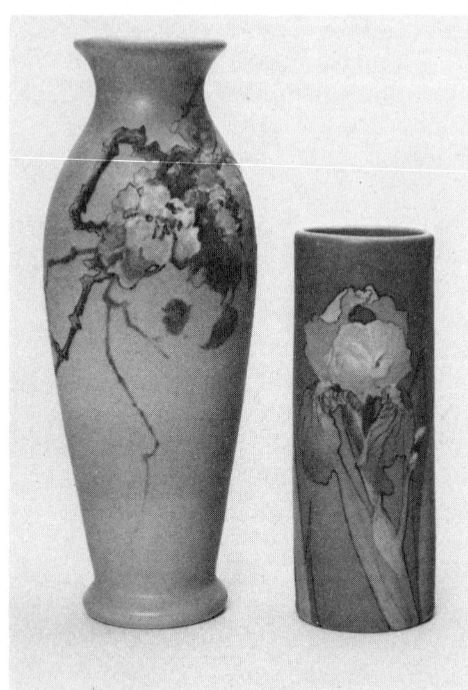

EARTHENWARE VASES from Weller, each impressed WELLER, decorated by Timberlake. (Left) pink ground, 12¾"H; *$300 A. (Right) blue ground, additional painted firm mark, 8¼"H; *$300 A. (Christie's)

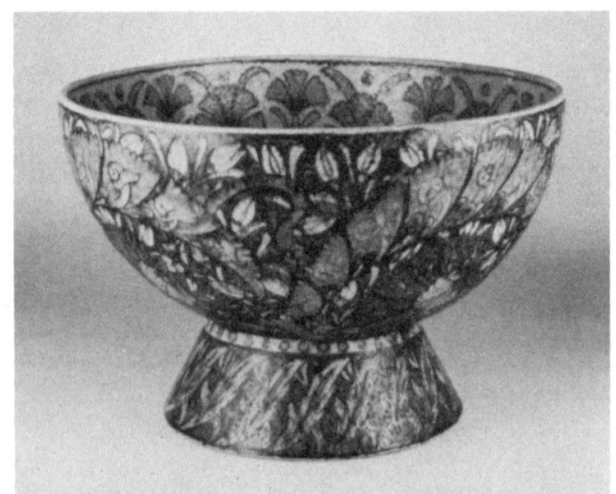

FOOTED BOWL in the style of William de Morgan; crackle glaze in turquoise/blue-green/blue on pale green ground, interior glazed with concentric rows of stylized flower heads; English, 17"D, late 19th century, some losses to glaze; *$2,000 A. (Sotheby's)

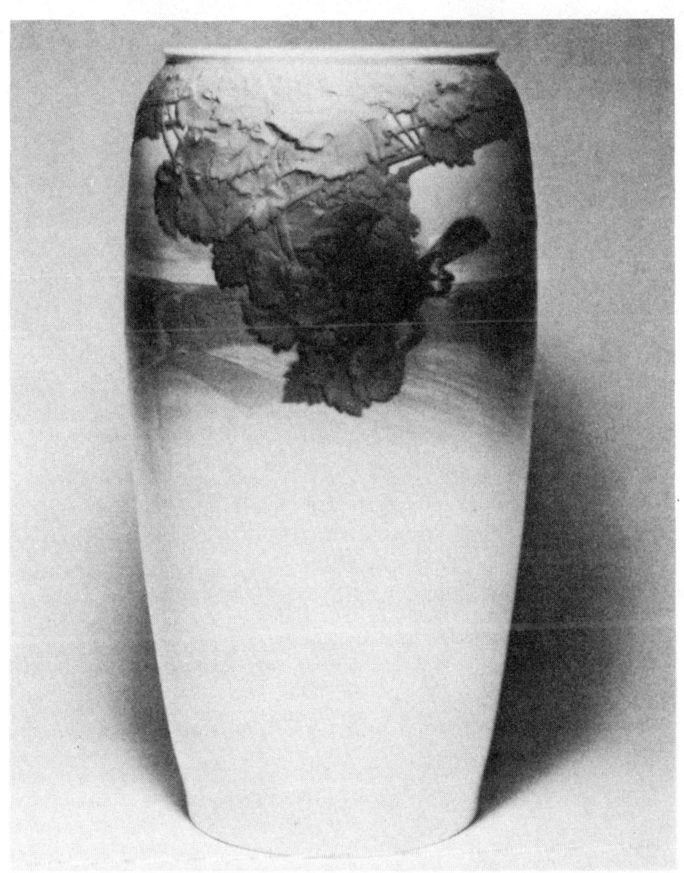

BERLIN PORCELAIN VASE, designed by Theo Schmuz-Baudiss; blended tones of dusty pale rose through smoke/pale grey to pale sea green/white; impressed N LA No. 13060 M15, incised "7448," produced by the Staatlichen Porzellan Manufaktur Berlin, c. 1903; 17¼"H; *$4,250 A. (Sotheby's)

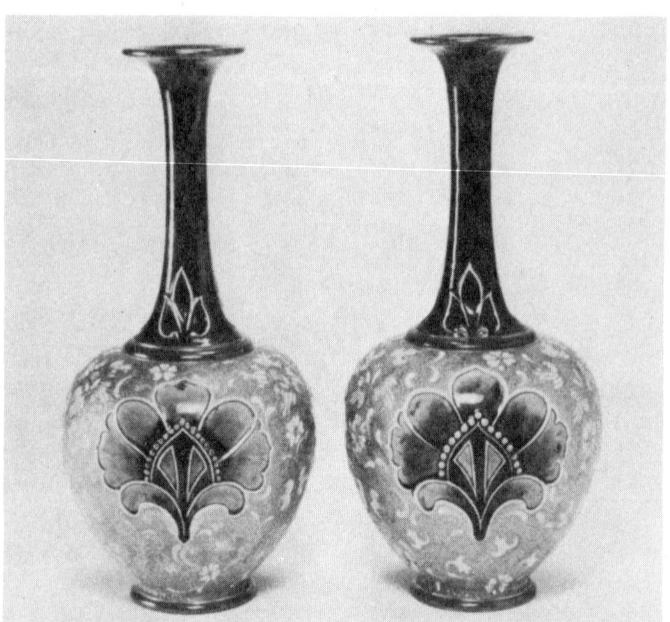

PAIR OF ROYAL DOULTON STONEWARE VASES, 1902-1914 period; olive/deep blue glaze reserved against tan/turquoise/white glaze, gilt-heightened; slender necks brown glazed with molded palmettes; impressed "DOULTON/& SLATERS PATENT," impressed artist & factory marks; 15½"H, minor chip on one palmette; an example of Doulton's "Chine" ware, developed by John Slater; *$350 A. (Sotheby's)

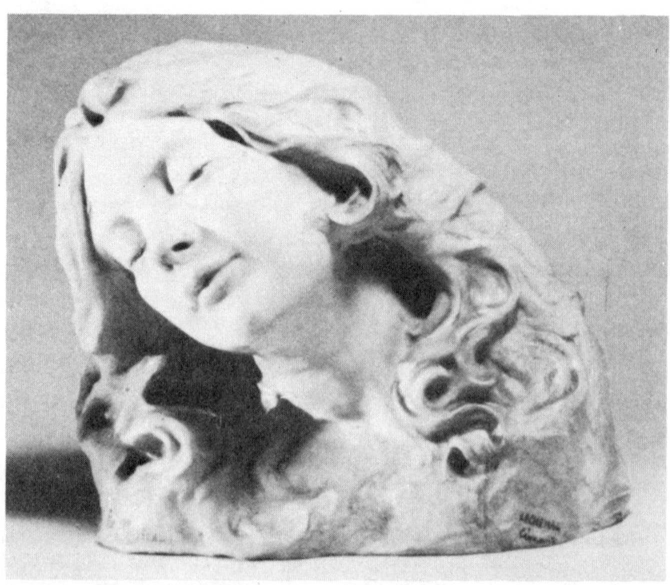

LACHENAL CERAMIC BUST, designed by Pierre-Felix Masseau, c. 1900; green-hued ivory glaze, the reverse in mottled blue/green; underglaze signature "Fix Masseau/Scteur," and "LACHENAL/Ceramiste"; 14"L; *$1,500 A. (Sotheby's)

GLASS INTRODUCTION

Glass represented one of the best — probably the most perfect — design elements for Art Nouveau craftsmen. Here was a substance which was plastic in its heated form, which could be made into innumerable shapes and colors, which could be decorated with other substances (inclusions of foil, enamels, gilding, and so forth), and which had the capacity of being both useful and decorative.

Just how much of the decorative glassware produced during the Art Nouveau period was truly "of the style" and how much was coincidental is now conjectural. Experimentation in glass coloring had been going on since the early Victorian period; certainly that phase of glass production was not new to the Art Nouveau years. It's become the fashion to lump all the glasses together as "art glass," and that may be the simplest and best solution; after all, it's a little late now for us to try to second-guess the intentions of the glassmakers and designers. Unless we know something of the background of a particular piece, and the background of its designer or artist, we're in a sort of limbo when assigning the designation "Art Nouveau" to many types.

Still, there are some common characteristics which Art Nouveau shared. A look at the history of glassmaking during this period, tying that together with some of the basic theories of Art Nouveau design, will prove instrumental in recognizing what might properly be called "Art Nouveau glass" — at least, called that by some.

Glass, depending upon the chemical constitutents used to make it, can vary greatly in its "natural" state. It may be a clear, transparent metal (glass), or it may be a transparent aqua, or it can be anything from olive-green to deep amber in color. Glassmakers learned very early that by controlling the type of sand, or the additives to the molten metal, or the percentages of these additives, the resulting glass could be changed in its final appearance. This represented one of the most basic means for changing the appearance of glass into something closer to what the glassmaker wanted.

The resurrection of the art of cameo and intaglio carving of glass brought about changes in glass fashion. It was in England that early efforts at cameo engraving resulted in a characteristic styling that continued into the early years of the 20th century, a style dominated by a white cameo raised portion (design) against a darker background. Once carried across the English Channel, especially in the city of Nancy, quite different carved effects were created. French engraved works might contain two, three, or more layers of glass, exquisitely carved to reveal sometimes startingly realistic scenic designs of floral motifs.

The carving of glass was a slow, skilled technique, really unsuited for mass-production of glass. A way had to be found to make it a speedier process, and the means was the use of acid-etching. The controlled application of a hydrofluoric acid mixture to the glass surface would chemically attack the silicate-based glass, removing enough of a layer or two in the proper places to produce the desired designs. In many cases it was still necessary to use carving tools on the glass after etching.

Two types of multi-layered glass should be noted and differentiated (although some dealers class them both together under the name "cameo"). In the first of these, the true "cameo" glass, the pattern or design of the glass is in a cameo effect, raised above the surface of the surrounding glass. When carved, that meant that all surrounding glass had to be removed; the same was true in the etching process, for in producing cameo glass by acid-etching, the design portion was masked off to protect it from the etching by the acid. In the second process, intaglio carving or intaglio-etching, the design itself was cut into the surface of the glass so that it was lower (deeper) than the surrounding glass. The difference between the two types of glass is an important one, both technologically and in today's market; all things being equal between two pieces of glass, the one which is intaglio-carved or etched should not bring as high a price as the cameo piece. Among dealers who fail to note this distinction, the collector can often make some good buys.

On the whole, French "cameo" or intaglio glass tended to be more realistic and naturalistic, and less stylized, than its British counterparts. The French products also exhibited greater asymmetry, more typical of the rococo heritage in France. Undulating lines, a hallmark of some forms of Art Nouveau, are seen in the French uses of flower stems and vining tendrils.

The multi-layered, overlay glass was only one characteristic type found in the Art Nouveau styles. Another typical treatment involved the uses of iridescent glass. Both Lobmeyr in Vienna and Loetz in Bohemia, as well as Tiffany in the United States, were among the leaders in this type of effect. The iridescence might extend over the entire surface of the glass vessels, or it might only be found in parts (as in the iridescent "oil-spotting" so typical of much of the Loetz production, or the "pulled feather" designs of Tiffany, Steuben, Durand *et al*). All types of iridescent glass relied upon the varying effects of light in movement over the surface to create differing appearances.

The application of enamel to glass was a technique which was found in both the best and worst of Art Nouveau glass. In its most basic form, enamels were applied to the surface of the glass as a final step in the decoration of the glass. This could entail the use of only a single color of enamel with a resulting crude design. On better glass, though, several different colors of enamels would be used, resulting in a true painting upon a canvas of glass. The enameling could be highlighted by gold (gilt-heightened) and when it was, the accompanying signature (when one was present) might also be in gold. Such was the case, for example, in many of the late 19th century transparent glass pieces attributed to Emile Galle. Enamel decoration was also used to augment and complement intaglio carving on specimens from the 20th century.

Often glass itself was added to a piece as a decorative element. Moser (among others) often used contrasting colors of glass handles on vessels. Tiffany, Loetz, Durand, and other makers applied glass stringing to the surface of some of their products. Tiffany, in particular, experimented with varying the surfaces of his glass to achieve unusual and desired effects.

When we speak of Art Nouveau glass we must also include the work of the most notable of 19th century French jewelers, Rene Lalique. Lalique began his experiments with glass in the opening years of the 20th century, eventually giving up his work in metals to concentrate on his glass productions. His glass, especially that produced by the moulding processes, represents a transitional facet of glass design, overlapping the Art Nouveau and later Art Deco styles. Good arguments can be advanced for placing the same glass piece by Lalique into both of these categories; for simplification, I've included only a few in this book. It can be stated fairly safely that his vases, boxes, and other items decorated with sinuous mermaids and maidens, as well as many of his floral-decorated pieces, fall within Art Nouveau consideration. Lalique's traditions in jewelry were not quickly abandoned, either, as he used glass in innovative ways in jewelry design (for that, see the Jewelry chapter). While most of the Lalique production was in clear glass (often made translucent through a surface etching process), some of his finer and more desirable works were in various pastel shades.

The stature of Louis Comfort Tiffany in the world of Art Nouveau glass is so great that his accomplishments in other design fields are occasionally overlooked. Tiffany represented the best of American glass not only to his American buyers but also to glass buyers in Europe; his early glass was carried by Bing at L'Art Nouveau in Paris, for example, competing with the finest decorative work to be gathered from around the world. Even if Tiffany received his inspiration from earlier iridescent glasses being produced in Europe; even if Tiffany's work wasn't executed by him but merely roughly designed by him; even if Tiffany's later works developed into a mass-produced commercialism which strayed from fundamental Art Nouveau tendencies; such is the nature of design, that we attribute all the works coming from his studios as being his (unless demonstrated otherwise), and give him just credit for bringing together disparate elements into the unified whole of his products.

Tiffany used his "Favrile" glass both for vessels themselves and for decorative elements on non-glass objects (brass, bronze, etc.). Primarily his glass objects will be found within this chapter; those objects containing other materials, such as the metals, will be found in the chapter on Lighting, the one on Metal objects, or the Miscellaneous chapter.

A word or two of caution should be noted regarding reproductions, frauds, forgeries, and other deceptions. As any field rises in value, the chances increase that some individuals will attempt to profit unfairly. Yes, there are reproductions on the market of many of the types of glass made in the Art Nouveau styles. Yes, there are frauds being perpetrated using these reproductions. They are still relatively minor in scope, though, and are seldom well-executed. Hand and visual contact with authenticated specimens will be enough to permit most collectors and dealers to differentiate the real from the rip-offs.

More complicated to analyze are the pieces altered by the later addition of a signature. We've seen pieces of verifiable Tiffany glass to which some person has mistakenly added a "Steuben" signature (engraved); some Loetz glass to which an engraved Tiffany signature was added; and a piece of Galle glass marked "L.C.T." In cases such as these, we may conclude that the deceiver didn't realize his or her mistake; the error was due to ignorance. Other added signatures may be added to glass in keeping with its origin, as when the familiar LCT is added to a piece of Tiffany glass. An engraving tool is an easy, inexpensive instrument, and in the hands of the unscrupulous may be used in attempts to improve the saleability of what is already a decent piece of glass.

Enameled signatures present much the same problems. Once a person learns to mix the enamel to produce a color in keeping with the rest of the decoration on the glass, almost any enameled signature can be added. Look carefully at the signature with a magnifying glass if there is any doubt; such a forged signature added at a later date may stand slightly higher than other enameling, or it may not have the wear one might expect, given the wear over the rest of the object.

Cameo signatures require a bit more skill, but they are still possible. Once a piece of overlay glass is made, and after the top layer is cut away either through etching or carving or both, the counterfeiter of signatures needs only find an area of the glass through which he may cut, and then add a new signature to an old piece. Even easier is a mild acid-etching of the surface of the glass, without cutting all the way through to an underlying layer of a different color of glass.

Faced with all these possibilities for deception, what's the collector to do? Does this mean we should steer clear of all types of glass from this period? Should we approach each piece of glass as if it is a fraudulent one?

Quite the contrary. Such deceptions are exceptions, not the rule. We just must remember that they do exist and be prepared for encountering them. Even so, almost any experienced collector (and many dealers, too!) can recount tales of the one that took them in; part of learning comes through making mistakes, just so the mistakes are not too costly.

What can be done to lessen the chances of being "taken in"? Several things, all of which are important to the collector. Among these:

* Study and learn the recognized signatures for the glassmakers you intend to collect;
* Learn to recognize the differences between, say, Austrian glass and American iridescent glass, so you won't fall for a good-looking signature on a type of glass for which it is completely out of context;
* Compile a reference library devoted to the glass you are collecting, including reprints or originals of catalogs when possible, giving you primary reference material on your glass;
* Although this chapter is organized by glass house alphabetically, don't place all your trust on a signature. Signatures should be used to help confirm attribution, not to initially assign it; and,
* Carefully observe the signature on any glass you are contemplating purchasing, looking for any signs that it may not be "right."

All pieces of glass listed under a maker's name in the following chapters can be assumed to have some sort of identifying mark, i.e., signature, unless otherwise stated. Following the alphabetical listing by maker is a section of glass which is unsigned — not identified by maker, or identified with only initials or some sort of cryptic mark so the average collector might have difficulty in identifying it.

Even unsigned pieces can be attributed in many cases, if not specifically by maker, at least according to country of origin. Many of the finest pieces of English cameo glass, for example, are not specifically attributed to particular makers with complete certainty. The unfortunate problem is, "signed" pieces will bring higher prices than comparable "unsigned" pieces over and over again. The collector who prizes a well-made glass item more than a few letters of a signature can capture their quarry at a lower price than the buyer looking for some sort of magical guarantee from a signature.

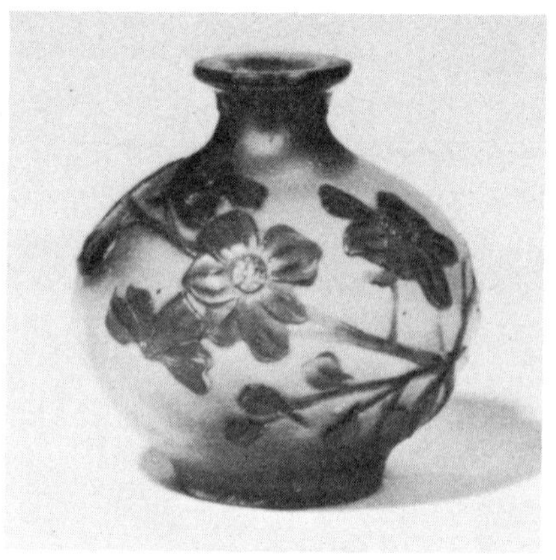

BURGUN, SCHVERER & CIE, cabinet vase; cameo, mottled grey & violet, overlaid in violet, wheel-cut with branch of wild flowers, gilt-heightened; gilt signature, "Verrerie D'Art/De Lorraine/B.S. & Cie./depose," 3¼"H, minor foot chip; *$1,000 A. (Sotheby's)

AKRO-AGATE

Box, Lidded — round, 2 female nudes with loin cloths wrapped around in high relief on cover, 3 women around sides; green; $115 D.

ARGY-ROUSSEAU

Ashtray — Pate de Verre, reds/purples with Egyptian head in center medallion, little flower buds all around edge & raised lattice work to bottom; 6¼"W x 3½", signed; $1,450 D.

— Pate de Verre, molded with flower head in shades of rose on leafy amber ground, molded signature, 3¾"D; *$720 A.

Comport — decorated with English Ivy in blue/green, molded signature, 3½"H; *$1,200 A.

Vase — wolf vase, molded in fine detail with 4 purple wolves silhouetted on pale mottled green ground pacing circumference of body on crested snow mounds; 9½"H; *$19,000 A.

— Baluster form, violet-streaked salmon ground moulded with mauve serrated scrolled handles; impressed G. ARGY-ROUSSEAU; 8¼"H; *$3,000 A.

— Pate de Verre, molded with Marguerite flower heads in shades of purple/blue on pale green ground, molded signature, 5¾"H; *$1,800 A.

— Pate de Verre, spherical, berry-laden boughs in autumnal shades, molded signature, 2½"H; *$1,050 A.

— Pate de Verre cabinet vase, gray flecked with pale green/amber/violet, the upper body with low relief blossoms in violet/green, signed "G. Argy-Rousseau", c. 1920, 4"H; *$900 A.

ARSALL

Vase — cameo waisted baluster rises from spreading circular foot; pink sides overlaid in dusty rose/olive, cut with berry-laden grape vines/tendrils/leaves; cameo signature "Arsall," 12½"H, c. 1900; $1,050 D.

BACCARAT

Centerpiece — silvered bronze & Baccarat crystal winged figure, signed; $1,250 D.

BIGELOW-KENNARD

Table Screen — leaded glass as white rabbit, 12"L x 6½"H, signed; $425 D.

BURGUN, SCHVERER & CO.

Compote — etched & enameled, transparent glass etched, gilded & enameled with floral decor, enameled signature, 5½"D; *$460 A.

Vase — cameo; deep lavender acid-etched & martele sides wheel-carved with pendant prunus blossoms over internal layer of pale rose/green/grey/yellow/white enamel; all gilded for emphasis; gilt signature VERRERIE D'ART/DE LORRAINE/B/S/&/Co. Depose, with thistle & croix de Lorraine, 5"D; *$2,800 A.

— cameo, celery-green body internally streaked with Oxblood red, enameled pink/white/green with wildflowers; sides overlaid in clear & carved over internal decoration; gilt signature, c. 1900, 7¾"H; *$2,100 A.

— cameo tapered cylinder, milky opalescent/lavender cased in clear glass, enclosing enameled white bellflower blossoms

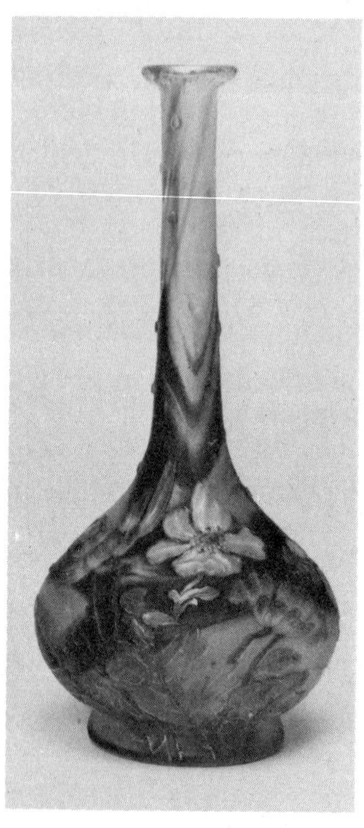

BURGUN, SCHVERER VASE, etched & enameled; green tinted glass with maroon swirls, with internally enameled/etched/ wheel-carved violet/white Anemones; gilt signature, 9¾"H; *$5,000 A. (Christie's)

& green leaves; partly wheel-cut, gilt-heightened elaborate floral motifs; silver-gilt mountings; gilt base signature; 5½"H, c. 1895, chips to exterior; *$750 A.

CARANZA, A. DUC DE

Shot Glass — 2"H, signed "A. Duc de Caranza"; $150 D.

Vase — slender tapering with metallic red & iridescent ochre; iridescent signature CARANZA; 8¼"H; *$450 A.

— flattened quatrefoil iridescent cameo, 6"H; *$375 A.

CHRISTIAN, DESIRE

Vase — cameo bud vase, deep ochre-lavender sides shade to pale ochre & olive green, overlaid in lavender; wheel carved in grasses/leafage/milkweed pods; all fire-polished, partly martele finished; intaglio body signature, "D. Christian"; base cameo signature, "D: Christian/Fecit," on bottom of bulbous body, 12 5/8"H; *$2,400 A.

DAMON

Vase — expanding cylindrical with flaring foot; clear shading to mint green at neck; enameled with swamp flora/fauna; heightened in gilt & with gilt foil inclusions; gilt signature "Damon/Blvd. Malesherbes/Paris," 9"H, c. 1900; *$950 A.

D'ARGENTAL

Bowl — scenic cameo with 3 cuttings, Autumn colors; 3½"H x 6"D; $795 D.

— cameo of yellow glass overlaid in maroon, cut with bunches of Rose blossoms; rose bowl, cameo signature "D' Argental" with cross of Lorraine, 8"D, c. 1900; *$600 A.

Box — cameo circular covered, body & cover of translucent yellow overlaid with brick red, etched Morning Glories; cameo signature, 5¼"D; $1,100 D.

— cameo circular covered, blooming Lilies in burgundy on plum-frosted ground, 5½"D, signed; $1,100 D.

— cameo circular covered, deep mustard sides overlaid with burnt umber/brown & cut in sprays of wildflower blossoms/ leaves; cover with knopped finial; 3¾"D, cameo signature; $990 D.

Perfumer — scenic cameo, birds/trees/river/marsh grass in dark greens & deep wine on frosted amber ground; heavy brass screw cap & collar stamped "Made in France"; atomizer works, metal top slightly dented; cylinder shape vase 4"H, 6" circumference; cameo signature; $875 D.

Vase — cameo, amber with maroon leaves/flowers, 12½"H x 5"D; $1,200 D.

— cameo, tapers outward from round pedestal base, then curves in toward mouth; deep cut cameo of brown on deep-amber ground; cameo signature, 12½"H; $1,150 D.

— cameo scenic, sky-blue sides overlaid in sienna mottled with green & cut with serene lake shore with leafy trees in foreground & purple mountains in distance; cameo signature, 11¾"H; *$1,000 A.

— cameo ovoid, frosted amber ground shading from deep rose at base, with detailed cameo berries/leaves of deep magenta; cameo signature, 10"H; $790 D.

— cameo vase, 3 cuttings, autumnal colors, 6"H; $750 D.

— cameo scenic, frosted purple to white to purple ground; many boats on moonlit water in 3 acid cuttings; cameo signature, 5¾"H x 3¼"D; $650 D.

— cameo scenic bowl shape, gold frosted ground, deep maroon cut to rose landscape by pond in 3 acid cuttings, signed, 3½"H; $550 D.

DAUM FRERES, NANCY, FRANCE

Bottle — 2-handled scent bottle, opalescent dusty violet overlaid in violet, cut with dragonfly & Iris stalk on reverse; 2 mottled green applied loop handles, supporting stopper with

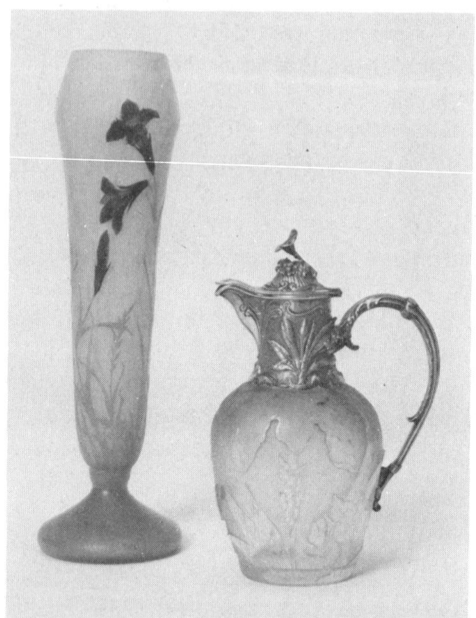

TWO PIECES FROM DAUM, NANCY, FRANCE. (Left) vase, enameled/etched/carved with Geraniums in naturalistic colors, engraved signature, 13¾"H; *$2,200 A. (Right) pitcher, green-tinted clear glass etched with Irises, gilt highlights, silver handle & mountings by Gorham, gilt signature on glass, 9¼"H; *$550 A. (Christie's)

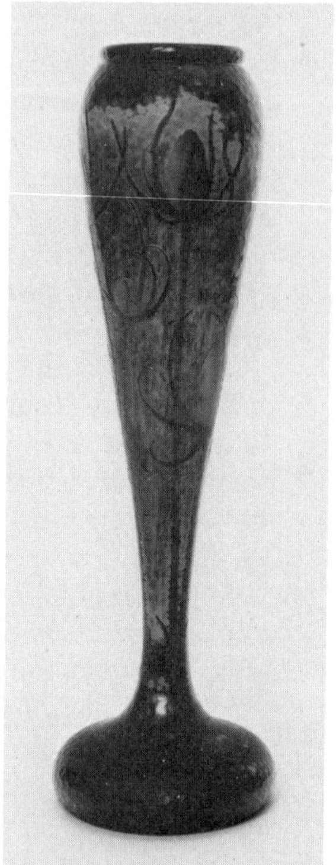

DAUM FRERES, NANCY — double overlay vase; *$4,000 A. (Christie's)

mottled green loop finial; 7½"H, inscribed "Daum/Nancy" with croix de Lorraine; one handle restored; *$700 A.

— scent bottle, translucent ground overlaid with amethyst etched with Irises & butterfly; silver overlay & silver cap with floral design; gilt signature; 8"H, chips to body & stopper; *$650 A.

Bowl — cameo & enameled, indented on 4 sides; baby Orchids in orange with green leaves on yellow ground, cameo signature, 3"H x 6"D; $850 D.

— cameo Summer scenic, blue sky, one acid cutting, clover top, 5"D x 2 3/8"H, signature; $850 D.

— cameo Winter scenic, frosted mottled ground in gold, bare forest trees with snow & snow on ground, 1 acid cutting & enameling; quatrefoil top, 2 5/8"H x 5 5/8"D, signed; $825 D.

— cameo quatrefoil with Columbine motif, frosted yellow/gold ground, cuttings of green/light wine; magenta crackle base, cameo signature "Daum Nancy France," 4½"H; $750 D.

— cameo footed, acid-etched mustard sides splashed with cranberry overlaid & enameled with Bleeding Hearts/vines/leafage in shades of Chinese red/ochre/avocado; spreading lime-green foot; cameo signature, 4"H; *$650 A.

— cameo & enameled rose bowl, red flowers/buds, green leaves/stems on green mottled ground, quatrefoil rim, 5½"D x 2½"H; $475 D.

— cameo & enameled, frosted aqua crackle glass ground with dainty gilt flowers, signed, 5½"D x 4"H; $450 D.

— cameo Winter scenic, lobed sides, cased mottled orange/yellow sides acid-cut & enameled in brown/gray/white; enamel signature; 6"D, c. 1910; *$450 A.

— rose bowl, square top, purple & gold, 2¾"H; $435 D.

— cameo trefoil, shading from apple-green to grey, interior acid-cut & enameled with Mistletoe buds/leafage & phrase "AU GUI/L'AN NEUF" in rust/white; gilt-heightened, gilt signature, 5½"D, c. 1900; *$250 A.

Box — covered, square with circular top, decorated as a Rose plant with pink blossoms, etched & engraved; engraved signature, 5¾"W; *$950 A.

— covered octagonal, decorated with yellow Iris plants, etched & enameled, cameo signature, 5"W; *$850 A.

— covered cameo, frosted ground covered in autumn leaves & small nutlike cones win brown with touches of yellow, 4"W; $395 D.

Compote — footed with triangular lip, mottled yellow/blue glass; Husson silver mounts, foliate scrolls; intaglio signature, 9"D; *$325 A.

Dish — low cameo of triangular section, clear invested with sky blue & yellow cut & enameled with Winter scene of birds in trees, enamel signature, 6"D, c. 1900; *$400 A.

Ewer — ribbed translucent white/yellow body with irregular gilded handle, enameled with many insects & snail, engraved siganture, 6¼"H; *$2,800 A.

Glasses — set of 10 signed "Daum Nancy" glasses, each with varicolored flared foot, 3"H; *$150 A.

Jar — cameo & enameled covered, round, green/yellow etched with Water Lilies applied with 2 dragonflies, enameled; engraved siganture, 3½"H; *$3,500 A.

Paperweight — Pate de Verre, circular, turquoise/violet streaked translucent ground moulded with brown/green beetle, moulded signature, 3½"H; *$1,400 A.

Pitcher — green-tinted clear glass etched with Irises with gilt highlights; silver handle & mount with floral repousse, cover with floral finial; glass has gilt signature, silver a Gorham hallmark; 9¼"H; *$550 A.

Salt — cameo & enameled Summer scenic forest scene, yellow ground, oval, 1"H; $525 D.

— cameo & enameled Winter scenic; rim may have been reground; $395 D.

— master salt on 4 applied ball feet, green clover with gold highlights, 1¾"H; $250 D.

Toothpick — cameo & enameled Winter scenic, 2"H; $385 D.

Tumbler — cameo Summer scenic, 5"H, 3"D at widest; $550 D.

Vase — monumental double overlay, mottled canary yellow ground overlaid with orange & brown, etched with wooded lakeland scene; cameo signature, 21¾"H; *$4,000 A.

— cameo rectangular with fish mouth rim, translucent purple/yellow ground etched & enameled with crimson/violet Orchids; gilt signature, 10"H; *$3,000 A.

— cameo, martele gray sides shade to purple & emerald at foot & neck; overlaid & wheel-carved with spray of Tiger Lilies/leafage; intaglio signature, 8"H; *$2,900 A.

— footed depicting naturalistically-colored Gentian blossoms, enameled, etched & carved; engraved signature, 13'¾"H; *$2,200 A.

— cameo decorated with pendant green boughs with large blue berries; enameled, etched & carved; engraved signature, 9¼"H; *$1,800 A.

— cameo mottled yellow overlaid in red, cut with exotic blossoms/leafage; cameo signature, underside inscribed "Made in France," 21 5/8"H; *$1,800 A.

— cameo pilgrim flask form, double overlay of matte gray overlaid with apple green & mauve, etched with lakeland scene, 12¼"H; *$1,800 A.

— blown-out inverted bullet shape, set into collared 4-footed metal frame; glass marbleized translucent with gold foil incrustations, upper lip everted; signed "Daum Nancy-Majorelle," 10"H; $1,775 D.

— cameo, red with internal dark green streakings, covered by lacy layer, decorated by huge Sunflowers with applied centers, some gold enameling, 16"H; $1,750 D.

— double overlay ovoid, translucent ground under red & crimson layers, etched with Poppies; engraved signature, 7¼"H; *$1,700 A.

— blown-out pineapple shape double gourd, mottled green with orange; in metal frame signed "L. Majorelle"; vase 5"D across base, 3½"D across mouth, 7"H overall; $1,675 D.

— blown-out oval tapering to narrow mouth, mottled orange/yellow/black set into 3-pronged metal base which is signed "L. Majorelle," 10"H; $1,675 D.

— cameo flattened spherical Vase Parlant; carved Ivy leaves outlined in gold, their veins carved with purple accents, all on grass-green ground; also carved are words, "Je meurs ou je m'attache," incised signature, date 1893 incised on base; $1,600 D.

— cameo acid-etched mottled pink/salmon sides turn to mottled orange/grey at base; cut & enameled with Bell-flower blossoms/leafage in pink/green; cameo signature DAUM/NANCY/FRANCE with croix de Lorraine, 13¾"H; *$1,600 A.

— elliptical columnar vase, etched with coral blossomed woodland plants with succulent leaves in loam-like earth, enameled; cameo signature 11¾"H; *$1,500 A.

— cameo baluster form, translucent ground overlaid with orange/brown; etched beetles/leaves/pods/etc; inscribed signature, 12½"H; $1,400 D.

— cameo Venice scenic, flattened oval cylinder, soft mottled blue-to-gold-to-blue frosted ground, gondola with man in foreground, 1 acid cutting & enameling; 8¼"H x 3 3/8"D; $1,200 D.

— cameo & enameled crackled amber frosted ground, polished brown/gold flowers/stems/leaves; trefoil mouth decorated in gold, base signature, 8"H; $1,100 D.

— cameo scenic on pedestal foot, rich mottled gold-frosted ground, trees along a river in dark brown cut to lighter brown in 3 cuttings; 13¾"H; x 4¾"D; $1,100 D.

— cameo cylindrical, translucent pale yellow ground overlaid with orange/dark green, etched with mountains/fir trees; cameo signature, 24¼"H; *$1,000 A.

— cameo & enameled, lavender to yellow ground, allover yellow/orange/green leaves with big red berries, 14½"H; $975 D.

— long neck cameo, apple green overlaid with olive & etched with Maidenhead Ferns, cameo signature, 27"H; *$900 A.

— cameo Winter scenic, etched & enameled, orange & yellow ground, engraved signature, 9¾"H; *$900 A.

— cameo Winter scenic flattened oval cylinder, one acid cutting and enameling, 6¾"H x 2½"D; $875 D.

— cameo flattened banjo form, pastel peach with mauve floral motif, 6½"H; $825 D.

— cameo Winter scenic, square form, clear sides mottled with citron, overlaid & carved with winter landscape in realistic tones; enamel signature, 3 1/8"H, c. 1910; *$800 A.
— circular form, etched & enameled, Bleeding Hearts in bloom, 7¾"D; *$800 A.
— cameo Autumn scenic, acid-etched clear sides enameled on interior in dusty rose, overlaid & realistically enameled in Autumn landscape; enamel signature, 4¼"H; *$700 A.
— stick vase, dainty bulbous vase tapered, green leaves/flowers on transparent pink, etched signature under base, 7¾"H; $700 D.
— cameo Winter scenic trumpet-form, orange & yellow-streaked body etched & enameled with brown bare trees in snow-covered forest, enameled signature, 10¼"H; *$700 A.
— cameo Winter scenic, orange & yellow with snow-laden trees, 4¼"H; $675 D.
— cameo Summer scenic, square form, green, cutting with enameling, 4¾"H; $650 D.
— cameo scenic ovoid, translucent lorange glass overlaid with brown, etched with lake scene; cameo signature, 7"H; *$650 A.
— cameo footed globular vase, acid-etched lemon-yellow sides splashed in purple, overlaid & cut with Bachelor Buttons/leafage in blue-gray/red/black; floret-carved foot & leafage heightened with gilding; gilt signature, 4"H; *$550 A.
— cameo spherical, clear glass overlaid with amethyst, etched with arcs & fans; engraved signature, 5¾"H; *$550 A.
— cameo, decorated with boughs of Fuschia in bloom, etched & enameled; cameo signature, 4¾"H; *$500 A.
— cameo Spring scenic, pastel coloring, trees & mountains, some enameling, 1½"H; $475 D.
— egg-shaped with uneven cracked-shell rim, pastel green/pink with blue enamel flowers, 3"H; $475 D.
— cameo oviform, mottled green/blue/yellow walls overlaid in deep lavender, cut flowers/leafage; cameo signature, 7 7/8"H; *$400 A.
— spherical miniature (or cabinet) vase, mottled orange ground, enameled with bare brown trees in snow-covered forest; enameled signature, 3"H; *$400 A.
— cameo & enameled, mottled lime green/lavender walls, etched with leaves & berries; cameo signature, 11½"H; *$375 A.

— trumpet form, multicolored, 25"H, drilled for lamp; *$275 A.

— enameled scenic, decorated in green & yellow with continuous riverscape on mottled pale blue ground; gilt signature, 4 1/2"H; *$225 A.

DECORCHEMONT

Coupe — amethyst-streaked grey glass moulded with rows of ivy-colored bricks impressed DECORCHEMONT, 3 3/4"H; *$1,600 A.

DEGUE

Vase — cameo scenic, peach & coral mottled satin ground, house in deep maroon with stag & 2 does in foreground, 2 acid cuttings; $750 D.

— cameo scenic, bulbous base with slim neck; brown-orange, mountains/trees/houses on mountain top; 3 strands leaves trail from top; $635 D.

— cameo bulbous, frosted amber ground with deep wine cameo highly polished Rose; scalloped pattern around rim, base indented; cameo signature, 5 1/2"H; $375 D.

DELATTE, A.

Sweetmeat Jar — gold-mottled frosted ground for mushrooms & large brown leaves in 2 acid cuttings; silver-plated top, rim, handle; 3 5/8"H x 4 3/8"D; $550 D.

Vase — spherical cameo, opalescent ground overlaid with light purple/plum, etched with Chrysanthemums; cameo signature, 6 3/4"H; $1,775 D.

— cameo on pedestal foot, dragonfly & floral motif, 4 1/2"H; $1,700 D.

— cameo on pedestal foot, tapered cylinder with everted rim, dragonfly & floral motif, 14"H; $1,450 D.

— cameo floral, 10"H; $995 D.

— cameo scenic, rich salmon-pink frosted ground with scene in deep mauve in 2 acid cuttings of trees along river edge; 7 1/2"H x 4 3/8"D; $695 D.

— cameo ovoid with slender cylindrical neck; purple to frosted ground overlaid in amber, etched with leaves/flowers; etched signature, 10 3/4"H; *$450 A.

— cameo, frosted mottled ground, large magenta florals & leaves in 2 acid cuttings; $425 D.

DE VEAU

Vase — cameo scenic, frosted pink-gold ground with scene & top in navy blue, peacock sits on fence with tail hanging; 10"H x 3 1/2"D; $1,150 D.

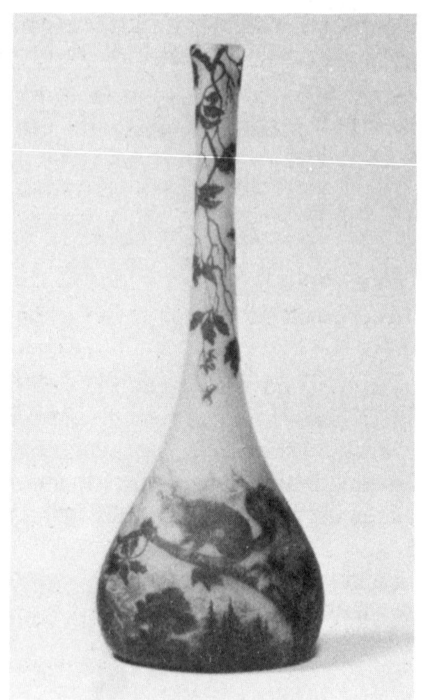

DE VEZ LANDSCAPE VASE, pale pink overlaid in yellow/blue, cut with mountainous landscape/trees/squirrel; 13"H, cameo signature "de Vez"; *$1,000 A. (Sotheby's)

DE VEZ

Vase — cameo scenic, soft pink translucent ground (richer at top) scene in navy blue cut to creamy yellow in 3 cuttings; covered boat on water in front of village, background mountains, leafy floral branches framing top; 16 1/8"H x 5¾"D; $2,250 D.

— cameo scenic trumpet form; navy blue cut to rose in 3 acid cuttings, gold iridescent ground; large long-beaked bird on branch, flowers, leafy branches frame top of scene; in original gold-plated brass base with leaves; 18¾"H x 6 3/8"D. $2,250 D.

— cameo scenic, frosted gold ground with navy blue cut to rose; scene of ornate Mosque on island, plus palm trees, in 3 acid cuttings; 11¾"H x 3"D; $775 D.

— cameo scenic, frosted gold ground for scene in deep green cut to rose in 3 acid cuttings; man in gondola in foreground, sailboats/shrine with Venice shoreline in back, flowers/leaves frame scene; 6 1/8"H x 2½"D; $775 D.

— cameo scenic trumpet form, pale yellow splashed with salmon; forest green/salmon overlay, cut with riverscape, stately trees in leaf in foreground; cameo signature, 5¼"H; *$750 A.

— cameo scenic, frosted gold ground with navy blue cut to lighter color (blue?); palm trees framing islands with buildings & mosque, dock to another island & village in background with mountains; 3 acid cuttings, 5"H, 4¾"D; $695 D.

— cameo Winter scenic, 2 people walking from house beneath ¾ moon with snow on house roof & ground; blue-green ground, 6"H; $502 D.

— cameo Winter scenic, 2 figures walking from house with snow on roof, 2 shades blue/green/and white; 5 7/8"H; $499 D.

— cameo, grey ground, black/amber cameo of butterflies/leaves, enamel heightened; 8¼"H, slight lip abrasion; $475 D.

DEVILBISS

Atomizer — iridescent honey color, original mesh bulb, 7"H; $235 D.

DUGUERSIL, PARIS

Vase — cameo square body with long slender neck, orange/yellow frosted ground, cameo & enamel brown thistles, 8½"H; $235 D.

DURAND

Bowl — blue iridescent rose bowl, ruffled top, signature V in pontil, 3½"H; $400 D.

Ginger Jar — "King Tut" pattern, green/gold, 10"H; $4,000 D.

Plate — "Pulled Feather" design, red, 8"D; $175 D.

— "Pulled Feather" design, blue, 8"D; $175 D.

Vase — inverted ovoid with small lip, "pulled feather" motif in black/white/gold on caramel amber ground, gold spider webbing; 8"H, signed "Durand 1970-8"; $1,250 D.

— baluster with everted lip, peacock blue iridescent with applied gold stringing; base signature DURAND in V, also "1812 7," 7¾"H; $850 D.

—"King Tut" design, top edge rolled; $750 D.

— "pulled feathers" in cream/gold/blue extend almost all the way up over gold iridescent ground with gold threading; signed "Durand 17," 9"H; $675 D.

— green hearts/vines on gold iridescent ground, signed & #d, 12¼"H; $650 D.

— baluster form, pink-gold iridescent, 7½"H; $650 D.

— ruby red with purple ribbon decor, 8"H; $570 D.

— footed vase, blue iridescent with white vines/hearts, 8 5/8"H, #2028-8; $550 D.

— ovoid body tapering to cylindrical neck/mouth, then everted again; deep red with turquoise "pulled feather" motif, 10"H; $525 D.

— purple-blue iridescent with random silver-blue allover design, 7"H; $450 D.

— baluster form, gold/green "pulled feather" design on opalescent white, applied gold threading; signed "V. Durand 1028 8", 8¾"H; *$380 A.

— squat bottle form, iridescent blue, #12-1974; *$375 A.

— ovoid, waisted foot, curling lip; blue iridescent, inscribed "DURAND/1968-6", 6"H, pontil chip; *$275 A.

— ovoid with curling lip, iridescent blue with iridescent stringing; inscribed "DURAND/V/1912 7," 7½"H, some stringing losses; *$250 A.

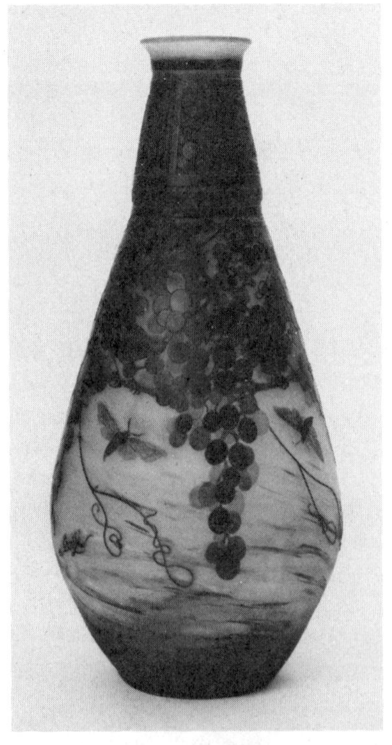

GALLE DOUBLE OVERLAY VASE, signed; *$7,800 A. (Christie's)

GALLE, EMILE

Beaker — obverse cut with cartouche enclosing seated lady flanked by 2 birds against gilt/floral ground; reverse with smaller panel of seated king; all on Islamic pattern ground, enameled iron-red/charcoal/white/blue/mauve, figures in citron yellow; enamel signature "E. Galle/a/Nancy", 4¼"H; c. 1890; *$1,500 A.

— enameled, clear topaz sides applied with 6 prunts, enameled in lavender /black/white with meandering leafage, gilt-heightened; gilt signature, 5"H, c. 1900; *$425 A.

Bottle — scent bottle with stopper, amber tones, deep cut shining clusters of berries/leaves cascading to base; 4¾" (with stopper); $498 D.

— scent bottle, light & dark burgundy, 5"H x 4¼"D, missing cap; $375 D.

Bowl — cameo, opalescent ground double overlaid with pastel blue/violet, etched with violets; cameo signature, 8½"D; *$2,200 A.

— cameo & enameled with quatrefoil rim, translucent mottled red/white ground with traces of yellow/blue, overlaid with maroon ferns, orchid, grasshopper with gold enamel details; enamel signature, 7"D; *$950 A.

— cameo swelling ovoid form, yellow ground overlaid in violet/blue cut with violets/leafage; cameo signature, 6"D, rim ground, c. 1900; *$800 A.

— trefoil type, mottled grey/yellow ground, overlaid in orange/brown/yellow; thick cuts of anemone blossoms/ leaves; cameo signature, 4¾"D; $650 D.

— cameo, frosted ground overlaid in pink in interior & cut with seed-laden Sycamore; outside overlaid in olive & cut with leafage; low bowl, intaglio signature, 11"D; *$450 A.

— cameo, frosted ground with deep red cuts of leaves/ berries; cameo signature, 4" D x 2"H (berry bowl); $275 D.

Box, Covered — cameo scenic, mottled grey/rose overlaid in sienna, cut with riverscape; conforming cover cut with butterflies; box cameo signature, 7 1/8"D, c. 1900, minor cover chips underside lip; *$1,200 A.

— cameo, frosted ground overlaid in amethyst, cut with 2 large dragonflies & Water Lilies; signed top & bottom, 6"D; $1,000 D.

Decanter — clear with enameled blues/aqua/wine/opal berries with trailing stems & leaves; with stopper having slight chip; script signature; $500 D.

Egg — light green ground, darker green ferns throughout; $1,500 D.

Ginger Jar — cameo, frosted ground tinged yellow, overlaid in Chinese red, sides cut with floral cartouches, top cut with dragon; jar & lid both with intaglio signatures; 7"H; *$2,600 A.

Pitcher — transparent green ground etched/gilded with flowers & enameled with multicolored arabesques; gilt signature, 5½"H; *$2,400 A.

— cameo & enameled, transparent green-tinted glass with silver- & gold foil inclusions; etched & enameled with small white-pink flowers & a cinnamon & gold carp; cameo inscription: "Galle 1879 1900 Histoire du Verre," 5½"H; *$2,000 A.

Shot Glass — multicolor floral enamel on amber-ribbed body, 1¾"H; $225 D.

Tumblers — group of 5, each with slightly different decoration on obverse and en verre parlant, enameled, enameled signatures; 4½"H; *$1,050 A.

Vase — handled, opalescent pink-tinted glass, applied handle of orange-brown extending to branches ending with green pine needles; inscribed signature, 6¼"H; *$43,000 A.

— monumental cameo, yellow ground double overlaid with pale blue/purple etched with Delphiniums beneath budding foliage; cameo signature, 24"H; *$22,000 A.

— elephant mould, cameo; band of dark brown elephants beneath pale green & brown foliage & palm fronds on amber ground; incised signature, 15 1/8"H; *$20,000 A.

— marqueterie-de-verre, finely applied & carved lavender/chartreuse/purple flowers, one enclosing gold foil, on violet/amber ground; inscribed signature, with paper label, 7"H; *$15,500 A.

— carved, enameled & gilt; diagonally faceted with martelle ground carved & enameled with dragonfly on obverse, frieze of Egyptian harvest scene around circumference enhanced by gold enameling; signed "E.G." and "E. Galle," 3¼"H, chip to foot of base; *$10,500 A.

— marqueterie-de-verre, 2-handled, obverse finely applied & carved with purple/amber/lilac Crocuses enclosing gold foil on beige/amethyst ground with mauve trailings; intaglio signature, 7"H; *$10,000 A.

— internally decorated marine cameo; internal decoration resembles green striations like seaweed, delicately cut with underwater leaves; all fire-polished with a silver-violet iridescence; cameo signature, 12"H; *$9,000 A.

— pilgrim flask cameo, 2-handled, body depicting 2 dragonflies above pond of Lily pads in shades of amber; cameo signature, 17"H; *$9,000 A.

— oviform, blue-streaked frosted citron & white ground, double overlaid with blue & puce, etched with peacock perched on balustrade overlooking Lake Como; cameo signature, 14"H; *$6,500 A.

— cameo, yellow ground, petals/leaves of Clematis in 2 shades of amber; cameo signature, 9¼"H; *$6,000 A.

— cameo cherry mould; pale blue fruit & chestnut brown leaves on translucent yellow ground; cameo signature, 11¼"H; *$6,000 A.

— cameo scenic, cut with scene of Rio de Janeiro, Copacabana in foreground, Sugarloaf in background; partly fire-polished, entitled in intaglio "Rio/de/Janeiro," cameo signature, 17¾"H; *$5,500 A.

— cameo, pumpkin-orange ground double overlaid in purple & amethyst, cuttings of Clematis vines in bloom; cameo signature, 6½"H; *$5,000 A.

— cameo footed, yellow to white ground, double overlaid in purple & deep pink; wheel-cuttings of branches of flowering Magnolias radiating from base; cameo signature, 16¾"H; *$5,000 A.

— teardrop shaped cameo, translucent yellow overlaid with lavender & green etched with Crocus flowers; cameo signature, 8½"H; $4,900 D.

— flask shape cameo, mould-blown Crocus pattern, outward tapering mouth, cameo of deep brown/yellow/amber; cameo signature, 8"H; $4,500 D.

— footed cameo, pale yellow ground overlaid with red & crimson, etched with Magnolia blossoms; cameo signature, 17"H *$4,000 A.

— pair of ovoid vases, each double overlaid in browns & purple, etched with mountainous landscapes; cameo signatures, 14½"H; *$4,000 A.

— ovoid marine vase, translucent ground overlaid with crackled brown-streaked beige, etched & wheel-carved with marine plants & shells; engraved signature, 8¾"H; *$4,000 A.

— spherical cameo, translucent yellow ground ovelaid with sapphire & amethyst, etched with Morning Glories; cameo signature, 8¼"H; *$3,600 A.

— mold-blown, off-white ground, double overlaid with reddish-orange & olive green, cut to ripening Tomatoes on vines; wheel-polished, 11¼"H, drilled & mounted as lamp; *$3,600 A.

— round pedestal foot and everted lip; deep wheel-cut fire-polished leaves/boughs in deep wine on greyish frost ground with blue interior; vertical "spaghetti" signature, 15"H; $3,600 D.

— cameo, mlky sides splashed with Chinese red, overlaid in Chinese red, wheel-carved Lotus blossoms/leaves; all fire-polished; cameo signature, 7½"H; *$3,500 A.

— cameo cylindrical, translucent citrine overlaid with blue & amethyst, etched with mountain & forest scene; cameo signature, 18½"H; *$3,500 A.

— tapered cylindrical cameo, translucent yellow ground overlaid with amber, etched with Tiger Lilies; cameo signature, 20"H; *$3,200 A.

— footed cameo, rosy yellow overlaid with Chinese red/maroon, carved Day Lily blossoms/leaves; partially fire-polished; cameo signature "Galle," 9¾"H; *$3,000 A.

— baluster form cameo, citron glass overlaid with burnt orange, etched with Prunus branches; cameo signature, 20"H; *$3,000 A.

— Verre Parlant cameo landscape; lower body with metallic inclusions, upper body intaglio carved with leafage on interior walls; cameo signature "Galle" and "Les arbres se parlent tout bas/Victor Hugo," 18¼"H; *$3,000 A.

— footed cameo, wheel-polished Clematis vines in bloom emerge from foot in shades of amber & yellow on paler yellow ground; cameo signature, 16¾"H; *$2,800 A.

— cameo, vanilla ground overlaid in salmon/rust, carved with pendant pods/leafage, partially fire-polished; cameo signature, 13½"H; *$2,750 A.

— cameo baluster form, translucent citrine triple overlaid with pale yellow/blue/purple, etched with Irises; cameo signature, 20"H; *$2,700 A.

— enameled, deep olive, with maroon/ochre mottling near lip; cut with long-stemmed flowers; enameled pale pink/white/olive blossoming Orchids with applied glass stamens, gilt-heightened; enamel signature, "Cristallerie d'Emile Galle/a Nancy/modele et decor deposes," 15¼"H, c. 1890; *$2,600 A.

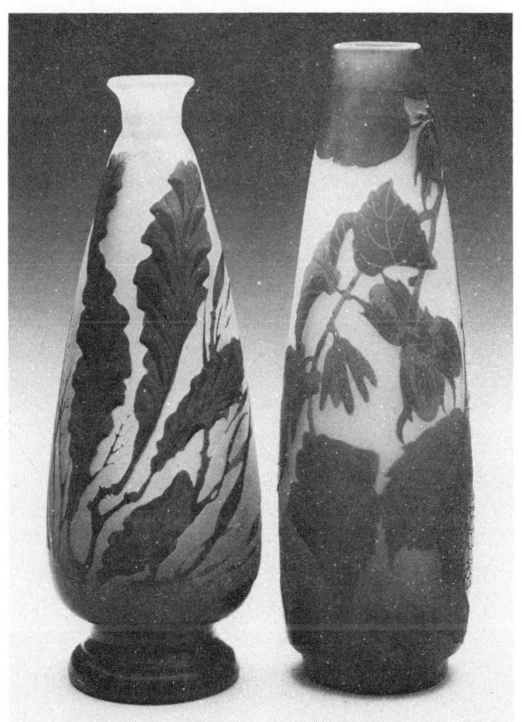

TWO GALLE CAMEO GLASS VASES. (Left) red leaf cutting, 10"H; *$900 A. (Right) green-to-purple cutting, 10½"H; *$900 A. (C.G. Sloan)

— cylindrical footed cameo, frosted citron/blue overlaid with purple, etched with branches of Lobelia; cameo signature, 20¼"H; *$2,400 A.

— cameo, translucent green-tint ground double overlaid with pale blue & violet, etched with mountains & trees; cameo signature, 18"H; *$2,200 A.

— cameo vase narrower at base than top, fire-polished grey sides overlaid in lavender & rust, cut with Iris blossoms/leafage; cameo signature "Galle," intaglio signature added later, 12"H; *$2,200 A.

— cameo, frosted ground shades to orange above & below, double overlaid with pale & dark brown, etched with pendant Gooseberry sprays; cameo signature, 21"H; *$2,200 A.

— cameo scenic pilgrim flask form, rounded; orange ground shading to white below & above, double overlaid with green & dark brown, etched with wooded lakeland scene; cameo signature, 9"H; *$2,000 A.

— cameo oviform with slender cylindrical neck, green/blue with red, etched Orchids; engraved signature, 10½"H; *$2,000 A.
— cameo square form on circular foot, white & orange-red matte ground overlaid with green & brown cherries among leaves; cameo signature, 5"H; $1,900 D.
— cameo oviform with slende cylindrical neck, green/blue ground double overlaid with blue & aubergine, cut Poppy plants, polished; intaglio signature, 12"H; $1,850 D.
— cameo elongated oviform, citron ground double overlaid with carmine Hibiscus & burgundy foliage; cameo signature, 15¼"H, bruise to neck & surface abrasions; *$1,800 A.
— scalloped rim cameo, translucent aqua ground overlaid with amber, etched with Irises; cameo signature, 14¾"H; *$1,800 A.
— cameo, translucent ground overlaid with amber & orange, etched with Lilies; cameo signature, 10¼"H; *$1,700 A.
— pedestaled cylinder cameo, shrimp-colored ground with two shades green; 18"H; $1,700 D.
— cameo, grey ground overlaid in dusty rose/mauve, cut with undulating Crocus/Tiger Lily blossoms/leafage; cameo signature, fire-polished, c. 1900, 11¾"H; *$1,700 A.
— cameo, 5 layers of glass with 3 acid cuttings, Fuschia decor; 24"H, Chinese-style vertical signature; $1,695 D.
— ovoid cameo, translucent yellow double overlaid with red & crimson, etched with Geraniums; cameo signature, 9¼"H; *$1,600 A.
— cameo slender oviform on pedestal foot, pale yellow ground, lake scene with mountains/trees in aubergine/blue Green; polished; intaglio signature, 7"H; $1,500 D.
— cameo stick vase, frosted yellow ground, deep wine overlay, cuttings of Lavender flowers/leaves; cameo signature, 13½"H; $1,500 D.
— cameo baluster form with tall flaring cylindrical neck; white & orange matte ground overlaid with yellow-green maple pods among leaves; cameo signature, 13½"H; $1,400 D.
— cameo, yellow ground with red/pink/maroon flowers/leaves; Chinese-style vertical signature, 8"H; $1,400 D.
— cameo fire-polished turqouise ground overlaid in lavender, cut with Morning Glory vines/leaves; cameo signature, 10¼"H; *$1,400 A.
— cameo, fire-polished grey ground overlaid in salmon, cut with Poppies/foliage; cameo signature, 13¾"H, c. 1900; *$1,300 A.

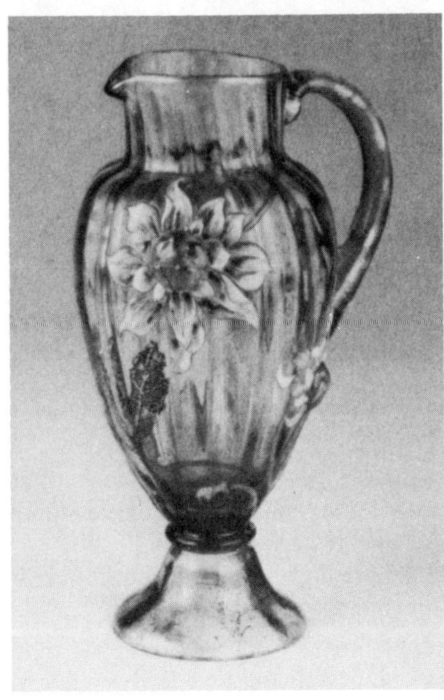

GALLE EWER, enameled with applied decoration, c. 1900; topaz sides decorated with acid-etched leaves & enameled in pastel lavender/yellow/ochre/dusty rose with Chrysanthemum blossoms with pistils in form of applied & enameled cabochons; enamel signature "Cristallerie/d'Emile Galle/Nancy 9," 8½"H; *$1,800 A. (Sotheby's)

— cameo baluster form, translucent yellow ground double overlaid with red & crimson, etched with Roses; cameo signature, 11½"H; *$1,300 A.

— pastel cameo baluster form; emerald green base with overall floral/leaf design, features cameo colors of deep blue/rose pink/frosted grey; cameo signature near base, 16 7/8"H; $1,250 D.

— cameo footed, pale yellow ground encased in reds & cut with Narcissus blossoms/leaves; intaglio signature "Galle," c. 1900, 10 5/8"H; rim & foot ground; *$1,200 A.

— cameo scenic, cut from brown to green to shaded yellow to frosted ground; 7¾"H; $1,200 D.

— cameo scenic bullet-shape, pale green/grey frosted ground, overlaid with brown trees & blue-grey panoramicc mountains; cameo signature, 7"H; $1,200 D.

— cameo tear-drop form, translucent yellow double overlaid with pale blue & plum, etched with trees & mountains; cameo signature, 8"H; *$1,200 A.

— cameo bulbous base stick vase, pink ground, overlaid in purple, cuttings of buds/leaves; cameo signature, 9¾"H; $1,125 D.

— cameo, tapered stem leads to bulbous top/candlestick-shaped mouth, with knop near decorated pedestal base; frosted ground, lavender & deep purple cameo leaves; cameo "spaghetti" signature, 11½"H; $1,100 D.

— cameo flattened ovoid form, frosted amber ground overlaid with burgundy, cut to florals & leaves; cameo signature, 7¾"H; *$1,050 A.

— cameo tapered ovoid form with trefoil top, pink walls overlaid with lavender & lime leafage; 12"H; *$1,000 A.

— cameo scenic of squat bulbous form, citron/yellow ground, scene of lake/lily pads in pale green/brown/beige tones; cameo signature, 4½"H x 4½" widest D; $975 D.

— cameo, white & light blue ground, royal blue overlay; "Chinese"-style signature cameo, 7"H; $975 D.

— cameo oviform with everted rim & pedestal foot; lime-green ground overlaid with aubergine, cut to leaves/pods, polished; cameo signature, 5¼"H; $950 D.

— cameo ovoid form, frosted grey ground overlaid in purple, cut to Sweet Pea buds/leaves; cameo signature, 9"H; $900

— cameo of slender shape, frosted ground overlaid with tangerine, depicting Poppy plants blooming, highly polished; cameo signature, 14½"H; *$900 A.

— cameo pedestaled, in reds/gold/burgundy; 6"H; $850 D.

— cameo, frosted ground overlaid in dark purple/plum, cut to lighter shades in Buttercup flowers; 10½"H; $825 D.

— cameo slender vase, pink ground double overlaid with olive and green, cut as pod-bearing plants; intaglio signature, 13¾"H; *$820 A.

— cameo 4-lobed body on circular foot, with cylindrical neck & trefoil lip; white matte ground shades to apricot at lip & foot; overlaid green etched with pendant vines; cameo signature, 10½"H; $800 D.

— pale green cut & enameled with Poppy blossoms/undulating stalks in pastel rose/purple/rust/yellow against acid-etched ground; on silver mounts; signed "Galle/depose/g.g." in intaglio (partly hidden by mounts), 9¾"H; *$800 A.

— enameled spherical form with tiered cylindrical neck, transparent glass enameled with insects/flowers/village scene; inscribed signature, 12"H; $800 D.

— cameo of elongated pear form, pink-to-frosted ground, double overlaid with purple & green, cut to Wisteria branches/leaves; cameo signature, 11½"H; *$800 A.

— cameo of jar form with oval mouth & everted lip; frosted pink ground overlaid with deep wine, cut to flowers/leaves; cameo signature, 5"H; $775 D.
— cameo stick vase with wide bulbous footed base, frosted citron-grey ground overlaid with deep brownish-wine, cut to pods/flowers/stems; cameo signature, 5½"H, 3½"D at base; $775 D.
— cameo waterscape scenic on rounded triangular form, mottled yellow-green ground overlaid in blue & purple, cut with scenic of junks at sail; cameo signature, 3½"H, rim ground; *$750 A.
— cameo tapered form, lime color walls overlaid with cut lavender leafage & grasses; cameo signature, 11¾"H; *$700 A.
— cameo cabinet vase of baluster form, frosted grey ground overlaid with brown, cut to grapevines; cameo signature, 3¼"H; $650 D.
— cameo stick vase of bulbous form on inverted tapered base; blue frosted ground overlaid with deep violet, cut to flowers; cameo signature, 6¾"H; $650 D.
— cameo with peaked rim, yellow ground shades to white & aubergine, wheel-polished vines of over-ripe grapes shown in 2 shades of amber; cameo signature, 7½"H; *$650 A.
— cameo flattened bulbous form with crescent-shaped top, frosted ground, burnt orange flowers/leaves in 2 acid cuttings; star signature, 5½"H x 4 3/8"D; $575 D.
— cameo cabinet vase, frosted aqua ground with deep detailed cameo of purple leaves/fruit boughs; incised signature, 3¼"H; $575 D.
— cameo ovoid body with tapering cylindrical neck & flaring mouth; orange to frosted ground, etched leaf/flower decor; etched signature, 12½"H; *$550 A.
— cameo of compote form with footed base; mixed frosted grey/orange ground, veined cameo leaves/blossoms in deep wine/green; cameo signature; under base is stamped FABRICATION FRANCAISE in circular stamp with cross of Lorraine at center; 3"H; $550 D.
— cameo ovoid form, green to frosted ground, olive-green flower/leaves decor; cameo signature, 4¾"H; *$525 A.
— cameo flattened ovoid, grey ground shading to pink at neck & base, overlaid in ochre-yellow/burnt orange, cut with wildflower blossoms/leafage; cameo signature, 6"H; *$500 A.

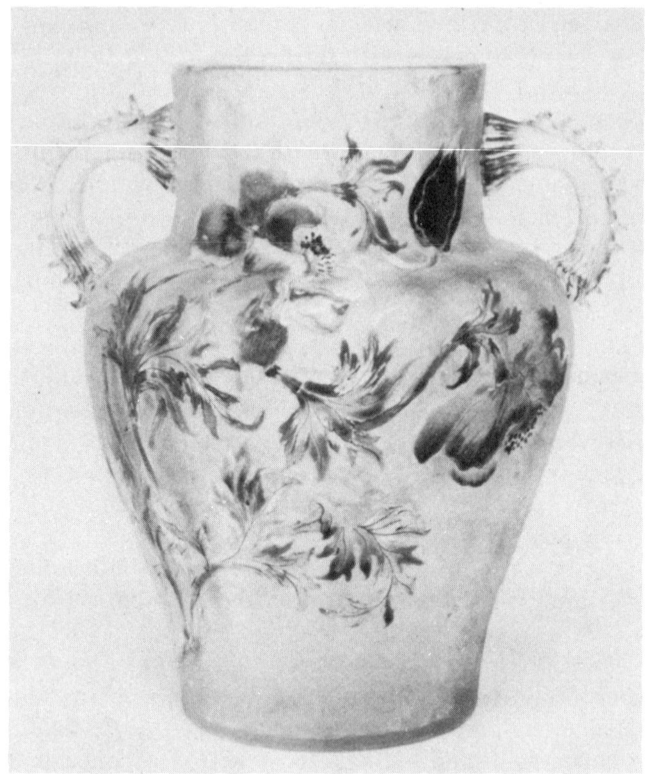

GALLE VASE, etched & enameled; green glass body with twin applied ridged handles; gilt detailed flowers & leaves etched & enameled in brown/green/yellow/purple; 9¾"H, etched GALLE DEPOSE: *$2,000 A. (Phillips)

— cameo banjo form, frosted ground with deep brown overlay cut to green ferns in 3 acid cuttings; star signature, 6½"H x 3 1/8"D; $495 D.
— cameo, pale yellow to lavender walls overlaid with lavender blossoms/leafage/vines; cameo signature, 9½"H; *$425 A.
— cameo, orange ferns with 2 acid cuttings, 4"H; $389 D.
— enameled domed foot vase, transparent yellow-tinted glass enameled with flowers/crown/lion in shades of blue & red; engraved signature, 5½"H; *$380 A.
— cameo baluster form, green-to-frosted ground, green floral cameo decoration; cameo signature, 4½"H; *$325 A.
— cameo, purple & yellow leaves/acorns, 2½"H; $325 D.

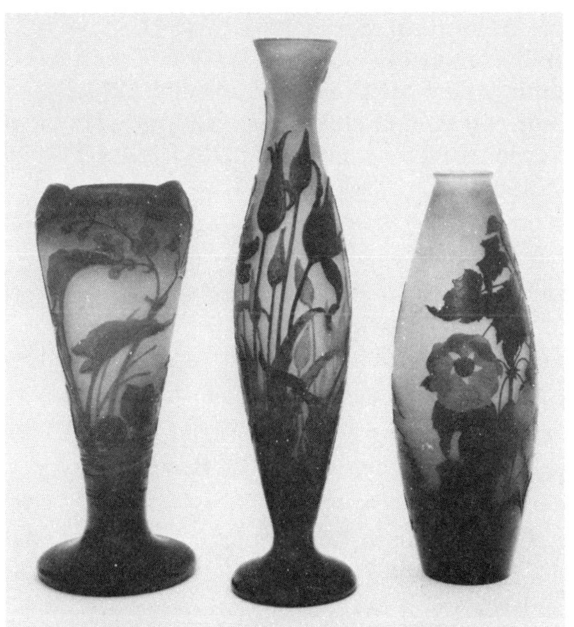

OVERLAY (CAMEO) GLASS VASE BY GALLE, all with cameo signatures. (Left) translucent aquamarine ground overlaid with amber, etched with Irises, 14¾"H; *$1,800 A. (Center) baluster form, translucent citrine ground overlaid with pale yellow/blue/purple, etched with Irises, 20"H; *$2,700 A. (Right) citron ground overlaid with carmine-burgundy, etched to Hibiscus, 15¼"H, neck bruise & surface wear; *$1,800 A. (Christie's)

— cameo cabinet vase, avocado & white, fern motif, 3"H, factory flaw; $245 D.

— cabinet vase, lime green swirl-molded glass with gilt accents, signed under foot, 2½"H; *$70 A.

GRUBER, J.

Etagere — semi-circular glass panel set above wooden shelf, opaque white glass overlaid with brown, etched with lake scene; cameo signature, 21"L; *$1,600 A.

HANDEL

Humdor — dark green ground, Indian on horseback spearing buffalo; $595 D.

— green ground, dark brown lioness with 3 cubs; $585 D.

— brown with green shading, Indian portrait, ornate brass-mounted hinged lid & rim; CIGARS on cover; 6"H; $395 D.

— same as above; $375 D.

— owl decoration; $350 D.

— 2 bears decoration, dated 1904; $345 D.

— moose decor, metal top; $275 D.

Tazza — opaque yellow, with orange flowers; $275 D.

Vase — cylindrical, etched clear glass painted with large violet spotted green lizard; painted "110/335 HANDEL WARE," 6¾"H; *$450 A.

HEISEY

Powder Jar & Hair Receiver — pair, with silverplated tops decorated with Art Nouveau woman & roses, patented May 14, 1890; plating worn; pair, $70 D.

Powder Jar — signed, with silverplated Art Nouveau lid; $35 D.

HONESDALE

Tazza — tri-cornered, clear & frosted, solid gilt/red/blue/green designs simulating leaded glass, 10"H; $175 D.

KEW BLAS

Compote — stemmed, baluster support on round footed base, flaring lip; gold iridescent, 3½"H x 4½"W, inside shows use; $550 D.

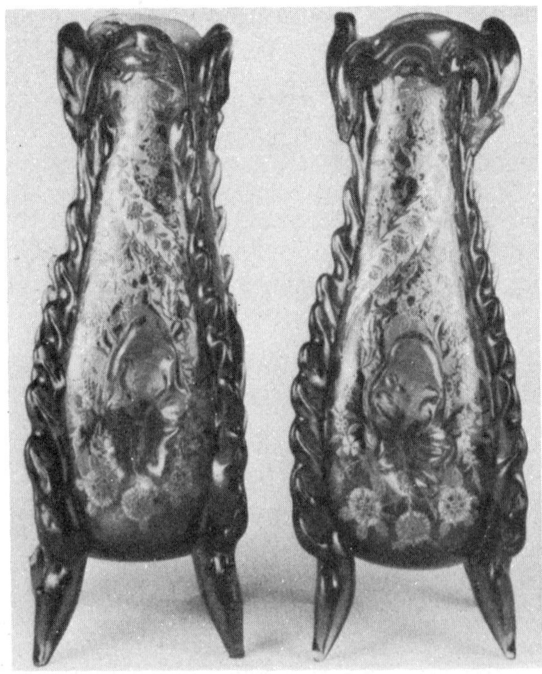

VASES BY AUGUSTE JEAN, olive-green, 4-sided, enameled & gilt-heightened, signed in red enamel "A Jean," c. 1880, 17¾"H; pair, with restorations & damages; *$650 A. (Sotheby's)

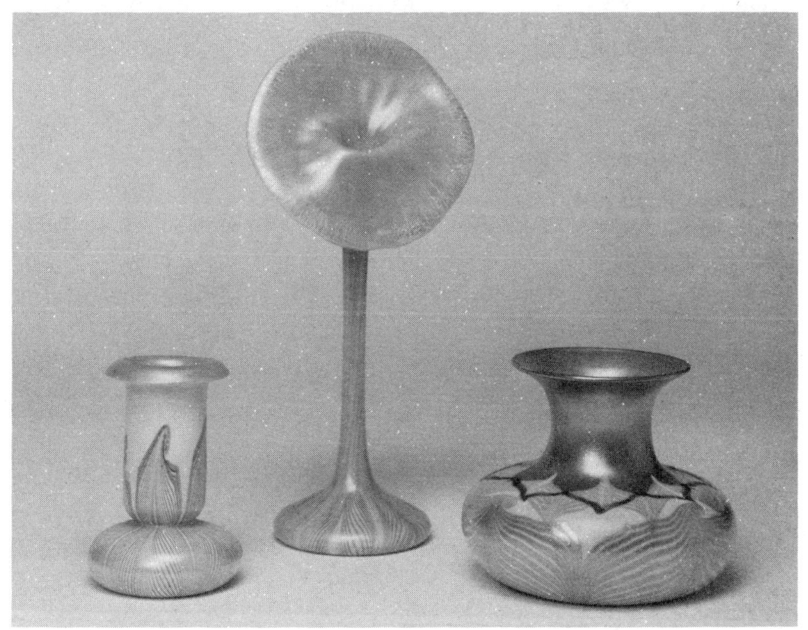

THREE AMERICAN IRIDESCENT GLASS VASES. (Left) green pulled-feather with gold everted rim, engraved "KEW BLAS," 5"H; *$360 A. (Center) "Jack-in-the-Pulpit" form green pulled feather with gold collar, engraved QUEZAL and A938; 12½"H; *$2,200 A. (Right) green & gold on white ground, engraved QUEZAL and 864; 5"H; *$1,100 A. (Christie's)

Vase — 11½"H, full signature; $1,700 D.

— cylindrical body over flattened wafer foot, wide shoulders taper back in at neck to rim; signed, 7¾"H; $1,450 D.

LALIQUE

Atomizer — frosted glass with 6 nude maidens, marked R. LALIQUE, 5¼"H; $475 D.

Box, Covered — "Primaveres," floral relief tinged with opalescence, traces of blue wash; molded R. LALIQUE/ FRANCE, 6½"D; *$750 A.

Figure — "Suzanne," opalescent milky glass amber-tinged, molded R. LALIQUE; 8¾"H; *$1,700 A.

— "Suzanne," same as above but yellow-tinged, mounted as lamp; *$1,100 A.

Flacon — "Douze Figurines," frosted, molded with embracing couples; stopper molded as a nude woman, washed in blue; acid-stamped "R. LALIQUE," inscribed "France," 11½"H; *$1,600 A.

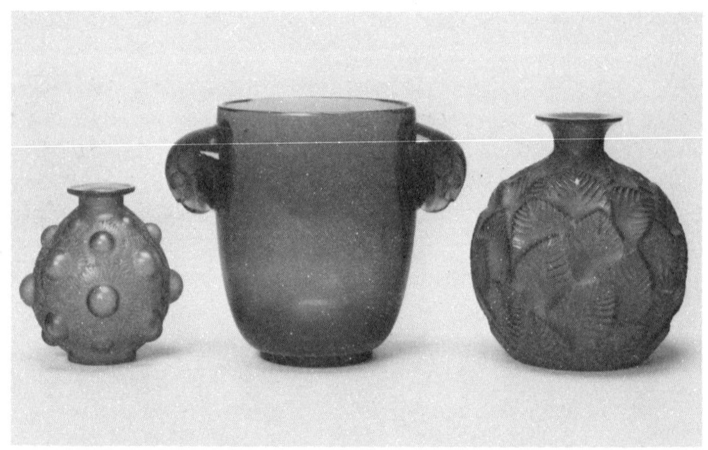

SPECIMENS OF LALIQUE GLASS. (Left) "Tournesol," blue glass, 4½"H, engraved "R. Lalique France No. 1007"; *$900 A. (Center) "Albert," deep topaz glass, handles depict hawks' heads, 6¾"H, marked R. LALIQUE FRANCE, engraved "No. 958"; *$1,100 A. (Right) "Ormeaux," amber glass, 6½"H, engraved "R. Lalique France No. 984"; *$750 A. All pieces are vases. (Christie's)

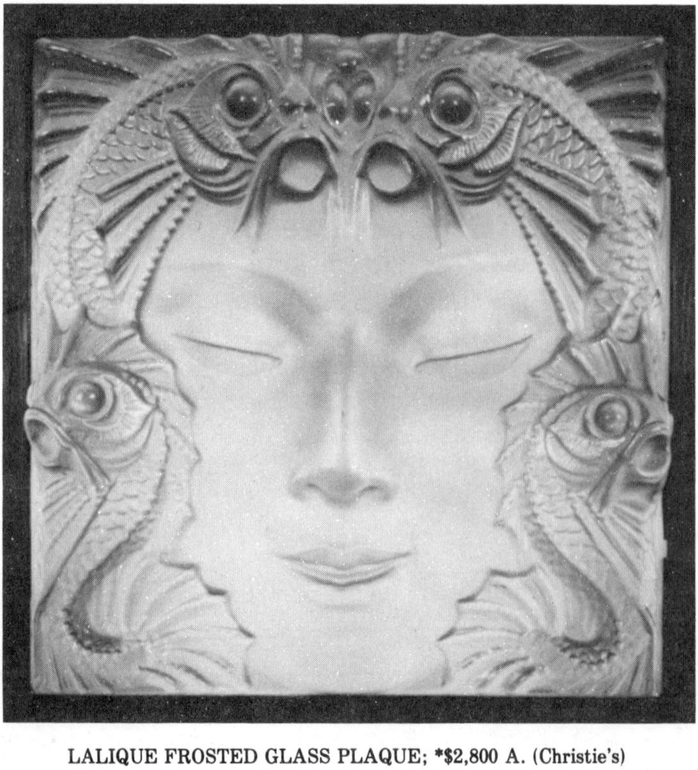

LALIQUE FROSTED GLASS PLAQUE; *$2,800 A. (Christie's)

Vase — "Serpent," amber, 10"H molded R. LALIQUE, minor inner rim chips; *$5,000 A.

— "Serpent," same as above but clear frosted; *$2,500 A.

— bulbous with tapering neck, upright leafage in medium relief; mint-green glass, inscribed "R. Lalique France No. 1014," 9"H; *$1,500 A.

— "Ceylan," parakeets (?), opalescent, 9½"H, inscribed R. LALIQUE/France; slight rim chip; *$1,200 A.

— "Formose," spherical orange glass with molded swimming fish, cased in ruby-red glass; impressed R. LALIQUE, inscribed "R. Lalique France," 7"H; *$1,200 A.

— "Poissons," rounded blue glass molded with large fish, molded R. LALIQUE (twice) & inscribed "R. Lalique France; drilled, 9"H; *$850 A.

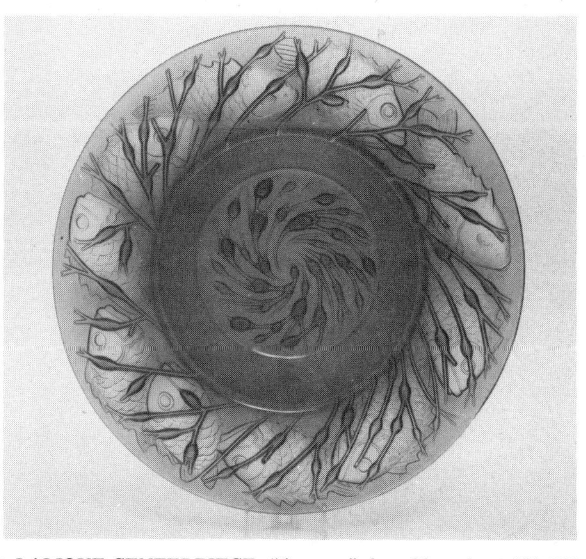

LALIQUE CENTERPIECE, "Anvers," deep blue glass; *$1,800 A. (Christie's)

— "Tulipes," clear on frosted ground, molded R. LALIQUE, inscribed "France," 8¼"H; *$800 A.

— "Sauge," leaf pattern covering, traces of brown wash; molded R. LALIQUE, inscribed "France," 10"H; *$750 A.

— bulbous with tapering neck, upright leafage in medium relief; amber glass, inscribed "R. Lalique France No. 1014," drilled, 9"H; *$550 A.

— milky opalescent with vertical leafage, 9½"H, acid-stamped "R. LALIQUE"; *$550 A.

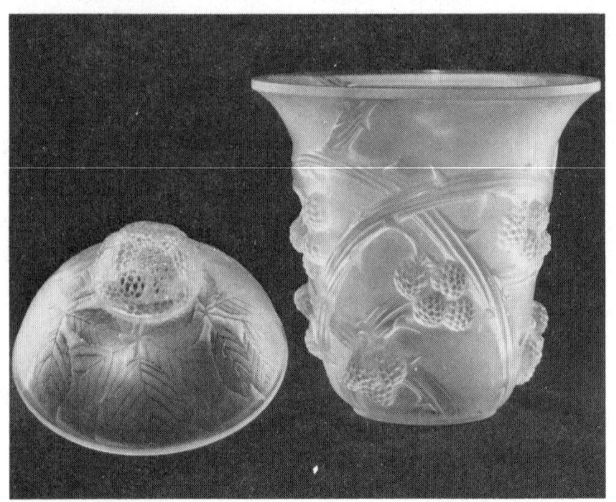

LALIQUE INKWELL, "Cernay," clear frosted glass; *$420 A. (Christie's)

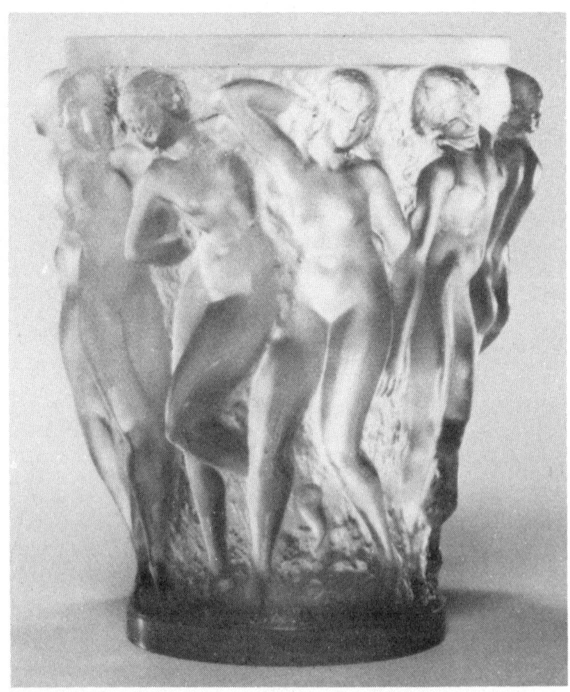

LALIQUE VASE, molded "Bacchantes," pearly opalescent, inscribed R. LALIQUE/FRANCE,9½"H, base chips; *$1,800 A. (Sotheby's)

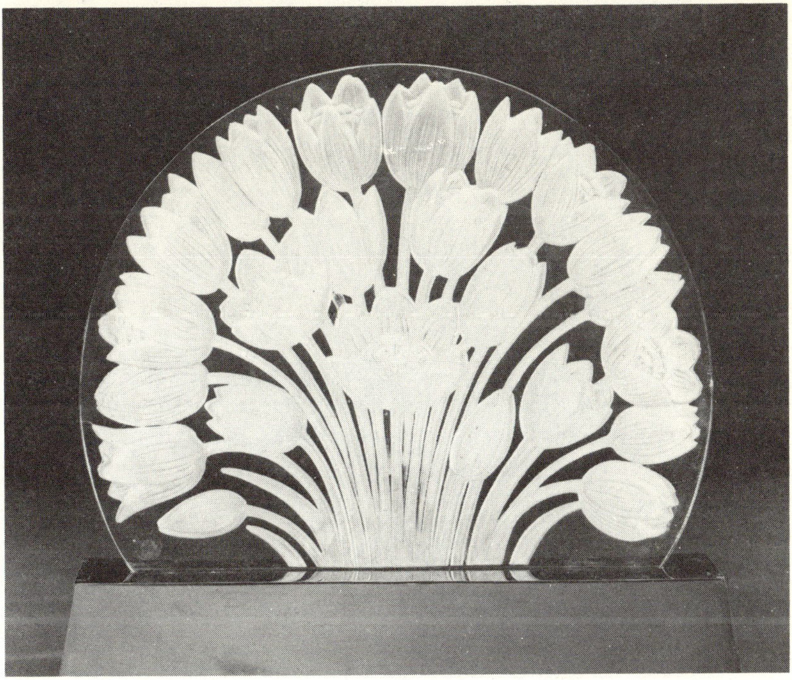

LALIQUE LUMINAIRE, "Tulipes," etched & clear glass; *$7,000 A. (Christie's)

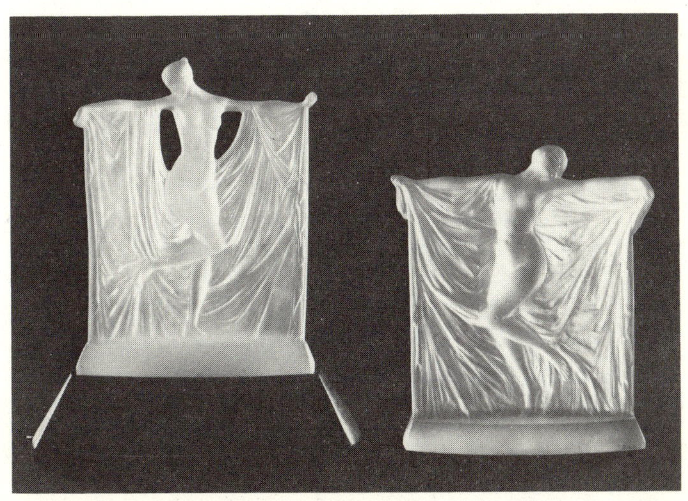

LALIQUE LUMINAIRES, glass. (Left) "Suzanne." (Right) "Thais." Each, *$3,800 A. (Christie's)

— "Druides," opalescent ball washed grey-blue, inscribed R. Lalique France," and moulded R. LALIQUE, 7"H, wash worn; *$350 A.

— "Esteral," ovoid oaplescent body molded in medium relief with leafy branches, blue-green wash; inscribed "R. Lalique France," 6¼"H; *$275 A.

— "Tulipes," script signature, mint; $225 D.

beaker form (like tumbler), grape motif, etched signature, 5¾"H; *$220 A.

— beaker form, crystal, raspberry motif; etched signature, 6¾"H; *$200 A.

Wine Set — decanter with pear-shaped body & tapering neck with frosted frieze figures of mermaids; 4 cups have flattened stems with frosted frieze figures of dancing nymphs; signed; *$425 A.

LEGRAS

Bowl — basket-shaped, cherry bunches cascading from leaf rim, 8½"D x 4½"H; $415 D.

— camphor glass rose bowl with enameled orange/brown leaf decor, 8 1/16"D; signature "Leg" believed to be partial "Legras" signature; $125 D.

Dish — open with serpentine top, scenic harbor view on amber/green ground; 5"H x 5"D; $425 D.

Jar, Cookie — cameo with warm peach ground overlaid with maroon & green, cut to stylized leaves & flower; brass-plated lid & handle; 7"H; $600 D.

Vase — cameo of bulbous form with triangular foot and long slender neck; pale blue ground overlaid with violet and olive-brown, cut with pendant Wisteria; cameo signature "Legras," c. 1900 23¾"H; *$1,300 A.

— cameo with martele finish; green ground overlaid with brownish-red, cut to scene of fawn browsing for leaves on tree; reverse shows bird in flight, several trees/shrubs; cameo signature, 8¾"H x 5½"D; $1,250 D.

— cameo of ovoid form with trefoil mouth & round base; salmon matte ground overlaid with deep wine/green, cut to bamboo shoots/pods & enameled; interior highly polished, cameo signature, 10½"H, 5½"D at widest, $875 D.

— cameo, beige ground with green & brown overlays, cut to seaweed & butterfly; 15½"H, $750 D.

— cameo of square form, acid-etched grey sides splashed with citron & pale blue, overlaid & enameled with realistic Autumn landscape; enamel signature "Legras," 12½"H; *$750 A.

— cameo, sea grasses motif, 13½"H; $685 D.

— cameo of cylindrical form, frosted orange & white ground etched/enameled with red plus among branches/leaves; inscribed signature, 8"H; $600 D.

— cameo of slender cylindrical form, flaring at neck and base; frosted orange ground, overlaid with purple, cut to grape/vine motif; cameo signature, 14"H; *$350 A.

— cameo Winter scenic, 9½"H; $340 D.

— cameo Winter scenic, woman walking in snowy terrain, enameled, 14¼"H; $319 D.

— cameo & enameled Winter scenic, same as above, 14¼"H; $310 D.

— cameo & enameled Winter scenic, same as above, 14¼"H; $285 D.

— cameo & enameled Winter scenic, same as above, 14¼"H; $220 D.

— enameled pot-shaped vessel with top edge inverted, mottled green/grey glass with heavy floral enameling around top; 2½"H; $195 D.

— enameled cylindrical form, mottled green/grey glass, enameled with floral & geometric shapes, 2"H x 2½"D; $185 D.

LOCKE ART

Glass, Cordial — Poppy pattern, 3¼"H; $65 D.

LOETZ

Bowl — rounded body fitting into pierced 2-handled silver stand; bowl is iridescent ruby-red decorated with iridescent blue loops/trails, inscribed "Loetz/Austria," length over handles 9"; *$1,300 A.

— low ruffled, iridescent salmon with silvery blue "oil spots"; $450 D.

— square form with fluted sides rolling inward, deep purple & green iridescence on red body, 10"W x 4"H; $375 D.

Box, Covered — compressed circular form, cased pale rose above flared domed circular black foot, overlaid in violet, cut with meandering blossoms/leaves; conforming knopped vover; cameo signature "L.A. Loetz," 6¼"D; *$450 A.

Centerpiece — foliate shaped & dimpled, painted floral vines, etc., 10"D; *$130 A.

Compote — iridescent bowl on green base; $250 D.

Inkwell — square green iridescent insert in pewter Lily pad frame; hinged brass lid & cover; initials & # in cover; original inner well; 3"H x 2½" square; $175 D.

Vase — dimpled oviform, translucent yellow glass with bands of iridescent gold dots & irregular gold & blue waves; inscribed mark, 6¾"H; *$2,800 A.

— translucent yellow & lavender, decorated with intricate gold network & applied "lily pads," inscribed mark, 13"H; *$2,800 A.

— iridescent blue shading to pale green at onion bulb-shape foot, striated silver-blue iridescent feathering; inscribed mark, 11¾"H; *$1,600 A.

— squat wide-mouth form, pale rose glass striated with silver-blue & with lappets of olive iridescence; inscribed mark, 7"H; *$1,500 A.

— pinched ship's decanter form, "oil spot" decor between alternating colored panels; engraved mark, 7"H; *$1,500 A.

— flattened bulbous body, iridescent with silver blue-green/ amber undulating trails; inscribed mark, 9"H; *$1,400 A.

— flattened bulbous body, iridescent amber with silvery-blue/green concentric waves; inscribed "Loetz/Austria," 12"H; *$1,400 A.

— double waisted form with double-lipped rim, 3 shades of blue; engraved mark, 6¾"H; *$1,100 A.

— ruby glass with mottled blue/green iridescence, with sterling overlay; 7"H; $1,095 D.

— hourglass form with applied handles, iridescent yellow glass with iridescent gold trails; inscribed mark, 6¾"H; *$950 A.

— silver overlay vase, 10"H; $900 D.

— waisted & pinched form with undulating horizontal bands in shades of blue; 9"H; *$820 A.

— cameo with brown pedestal foot, chartreuse ground overlaid with brown, floral cuttings, ruffled top, 8"H; $750 D.

— yellow ground with blue iridescent undulating bands; engraved mark, 6"H; *$580 A.

— lobed form with quatrefoil everted rim, shades of blue & purple, 10¼"H; *$550 A.

— purple "pulled feather," 5"H; $500 D.

— pinched at waist & base, iridescent, 9¼"H; *$500 A.

— double gourd form, blue iridescent with "raindrops," crossed arrow mark, 7"H; $500 D.

— dimpled spherical form with spiral ribbing, transparent navy blue glass with violet-green iridescence, 8¼"H; *$450 A.

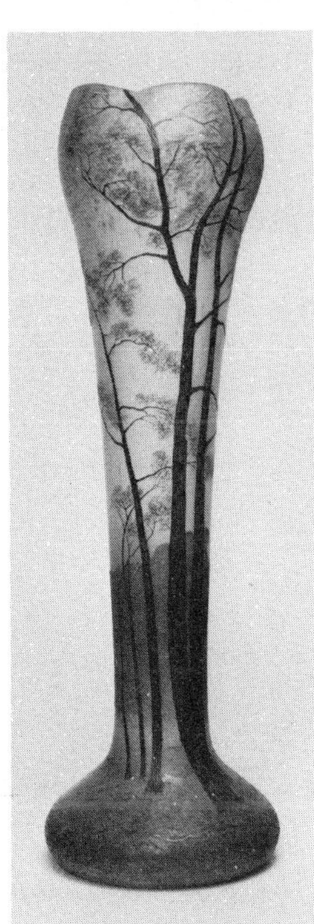

LEGRAS VASE, etched & enameled; signed; *$1,000 A. (Christie's)

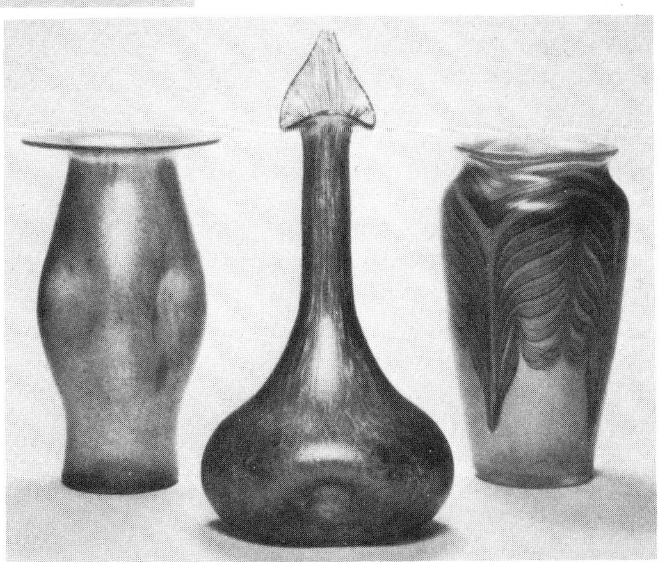

THREE IRIDESCENT AUSTRIAN VASES, c.1900. (Left) decorated with apricot & silvery-amber iridescent spotting, 7¼"H, attributed to Loetz but unsigned; *$275 A. (Center) decorated with amber & silvery-blue iridescent spotting, 10"H, unsigned but attributed to Loetz; *$550 A. (Right) feathered with yellow iridescence around pale opalescent body, inscribed "Loetz," 7"H; *$800 A. (Sotheby's)

— bottle shape with 4 pinches, iridescent with aqua/lavender/green highlights, 4¼"H; $450 D.

— elongated form, slightly flaring lip, spreading foot, 12¼"H; *$425 A.

— green iridescence in bronze Art Nouveau holder, 14"H; $395 D.

— green iridescence with "oil spots," 9¼"H; $325 D.

— trefoil everted rim and pinched body with "oil spot" decoration in amber shades; engraved signature, 3½"H; *$300 A.

— waisted oviform, amber-mottled clear with blue scrollwork, 5¼"H; *$280 A.

— paperweight vase, clear bulbous shape enclosing what looks like moire, shading from red to fuschia contrasting with green; 3½"H x about 4"D at widest; $225 D.

— Verre de Soie with heavily applied green cord & oval discs, 8"H x 3½"D top; $210 D.

— pearl iridescent with gold; $150 D.

— 2 green iridescent graduated vases, each with spiraling snake accent, 9"H; *$90 A.

MICHEL, J.

Vase — cameo with leaves/flowers, 11"H; $975 DD.

— tapered stick vase with flat front & back, decorated round pedestal foot; frosted citron-amber ground, with 2 acid cuttings of raspberry & wine leaves; cameo signature "J. Michel Paris," 10¾"H; $950 D.

MONT JOYE

Bowl — enameled Iris blossoms in bright colors on frosted ground with gilt borders; 8"D x 2½"H; $225 D.

Loving Cup — 3 deep purple handles, amethyst matte ground with glossy Art Nouveau designs & 3 goldfish, with gilt accents; 6"H; $110 D.

Vase — wavy background, vine/stems/leaves, deep Rose flowers, gold on top rim, 10"H; $550 D.

— green frosted with gold enamel leaves/acorns; $295 D.

— green acid cutback, gold Mums, 7½"H; $185 D.

— Irises, gold decor, 10"H, small top flake; $165 D.

MOSER

Bottle — cranberry glass, carved & gilded, ground pontil, 6½"H with stopper; $265 D.

Bowl — shallow, fleur-de-lis design in orange/blue with 22 ruby glass jewels on clear glass; multiple gold fields, kaleidoscopic snowflake symmetry; 9"D x 1¼"H; $235 D.

Box, Dresser — round hinged, amber with allover multicolor enameling, 5"D; $225 D.

Glass, Wine — vaseline glass, intaglio birds/foliage; $85 D.

Table Set — 18 pieces: water goblets, sherbets, wines; green & crystal with cut flowers & foliage; $1,650 D.

Vase — trumpet form, rubina verde, enamel/gold decor & glass acorns; artist signed, 15"H; $1,350 A.

— cameo jeweled oviform with cylindrical neck; clear frosted glass, neck/foot enameled in orange within magenta bands, flower heads with yellow centers beneath applied glass centers; side cut with Poppies enameled in maroon & green; acid stamped "Moser Karlsbad," 15½"H; *$1,100 A.

— 12 pinched sections around trumpet-shaped vase on pedestal foot with conventional metal band showing fish/fauna, deep amber 7½"H x 5½"D at widest; $750 D.

— paneled translucent green with swamp flowers & crane enameled; 3 bees in goldtone metal; 8"H; 2 available for $575 or, each $300 D.

— pedestaled, deep purple with mitred cuts around; frieze above foot has well-defined figures impressed in gold; 20"H; $395 D.

— pedestaled foot, ruby glass, highly enameled, 8¾"H; pair, $395 D.

— pink-swirled ribs with gold decor, 13¼"H; $175 D.

— "Heliot," color changes from pale orange to pale blue depending upon light, 8"H; $90 D.

— paneled purple, 5" x 4"; $79 D.

MULLER FRERES, LUNEVILLE (later CROISMARE), FRANCE

Vase — oviform leading to gently flaring lip, frosted whitish ground with 3-color cameo cuttings of orange/brown/gold Roses & leaves; 11"H, with cameo Luneville mark; $2,200 D.

— baluster form of translucent red/blue/yellow-streaked ground, overlaid with brown & lavender, etched with Oak leaves & acorns; cameo & engraved mark, 15¾"H; *$2,000 A.

— cameo, pale sky-blue overlaid in plum, wheel-carved with Convolvulus blossoms/leaves, all fire-polished; inscribed "Croismare/Nancy," 11¼"H; *$1,500 A.

— baluster form cameo, translucent pink/chartreuse ground, double overlaid in white & caramel, etched with leaves/melons/grasshopper; cameo mark, 8"H; *$1,500 A.

— bulbous form cameo, pale frosted blue ground, flowers/leaves in blue shades in 3 acid cuttings; cameo Luneville mark, 7¼"H; $1,100 D.

— white/red ground, overlaid in red, etched flowers, all fire-polished & signed "Muller Croismare, Depot Nancy," 6"H; $950 D.

— baluster form, translucent yellow ground overlaid with umber, etched windmill & lake scene; cameo mark, 8½"H; *$850 A.

— etched & enameled cabinet vase, white ground enameled with lakeland scene in blue tones, with 2 sheep grazing; enameled signature, 3 1/8"H; *$320 A.

— round form with narrower short neck, amber mottled ground shading to burgundy, pewter overlay in stylized florals & swags; $300 D.

— flaring trumpet form, harlequin colors, 12"H; *$150 A.

NASH

Nut Dish — gold iridescent, ribbed body, 4"D x 1"H; $165 D.

Vase — flower form, gold iridescent ruffled edge on body with ruffled relief work, 5¼"H; $490 D.

— amber iridescent, flared lip, marked "544-NASH," 4¼"H; $400 D.

— amber iridescent, smooth scalloped lip, marked "543 NASH," 4½"H; $400 D.

— cabinet vase, ruffled step pattern in gold iridescence, marked "Adna" and #d, 1¼"H x 4"W; $350 D.

— ribbed flared body with scalloped top & pedestal foot; gold iridescence with fiery purple iridescent interior, 4"H; $275 D.

NICHOLAS, P.

Vase — slender double overlay, purple & blue etched with 3 fish; cameo signature, 9½"H; *$1,500 A.

PANTIN

Vase — deeply cut in gold/orange flowers & leaves & 2 large dragonflies, with gold enamel accents, 18"H; marked "Pantin, 1225," and factory mark; $975 D.

QUEZAL

Bottle — scent bottle, gold iridescent with red highlights; $175 D.

Bowl — deep bowl, blue iridescent, 3¾"H x 5½"D mouth, marked QUEZAL; $450 D.

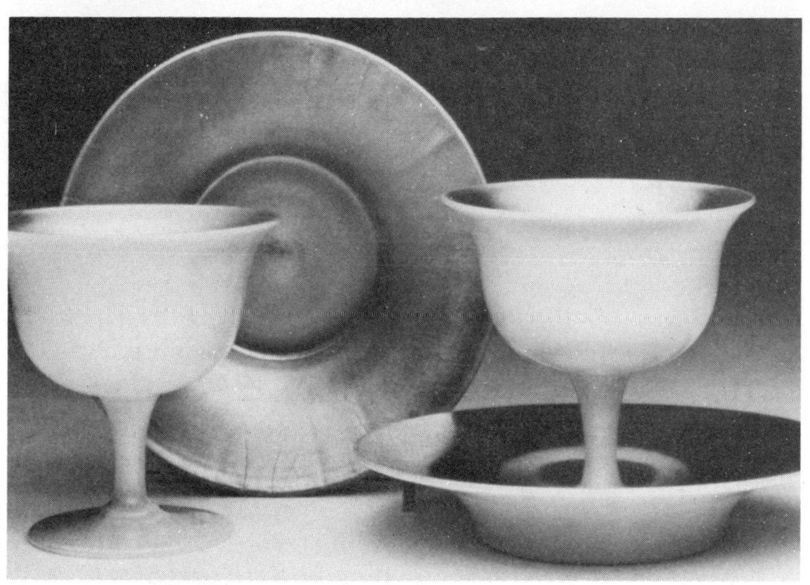

STEUBEN, six pair of Aurene & Calcite sherbets & undertrays; the undertrays, 6"D; *$550 A. (C.G. Sloan)

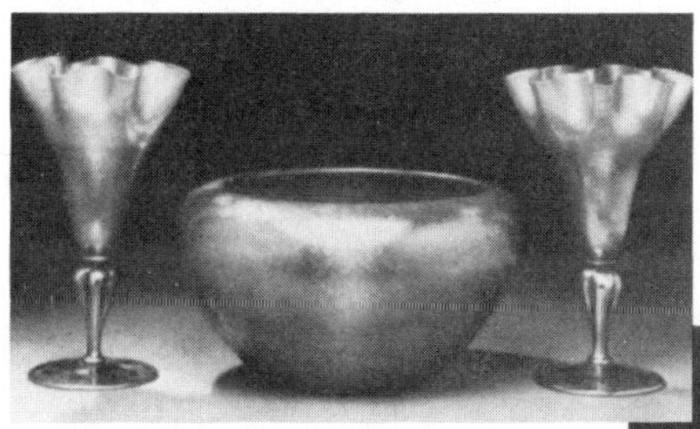

THREE PIECES signed Steuben Aurene gold iridescent glass. (Center) bowl, #2687, 11½"D; *$450 A. (Left and Right) pair of compotes, each #2708, 10"H; the pair, *$625 A. (C.G. Sloan)

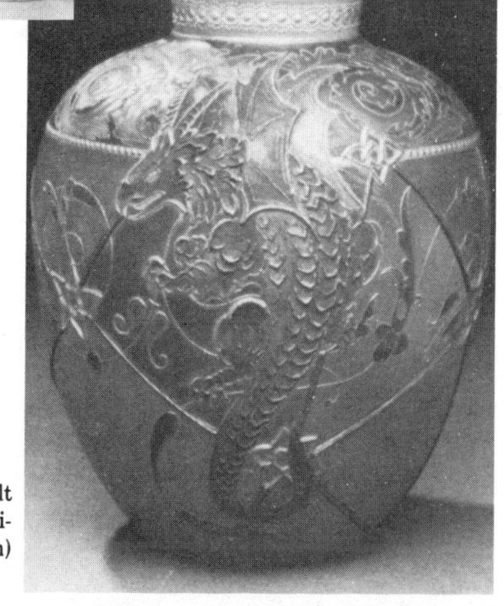

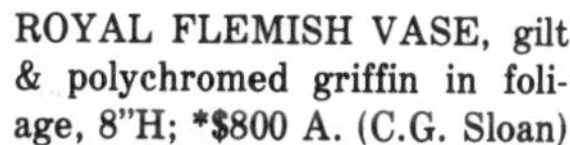

ROYAL FLEMISH VASE, gilt & polychromed griffin in foliage, 8"H; *$800 A. (C.G. Sloan)

Compote — long slender stem, gold iridescent, 5"H; $275 D.

Plate — deep orange-gold iridescent, with blue highlights on underside, 8 5/8"D; $157 D.

Salt — extra large master salt, amber shading to purple iridescence at base; 2¼"H, 4" at widest, 2¾" at mouth; $245 D.

— gold iridescence, pink/blue highlights, ribbed effect; 1"H x 2¾"D; $175 D.

Toothpick — iridescent; $200 D.

Vase — Jack-in-the-Pulpit form, stem tapers gradually to graceful rounded body, where it widens; body decorated in swirling silver/platinum/white, with colorful petals; 11¼"H; $4,200 D.

— "King Tut" design on classic-styled vase, gold on opal, 12½"H; $1,250 D.

— classical shape, platinum amber ground with blue swirls, caramel colored interior; 6½"H, marked "Quezal"; $1,150 D.

— gently flattened spherical form with tall flaring cylindrical neck; overall iridescence, interior gold iridescence, neck with green/gold iridescent threading; inscribed mark, 8"H; $1,100 D.

— green "pulled feather" on blue, 7½"H; $975 D.

— urn-form, multi-colored ground with trailing brown tendrils, inscribed mark, 4¾"H; *$950 A.

— baluster form, swirling streaked yellow-green decoration, inscribed mark, 5"H; *$950 A.

— green random-pulled on gold, 6½"H; $850 D.

— trumpet form with flared & ruffled rim & flat spherical base, pink & amber iridescence, inscribed "QUEZAL 297," 6"H; $525 D.

— gold feathers edged in green pulled down from top on opal ground, with pale gold interior, 3½"H x 5"D at widest; $475 D.

— Lily form, gold iridescence, 8½"H; $450 D.

— globular body with short spherical neck, amber iridescence; base inscribed QUEZAL 1280; 4½"H; $375 D.

— bulbous form, gold to lavender iridescence, 5½"H; $300 $300 D.
D.

— ruffled top bud vase, orange iridescence, 10¼"H; $250 D.

— lobed form, blue iridescent, 4"H; *$225 A.

RICHARD

Box, Covered — cameo scenic, round; orange satin ground with sailboats in cove & mountains/trees on shore in 2 navy blue cuttings; signed plus original Richard paper label, 5"D x 2¾"H; $650 D.

Vase — trumpet form on circular foot, mottled amber overlaid with chestnut, cut with berry-laden pendant branches, footed with leaves; cameo signature of "Richard," 13¼"H, c. 1925; $1,100 D.

— baluster form, white frosted ground, cobalt blue leaves, 3½"H, cameo mark; $375 D.

RIGOR, E.

Vase — cameo with semi-everted lip, orange ground with pine boughs & cones in 2 colors; 5¼"H x 6"W at widest point; cameo mark; $375 D.

ROYAL FLEMISH

Cracker Jar — raised gold ribs with cobalt blue intersections, frosted ground, allover floral in stained-glass colors; cover signed "Pairpoint"; $875 D.

Vase — flattened globular form with broad everted oval rim; obverse enameled with armorial shield among scrolling gold leaves; reverse with coat of arms; 9¾"H; $3,950 D.

— globular form, 2-handled, decorated in green/lavender/coin gold; medallions in classic designs; by Mt. Washington Glass Co., c. 1890; 8½"H; $2,800 D.

— gold/black/rust/tan enameling, with raised jewels of red/blue/gold; 12½"H; $2,500 D.

SABINO

Bottle, Scent — opal lustre glass decorated with 5 dancing Art Nouveau ladies, 6¾"H; pair, $155 D.

SAINT LOUIS

Vase — inverted pear-shape body with bulbous trumpeted neck, decorated with red/gilded Chrysanthemums on frosted ground; signed "St. Louis," 11"H; pair, *$400 A.

SCHNEIDER

Bowl — low bowl on 3 bun feet, mottled burgundy/pink shades, 15¾"D; $250 D.

Ewer — mottled gloss purple-to-mottled cream with purple applied handle; French, 4"D x 5 5/8"H; $195 D.

Vase — blown-out mottled pink/orange/lavender glass in signed Majorelle stylized iron floral holder, 5 3/4"H; $465 D.

— pillow-shaped, pink/yellow mottled body with amethyst base, 7¼"H; $350 D.

— squared oval pedestaled form, mottled deep pin to purple; 13½"H; $295 D.

— clear bubbly glass with applied clear decor with amethyst foot, 15"H; $275 D.

— mottled orange/yellow/blue/purple with 2 applied purple handles, 11½"H; *$150 A.

SEVRES

Cracker Jar — cameo, translucent clambroth ground with large purple Irises/leaves in one cutting; heavy raised gold on flowers/leaves; hammered silverplated top, rim handle; engraved base signature of flowers/scrolls/Sevres; $595 D.

SMITH BROTHERS

Bowl — melon-ribbed creamy satin ground, gold strands trail, elaborate floral & leaf decor, enamel drops, brass, gold-beaded rim, 9"D; $359 D.

Box — melon-ribbed cream color, painted daisy decor; signed with Rampant lion; $325 A.

Cracker Jar — melon-ribbed, Art Nouveau woman's portrait in gold; silver lid & bail; $500 D.

Powder Box — melon-ribbed, shading from white to pale blue satin; decorated with trailing pink blossoms with yellow centers, other blue flowers, green leaves; 3¾"H x 5½"D, signed with Rampant lion; $225 D.

STEUBEN

Bon-Bon — clover-shaped & pulled to point, 4 applied feet, flared & ruffled rim, gold iridescent; 3¾"D x 1½"H, Aurene signature; $175 D.

Bottle — scent bottle, Verre de Soie, melon ribbed with flame stopper; signed by F. CARDER, 6½"H; $150 D.

Bowl — bell-shaped, deep blue iridescent with deep orange random streaks, 7¾"D; marked "Aurene 2851"; $575 D.

— fruit bowl with rolled lip & stretched edge, gold iridescent with blue highlights, 12"D x 4½"H; $450 D.

— footed, lustre green/gold/blue iridescence with stretch-glass effect around border, 10"D x 4"H; $375 D.

— bulbous base, gold iridescent & calcite, 12"D; $365 D.

— Ivrene exterior, interior of iridescent gold with red highlights, 10"D x 2½"H; $175 D.

Centerpiece — footed, 13½"D x 5"H; *$200 A.

Comport — twisted stem with crimped lip, silvery-blue iridescence shading to mirror blue at foot, inscribed "aurene/ 367," 8"H; *$500 A.

Compote — footed, 9"H; *$150 A.

Decanter — iridescent gold, 4 pinched sides, 11"H; $550 D.

Dish — circular Calcite with amber iridescent interior, 5¾"D; $175 D.

Finger Bowl — gold iridescent (Aurene) on calcite, 4¾"D; $85 D.

Punch Set — punch bowl, ladle, & 10 goblets; punchbowl & goblets inscribed "Aurene 2772," silverplated & glass ladle impressed "Pairpoint," all glass is gold iridescent; 10½"H punchbowl, bowl & 8 goblets with original paper labels; *$2,800 A.

Salt — fluted with 4 reeded applied feet, gold iridescent, 1 3/4"H x 3¾"D; $225 D.

Sherbert & Undertray — calcite, rainbow on gold iridescence, white calcite beneath; sherbert 4"H, dish 5¾"D; $300 D.

— Aurene glass, twisted stem, undertray 6¼"D; *$275 A.

— calcite, 4"H sherbert; *$145 A.

Vase — footed elongated ovoid form, ivory glass with green feathering decorated allover with amber iridescent hearts & trails; inscribed "aurene/509," 10"H; *$3,250 A.

— inverted baluster form with wide everted lip; transparent amber with vertical swirls of lavender/blue/red/white/aqua extending the length of the body; 11"H x 5½"D at lip and foot, signed with name & fleur de lis; $1,350 D.

— covered baluster form, gold iridescence; engraved signature & "3114," 14½"H, interior rim slightly ground; *$750 A.

— tulip shape, optic rib pattern, iridescent gold with heavy blue/pink highlights; 7"H, base inscribed STEUBEN in script; $575 D.

— floriform, amber iridescence; 8½"H, printed STEUBEN; *$450 A.

— chalice form, gold iridescence; 13"H, 3"D at widest, AURENE in block lettering; $390 D.

— blue iridescence, 8"H, #1755; $375 D.

— bud vase, gold iridescence with blue highlights, 8¼"H, #2556; $165 D.

— bulbous form, gold iridescent, 2¾"H; *$160 A.

— ovoid widemouth form, gold iridescent, 4¼"H; *$150 A.

— spill vase, 10¼"H; *$140 A.

— footed with everted lip, clear amber in optic rib pattern; marked STEUBEN and fleur de lis; $135 D.

STEVENS & WILLIAMS

Vase — cameo, white-to-frosted blue with Art Nouveau Morning Glory design, ribbed, 8"H; base numbered "674/4½"; $1,400 D.

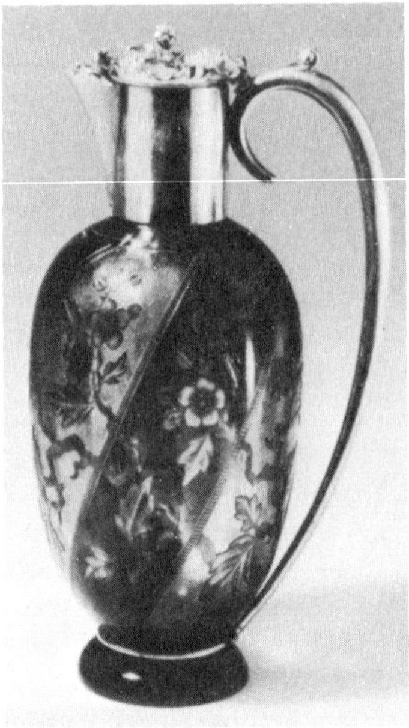

STEVENS & WILLIAMS cameo & intaglio-carved vase, lime-yellow overlaid with brown, carved & fire-polished; stamped STEVENS & WILLIAMS STOURBRIDGE /ART GLASS; silver-gilt mounts possibly by Richard Hennell, London, 1892; 9¾"H, gilding worn; *$2,000 A. (Sotheby's)

— cameo, white blossoms & leaves cut back to yellow satin finish, 7"H; $800 D.

— footed; amber with applied crystal alligator at middle, 4" of crystal drippings at top, heavy crystal decoration at bottom and forming foot; 12"H, foot with normal wear; $265 D.

TIFFANY, LOUIS C. (America's premiere manufacturer of outstanding glass was also an innovator when it came to glass design. His Favrile glass is now collected not only in this country but also abroad; Europeans consider it representative of the best of commercial Art Nouveau glass design. With such attention, it's no wonder that prices have skyrocketed. Personnel at a couple of major auction houses announced they felt the glass had peaked, but apparently their words never trickled down to the buying public, which continues to set records.)

Bottle — red striated feathering with deep blue & amber peacock eyes, with stopper; inscribed "L.C.T. F2055," silver mounts by J.E. Caldwell Co.; 9¼"H; *$7,750 A.

— scent bottle, stoppered, iridescent blue with lily pad decor, 4"H; *$650 A.

Bowl & Undertray — 10 signed iridescent gold bowls & undertrays, undertrays 6"D; *$750 A.

— foliate shape, gold iridescent; undertray, 6¼"D; *$375 A.

Bowl — blossom shape raised on 4 short legs, gold iridescent, inscribed "L.C. Tiffany Favrile 2787C," 3"; *$300 A.

— ribbed with flaring lip, gold iridescent, 8"D; on gilt-metal stand of different origin; *$300 A.

— rose bowl, gold iridescent with pulled up green stripe, 3"H; $295 D.

— ruffled edge, gold iridescent, 4½"D, marked "LCT"; $260 D.

— foliate gold iridescent, 4½"D; *$175 A.

Butter Pat — scalloped rim, deep blue iridescent, 3"D; $225 D.

— scalloped rim, gold iridescent, 3"D; $165 D.

Centerpiece — circular with folded rim, transparent blue decorated with lime green vines & lily pads, & a crackled multi-colored iridescence; inscribed "1753L L.C. Tiffany Favrile," 13"D, with iridescent blue flower frog; *$1,700 A.

Cigarette Holder — amber iridescent cylindrical mounted with silver rim, hinged cover, & crescent handle; 6"H over handle, c. 1920; *$275 A.

Compote — circular foot, flaring oval form, blue iridescence, 13½" x 10½", with original paper label, etched signature; $1,850 D.

— bulbous body with ruffled rim is opalescent decorated with striated green feathering continuing on short cylindrical stem, raised on domed circular amber foot; interior washed in amber iridescence; 5¼"D; $1,600 D.

— peacock blue with self-quilted pattern on underside of upper bowl, 5¾"D x 6"H; $1,400 D.

— transparent dark blue with heavy crackled multicolored iridescence, 9¾"D; *$900 A.

— blue iridescent with knobbed stem, 5" x 6½"; $750 D.

— iridescent amber, flaring scalloped top on round ribbed pedestal base with knopped stem, 4"H x 8½"D; $650 D.

— green pastel, ribbed, 4¼" x 5½"; $595 D.

— footed with quilted sides in amber iridescence shading to blue, intaglio cut with Ivy leafage at rim; 8"D, inscribed mark, #1561; *$450 A.

— flower form, iridescent gold, 9"H; *$425 A.

— gold iridescence, 7¾"H; *$175 A.

Cordial — stemmed, gold iridescent, 4½"H; $175 D.

Cup — amber iridescent decorated with wide green leaves & stems extending up from underside of base; handled, 2¼"H, #7423 D; $850 D.

— footed ivory with green feathering & widely flaring crenated rim washed in amber iridescence, 5"D, #3334E; *$475 A.

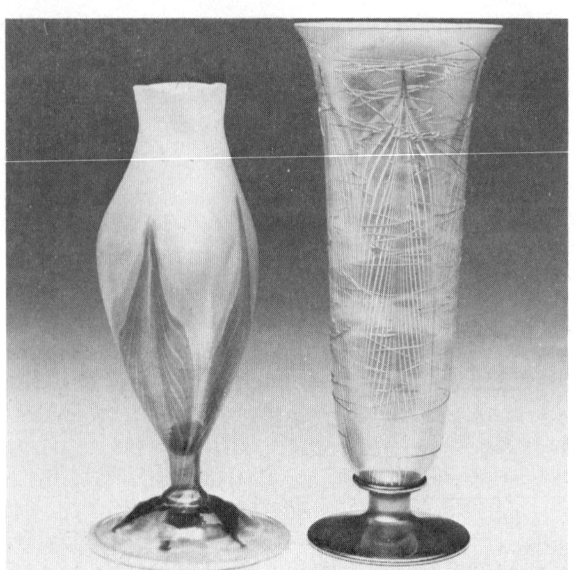

TWO EARLY 20th CENTURY iridescent American glass vases. (Left) green leaf design, marked under base "Q2101," attributed to Tiffany, 10½"H; *$500 A. (Right) Durand flared-form, with gold iridescent feather decor with threaded overlay, signed, 12"H; *$425 A. (C.G. Sloan)

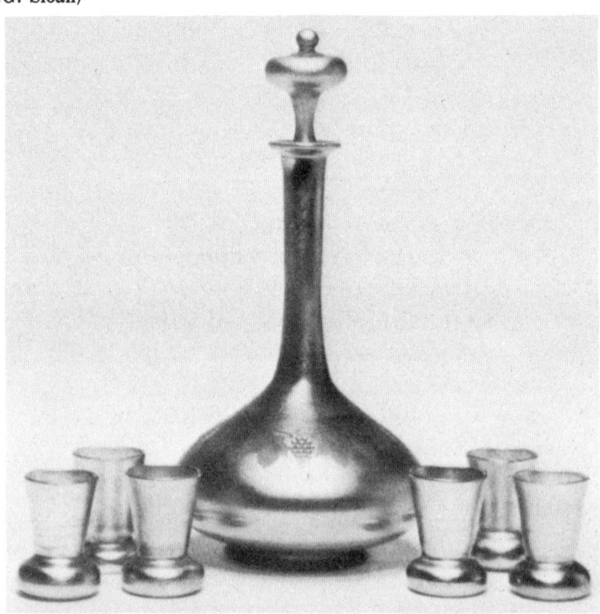

TIFFANY DECANTER WITH 6 LIQUEURS, c. 1910;amber iridescent, the decanter with intaglio cutting at shoulder of scrolled grapevine, decanter & stopper 10"H, each piece with company mark; *$1,800 A. (Sotheby's)

Decanter Set — decanter, 12 liqueurs, & bronze tray; decanter iridescent gold with dimpled square body & matching stopper, inscribed mark & #632; liqueurs iridescent gold, inscribed marks; circular bronze tray (gilded) with etched finish, impressed "Tiffany Studios New York 1721," with decanter of 10"H; *$1,700 A.

— decanter & 4 wines; transparent yellow with bright gold iridescence, decanter 9¼"H numbered 327 as is matching stopper; *$800 A.

Dish — gold iridescent, 7"D; *$200 A.

Finger Bowl & Undertray — striated with ruffled lip, gold iridescent, undertray 6½"D; pair of each, *$575 A.

— foliate shaped bowl, gold iridescent, undertray 6"D; *$425 A.

Flower Frog — Verre-de-soie, 3"H, #4260K; $200 D.

Glass, Wine — inverted bell-shaped bowl is pink-gold iridescent, white exterior on clear yellow stem & circular foot, 5¼"H; $250 D.

Goblet — foliate shape, iridescent green, #1872, 14½"H; *$325 A.

Liqueurs — 9, each iridescent gold with small "pig tails," 2 unsigned, one #5761, one #R2912, each 3"H; *$1,500 A.

— 11 gold iridescent, pinched sides, slightly flared lips, 1¾"H; *$600 A.

— 5 gold iridescent; *$300 A.

— dimpled liqueur & foliate undertray, tray 3"D; *$200 A.

Loving Cup — baluster form with 3 applied handles; iridescent yellow with green vines/leaves; inscribed mark & "8557C," 6"H; *$950 A.

Nut Dish — blue iridescent with ruffled edge, 3"D; $210 D.

— gold with blue highlights, 4½"D x 2½"H; $200 D.

— blue iridescent with ruffled edge, 3"D; $195 D.

Paperweight — obelisk, tan-swirled chartreuse, #1055A, 2¾"H; *$260 A.

Pitcher — cylindrical with applied handles, gold iridescent engraved with grape leaves/clusters, 7¾"H; *$900 A.

Salt — blue iridescent scalloped, about 3"W, #1255; $275 D.

— bean pot shape, 2 handles, gold iridescent; $200 D.

— master salt, gold iridescent; $180 D.

— gold iridescent scalloped rim, about 3"W; $175 D.

— gold iridescent ruffled rim; $145 D.

Scarab Seal (letter seal for wax) — form of 3 beetles, single letter, 1¾"H; $265 D.

— form of 3 beetles, single letter, 1 3/4"H; $255 D.

Sherry — amber iridescent, circular footed & faceted paneled standard bell-form bowl with faceted arches at base, 4½"H; $225 D.

— same as above but burnt gold; $225 D.

Snifter — miniature iridescent gold, 3¾"H; $350 D.

Stand, Vase — emerald-green with amber iridescent wash & black surface, inscribed "L.C. Tiffany-Favrile 214A/Coll.," 3 1/8"D; *$950 A.

Tazza — bowl, long narrow stem, & ribbed domed foot of transparent yellow glass with gold iridescence, 15"H; *$1,100 A.

Tile — blue iridescent, 4" x 4", marked "patent Applied For"; $125 D.

— yellow iridescent with floret center, 3" x 3", marked "L.C.T. CO.," & dated Feb. 8, 1881; $75 D.

— red with floret center, 3" x 3"; $65 DD.

— marbleized red/green/brown/yellow with raised 4-lobed floret, 3" x 3"; $60

— marbleized as above; $55 DD.

Toothpick — dimpled, gold iridescent, 1¾"H; $125 D.

Tumbler — pink highlights on iridescent gold, pushed in on 4 sides, 3½"H; $155 D.

Vase — small Lava Glass; $32,000 A.

— "Lava Glass," inscribed "L.C. Tiffany-Favrile 9770K," pontil marked "C," 5¾"H, c. 1915; *$18,000 A.

— aquamarine, 4 gold fish in solid green-tinted body & 2 blue-green dragonflies with engraved features; inscribed "1977H" & mark, 10¼"H; *$13,000 A.

— paperweight vase, gently sloping waisted form with 10 deep white Narcissus flowers about top area, with paperweight canes in red/white; around body 23 green stems like bamboo shoots from near top to underside of base, all on translucent ground; 18½"H, marked & #3011, c. 1912; $9,500 D.

— Jack-in-the-Pulpit vase, broad scalloped & undulating rim of transparent yellow, with heavy crackled gold iridescence, 20"H, marked with firm name & #6366H; *$6,000 A.

— Jack-in-the-Pulpit vase, opalescent white with green leaves decorating the reverse of a broad ruffled rim; 16"H, #W4756; *$6,000 A.

— Jack-in-the-Pulpit vase, scalloped foot of transparent yellow with opalescent white columns & heavy crackled gold iridescence on broad, undulating rim; 15"H, inscribed "08261"; *$4,500 A.

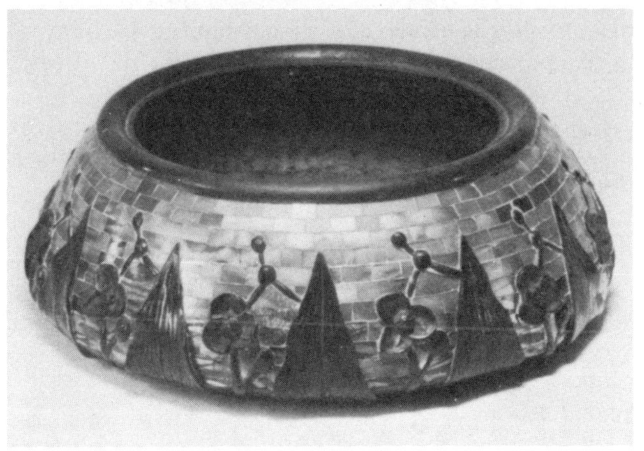

TIFFANY PLANTER, Favrile glass & bronze, c. 1900; iridescent olive/silvery-blue glass tiles; impressed with firm mark & #835; 12"D, lacks liner; *$4,000 A. (Sotheby's)

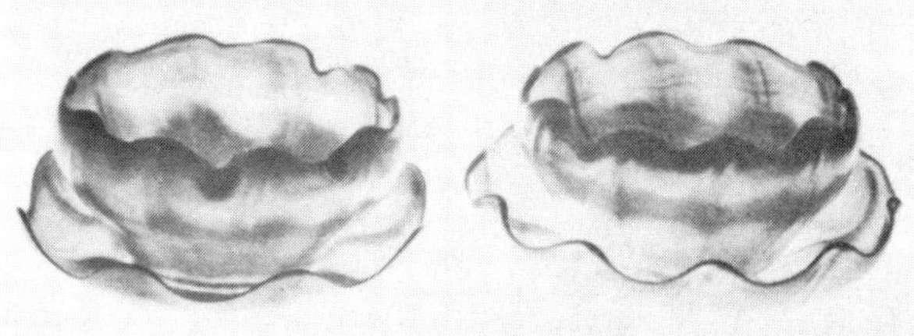

TIFFANY BOWLS & MATCHING SAUCERS, set of 8 (16 pieces in all), iridescent, each about 4½"D; *$1,950 A. (Morton's)

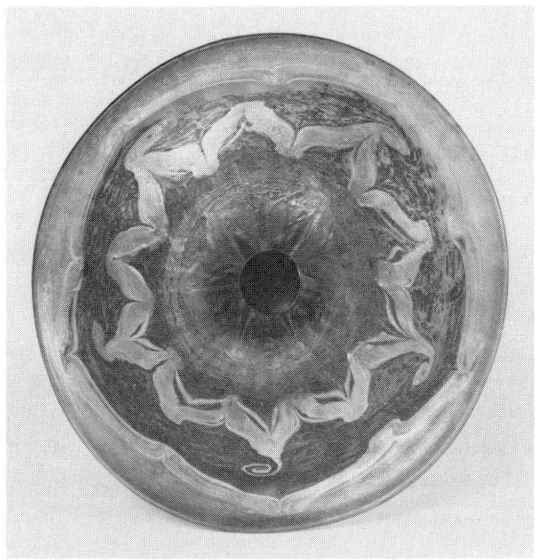

TIFFANY GLASS Plaque, "Cypriote" glass with pitted surface of amber glass, brown mottled with concentric iridescent gold waves/scrollwork; signed, #F916, 17½"D; *$2,500 A. (Christie's)

— paperweight vase, 1½"W marbleized banding of shades of green/turquoise/yellow/black, all on brown/amber ground; 5½"H, #V143; $4,500 D.
— pedestaled foot of pale yellow, translucent red body with central cobalt-bordered band of purple scrollwork; 4"H, #5055L; *$4,500 A.
— spherical with cylindrical neck, red; 12"H, #9588H; *$4,400 A.
— "Tel El Amarna" pattern, ovoid form; deep purplish/ black-blue with overlapping herringbone bands of black/ ivory/gold tones at Egyptian collar; black round footed base; 7¾"H, #3801P; $4,200 D.
— "Tel El Amarna" pattern, ovoid form; dark green with black & gold overlapping herringbone bands at neck; Egyptian collar, black round footed base; 8½"H, #6458E; $4,200 D.
— Jack-in-the-Pulpit form, transparent green-tinted glass with opalescent white ribbing, crackled gold iridescence on broad undulating mouth & gold-orange iridescence on foot; 17"H, #T5003, with original paper label; *$4,000 A.
— Cypriote-type baluster form, transparent green with pitted violet overlay; green plumes & iridescent eyes of blue/gold/green; 12"H, #F2013; *$4,000 A.
— paperweight vase, baluster form, decorated with long green/brown leaves & 4 yellow-centered white daffodils encased in clear glass; 14¾"H, engraved mark & "2996G"; *$3,800 A.
— floriform, opalescent ruffled bowl with green-striated leaves outlined in gold; domed foot has 5 leaves; mark & "R9650",16¾H; *$3,800 A.
— paperweight vase, broad green leaves & bright yellow flowers with brown & navy millefiori centers; 8¼"H, #5473J; *$3,500 A.
— agate Favrile, transparent yellow with blue bands & turquiose/lavender grey bands; heavy orange-gold opalescence; 5"H, #V299; *$3,500 A.
— floriform, opalescent iridescent top covered with green feathering; stem is green with striations ending in foot of gold with opal border; 15"H; $3,500 D.
— Jack-in-the-Pulpit vase, broad ruffled rim of transparent yellow, with crackled gold iridescence on slender stem sitting upon domed foot; 16½"H, #9467A, with original paper label; *$3,200 A.

— millefiori decor, gray-green sides decorated with silvery-blue iridescent leaves/trailings, with ivory/ochre millefiori blossoms; 6¾"H, #R2514, c. 1902; *$3,100 A.
— double gourd form, khaki-green ground with ochre/gold scrollwork & band of burnished gold-violet waves peaking to rim; 9¼"H, #E1742; *$3,000 A.
— mirror lustre decor; abstract leaves/floral design in dark green/turquiose/bright gold; red leaf streamers & veining; round footed base; 6"H, inscribed LCT N7248," with partial TGC paper label; $2,950 D.
— pinched, almost flower-form body spreads to quatrefoil scalloped neck; alabaster with green pulled feather edged with gold; caramel interior; 9½"H, #624D"; $2,900 D.
— ribbed double gourd form, translucnt green with thin gold scrollwork & wide band of gold arches; 9 3/4"H, #E1741; *$2,900 A.
— Egyptian onion-shaped floriform; onion-colored & shaped with slender neck rising toward bulbous flaring, gently receding to narrow neck; ribbed vertical surface; green/purple stripes run vertically from base to bulbous neck; 12"H x 4¾"D at wides, #N7380, original TGDC paper label; $2,850 D.
— floriform, ribbed opalescent bowl with striated green leaves & orange-gold iridescence, supported by iridescent gold domed base; 13"H, #4486A; *$2,800 A.
— flower form with iridescent ribbed domed foot; stem with yellow/gold striations extending to gold-outlined green leaves on opalescent bowl; 15½"H, #T1213; *$2,600 A.
— floriform, gold iridescence, inside of top a rainbow of multicoloring; 11"H, #Y2218; $2,500 D.
— floriform, opalescent mouth continues into striated green lappets edged in amber; domed foot with radiating striated lappets; 16"H, #Y9143, c. 1905; *$2,500 A.
— Clear with orange iridescence, enclosing green-brown stems & leaves & orange flowers with purple-green millefiori centers; 8½"H, #3037; *$2,400 A.
— flower form with ribbed pattern on round pedestal foot, amber iridescent; 12½"H, #2354; $1,950 D.
— shouldered body with flaring collared mouth; iridescent gold with green feather-edge motifs extending downward from neck; iridescent amber ground shades to gold at foot; 7½"H, pontil monogrammed "TGC," a specimen from the early Tiffany Glass & Decorating Co.; $1,900 D.

— flower form raised upon knopped stem with applied circular foot; trailing green lily pads on iridescent gold ground; 9"H, #4834G; $1,900 D.
— cylindrical, pale yellow opalescent with caramel threading & large iridescent gold flowers; 10¼"H, #M7057; *$1,900 A.
— gooseneck ribbed, gold iridescent glass with scalloped/pointed rim; 10¾"H, #W4733; *$1,700 A.
— long neck ovoid form, transparent green glass with pointed gold links & heavy blue-green iridescence; 9"H, #K961, original paper label; *$1,700 A.
— floriform, green feather on white ground with gold interior; 11½"H, #1014; $1,650 D.
— floriform, amber iridescent with green leaves/trailings; 6"H, #8038D; $1,500 D.
— transparent green decorated with brick red pulled feathers; 20¾"H, #X1164; *$1,500 A.
— baluster form, red, stylized, 9 3/4"H, #7123A; *$1,500 A.
— millefiori oviform, gold iridescent decorated with brown vines, green leaves, numerous small white flowers; 5¾"H, #7895B; *$1,400 A.
— trumpet form (pair) opalescent with gold-outlined green feather-pulled design; each bronze-mounted, the etched bases impressed "Tiffany Studios New York 1043," 15"H; pair, *$1,400 A.
— floriform, amber iridescent, 8"H, #A3174; $1,350 D.
— flattened cylindrical, iridescent gold decorated with blue/gold swirling & heightened with multicolored iridescence; 2"H (?), #K615; $1,350 D.
— floriform, gold with blue highlights, 9 7/8'"H; $1,200 D.
— spherical form, opalescent pale yellow with band of gold waves & chain of gold hearts; 7½"H, #K2432; *$1,200 A.
— oviform, opalescent with large gold leaves & gold-violet iridescence; 4½"H, #E714; *$1,000 A.
— freeform, appears to have 3 handles; amber iridescent, 4½"H, #9480C; $950 D.
— pinched open lattice-work around top in double row; iridescent gold with blue/purple highlights, just over 4"H, #3703P; $950 D.
— balustered paperweight vase; white & amber-centered beige flowers among green leaves encased in gold iridized clear glass; 4½"H, #U6008, minor rim crack; *$750 A.
— gourd-form, transparent green with large gold-brown plumes; 8¾"H, #X1937; *$750 A.

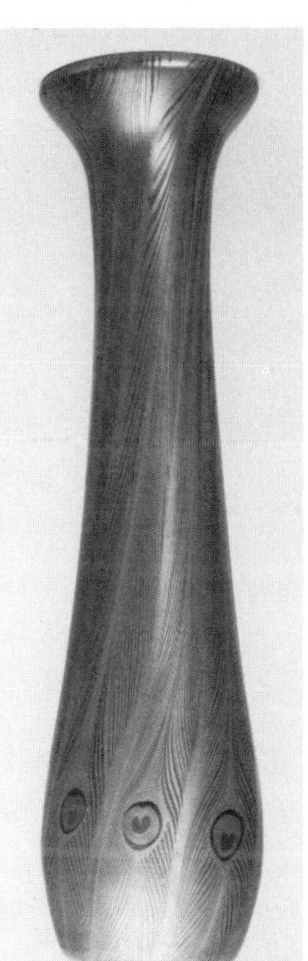

TIFFANY VASE, "Peacock feather" design, signed; *$4,200 A. (Christie's)

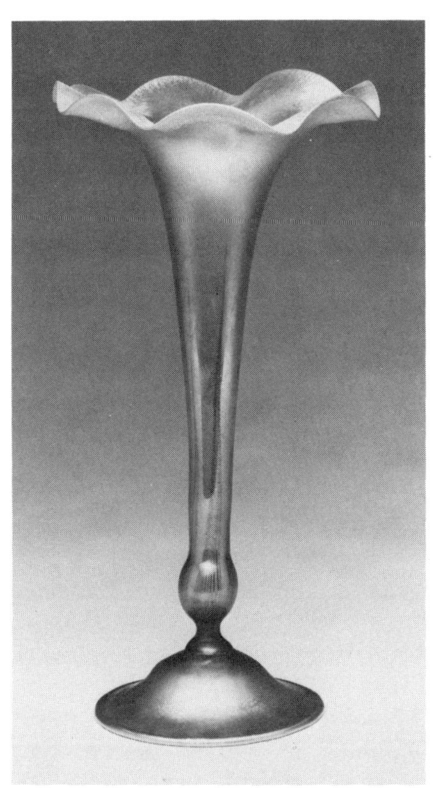

TIFFANY VASE, trumpet form with flaring, ruffled mouth; green feathered design, #W 5400, 15½"H; *$650 A. (C.G. Sloan)

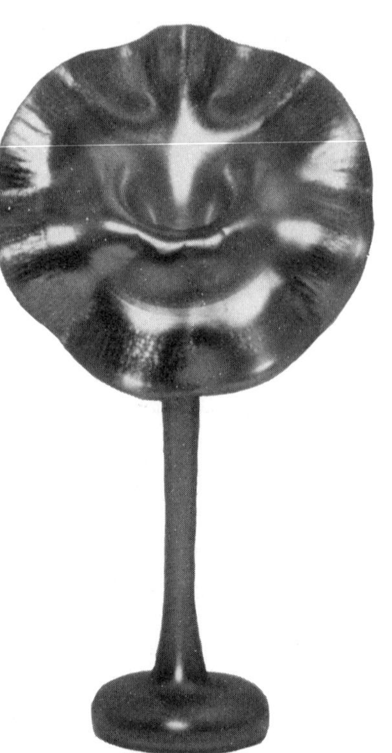

TIFFANY "Jack-in-the-Pulpit" vase, transparent yellow with crackled gold iridescence, signed, #6366 H, 20"H; *$6,000 A. (Christie's)

— trumpet form, green/gold pulled feather design, in bronze holder, both signed, 9½"H; $725 D.
— ribbed baluster form, translucent ruby applied with spiralled threading & heavy silvery-blue iridescence; 3½"H, #R5406; *$700 A.
— waisted baluster form, transparent green-tint with red pulled feather design; 11¾"H, #X1170; *$650 A.
— free-form, 11 pinches at waist turning up to neck having inverted rim with more pinches; gold & orange iridescence with blue highlights, 5"H x 4"W; $650 D.
— trumpet form, green/gold feathering on alabaster ground, 14½", in bronze holder; $648 D.
— 3 small handles, opalescent body with green scrollwork bordered by gold bands; 4"H, #Y1597; *$600 A.
— yellow pulled feather on alabaster, 8"H; $550 D.
— oviform with lobed shoulders & everted mouth, gold iridescent; 6"H, #5191A, with original paper label & inscribed mark; *$500 A.

— Lily-like floriform top on ball stem & flat pedestal; pastel yellow with iridescent stretched edge; $425 D.

— balustered with folded rim, transparent yellow with gold iridescence; inscribed "472P 1538 Louis C. Tiffany, Inc. Favrile," 12¾"H; *$420 A.

— double gourd form, transparent green glass with reddish-brown & cream pulled feather motif; 13½"H, inscribed "X1193"; *$420 A.

— hexagonal bowl bud vase, ball stem, pedestal foot, in iridescent gold; 6"H; $395 D.

— bud vase, green flames on frosted iridescent ground, 16"H; in Dore bronze holder, base signed Tiffany; $325 D.

— paperweight vase of "Cyriote" glass, swirl & patches of green/olive/tan with irregular overlay of pock-marked dark purple; 7"H, #700V, body crack; *$300 A.

— baluster form with fluting at shoulder, gold iridescent, 9¼"H; *$275 A.

— bowl-like, gold iridescent outside with inner pale blue iridescence, ribbed & with deep dimples; 2½"H x 4"D, marked & #d, with original paper label; $250 D.

— miniature globular of gold iridescence, 2"H, #6178A; *$175 A.

— blue cased, marked, 3¼"H; *$160 A.

TOMA

Vase — enameled scenic, boar walking across winter scene of lake & castle; 12"H, French, signed "Toma"; $245 D.

VAL ST. LAMBERT

Vase — translucent beige-mottled ground overlaid with khaki-green/brown thistles; cameo signature "V.S.L.," 11½"H; *$750 A.

— cameo, flattened vessel with lobed sides & waisted neck in lime green cut with large red Poinsettia blossom/leaves against hatched ground, heightened with gilding; gilt signature "S," 8"H, c. 1900; *$250 A.

VERRE FRANCAIS, LE

Pitcher — 12½"H; $850 D.

Planter — cameo, shades of green/deep red/clear glass; $275 D.

Vase — cameo, baluster form on round pedestal wafer foot of orange; Surrealist floral design, deep grape/bright orange cameo on greenish-yellow frosted ground; script signature; $1,350 D.

— cameo, burnt orange ground with mottled brown/white design, 5½"H; $650 D.

— cameo, yellow-reds & browns, 14"H; $595 D.

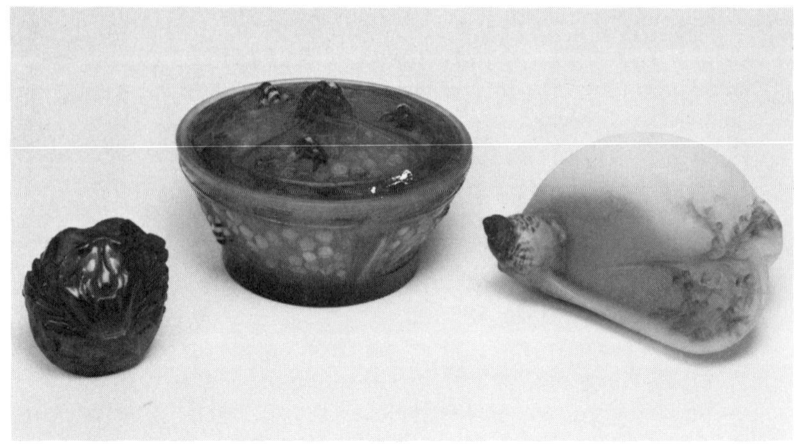

PATE-DE-VERRE PIECES, all signed A WALTER (two on right also marked NANCY) and "Berge Sc." (Left) Paperweight, circular yellow ground moulded with chocolate/yellow/turquoise crab, overall 2¾"D; *($1,500 A. (Center) Covered box, green-streaked yellow body & cover moulded with honeycomb pattern & bees, 7¼"D, cover repaired; *$1,300 A. (Right) Vide Poche, moulded with speckled yellow shell to rear of green-yellow tray with brown seaweek, 7"L; *$1,400 A. (Christie's)

WALTER, ALMARIC

Bowl — mustard pate-de-verre streaked with avocado cast in medium relief with Bacchus head at center in realistic tones; signed "A. Walter Nancy/N. MERCIER," 6¼"D, c. 1920; *$850 A.

— trefoil lip pate-de-verre, high relief berries/foliage in green/russet against mottled midnight blue/turquoise ground; signed "AWalter/Nancy/Berge/Sc," 5½"D, minor wear/chips to leafage; *$700 A.

Box, Covered — square, molded with winged insects on 2 sides in shades of blue/yellow; designed by Henri Berge; 3¼"H; pate-de-verre; *$1,900 A.

Coupe — pate-de-verre, molded with pale violet Holly branches/ green leaves against grey-blue ground, the base with mottled yellow/green snails; 8"H, marked "A WALTER/ NANCY/H Berge"; *$1,000 A.

Figure — pate-de-verre cicada, in red/green/brown, with yellow underside, 3"W, molded signature; *$520 A.

Plaque — pate-de-verre portrait bust of Joan of Arc, hands raised in prayer; plaque in mottled mauve; face/hands in alabaster/shades of pink; rust-colored hair, pale green tunic; head encircled in deeper green with Verrerrie Parlant, "St. Jeanne D'Arc Priez Pout Vous," with base inscribed "A.W.N."; 5¾"W x 9"H; $1,850 D.

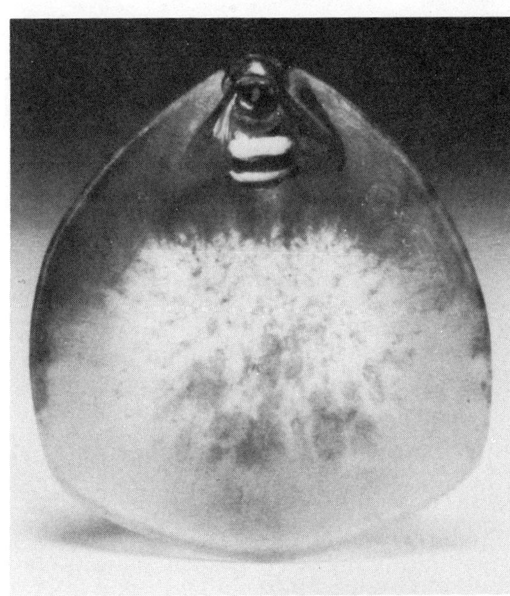

WALTER FIGURAL dish, pate-de-verre, moulded with green/yellow/black decoration to one side of yellow/ochre dish; marked "AWalter/Nancy" and "Berge/Sc," 4½"H; *$1,000 A. (Sotheby's)

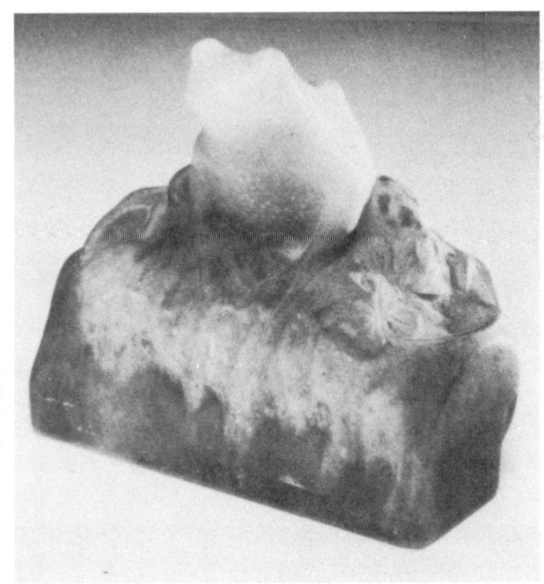

WALTER Paperweight, pate-de-verre figural in blue/green shades, signed AWALTER/NANCY and "Berge/Sc," 4½"L; *$1,600 A. (Sotheby's)

Vide Poche — pate-de-verre triangular ochre/yellow tray molded with turquiose-winged brown/black moth; impressed A. WALTER NANCY and "Berge Sc," 6¾"L; *$2,600 A.

WEBB, THOMAS, AND SONS

Bottle — scent bottle, citron cameo, white flowers with design repeated on elaborate silver stopper (hinged); signed "Thomas Webb and Sons, 5½"H; $1,500 D.

Creamer — cameo, white over yellow; floral motif on front, butterfly on back, carved handle; 3½"H, signed "Thos. Webb & Sons"; $1,300 D.

Pitcher — cameo satin glass, citron with white flowers/butterfly, shiny white interior & handle, scalloped rim, 5½"H; $565 D.

Vase — flattened spherical form, blue ground overlaid with white, etched with Prunus blossoms & butterfly; etched signature, 7½"H; *$1,700 A.

— ivory cameo, ovoid form, ivory sides carved on the obverse with Sweet Pea blossoms/leaves; acid-etched signature, 6¼"H, c. 1890; *$1,000 A.

— Coralene with jeweled red flowers, blue on white with teardrops, fluted top, 6¾"H; $475 D.

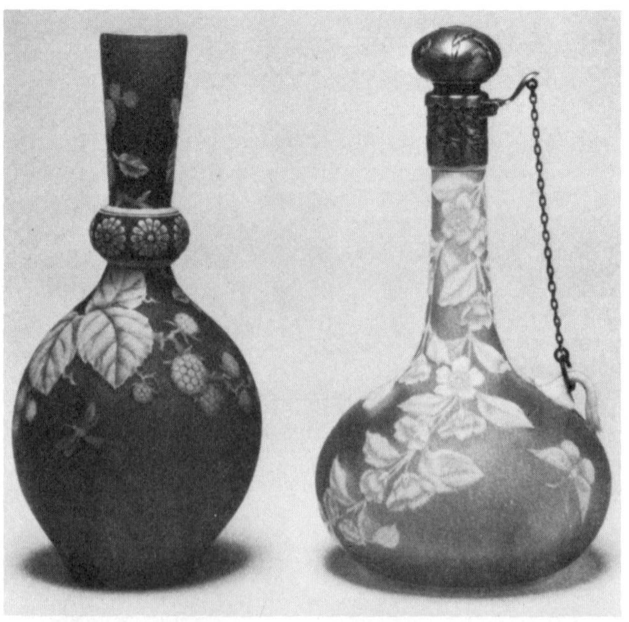

TWO PIECES ENGLISH CAMEO GLASS, late 19th century, each 9"H. (Left) unsigned cased raspberry glass overlaid in white, carved with blossoming/fruiting raspberry branches/bee/butterfly; knop also carved with band of stylized flowers; attributed to Stevens & Williams; *$1,300 A. (Right) yellow body overlaid in white, cut with pendant apple blossoms/leafage, by Thomas Webb & Sons (signed); with Gorham silver mounts, 1886; minor handle chip; *$1,400 A. (Sotheby's)

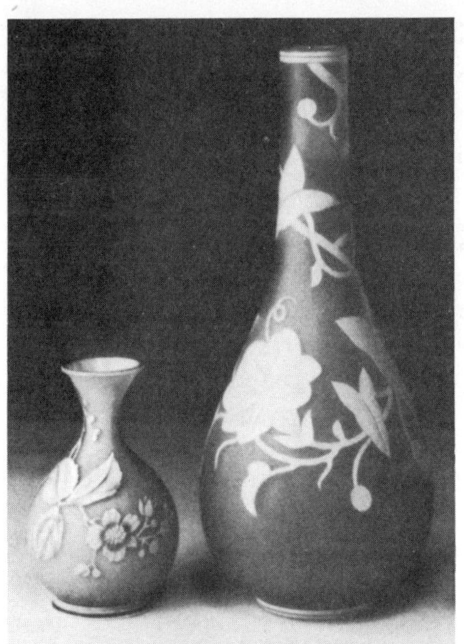

TWO UNSIGNED ENGLISH CAMEO VASES, attributed to Thomas Webb & Sons, c. 1900. (Left) yellow glass overlaid in red & white, carved with blossoming apple branch, the reverse with butterfly; 5"H, rim ground; *$700 A. (Right) pale lime-yellow overlaid with white, carved with Convolvulvus blossoms/leaves; neck & foot with ring turnings, 11¾"H; *$950 A. (Sotheby's)

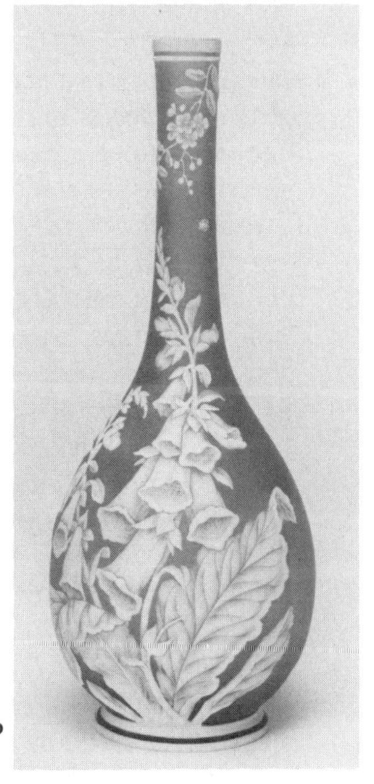

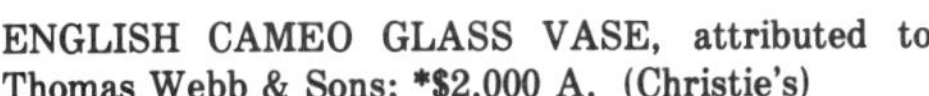

ENGLISH CAMEO GLASS VASE, attributed to Thomas Webb & Sons; *$2,000 A. (Christie's)

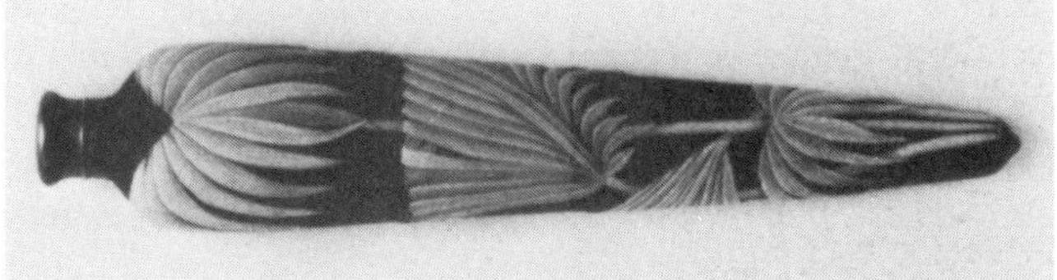

ENGLISH CAMEO GLASS PERFUME VIAL, red overlaid in white, cut with Palm leaves & a butterfly, monogrammed silver top by Gorham; 9½"L, attributed to Thomas Webb & Sons; *$750 A. (Sotheby's)

WEISS

Vase — flattened ovalfrosted gold ground with overlays of purple to brown, trees along river in 3 acid cuttings; 5 7/8"H; $550 D.

UNSIGNED PIECES: MISCELLANEOUS (The organization of this chapter has been upon the basis of the readily-identifiable, signed pieces, arranged alphabetically. For many fine examples of glass, though, this may almost beg the question, especially when the user cannot readily identify a particular piece as to its maker.

Every major art glass maker turned out glass which, for one reason or another, wasn't signed, which didn't carry the "mark" of the company. Today's collector, faced with the many, many pieces of unsigned (unmarked) glassware from the Art Nouveau styles, can well be puzzled as to the origins of them. Oh, it may be possible to say a particular piece is German, or English, or French, but getting much more specific may become a matter of specualation.

We'll have to say, for many fine glass items, that they are just that: fine examples of the glassmaker's or glass decorator's art. Other pieces can often be attributed by similarities to known pieces which *are* signed, but that presupposes prior knowledge of this field by the reader. Somehow, that seems to defeat the purpose of this book — to present an overview of both identification and pricing for the Art Nouveau styles.

The following glass items are either unsigned by factory marks, or they are signed in a manner so esoteric as not to be readily recognizable by most collectors who are not specialized in the glass field. Organization is by the type of object.)

Basket, Miniature — Peach Blow glass, attributed to Sandwich; body with raised swirls & ruffled rim, applied camphor glass handle; 3½"D, 5½"H to top of handle; $895 D.

Biscuit Jar — domed cover with floral chasing, jar with similar Lily-of-the-Valley & wheel-cut intaglio decor; silver mounted, attributed to Hawkes, 12½"H; *$275 A.

Bottle — cameo with silver cap; white against olive-greenish ground, shell motif both sides, 2½"H to top of cap; unsigned but considered English; $750 D.

— scent bottle, silver overlay in Art Nouveau Dogwood pattern, original ball stopper, 4½"H; $72 D.

— scent bottle, frosted nude on front, marked "Melba," small flake on back; $20 D.

Bowl — rose bowl, enameled and cut to cranberry glass, 7"D; unsigned but attributed to Moser; $155 D.

— heavy compressed ovoid form in opalescent glass washed in iridescence, 8", unsigned but attributed to Steuben; *$150 A.

— ruffled, green with blue & gold, 4"H x 8"D; unsigned but attributed to Loetz; $120 D.

Bowl & Saucer — both yellow overlaid with white, etched with Orange blossoms/butterflies; saucer 4½"D; English, c. 1900; *$700 A.

Box, Covered — cameo Winter scenic, tangerine ground, 3'W, attributed to Daum; $595 D.

— deep blue Art Nouveau blown-out pattern covered with gold & raised porcelain flowers, hinged; $179 D.

Box, Trinket — 3 brass ormolu scrolled feet & similar rim, colorful heavy enamel against transparent glass; unsigned, but paper label remnant shows it was from Austria; attributed to Moser; $150 D.

Centerpiece — blue enamel on amber ground, intaglio cut, 12" x 5", compote with matching pair candlesticks; 3 pieces, $295 D.

Compote — ruffled edge blue opalescent shading to apple green, 9½"D; Art Nouveau women's heads on spelter base; $125 D.

— white frosted, scalloped deep blue edge with metal Art Nouveau base, 7½"H x 8"D; $65 D.

Cookie Jar — green iridescent, melon-ribbed, with brass rim/top/handle; 6 7/8"H x 5 3/8" F; unsigned but attributed to Loetz; $150 D.

Decanter — emerald green, presentation August 12, 1898; silver network of vines/florals by Alvin Silversmiths (signed); 11½"H to top of repoussc silver on cork stopper; $695 D.

Ewer — crystal in silvered mounts, 10½"H; *$150 A.

Glass, Wine — enameled with iridescent flower in shades of orange/tangerine; gold eneameling on outer side of bowl, ruffled foot, about 6 7/8"H; unsigned but attributed to Lobmeyr; $165 D.

Humidor — Knights of Columbus; Art Nouveau gold-colored metal cover with K of C emblem, zipper cutting; made for presentation to K of C officer, c. 1915; $189 D.

Inkwell — cut crystal with Continental silver top with applied flowers; button-cut base, 6¾"H; *$750 A.

— red-orange with sections of random gold throughout, & darker at base; glossy outer casing; 5"H, almost as wide, square base, large round knob top; attributed to Daum; $750 D.

— geometric; 3 triangular formations protrude on upper part, with 3 protruding opposite on lower part, all iridescent; brass collar & hinged Art Nouveau lid with clear glass insert; 3½"H x 4½"W; $250 D.

— green iridescent with webbing; brass collar & hinged lid; 2¼" square, 2¾"H; no insert; $140 D.

— cut crystal glass with waffle bottom; sterling Art Nouveau top; 1¾"H; $39 D.

Pitcher — Pomona glass, with small braided crystal rope wrapping around collar, enameled with flowers/leaves; $195 D.

— lemonade pitcher, sterling overlay on cut glass in grapes/vines decor; $195 D.

Plaque — transparent green with ochre highlights & blue-purple iridescence, moulded with Irises, 8¾"H; unsigned but attributed to Tiffany; *$220 A.

Plate — orange stretched obverse, with gold stretched reverse, and applied blue stretch edge, 8"D; unsigned but attributed to Durand; $185 D.

Powder Box — flattened spherical form; translucent ruby glass with iridescent silvery-blue mottling & chased floral silver overlay; monogrammed silver cover; 3"H, unsigned but attributed to Loetz; *$380 A.

Salt — pedestaled with lid, Art Nouveau cherub, 4½"H; $23 D.

Salt & Pepper — cut crystal in prism, honeycomb & fan; ornate Art Nouveau sterling tops; pair, $95 D.

Tumbler — enamel decorated; deep amber glass with multicolored enamel dragon/flowers in green/ruby/brown/opal; 2½"H, attributed to Galle; $800 D.

Vase — baluster form in clear overlaid & applied with yellow/purple/red/green/blue, all finely carved with flowering Peonies/Irises/Violets/Lilies; ground is carved with leaves; 9½"H, unsigned but attributed to Eugene Michel, Lorraine, c. 1895; *$8,200 A.

— oviform, black glass overlaid with gold etched with stylized flowering trees, 8"H, interior scratch; possibly Steuben; *$4,500 A.

— red quilted satin glass overlaid in white & etched back to depict Iris plants blooming; 8"H, English; *$3,500 A.

— cameo, red ground overlaid with white, Passion Flower on front, dragonfly on reverse; 5"H, almost as wide; English; $1,950 D.

— cameo, blue-aqua ground on baluster form, terminating in 1½"-W collar with stems/flowers in white/lavender; cased opal liner; 5½"H, English; $1,850 D.

— spherical form, translucent yellow decorated with violet/olive-green waves & gold mottling; chased silver floral overlay; 8½"H, unsigned but attributed to Loetz; *$1,800 A.

— cameo, blue with cameo carved flower/buds/leaves, with 3 bands at top and bottom; 5"H, attributed to Webb; $1,750 D.

— cameo scenic, man rowing across lake; blue sky, light green water, trees/foliage in brown shades; 4½"H x 7"W; attributed to Galle; $1,750 D.

— cameo, citron ground with white floral, 15"H, English; $1,500 D.

— ovoid form, pink ground overlaid with white, etched with Geraniums/butterfly; 8"H, English, c. 1900; *$1,200 A.

— ruby glass with blue-green mottled iridescence, with meandering silver overlay marked "999/1000 fine silver," 7"H, unsigned but attributed to Loetz; $1,200 D.

— teardrop form, blue ground overlaid with white, etched with Prunus blossoms & a butterfly; 7"H, English, c. 1900; *$900 A.

— emerald green with silver overlay, 13¼"H; $695 D.

— cameo, teardrop form, pale lime glass overlaid in white, cut with blossoming Morning Glory vines, the lip & base ring turnings; 9½"H, English, probably Thomas Webb & Sons, c. 1900; *$500 A.

— compressed bulbous form, rose glass decorated with rose-tinged amber iridescent spotting, overlaid with scrolling pewter mounts case with blossoms/undulating strapwork forming loop handles; 9"H, Austrian, c. 1900; *$450 A.

— bottle form, rose & scrolling trellis design over green-to-blue ground, the decorative design in silver overlay; 10½"H; *$450 A.

— random swirl purple iridescent pattern, set into Art Nouveau bronze "tree" blossoming at top; 6¼"H, unsigned but attributed to Loetz; $450 D.

— baluster form, transparent green with white threading/leaves, with bright silvery-blue iridescence; 10½"H, unsigned but attributed to Durand; *$420 A.

— pinched form with quatrefoil rim, blue & purple; unsigned but attributed to Loetz, 8"H; *$380 A.

— double gourd form with 8-petal fluted top; 6"D bulbous base with 3 circular concave areas; overall silver-blue amber "oil spots" on green polished pontil, unsigned but attributed to Loetz; $375 D.

— baluster form, bright yellow & iridescent blue-silver mottled brown, 7"H; unsigned but attributed to Loetz; *$350 A.

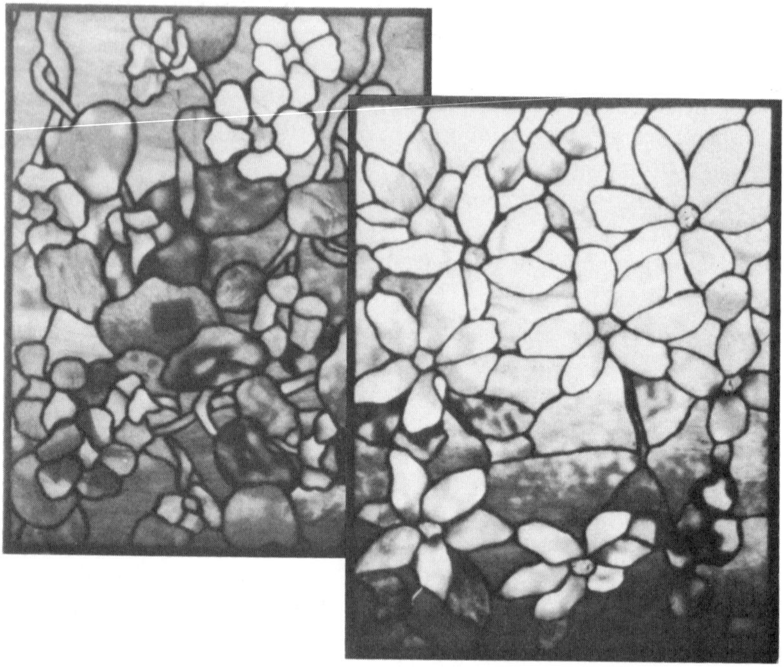

THREE LEADED GLASS PANELS (only two shown), each 15" x 12", early 20th Century; *$1,600 A. (Sotheby's)

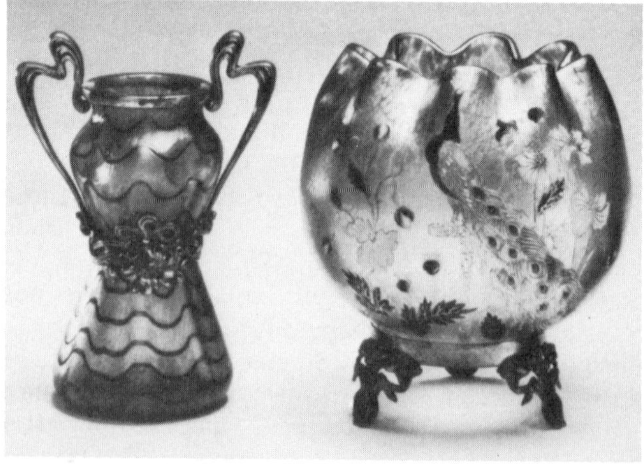

TWO AUSTRIAN-STYLED unsigned iridescent glass vases, c. 1900, both attributed to Loetz. (Left) apricot glass with wavy blue striations, silver mounts in scrolling floral motif, 6"H; *$225 A. (Right) bulbous lemon-yellow vessel enameled with peacock amid flowers, gilt-heightened, raised on gilt-bronze feet, 6"H; *$350 A. (Sotheby's)

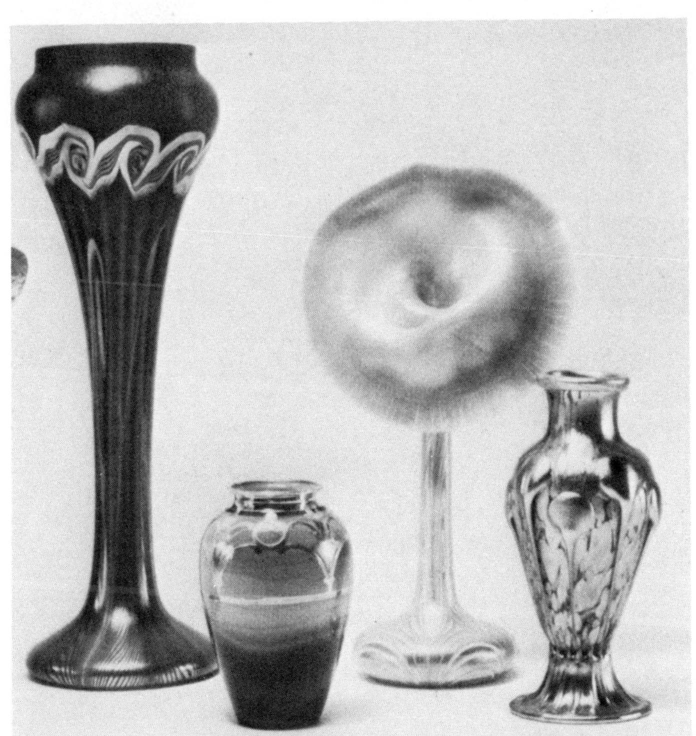

FOUR EXAMPLES OF AMERICAN GLASS; from left: Pale lemon cased in green glass, with silver-iridescent lappets at shoulder, 13¼"H, inscribed "Quezal," with neck restoration, *$650 A; silver-overlay 'Agate' vase, striated ochre/green overlaid with scrolling foliate motifs, inscribed "Quezal/M/862," 4½"H, *$700 A; ivory "Jack-in-the-Pulpit" vase with orangish rim, 10¾"H, inscribed "Quezal," *$1,100; striated ivory/green with amber iridescent foot/lappets/mottled wash, inscribed "Quezal E807," 6½"H, damaged rim, *$375 A. (Sotheby's)

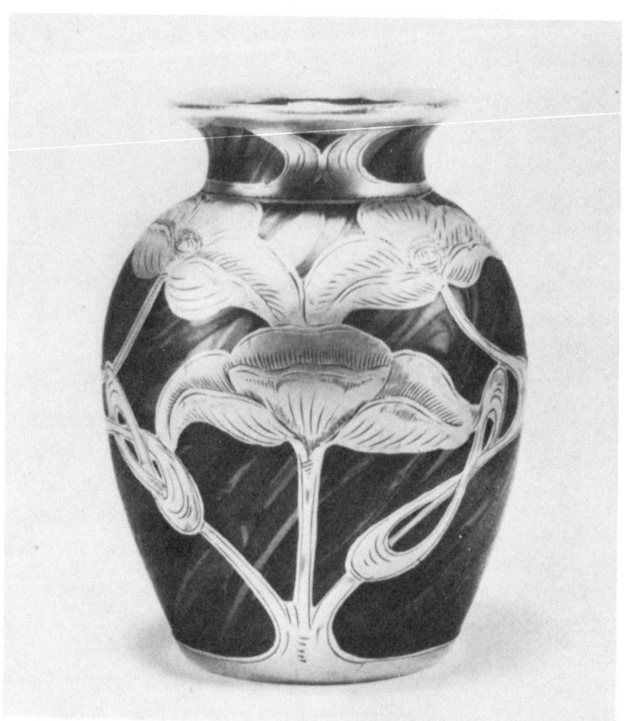

LOETZ SILVER-OVERLAY IRIDESCENT GLASS VASE; silvery-blue/ochre/salmon/deep blue iridescence; inscribed "Loetz/Austria," c. 1900, 5¼"H; *$1,600 A. (Sotheby's)

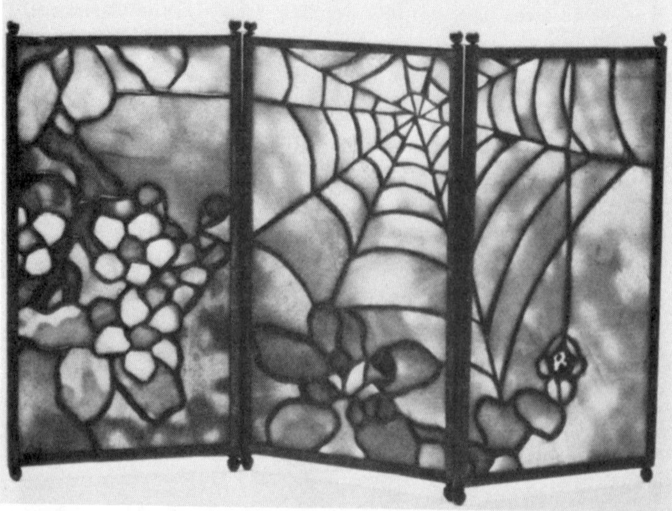

SCREEN, MINIATURE; three-fold of Tiffany Favrile glass and bronze, with leaded spider web against mottled blue/blue-grey sky, with pink/red apple blossoms, green leaves; tag impressed TIFFANY STUDIOS/NEW YORK; 7¾"H x 12 1/8"L; *$3,500 A.

— cameo, grey trumpet flowers/berries on vine against frosted yellow ground; 4½"H, French, attributed to D'Argental; $310 D.

— classical urn shape with everted rim, amber/green iridescent body with over iridescent "oil spots" & gold trailings; 10"H, attributed to Loetz; $260 D.

— cameo, carved emerald green iridescent, with large thistles & branches with pinkish iridescence covering the front; bulbous with short slender neck, 11½"H overall, unsigned but attributed to Loetz; $230 D.

— crystal, fluted & engraved with sheaf of wheat alternating with sunflowers, 12"H; *$225 A.

— marigolds on green ground, 13½"H, Austrian; *$170 A.

— translucent ruby with intricate blue/violet pale yellow swirls; 3¼"H, unsigned but attributed to Loetz; *$160 A.

— green glass with silver overlay of detailed Poppies/leaves; overlay marked "999/1000," with Alvin hallmark; $155 D.

— baluster form, gold iridescence with green iridescent leaves/trails, fitted for electricity, 10"H; *$150 A.

— footed baluster form, iridescent gold with foliate designs, 12"H; *$150 A.

— green fluted with lavish trailing blossoms, 10½"H; $139 D.

— crystal with gilt intaglio flowers, 7¼"H; $125 D.

— cranberry iridescent, 4¾"H x 4¾"D top opening; sitting in pewter Art Nouveau holder; unsigned but attributed to Loetz; $125 D.

— bottle form, Art Nouveau-inspired, 10"H; *$75 A.

— compressed double gourd form with narrow straight neck, blue iridescence, 8½"H; *$40 A.

— dimpled, with trailing lily pads below flared rim, 6¼"H; *$40 A.

— squat globular body with "stiff" neck, iridescent, 5"H; $40 D.

FURNITURE

Art Nouveau was an art most used on smaller pieces than on larger ones. That didn't mean that there were no successful Art Nouveau designs in such "large" things as building design (architecture) or in furniture. Today, however, furniture is, minor collecting area for lovers of Art Nouveau. Attribute this to a scarcity of true Art Nouveau-inspired designs in furniture; to the possibilities of not recognizing some Art Nouveau pieces for what they are; to increasing prices for some types of Art Nouveau items, pushing them beyond the price ranges of some buyers.

Much of the Art Nouveau furniture can be recognized by its use of tendril forms, but to leave the statement there without amplification would be misleading. Not only did national tendencies develop in furniture design; individiual designers also bucked the prevailing tendencies within their own countries, often helping change the concepts of what could or should be done with furniture.

The British Isles, for instance, can't be characterized as a whole due to different tendencies there. The Arts and Crafts Movement, instrumental in bringing about an increased awareness of the "minor" decorative arts, led also to an essentially conservative approach to design, especially in England. Furniture following in its wake was far more symmetrical than that found in some other European areas. Plant forms, when used, were derived from the flower. Lines of furniture were graceful, undulating, but predictably regular. Gothic (or neo-Gothic) influences appeared in both Arts and Crafts and later Art Nouveau furniture. Woods used tended to be light in color, primarily oak or ash, their natural colors being shown.

But in neighboring Scotland, Art Nouveau furniture design got off to a later and different start. Under the tutelage and examples of Charles Rennie Mackintosh in Glasgow, several tendencies developed in the early 1900s. Like the ash and oak used in England, furniture tended toward the light in color, but in Scotland the lightness came from paint in what were unusual color schemes for the day: white, off white, light gray, or several pastel hues. Squared geometric forms were used, in some ways similar to and perhaps derivative of the Arts and Crafts stylings of an earlier day. The line itself assumed primary importance, but lines were used as decorative features. One Mackintosh idea that spread only slightly was the use of vertical parallel lines as decorative devices, particularly on chairs. Part and parcel of Scottish design under Mackintosh was extensive symbolic treatment. Furniture might have a bud, an egg, a heart — all figures with symbolic meaning.

The French adapted the English predilection for the Gothic styles but gave them the peculiar neo-rococo touches so common in that country. Divided as the country was between the artistic centers of Paris and Nancy, it was natural that two distinctive styles would develop there. Both styles remained firmly rooted in nature.

Galle and Majorelle, working in Nancy, presented naturalistic renderings of flowers and plants (as the English did) but used them much more asymmetrically. The Iris was a common Galle motif in his marquetry furniture (often utilizing essentially Louis XV stylings), while animal life portrayed might include dragonflies or even frogs. Majorelle extracted nature from its 2-dimensional effect as portrayed by Galle, bringing it back into the three dimensions found within nature.

Parisian furniture also relied upon nature for its inspiration; unlike the Nancy production, Parisian furniture often stylized and abstracted natural symbols in somewhat the same way Mackintosh did in Scotland. Seldom did Parisian designers give free reign to their ideas in the way those of Nancy did; the result: a more restrained, less decorative group of stylings.

Belgian furniture was still more diverse. Borrowing from the plastic, dynamic traditions of French Art Nouveau, and freely taking from the more staid constructions of Great Britain, Belgium produced a trio of major designers, each working somewhat differently. Victor Horta seemed to wage war upon right angles. His work was an attempt to have his designs seen in their entirety rather than piece by piece. Part of his dynamism can be seen in his use of the device of having a single point (or egg) serve as the embryo for a group of lines springing from it. Gustav Serrurier-Bovy, on the other hand, restrained his designs, enclosing them with arches drawn from the medieval periods. Henry Van de Velde, working in Belgium, developed a rectilinearism completely out of keeping with the rest of the nation's furniture designers.

Yet the rectilinear design concept was not out of touch with work done in Germany and Austria. German design was spread out but furniture was centered in two main areas, Munich and Darmstadt. Early design concepts included such ideas as that of Otto Eckmann and others, of using curved lines with distinctive thickenings within the curves, and the use of arched struts. Furniture of the Jugendstil, far from being the rather light-appearing pieces of the French, tended toward the massive and ponderous. Decorations included an entrelac-like design, although later pieces reflect geometric designs rather than naturalistic ones. However, when nature, in the form of flowers, was used as a decorative device, it was the flower itself that caught the German designers' attentions, rather than the stems and tendrils. A heavy debt was owed to the Vienna Secessionists, especially in the Darmstadt area.

Austrian Secessionists centered at Vienna developed what was to be a new, novel approach to design; in some ways it can be said to presage the coming Art Deco movement, even serving as a partial bridge between naturalistic Art Nouveau and geometric Art Deco. The square and rectangle were predominant decorative devices, both in detail and in the whole. Use was made of such symbolic elements as the bud of the flower and the circle filled with flames. Trees with clusters of circles on their limbs (sometimes referred to incorrectly as "apples") were also used. No fear was evidenced of the right angle or the corner, and accordingly, German design picked up this aspect as well.

America was pretty much bypassed by the Art Nouveau movement when it came to furniture. Much more influential here was the American adaptation of the English Arts and Crafts movement. The major designer, Gustave Stickley, worked in what was to be known as the "Craftsman" or "Mission" style, soon followed by a host of imitators.

No matter which country is discussed, furniture in the Art Nouveau styles was seldom mass-produced (American Mission-style furniture was, of course, not exactly in the Art Noueau mode, but it was mass-market.) My personal opinion is that, as a group, much of this furniture is currently under-valued.

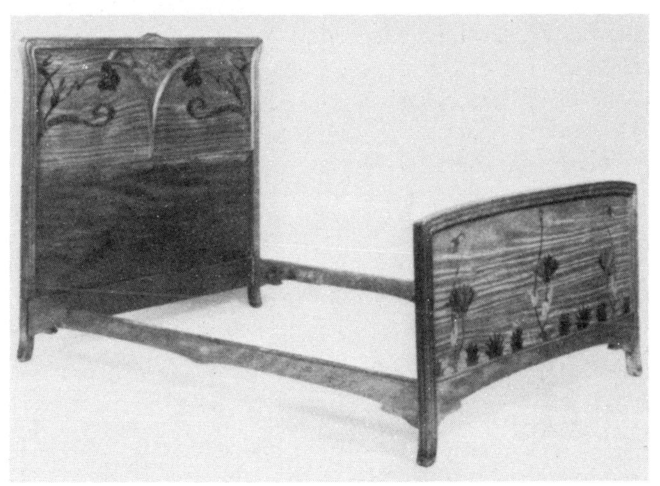

BED FRAME, c. 1900, fruitwood marquetry inlaid with Poppy & Iris blossoms; 57"H x 51"W x 78½"L; *$1,000 A. (Sotheby's)

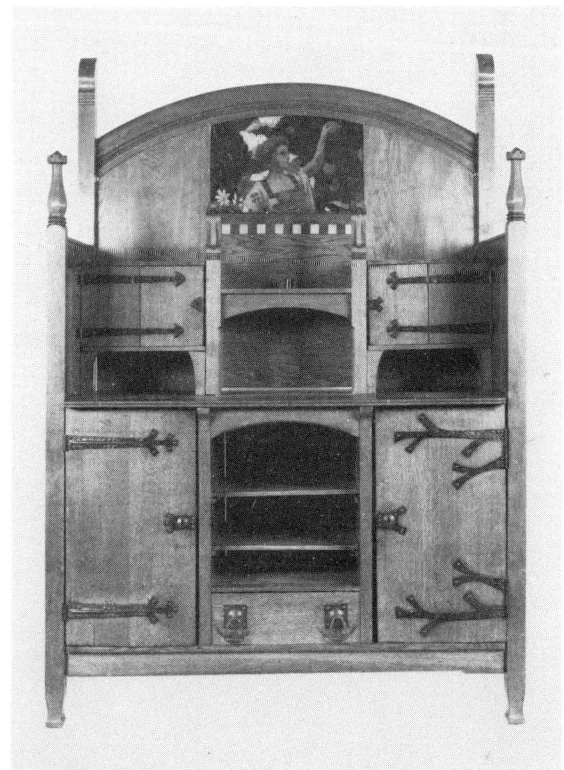

BUFFET, oak, by Henri-Jules-Ferdinand Bellery-Desfontaines, c. 1900; *$1,800 A. (Christie's)

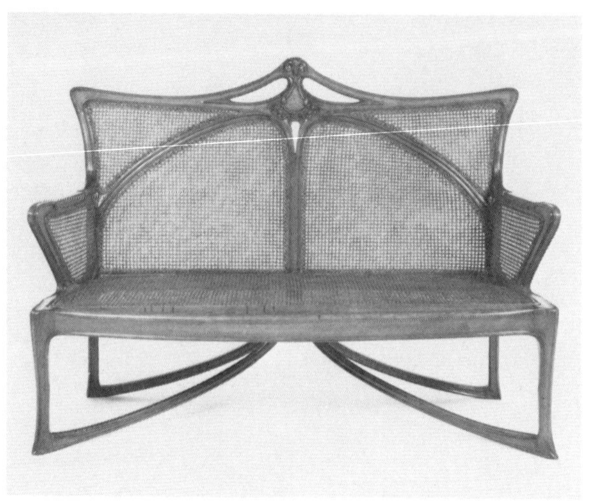

CANAPE, French stained walnut, c. 1900; *$2,200 A. (Christie's)

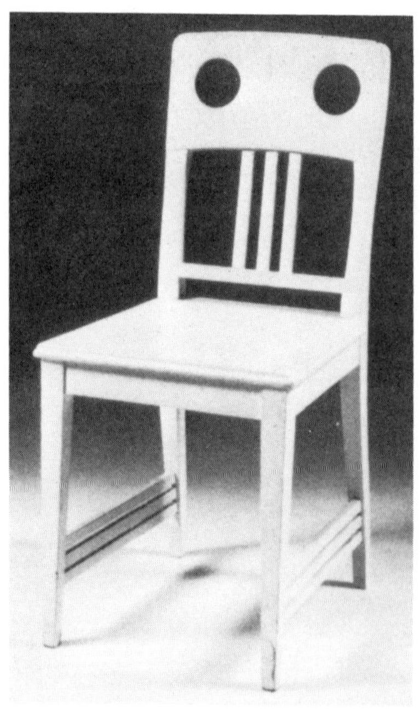

CHAIR, painted wood; Viennese Secessionist, designed by Olbrich, 1899, painted white; *$1,700 A. (Sotheby's)

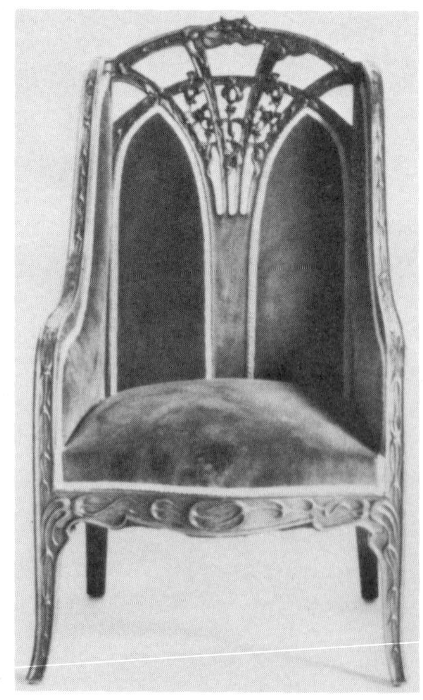

CHAIR, ARMCHAIR, carved walnut by Marjorelle in the Clematis pattern, brown velvet upholstery, c. 1900; *$5,250 A. (Sotheby's)

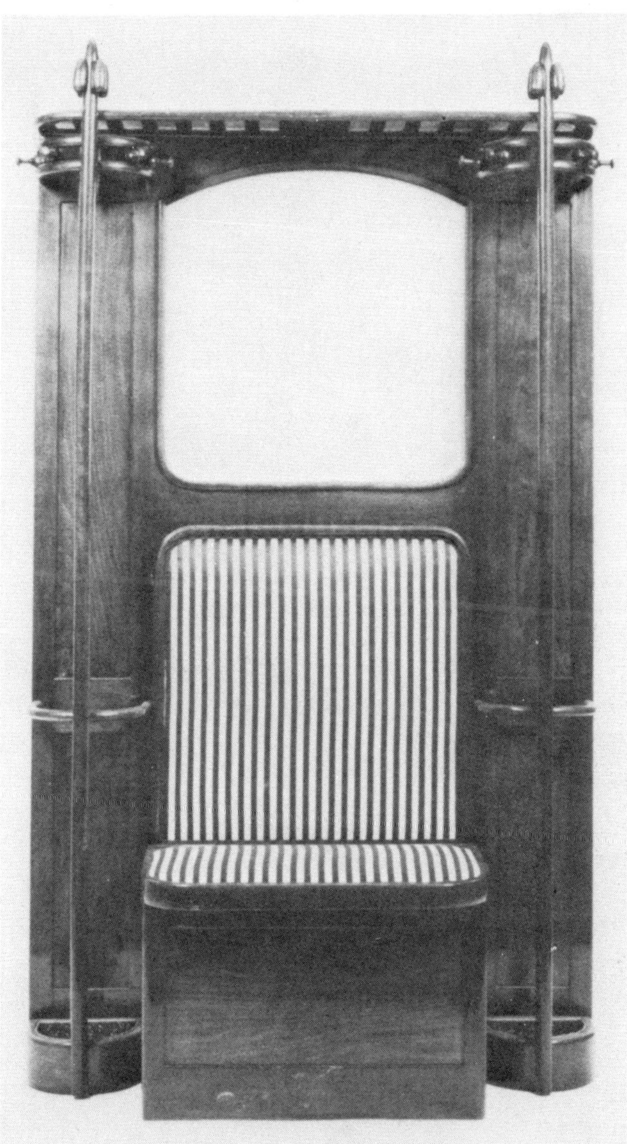

HALL PIECE, designed by Josef Hoffmann, made by Thonet (Austria); ivory & black silk upholstery; paper label remnants printed THONET; 85"H x 47½"W; c. 1905; *$6,500 A. (Sotheby's)

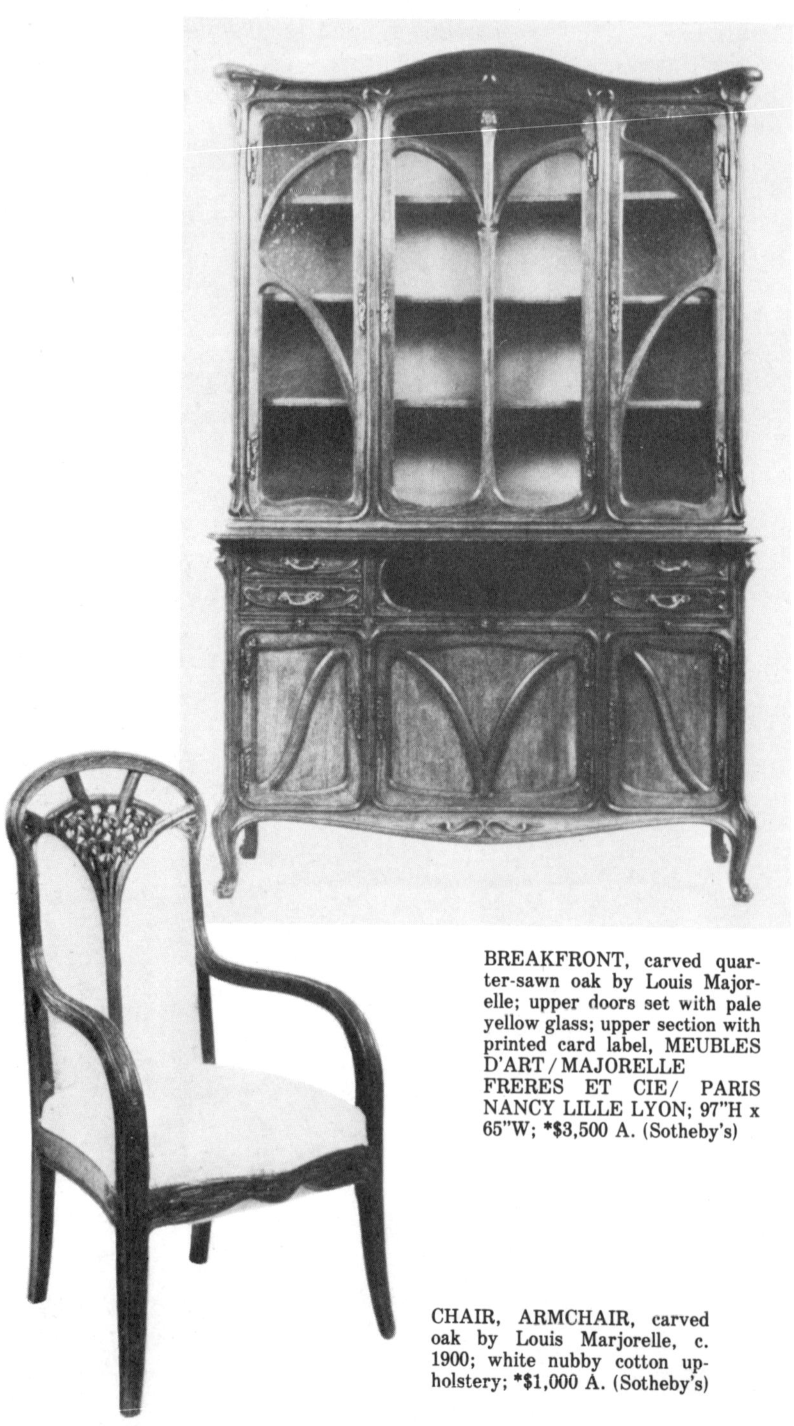

BREAKFRONT, carved quarter-sawn oak by Louis Majorelle; upper doors set with pale yellow glass; upper section with printed card label, MEUBLES D'ART / MAJORELLE FRERES ET CIE/ PARIS NANCY LILLE LYON; 97"H x 65"W; *$3,500 A. (Sotheby's)

CHAIR, ARMCHAIR, carved oak by Louis Marjorelle, c. 1900; white nubby cotton upholstery; *$1,000 A. (Sotheby's)

ARMOIRE — inlaid rosewood, molded cornice flanked by poppy seed-pod finials above frieze inlaid with purple-heart dragonflies having eyes designed as trefoil clusters; beveled mirror in rosewood borders inlaid with dragonflies, flanked by twisted columns continuing to square feet below drawer with 2 brass foliate pulls; 103" x 47", by Louis Majorelle; mirror broken; *$5,500 A.

BOOKCASE CABINET — Mission oak, paneled glazed door enclosing shelves, painted black trim; by Gustav Stickley, c. 1900; 56"H x 36"W, *$700 A.

BOOKRACK — desktop style, carving on top and sides; 18" x 8"; $75 D.

CHAIR, DINING — set of 6, all carved at crests, aprons, and knees with flowers; shield-shaped splats and seats upholstered in nailed leather decorated with tooled fuchsia sprays; some chairs with metal retailer's tag, "A. Bastea Lyon;" each chair 36"H; *$5,200 A.

CHAIR, ROCKING— lady's model, oak, the concave back with 3 splats above original nailed leather seat; 30¾"H, with red decal of Gustav Stickley; *$280 A.

CHAIR, SIDE — pair of Arts and Crafts upholstered seat side chairs, shaped back crests with pierced sunflower designs, ebonized wood finish; *$400 A.

CHINA CABINET — Mission style stained oak, 3/4-galleried top above latticed glass doors opening to adjustable shelf space; lower doors open to more space, with hammered black-painted brass key plates, hinges, bail handles; joints have pierced tenons on short legs; 62½"H x 35"W, red decal of Gustav Stickley; *$3,000 A.

CLOTHES CHEST — oak with hammered copper hinges, key plate, handle; oak top and metal with mark of Roycroft firm; 23"L x 9½"W; *$280 A.

DESK, WRITING — oak, rectangular top over 2 short frieze drawers; sides with vertical supports joined by lower medial shelf; 30"H x 54"W x 30" deep; by L. & J.G. Stickley; *$375 A.

FIRE SCREEN — Arts and Crafts oak, 36 3/4"H; *$150 A.

SIDEBOARD — oak, metal mounts, 2 cupboard doors, 2 short & 1 wider drawer, label in top center drawer of L. & J.G. Stickley; 36"H x 49"W x 19½" deep; *$850 A.$

SIDEBOARD — oak, 2 short and 2 long drawers, matching brass key plates, bail handles; model #735 by L. & J.G. Stickley, 46¼"H x 55¾"W; *$1,500 A.

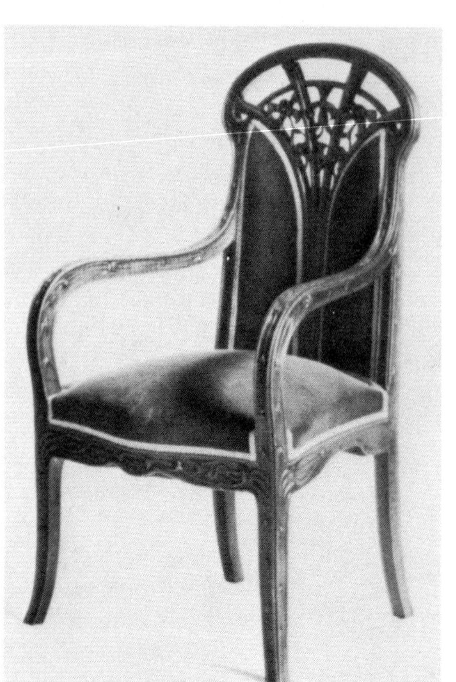

CHAIR, ARMCHAIR, carved walnut by Marjorelle in the Clematis pattern, brown velvet upholstery, c. 1900; pair, *$4,100 A. (Sotheby's)

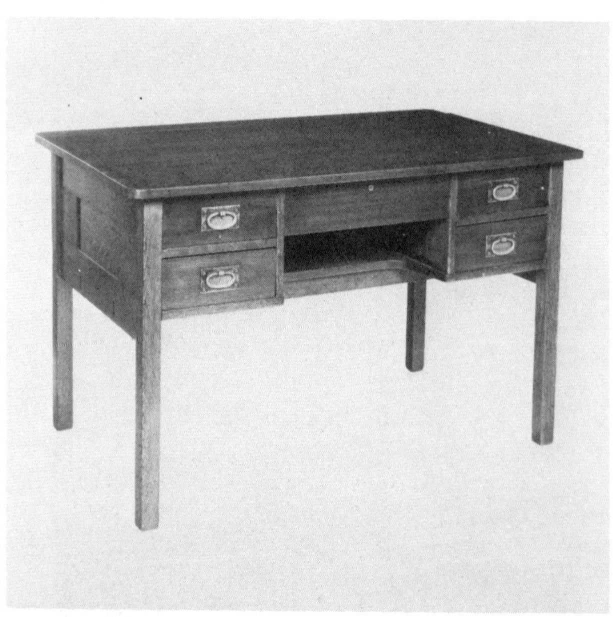

DESK, AMERICAN MISSION STYLE OAK by Gustav Stickley; *$1,200 A. (Christie's)
(Christie's)

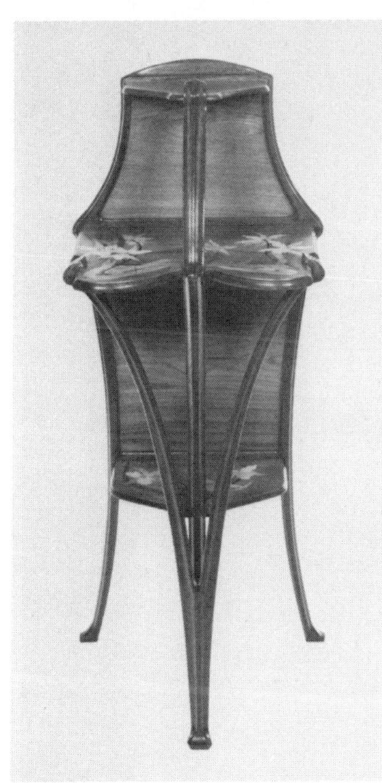

ETAGERE, mahogany with floral inlay on all three tiers, by Emile Galle; *$4,600 A. (Christie's)

Below,
HALLWAY PIECE, massive carved oak, French, c. 1900; *$1,200 A. (Christie's)

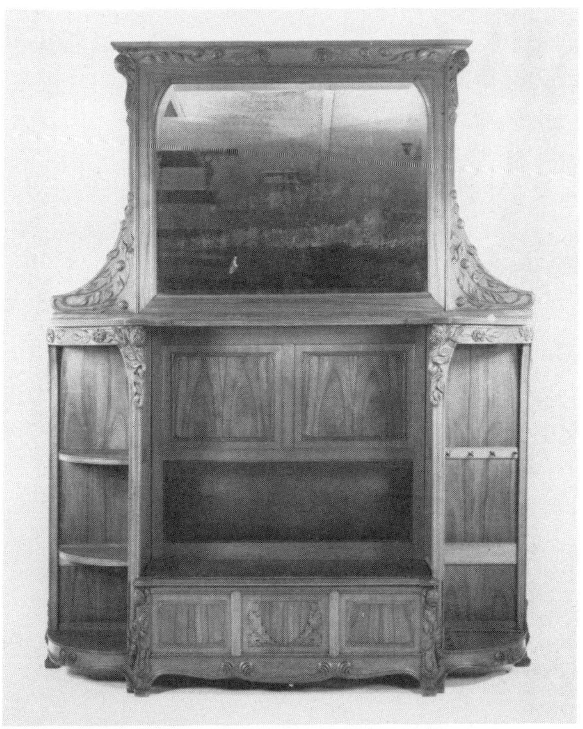

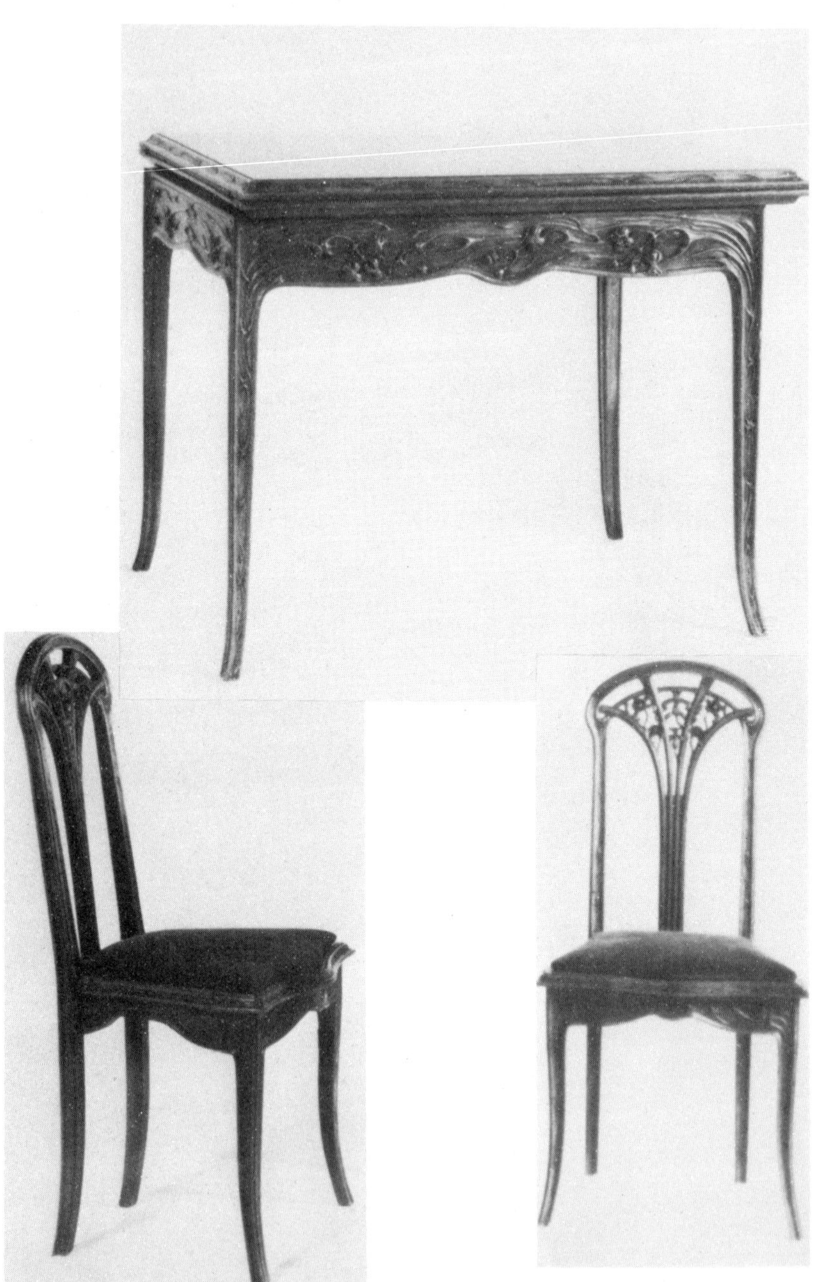

GAMING SET comprising a gaming table and three sidechairs (2 shown), carved walnut by Louis Marjorelle in the Clematis pattern, the chairs with brown velvet upholstery; table, 39½"H; *$3,750 A. (Sotheby's)

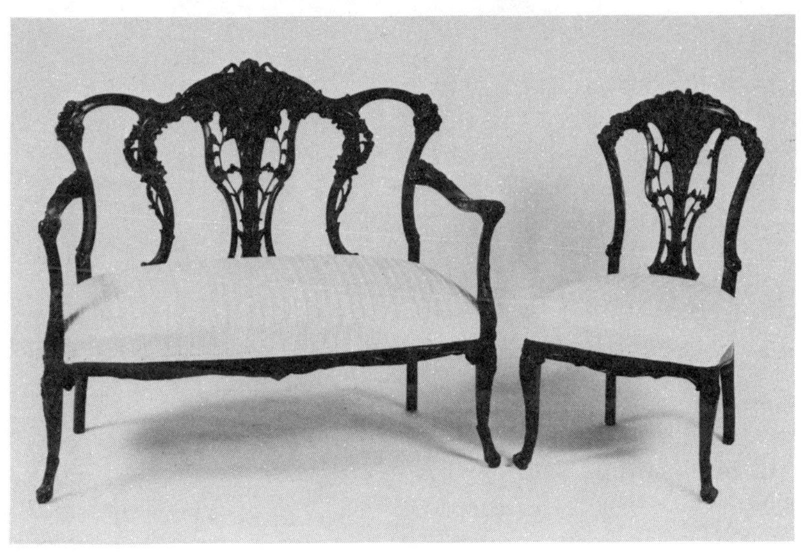

SUITE, SETTE AND CHAIR, each of carved mahogany with backs carved with Lily & Cattail motif, animal paw feet; settee, 49"L; *$1,000 A. (C.G. Sloan)

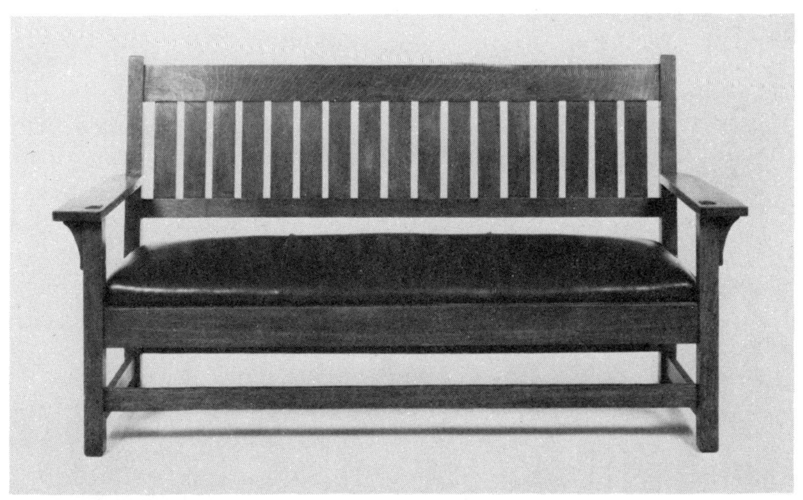

SETTEE, AMERICAN MISSION STYLE OAK by Gustav Stickley; *$2,500 A. (Christie's)

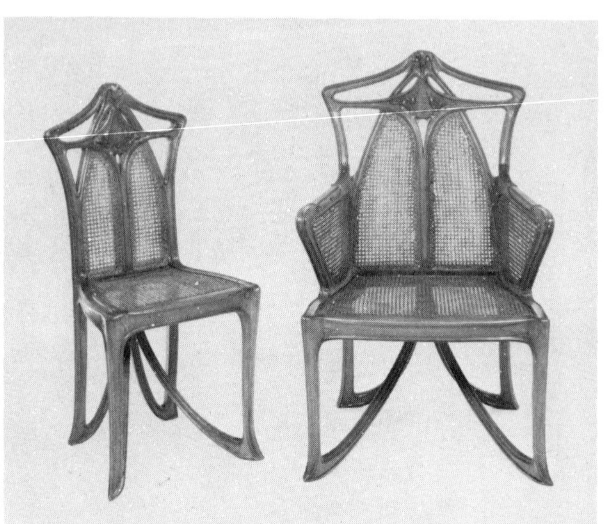

SUITE, FRENCH, WALNUT, c. 1900. (Left) one of a set of four simple chairs, their legs joined by stretchers issuing from the center back splat, 36½"H; the set of four, *$2,200 A. (Right) one of a pair of matching fauteuils, 39"H; the pair, *$2,200 A. (Christie's)

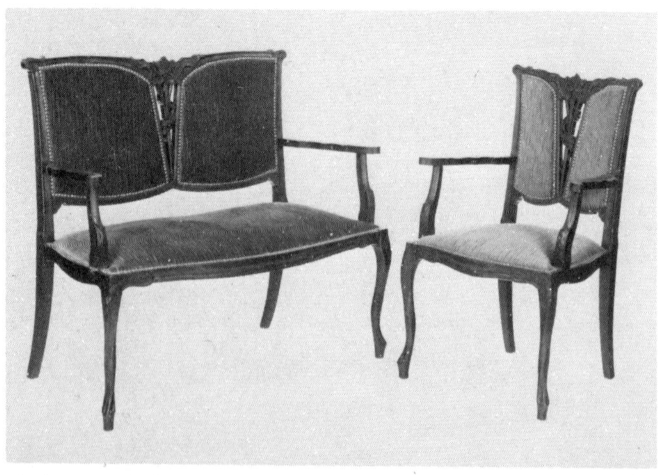

SUITE OF STAINED MAHOGANY, French, probably from Nancy, c. 1900; 4 pieces: a canape, a fauteuil, two chaises; backs carved with central pierced Lily sprays flanked by padded panels above cushioned seats upholstered in lined green corduroy, with leaf-carved armrests & feet; 45½"H, canape 38"W; *$2,200 A. (Christie's)

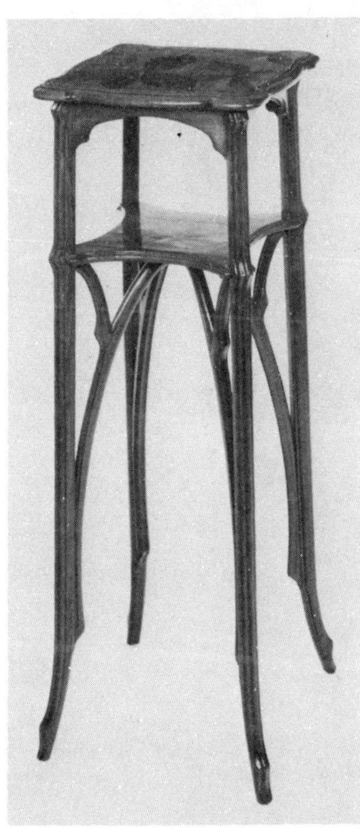

TABLE; 2-tiered mahogany with inlay on both tiers, by Emile Galle; *$2,200 A. (Christie's)

Below, TABLE, LIBRARY; 10 ivory & copper-clad columns, vellum top, inlaid pewter in both Near and Far Eastern motifs; by Carlo Bugatti, c. 1895; 31½"H x 49"W x 31" deep; *$4,200 A. (Phillips)

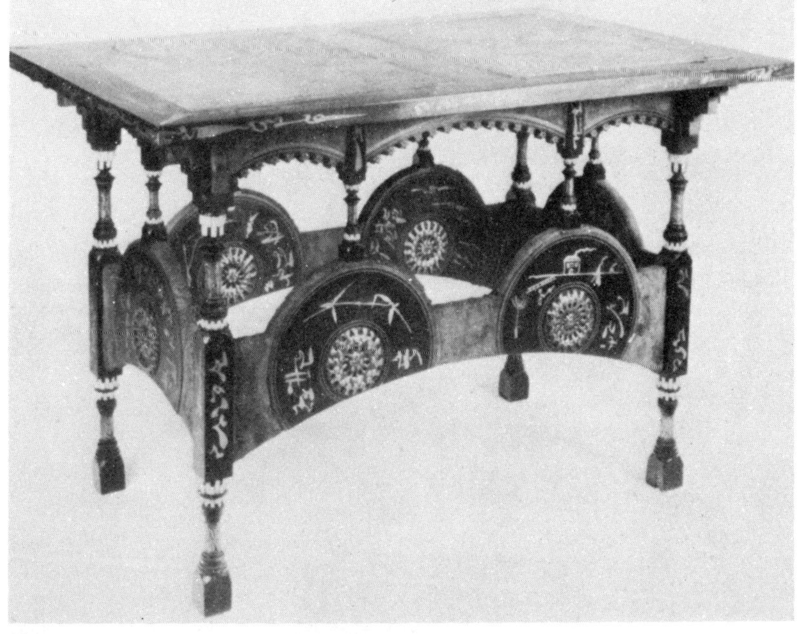

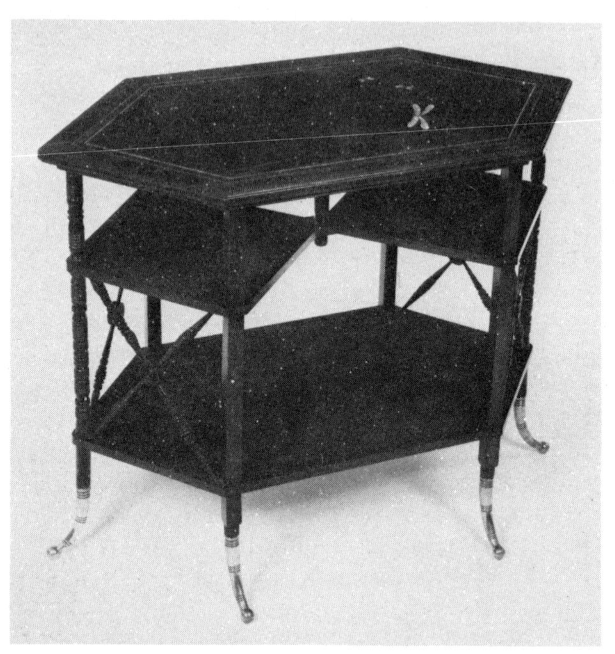

TABLE, TEA; 3-tiered mahogany with inlaid butterflies & spider in web; European, c. 1900; *$1,100 A. (Christie's)

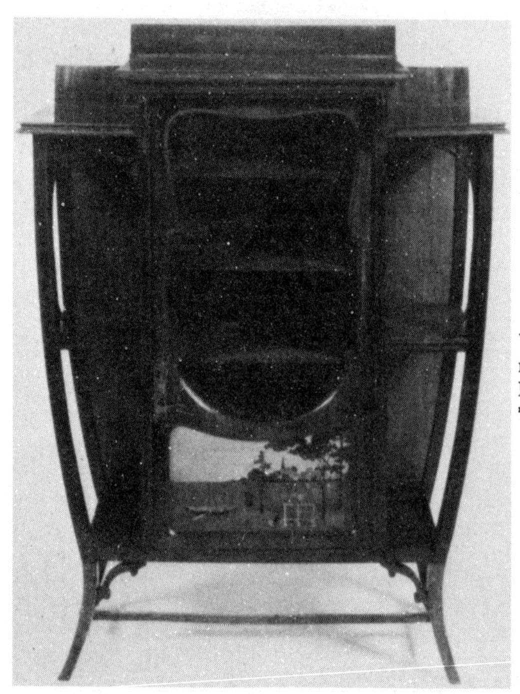

VITRINE, fruitwood marquetry, probably from the School of Nancy, c. 1900; 46"H x 35½"W; *$750 A. (Sotheby's)

TABLE, CENTER — oak, canted square top above 4 legs linked by stretchers supporting a diagonally-set smaller undertier, with paper label of L. & J.G. Stickley; 36" square x 29½"H; *$450 A.

TABLE, DRESSING — ladies' table central arched dressing glass with hinged flanking panels above enclosed shelf flanked by 4 short drawers; lower part with kneehole flanked by 4 drawers; on square feet; branded STICKLEY BROS CO. GRAND RAPIDS; *$1,800 A.

TABLES, NESTING — fine mahogany inlaid set of 4, the largest with eared top inlaid in walnut & stained fruitwoods with banjo-playing frog serenading another on lily pad among water lilies/leaves on green-tinted stems; 3 smaller tables also with frog courting scenes; all on fluted X-shaped trestle ends, all with marquetry signature of Emile Galle; largest, 28"H x 23½"W; *$6,200 A.

TABLE, NIGHT — rosewood and mahogany, with 3/4-galleried square marble top fitted with drawer, above undertier shelf & cupboard door inlaid with entrelac ribbons and mother of pearl florets; by Louis Majorelle; 37¼"H x 16½"W; *$3,200 A.

TABLE, OCCASIONAL — signed Roycroft; $175 D.

TABLE, TWO-TIER — rectangular with lobed corners inlaid with various woods in Spider Chrysanthemum blossoms/leaves; 4 cylindrical legs center a lower shelf with 4 conforming blossoms/leaves; marquetry signature "Galle", c. 1900; 28¾"H x 28¼"W; *$2,000 A.

JEWELRY

Jewelry, designed purely as decorative pieces, with no intent of greater utility than mere adornment, presented a perfect field for Art Nouveau designers. Prior to this time gold (or at very least, silver) was combined with diamonds (the larger and more ostentatious, the better) to produce a rather sterile world of design.

Enter the heretical Art Nouveau designers. Like the Arts and Crafts adherents, they felt no allegiance to the idol of gold, turning to bronze, brass, iron, the new plastics, and even occasionally aluminum to serve as settings and frames. They looked for the beauty inherent in their materials, and many concluded that, while the diamond may be beautiful, it may also be redundant and superfluous. In its place the new designers used a variety of semi-precious stones, common gems, and, in general, stones valued more for their beauty than for their monetary value.

There laid the primary focus of the Art Nouveau movement in jewelry design. The monetary value of the jewelry was no longer so important as the artistry of design that went into it. The lines of the jewelry, and the colors used in it, became paramount. While precious gems might still be used, they may be placed beside stones of negligible value which were selected for their natural beauty and color.

At least one contemporary writer (Aymer Vallance) strongly hinted that the search by Art Nouveau jewelry designers for new, different stones to use for special jewelry effects gave impetus to the growing field of gemology. No longer content to use the same old stones, designers helped launch the inquiry into the possibilities of using many of the less-well-known, less considered stones.

The white pearl, used alone or in combination with other pearls or other stones, grew in importance. Pastel-shaded stones (including coral) were used. Plain glass (yes, the same glass which would later be so common in cheap "costume" jewelry) was substituted for natural stones when the color was "right." Cabochon cuts for stones required less work than cutting many facets into a stone, and the cabochon stone became preeminent (although not exclusively used).

Jewelry designers were most active in Continental Europe and the British Isles. Activity was not at the same level throughout the area, though, nor did it follow the same patterns. In most areas, and at most times during the Art Nouveau movement's influence, curvilinearity reigned supreme over rectilinearity (even in the areas were rectinear design prevailed in other decorative arts).

France, the supreme home of jewelry designers, had a jewelry design industry not only centered at but almost wholly contained in the Paris area. Art Nouveau design began appearing in the 1880s, furthered by such world-reknowned leaders in the field as Rene Lalique, Georges Fouquet, Maurice Dufrene and others.

British jewelry design was much more diversified. Rather than being centered at London, it was spread out in cities such as Liverpool, Edinburgh, Glasgow, Nottingham, as well as London and environs. Silver was substituted for gold in many instances; the English Arts and Crafts Movement gave the British their greater appreciation of metals such as bronze, brass, iron, and pewter.

German jewelry design was scattered throughout the country, finding a number of homes in cities such as Munich, Berlin, and Dresden. Austria and Belgium, both important jewelry-producing nations, represented the opposite pattern, centered (respectively) at Vienna — which writer W. Fred felt had a "distinctive psychic character" — and Brussels.

Brooches and pendants gained increasing importance during the Art Nouveau period. Bracelets became lighter in weight and styling; sporting jewelry — featuring the shapes of game animals, horses, and dogs — became prominent, especially in England; a resurrection of enamel work took place both on the Continent and in the British Isles, only to be supplanted by the turn of the century by the increased use of semi-precious gem stones. The asymmetry which seemed a keynote of some facets of Art Nouveau did not always manifest itself in jewelry; highly symmetrical designs were sold side-by-side with the newer, asymmetric styles.

One cornerstone of French design, and the designs in areas which underwent French influence during this period, was the use of naturalistic forms. This is similar to what occured in glass, where French styles tended more toward the natural than the abstract in most cases. Florals and insects (with shimmering multi-colored wings, such as the dragonfly) were common motifs. Like the British, the French also made use of the entrelac windings brought back from the Gothic period.

Pricing can be very erratic in this field. Many dealers, faced with a piece of jewelry they believe to be Art Nouveau-influenced, will tack on a nominal premium to the price, perhaps not recognizing that they are looking at a piece by a major designer. Yes, you can still find bargains, but be prepared to pay major prices for major pieces.

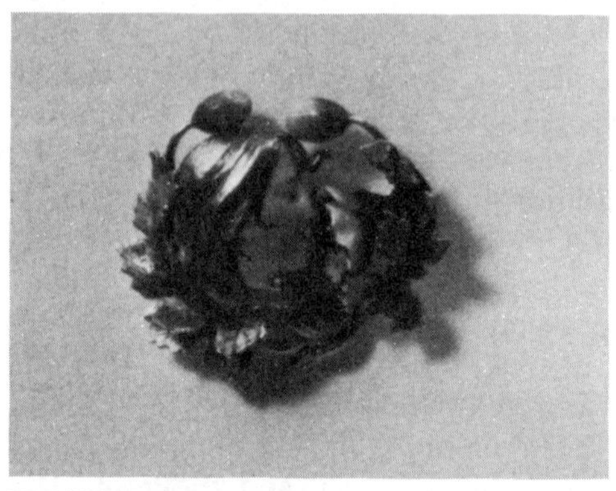

BROOCH; gold, enamel & diamond; young female head surrounded by Poppy blossoms/leaves, sniffing one bloom set with diamond; American, c. 1900, 1½"L; *$1,700 A. (Sotheby's)

Bracelet — sterling clamp on heavy, wide Art Nouveau cut-out flower; $22 D.

Brooch — 14k y.g. with single white .28 ct diamond; graceful lines, original patina, 1¼"; $275 D.

— Arts and Crafts style, by Brandt Metal Crafters; $40 D.

Chatelaine — y.g. & pearl griffin chatelaine; *$275 A.

Cuff Links — iridescent blue scarabs set in 14k gold mounting, unsigned, pair; *$240 A.

— 14k y.g. with raised face having long flowing hair, scroll edge, 2 diamonds, pair; $225 D.

Earring — 14k y.g. hand engraved cups with distinctly Art Nouveau styling, each containing a deep set freshwater pearl; $134 D.

— 14k gold full dragon with ruby eyes, c. 1900; $84 D.

Fob, Watch — very ornate with woman's face; $35 D.

— Art Nouveau lady, advertising Belmont Packing, Philadelphia; $30

— woman's face as decor; $15 D.

Fob Chain — round disc of solid profile of Art Nouveau woman in crescent moon with flowing hair; above, held by small chains, are double heads of angels; above them, a somewhat smaller angel head; above that, an even smaller angel head; sterling silver with gold wash, swivel to hold watch, good patina; $210 D.

Hatpin — sterling silver, Art Nouveau lady's head; $49 D.

— 3-sided woman's face, Art Nouveau styling; $45 D.

— gold iridescent flying bat on large dark ground; $35 D.

— diamond-shaped Art Nouveau sterling silver decoration at top, measuring 1"; overall, 9"L; $30 D.

— sterling silver, Art Nouveau; $25 D.

Lavalier — composed of diamonds/sapphire/pearl/gold; set in floral motif with one diamond-shaped Sapphire, with 2 European-cut diamonds & 37 Rose-cut diamonds; y.g. mount with one pearl suspending, 14k y.g. twisted foxtail chain, in fitted leather box; *$1,200 A.

— 10k y.g. with 3½mm center pearl, seed pearl & dangling baroque ornamentation; overall, 15mm x 40mm (about 5 7/8" x 17¾"); $58 D.

Locket — circular applied with openwork spray of flowers with shaded green enamel leaves and pearl berries; back pierced to match, suspended from iris-form pin similarly enameled & set with pearl; 55mm L (about 21 9/16"), of French origin; *$1,200 A.

— y.g. filled, flower/leaf motif set with glass "brilliants," 1¼"D; $30 D.

Necklace — set with 5 sections accented by one marquise-shaped cabochon opal enhanced by 15 small diamonds, with 6 sections set with 1 oval cabochon-cut opal accented by 8 rose-cut diamonds; all in y.g. mount; *$5,500 A.

— 14k gold with genuine aquamarine center & draped 15" cable chain, trimmed with 3 pearls & freshwater pearl drop, and green opaque enamel leaves; $420 D.

— sterling silver, pendant a blown-out head of Gibson girl-type with figural roses at neckline, with 2 small rubies centering each; necklace 14"L, pendant 2" x 1¼"; $45 D.

— sterling silver with dancing fairy; $22 D.

— pendant-type necklace, silveroid metal; $10 D.

Pendant — combined pendant/brooch of coral/diamond/gold with chain; centered by one oval orange-pink coral cabochon accented by 5 European-cut diamonds (total weight of diamonds, about 80/100 cts., with one pear-shaped coral cabochon suspended; enhanced by 14k gold & coral beaded chain; pendant/brooch signed "Leboit"; *$1,300 A.

— Dragonfly of Favrile glass and bronze, 6" body, 10" wingspan; attributed to Tiffany; $1,250 D.

— Dragonfly, Favrile glass & bronze, in olive and ochre, with link chain; *$600 A.

— 18k y.g. woman's profile with flowing hair; $79 D.

Pin — 14k green gold, 3 raised women's heads with long flowing hair facing each other, with pink enamel cheeks & enamel faces; 1¾"L; $350 D.

— triple leaf pin, handmade, with multicolor gold leaves pierced by stick pin with white old mine-cut diamond; 1½"; $200 D.

— 14k y.g., twisted candy cane bar pin, 2 3/8"; $77 D.

— enamel on sterling silver scarab pin, Arts & Crafts mode; $75 D.

— 10k y.g. oval circle pin with raised floral design & 17 seed pearls; $69 D.

— 14k green gold lapel pin with loop for drop, flowers with purple petals & green/orange enameled leaves; damaged by testing nick; $65 D.

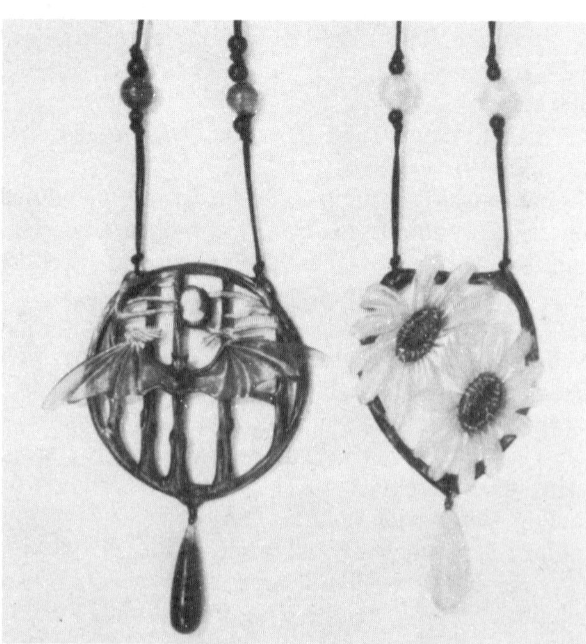

PENDANTS, both carved & stained horn, French, c. 1900; one signed "Bonte," the other with illegible inscription (possibly Bonte), lengths 2¾" and 3"; *$900 A. (Sotheby's)

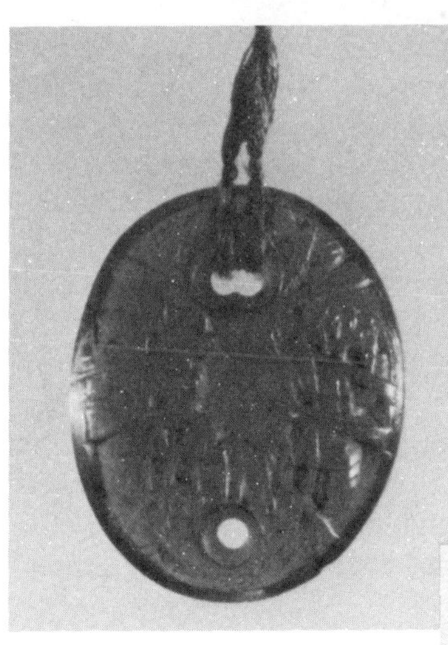

PENDANT, blue glass, by Lalique; molded obverse with opposing rows of hornets, inscribed "Lalique," 2¼"L; *$750 A. (Sotheby's)

PENDANT, pate-de-verre, by G. Argy-Rousseau, c. 1925; ochre-amber pine cone molded against shaded green leaves, hung with original silk cord & tassel; signed "GAR," 2¼"L; *$900 A. (Sotheby's)

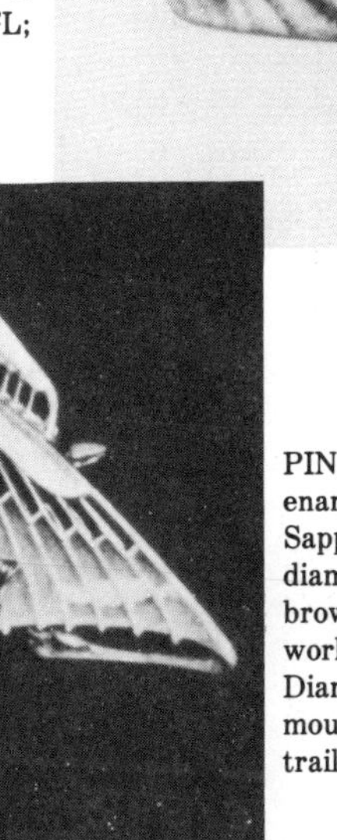

PIN, plique-a-jour blue & green enamel wings center a golden Sapphire, enhanced by rose-cut diamonds accented by lavender/brown/white/green enamel work, topped by 2 European-cut Diamonds, set in yellow gold mount, c. 1910; signed L. Grautrails; *$9,000 A. (Butterfield's)

— 14k green gold $1\frac{1}{4}$" oval mounting with center faceted amethyst (7mm x 6mm); $65 D.
— sterling silver, lady with flowing hair in Art Nouveau flower; $55 D.
— 10k y.g. woman's head with flowing hair, clover, & 7 seed pearls, 7/8"L; $54 D.
— 14k green gold bar pin, 1"L, with sapphire center; $44 D.
— carved jet cameo pin; $40 D.
— sterling silver, heavy; $23 D.
— by Forest Craft Guild; $15 D.
— swirled brass with blue stone; $15 D.

Ring — gold, opal, & plique-a-jour enamel; central cabochon flanked by 4 irregular rectangular forms encasing the plique-a-jour enamel, gold foliate setting; 7/8"D, stamped LALIQUE; *$3,400 A.
— 14k y.g., with oval blue topaz (2.5 cts.) in deep solid gold bezel with deeply engraved design on sides; $285 D.
— 10k gold, cabochon-cut Siberian amethyst set in deep oval gold bezel having detailed repousse design on each side; $240 D.
— 14k gold, with small round emerald & 2 little rose-cut diamonds in design; a small ring; $155 D.
— 14k gold Art Nouveau shank becomes 2 bands on top; sides overlaid leaves holding bezel-set emerald-cut green tourmaline, with double band all around; $140 D.
— 14k gold, late Art Nouveau, heavy swirl setting with full pearl, small diamond on either side of bypass; $110 D.
— 3-faceted round peridots set in gold half-cups, those set in prongs, 3 leaves flow besides them with rose-cut diamonds; heavy mounting, c. 1890; $115 D.
— 14k y.g., emerald in floral design; $95 D.
— 14k y.g., 2 large pearls bow in middle with ends surrounding pearls; from 1930s, characterized by dealer as "late Art Nouveau look"; $85 D.
— sterling silver, woman with flowing hair; $36 D.

Stick Pin — 14k y.g. with Art Nouveau woman's head; $32 D.
— with carved ivory skull characterized as transitional between Art Nouveau and Art Deco; $10 D.

Tiara — Art-Nouveau styled crystal & metal thread; $22 D.

LIGHTING DEVICES

Found within this chaper are all manner of lighting devices: candlesticks, wall sconces, hanging lanterns, floor lamps, table lamps, desk lamps, piano or mantel lamps, candelabra, ceiling domes, chandeliers, plus lamp bases and isolated shades without their matching bases.

Lighting during the revolution of the "new art" was undergoing its own revolution, both in America and across the Atlantic Ocean. The revolutionary factor in lighting was electricity, first utilized commercially in lighting in the 1870s and ready for home use in the 1880s. By the turn of the century, much of urban America and Europe were already electrified. Coincidentally, Art Nouveau was enjoying its major artistic influence at just the same time. Art Nouveau pieces in the lighting field therefore include both electric lights and pre-electric types, even though oil lamp and candle lamp production continued well into the 20th century.

Many of the finest, most collectible lamps were made by firms whose fame was already established through their work in other fields. Primary among these in the United States was Tiffany Studios (with their Favrile glass, ceramics, and bronze items making them the best-known manufacturer of artistic ware in the nation). European makers included the glass firms of Gallc and Daum and Muller Freres. For additional information on these houses, see the chapter on Glass.

Glass is the most important medium when discussing lighting, although it is by no means the only one. Art Nouveau designers did the same things with lighting glass that they did with other decorative glasses, namely, making it look like everything **but** glass. For that reason, lamps made with clear bodies and shades are found from this period with reverse painting, external enameling, cased or overlayed bodies with etched or carved designs, leaded stained glass, gilding, and so forth.

And when one speaks of glass lamps, the name of Louis Comfort Tiffany inevitably comes up quickly, as it does in so many other areas of decorative arts. The now-famous Tiffany lamps are mostly products of the first two decades of the 20th century. Love 'em or leave 'em, one fact remains: they hold the records for high auction prices in both lighting fixtures and glass objects at many major auction houses.

One question often arising concerning the Tiffany lamps concerns their bases. Which base is the "right" base for a particular shade? The answer: in most cases, there is none. Lamp bases and shades were available separately, and a customer could choose both the shade and the lamp desired. A particular base might be "suggested" to accompany a certain shade, but it was generally not a "must." As a result, the same shade might be found on several different bases — each "right" for the shade.

The bases from one shade to another could vary, but two shades in the same pattern would also vary. Each was hand-crafted and assembled following general color and design schemes. Variations were frequent, and the same design might be found in several color schemes. Some of these color combinations were more successful than others. The same shade, in the same size, on the same base, might vary in price today according to the collector's perception of how successful or desirable the particular combination actually was.

Currently underpriced in the market are many of the turtle-back tile lamps. These were produced in both floor and table models, although the counterweighted table or desk models predominate. The number and color of tiles directly affect the prices of the lamps.

Tffany might be the best-known name in lighting devices in America, but it was far from the only one. Bradley & Hubbard lamps are commonly seen with both their "chipped ice" effect shades as well as slag glass inserts (especially caramel slag). Handel, Moe Bridges, and Jefferson lamps are most commonly seen in reverse-painted specimens. Quezal and Durand, like some of the Tiffany lamps, used iridescent glass extensively, although their total output is comparatively minor.

European lamps currently collected include some of the most attractive specimens of intaglio-etched overlay glass to be found. Practically every major glass maker in Continental Europe made glass-shaded or based lamps as part of their standard production by the 20th century. Most noteworthy was the tremendous factory production of firms such as Galle and Daum.

Floral-decorated European etched or cut patterns on overlay glass were relatively easy to produce. The true beauties in this medium were the "scenics," a term applied these days to virtually any piece depicting some sort of scene — harbors, mountains, ponds, streams, oceans, animals, houses, and the like.

As with other types of glassware, collectors (and dealers) should be aware of — although not necessarily "beware" of — the possibilities for "faking" signatures on an unsigned piece of glass to enhance its collector appeal. (See the chapter on Glass for more details.) Also, due to the combination of different manufacture, avoid referring to the entire lamp as being from the "X" company unless your evidence indicates that all major components visible to the eye are indeed from that company. Over the years many shades found their ways onto lamps from other firms. That still happens in antique shops today, with perfectly honorable motives; it's often easier to sell a complete lamp, for instance, than a base **sans** shade.

The field of candlesticks opens the collector to a full array of materials — ceramics, glass, metals, and combinations. As used by collectors, "candlestick" seldom refers to the candle itself, but rather to the candlestick **holder**. (In the same way, toothpick holders are referred to as "toothpicks," creating confusion when one wishes to speak of a silver toothpick — is it a pick for the teeth made of silver, or a holder for toothpicks made from silver?)

The small (in comparison with most lamps) candle holders are relatively low in price. They are also relatively common as a group, although individual pieces may be scarce to rare.

Hanging lighting fixtures in Art Nouveau styles may be expensive indeed, running into many thousands of dollars. The pricing is due, in part, to the comparatively large surface areas of glass represented in such fixtures. Another reason for steep prices include the comparative scarcity of such fixtures. Chandeliers generally command higher prices than curved ceiling domes. Other hanging fixtures (such as candle lanterns) may be underpriced.

As long as collectors purchase lamps with multiple small shades, there will be a ready market for the individual shades. Breakage, chipping, and the desire on the parts of some collectors to "upgrade" their collection by having only signed specimens of shades result in one type of demand upon the available supply. The shades also present the collector of average (or not so average) means a way of collecting different types of art glass at relatively low prices. Used thus as cabinet pieces (small pieces designed for display in a cabinet rather than for use), shades are experiencing demand from a different group of collectors.

The iridescent glass shades so characteristic of the early 1900s were produced by a variety of makers both in this country and abroad. Tiffany, Quezal, Durand, Steuben, and Lustre Art were the major makers within this country, and some of their products look virtually identical. (Considering the movement of personnel from one glass maker to another, that's not hard to understand.) Without signatures of some sort, it may be impossible to differentiate between some specimens.

Other shades had decorations more characteristic of one or two of the firms than others. Every maker of iridescent shades used the "pulled feather" design, usually with color variations. Small green leaves were often found on Lustre Art shades (but were seen on other makes as well). Applied spider webbing or threading was characteristic of Quezal and Lustre Art but was seen on Tiffany shades as well. When buying a shade to match a particular lamp, be sure to measure the fitter rim so it fits the lamp you have in mind.

Which brings us to lamp bases, the black sheep of the lighting field. These bases are essential to all forms of lighting except hanging and wall-mounted models, and candlesticks or candle holders. There simply is no comparison in prices between the sometimes sky-high levels which lamp shades can attain, and the much more modest figures attached to lamp bases. Even the "best" bases — those with excellent workmanship, carrying desirable signatures, made of the finest of cut overlay glass — will not come near the comparable shade in price.

That's not to say many lamp bases are not worthy pieces to add to a collection; they are, and some will even bring respectable prices in the market. However, collector interest centers around the attractive shades, rather than upon the more utilitarian bases. That explains (at least partially) why a signed shade on an unsigned base will usually bring more than the type of shade which is unsigned on a base which is signed.

For collectors that's both good news and bad news. Bases have a much higher survival rate than shades do, and their greater supply helps keep prices down — a plus if you're buying, but a minus when it comes time to sell. It also means that collectors with good shades already in their collections can pick and choose between available bases, perhaps using the same shade on more than one base as the mood dictates.

Ceramic bases are seldom prized by collectors and may represent a good field for the collector interested in the esoteric. Strangely, some of the cast metal bases (whether in bronze or white metal) are as artistic as their counterparts in bronze or white metal cast figures, but these, too fail to meet the same price standards.

The importance one places upon total originality of a piece will determine how much importance is given to replacement electrical fittings and wiring on a lamp. The collector seeking a lamp which can be used immediately will probably not mind changes making a lamp more useful.

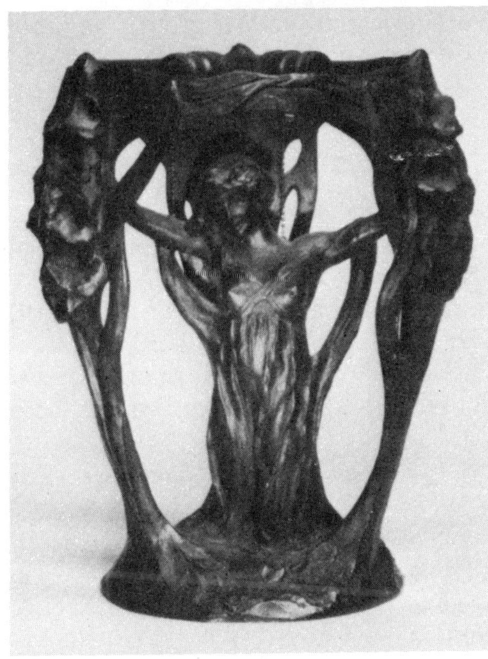

BASE, LAMP; After Alice Nordin, black patinated bronze, inscribed "Alice Nordin/1912" and "Bergman Fud.," Swedish, 14¾"H; *$2,300 A. (Sotheby's)

LAMP BASES (ALL TYPES)

opaque green iridescent Favrile glass blown into reticulated body raised on 4 curved feet; impressed TIFFANY STUDIOS NEW YORK 21667; 19"H, minor restoration; *$6,000 A.

bronze base with finial; impressed TIFFANY STUDIOS NEW YORK 557; for the "Four Seasons" pattern shade, 24½"H; *$2,800 A.

jeweled table lamp base, 3 sockets, finial, greenish-brown patina to bronze; 22"H, for 16" shade; *$2,700 A.

bronze and pate-de-verre, with original harp and finial; features 48 red poppies through "windows," total 9"H; $1,995 D.

counterweight desk lamp base for 7" shade, impressed TIFFANY STUDIOS NEW YORK 5871; 15¾"H; *$950 A.

baluster form iridescent gold table lamp base, decorated with green vines/leaves; inscribed "L.C. Tiffany Favrile," 11½"H; *$550 A.

bronze Dore seedpod base, Tiffany Studios mark, 13½"H; *$500 A.

baluster cameo glass, grey mottled with pink, lime green overlay, cut with spiked blossoms/leafage, cameo Galle signature, 10"H, c. 1900; *$500 A.

cameo, pink-tinged frosted overlaid in amber/green, cut with Gingko leaves, cameo signature "*Galle", 11"H, 1904-1914 period; *$475 A.

bronze desk lamp base, marked TIFFANY STUDIOS NEW YORK 28609; *$425 A.

waisted cylindrical form, table lamp base, earthenware; painted with profusion of red/purple/yellow/blue flowers on navy/pale blue ground; impressed Moorcroft mark, and original paper label, 11¼"H; *$300 A.

bronze lily pad floor lamp base, stamped TIFFANY STUDIOS NEW YORK 428; 55"H; *$300 A.

blue "King Tut" design with 9"H gold-lustred shaft, original finial with King Tut mask, overall 24"H, from Durand; $275 D.

CANDELABRA, CANDLE LIGHTS, CANDLE STICKS, AND WALL SCONCES

Candelabrum — 6-light bell-shaped shades, opalescent with white latticework, striated green leaves/heavy gold & blue iridescence, each inscribed "L.C.T. Favrile"; bronze base with thick central column is impressed TIFFANY STUDIOS NEW YORK 496 13058; 16½"H; *$5,000 A.

Candelabrum — half-nude woman holds figural grape vine, portions below hips forming scrolling Art Nouveau lines; open work & flowers in relief; 3-light, 10"W, 16"H; pair, $295 D.

Candle Lamp — Queen Anne's lace bronze base, with gold-ribbed unsigned shade; Tiffany-signed base, overall 25¼"H; $1,350 D.

— gold iridescent, signed shade & base, 13"H; Tiffany mark; $675 D.

— gold iridescent shade, signed; chip on fitter rim; Tiffany; $345 D.

Candle Sticks — pair, pink pastel, striped opalescent foot & hollow-lobed stem, pink iridescent cup with stretched edge, 4¼"H; marked Tiffany; pair, $575 D.

— amber iridescent glass, flat drip pan, bulbous candle socket; raised on inverted teardrop ribbed standard & ribbed domed circular foot, 11¾", inscribed "L.C.T. Favrile 1826"; pair, *$550 A.

— pewter & brass, girl in flowing robes holds 2 candles aloft, one in each hand, 11"H; $450 D.

— gold iridescent glass with solid-colored swirled stem, 8"H; Kew Blas; pair, $450 D.

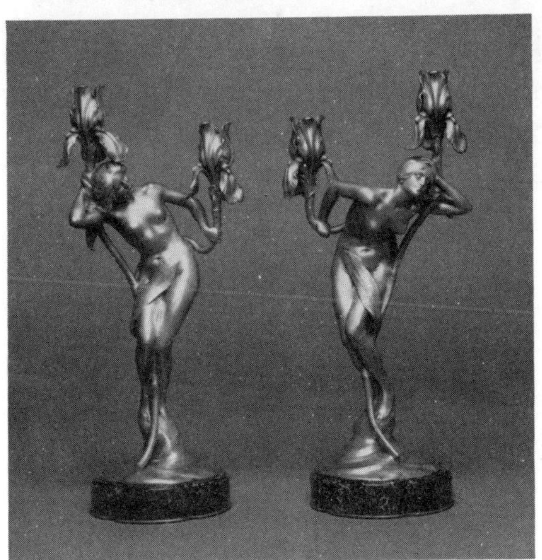

CANDELABRA, pair, after Maurice Bouval; "Le Reve" and "L'Obsession," gilt-bronze allegorical, c. 1900; *$15,000 A. (Christie's)

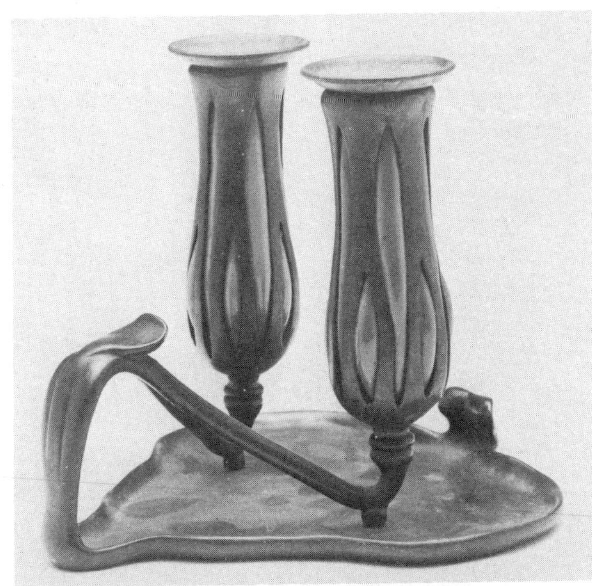

CANDLESTICK, 2-light, by Tiffany; foliate-form handle, blown-out green glass, 6"H; *$700 A. (C.G. Sloan)

CANDELABRUM, silvered copper, probably German, possibly by WMF, c. 1900; 15½"H; *$600 A. (Sotheby's)

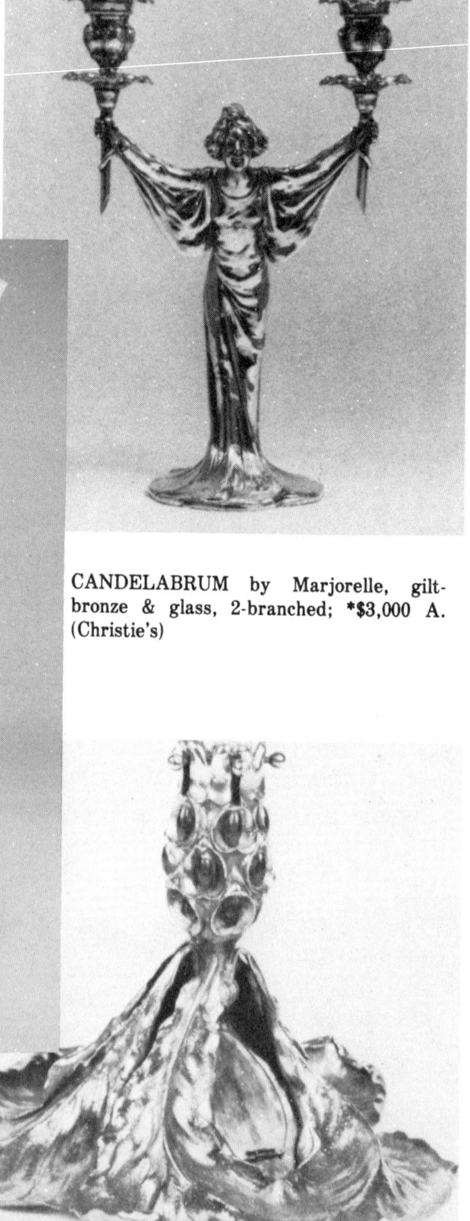

CANDELABRUM by Marjorelle, gilt-bronze & glass, 2-branched; *$3,000 A. (Christie's)

CANDLESTICK WITH CIGAR CUTTER, formed as tobacco plant; copper finish, impressed Tiffany mark, 8½"H; red glass jewel-like insets; levers at top open a matchbox; *$800 A. (Phillips)

— bronze, spirit rising from scrolling base with covered bundle forming candle socket, with brown patina, 9½"H; in the style of Gustav Gurschner, c. 1900; *$425 A.

— glass, red flared chintz pattern top on aquamarine bases, 4½"H, marked Nash & #d; pair, $425 D.

— wide everted drip pan in iridescent blue continues to baluster socket decorated with striated blue/opalescent feathering, raised on flattened amber foot; 4 5/8"D, attributed to Durand; *$250 A.

Candle Holder — Weller Louwelsa, floral motif; $145 D.

Wall Sconce — glass & bronze, 5 3-light lilies; 15 shades of gold iridescent yellow glass, each inscribed "L.C.T."; green-patinated electrified sconces cast with central flower bordered with bayberries; 16½"H each; set, *$9,000 A.

— pair, each with 5 foliate Tiffany glass shades, on gilt bronze, 15½"H; *$2,400 A.

— pair as above, each with 5 Tiffany shades, 15½"H; *$2,050 A.

— single sconce, Cypriote glass in two shades of pitted amber glass with green/red patches, inscribed "L.C.T.," bronze wall sconce, mounting wired for electricity; *$1,300 A.

— pair, each with 3-sided shades of iridescent gold glass, the bronze mounts electrified, shades marked "L.C.T."; *$1,200 A.

— single sconce, 2-arm, with 2 tapering/bulging socket supports joined to domed circular wall plate by horizontal baluster standard with orb terminal; *$375 A.

HANGING LIGHTING

Ceiling Dome — cameo with 3 acid acutbacks & wheel-engraving in yellow/red/white; 17"D, original ceiling cap, silk hangers; marked Galle; $3,500 D.

Chandelier — "Dogwood" pattern, pink & green-tinted white flowers among streaked green leaves on multicolored midnight blue/green "fractured" ground; impressed TIFFANY STUDIOS NEW YORK; 28"D, replaced sockets & chains; *$18,000 A.

— cupola shape in the Chinoiserie manner, emerald green glass; ceiling rod extends beneath shade to support opaque white glass bowl concealing 6 light sockets; leaded glass & bronze; marked Tiffany; 46"H to ceiling, 29½"D; *$10,000 A.

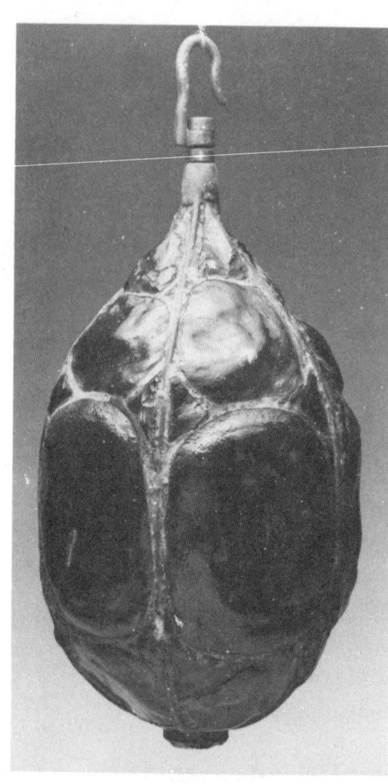

CANDLE LANTERN, hanging; red turtle-back tiles, attributed to Tiffany (possibly a prototype?); *$1,200 A. (C.G. Sloan)

— gold turtle-back tile chandelier with original chains & hook, 20"D; unsigned but attributed to Tiffany; *$6,000 A.

— 10 bell-shaped shades of iridescent yellow glass, suspended from bronze fixture with numerous hanging balls, the shades inscribed "L.C.T."; 34"H, original ceiling cap; *$5,500 A.

— cream-colored 12-sided leaded chandelier, with a 1¼" red band above 2" border; 23"D, signed Handel, mint condition; $2,200 D.

— leaded glass globe with 2 central bands of pink flowers among white-streaked green leaves on white & butterscotch ground; 14"D, unsigned but attributed to Handel; *$2,000 A.

— 4-piece, metal leaf holder with white frosted glass; $600 D.

FLOOR LAMPS

"Laburnum" pattern leaded glass & bronze; shade with mottled yellow flower clusters in streaked dark green leaves on blue ground; bronze base impressed TIFFANY STUDIOS NEW YORK 387; 63"H, 22¼"D shade; *$43,000 A.

"Nasturtium" pattern, both base & shade marked Tiffany; 63½"H, 23"D shade; *$32,500 A.

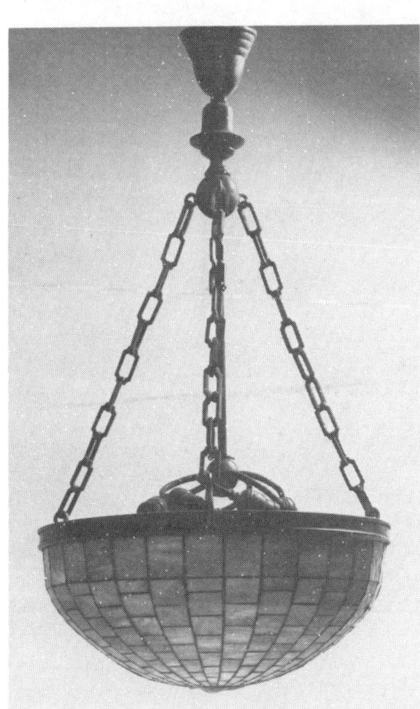

SHADE, HANGING, basket form by Tiffany; caramel color with center green glass inset, fitted for 7 sockets; 21"D shade, 50"H supporting shaft; *$2,500 A. (C.G. Sloan)

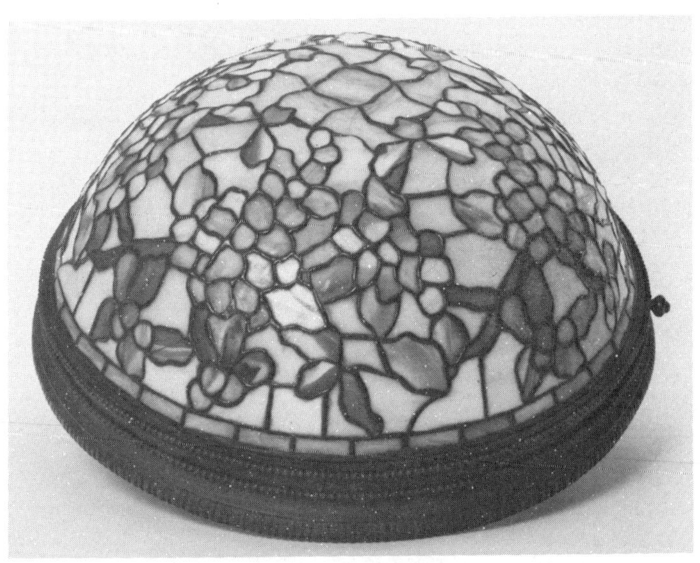

CEILING FIXTURE, DOMED, by Tiffany; "Apple Blossom" pattern; *$5,000 A. (Christie's)

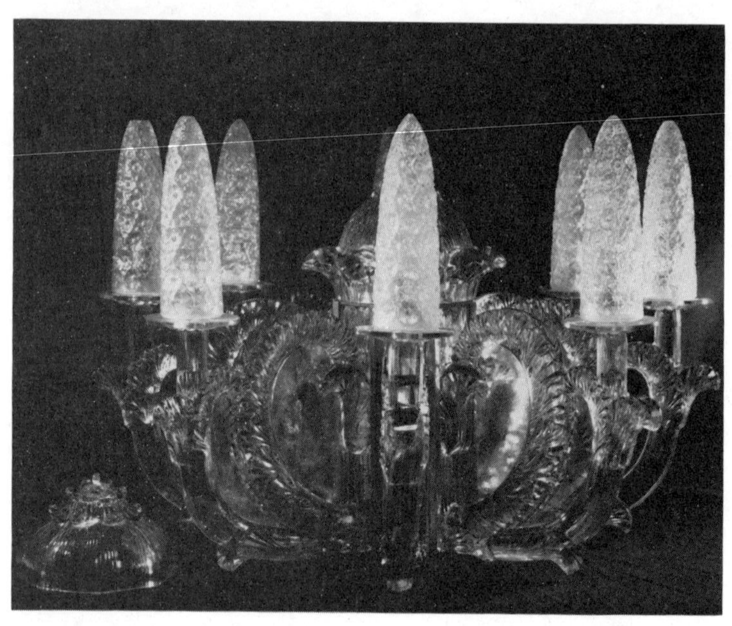

CHANDELIERS; pair of monumental Lalique chandeliers (only one shown); *$36,000 A. (Christie's)

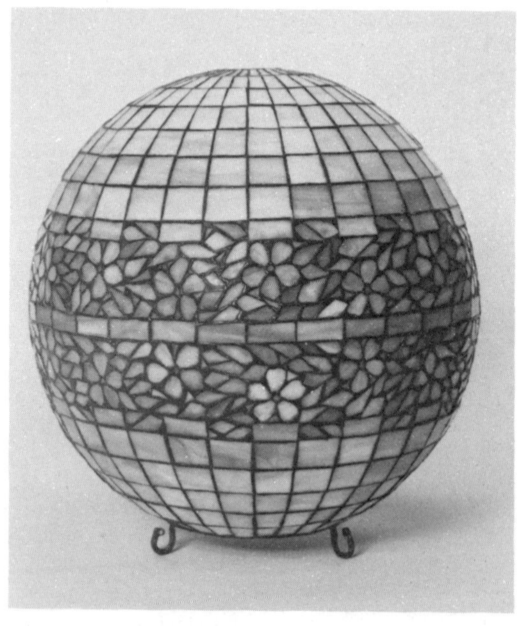

CHANDELIER, leaded glass, attributed to Handel; *$2,000 A. (Christie's)

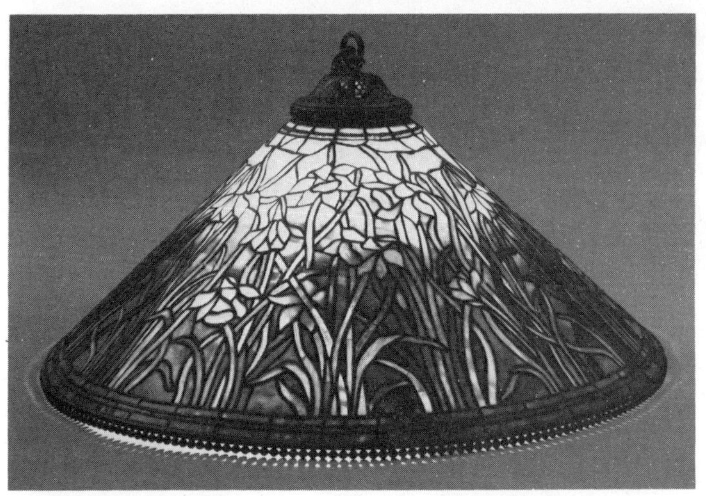

CHANDELIER (hanging shade), "Daffodil" pattern by Tiffany; *$19,000 A. (Christie's)

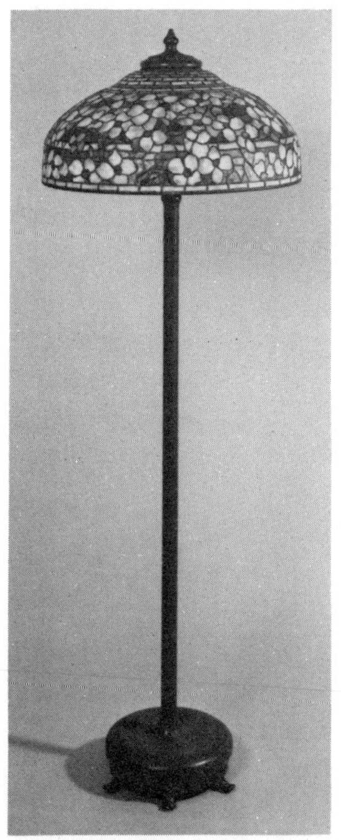

FLOOR LAMP, "Dogwood" pattern shade; by Tiffany; *$22,000 A. (Christie's)

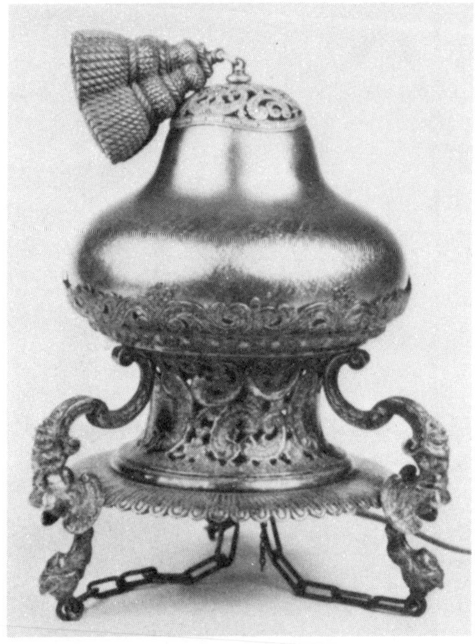

CHANDELIER, iridescent gold Quezal glass shade (signed QUEZAL) in elaborate metal mounting; 15"H, shade 7"D; *$800 A. (Phillips)

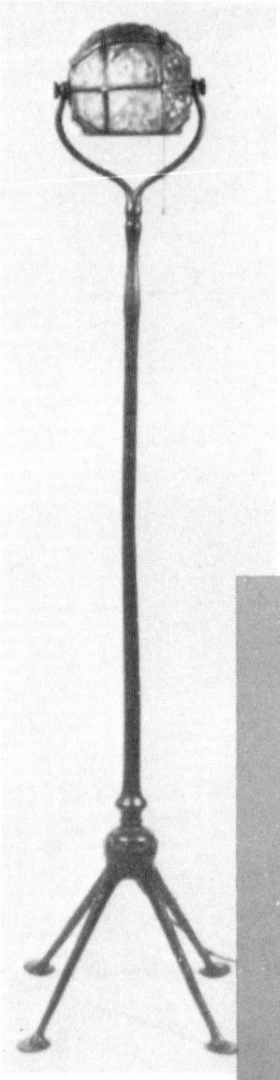

FLOOR LAMP, Tiffany, bronze with turtle-back tiles/spherical shade; gold iridescent shade (unsigned), foot stamped TIFFANY STUDIOS NEW YORK 430; 54"H; *$5,000 A. (Phillips)

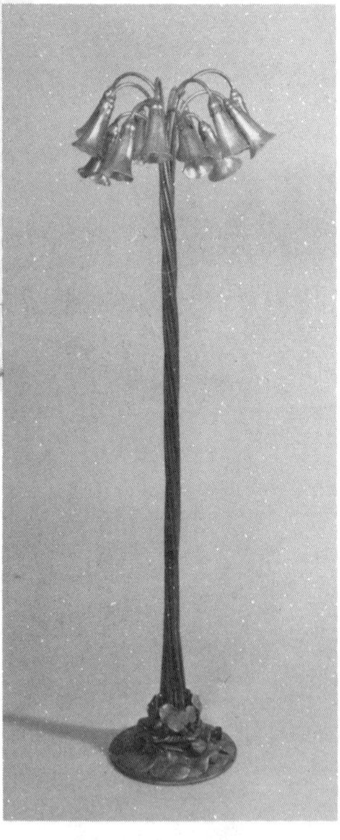

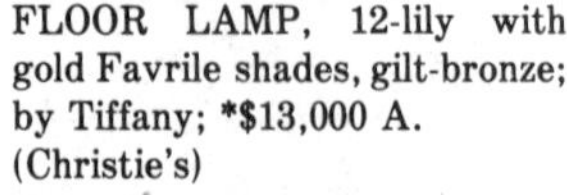

FLOOR LAMP, 12-lily with gold Favrile shades, gilt-bronze; by Tiffany; *$13,000 A. (Christie's)

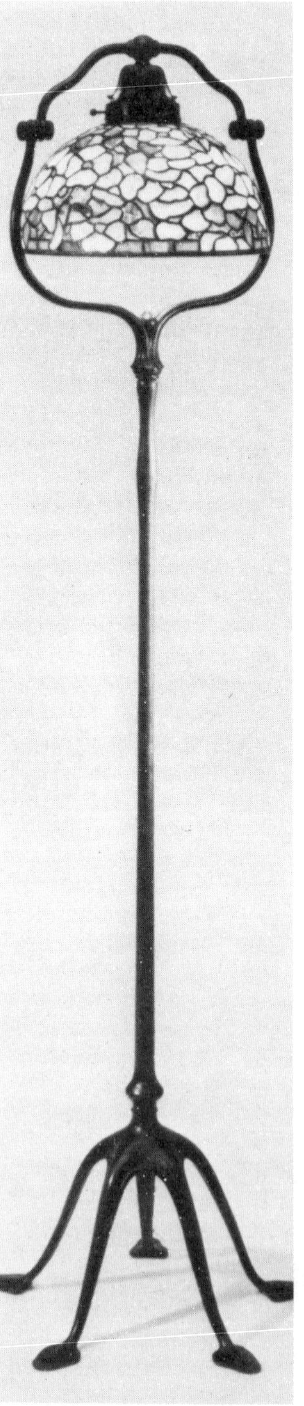

FLOOR LAMP, Tiffany "Dogwood" pattern shade; shade & bronze base impressed with marks; 57"H, 11¾"D shade; *$5,000 A. (Sotheby's) (NOTE: another Dogwood floor lamp is pictured at a drastically different price!)

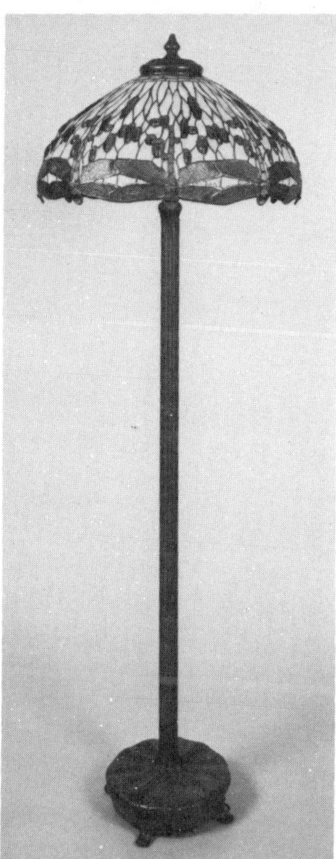

FLOOR LAMP, leaded glass & bronze, "Dragonfly" pattern by Tiffany; *$14,000 A. (Christie's)

FLOOR LAMP, Tiffany, "Magnolia" pattern shade signed & #d #1599, base signed (#376); original pigtail cap; 77"H, shade 28"D; *$97,000 A. (C.G. Sloan)

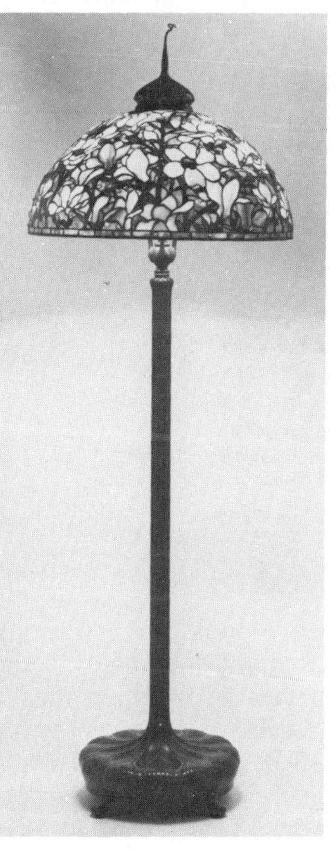

"Peony" pattern, shade with multi-hued red flowers among bright mottled green leaves on variegated beige/pale mauve ground, impressed TIFFANY STUDIOS NEW YORK 1505; junior floor base, impressed TIFFANY STUDIOS NEW YORK 379; 64"H, 22"D shade; *$32,000 A.

Curtain border lamp, shade with rippled yellow-orange border beneath radiating emerald green panels, impressed TIFFANY STUDIOS NEW YORK; base impressed TIFFANY STUDIOS NEW YORK 377; 74"H, 24"D shade; *$15,000 A.

Jeweled shade of variegated green & orange hues, with 24 red jewels at lower edge, with orange scrollwork, containing 2,000 plus pieces leaded stained glass, marked Handel; base marked Handel; 64"H, 25¼"D shade; $12,500 D.

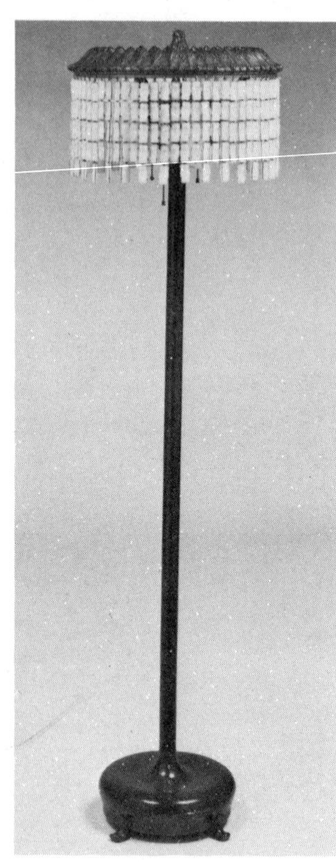

FLOOR LAMP, Tiffany, bronze with pendant opalescent beads; signed; *$2,800 A. (C.G. Sloan)

Harp lamp, bright blue shade with swagged bands & intaglio carved with dragonflies & butterflies, inscribed "L.C.T. Favrile"; base impressed TIFFANY STUDIOS NEW YORK 423 H; 58½"H, 12"D shade; *$3,800 A.

Counterweight lamp, iridescent blue shade decorated with blue swirls & engraved moth, inscribed "L.C.T. Favrile"; base unsigned bronze; 54½"H, 10"D shade; *$3,800 A.

Harp lamp, shade with striated green leaves on cream ground, inscribed "L.C.T."; bronze base impressed TIFFANY STUDIOS NEW YORK 423; 58"H, 11¾"D shade; *$3,000 A.

Green-etched shade surrounded by bell-shaped metal frame resting on tapering cylindrical central standard resting on Handel-signed circular base; 58"H; *$425 A.

DESK LAMPS, TABLE LAMPS, PIANO LAMPS, AND OTHER SMALL LAMPS (Due to the extensive listings contained within this section, organization will be by manufacturer alphabetically. Following the alphabetical listing will be a listing of those unsigned or otherwise unidentifiable specimens.)

ALADDIN

Reverse-painted tree scenic, 13½", slight wear; $175 D.

ARGY-ROUSSEAU

Pate-de-verre mounted **veilleuse** of slightly swelling cylindrical form, on which stylized fern scrolls descend in pyramidal panels of frosted glass; all mounted on tripod wrought iron base as a night light; moulded signature; $3,500 D.

BRADLEY & HUBBARD

Table lamp, 3-shade, of red/orange/yellow oval chipped jewels with a lead surround, on original Art Nouveau base; $700 D.

Table lamp, reverse-painted 4-panel, "chipped ice" shade with brown/black as border, pink/green Gardenias, acorn pulls, 14", mint condition; $695 D.

Table lamp, panels of fiery orange on elegant tree trunk base surrounded with raised Irises; 22"H, 17½"D; $525 D.

Table lamp, caramel slag panels under spelter frame of urns/drapery; signed & dated; $365 D.

Table lamp, slag glass panels under patinated metal, 21"H; *$325 A.

MOE BRIDGES

Table lamp, reverse-painted woodland scenic; $1,400 D.

Table lamp, paneled, scenic; $400 D.

BUFFALO METAL WORKS

3-light Daffodil table lamp, bronze base marked by Buffalo Metal Works, California; shades are striated iridescent green; *$425 A.

DAUM FRERES

Table lamp, double overlay, base & shade of yellow-mottled translucent glass overlaid with red & amethyst, etched with forest landscape; shade with cameo signature; 27"H, 12¾"D shade; *$12,000 A.

Table lamp, orange-mottled translucent ochre base & tiered domed shade overlaid with brown etched with orchids, both with cameo signatures; 13¾"H, 7½"D shade; *$3,000 A.

Table lamp, base & shade of stained translucent peach glass with large purple patches; shade with engraved signature; 17"H, 8¾"D shade; *$1,900 A.

Table lamp, base & shade of purple & orange-streaked crimson glass with large gold foil inclusions; shade with engraved signature; 20"H, 12"D shade; *$1,300 A.

Table lamp, domed shade & trumpet-form base of purple-streaked red with gold foil inclusions; shade with engraved signature; 14½"H; *$1,000 A.

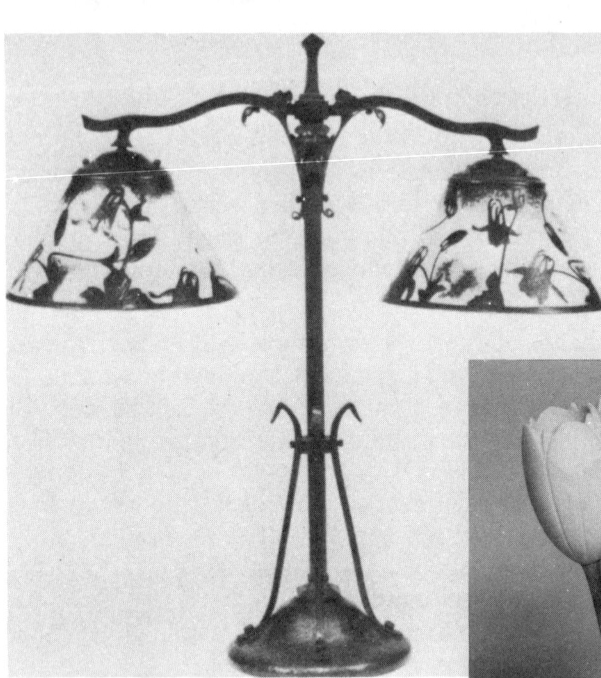

DAUM 2-LIGHT STUDENT LAMP, c. 1910, cameo glass shades inscribed DAUM/NANCY, the bronze base in Louis Majorelle's style; 26"H, 10"D; *$6,000 A. (Sotheby's)

TABLE LAMPS, pair, by Albert Cheuret, c. 1920; carved alabaster shades on 3 curved stems issuing from plant-form base, 14½"H, inscribed "Albert Cheuret," 2 shades damaged; the pair, *$2,200 A. (Christie's)

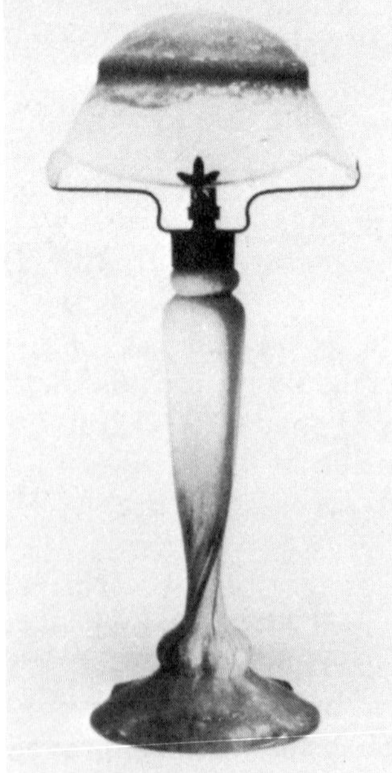

DAUM TABLE LAMP, mottled blue shading to pale green, with wrought iron fittings; shade & base acid-stamped DAUM/NANCY with croix de Lorraine, c. 1915; 21½"H; *$1,300 A. (Sotheby's)

DEGUE

Table lamp, base & shade pink-streaked translucent blue glass overlaid with purple-navy, etched with large overlapping trees; both pieces with cameo signatures; 26"H, 19½"H; *$14,000 A.

DUFFNER

Table lamp, filigree & caramel slag panels, bronze base; $775 D.

DURAND

Mantel lamp, pair of gold iridescent glass shades with gilt-metal bases, 8½"H; pair, *$225 A.

GALLE

Table lamp, triple overlay glass & bronze flower form; deep amber-brown shading to chartreuse green & pink on white, wheel polished & set on bronze mounting; chinoiserie cameo signature, c. 1900; 13½"H; *$20,000 A.

Table lamp, trible overlay glass, shade with flowering pink/magenta Wild Roses among pale/dark orange branches on brilliant yellow ground; base with matching motif, both with cameo signatures; 23½"H, 14½"D shade; *$18,000 A.

Table lamp, cubic base & conical shade of cased translucent powder blue glass overlaid with plum, etched with Morning Glories; both base and shade with cameo signatures; 11"H, 10¼"D shade; *$10,000 A.

Table lamp, depicting Wisteria in purples etched to off-white & yellow ground, wheel polished; cameo signature; 22½"H, 11¼"D shade; *$7,500 A.

Table lamp, conical shade of translucent glass overlaid with sky blue & plum, etched with 2 eagles; trumpet-form base overlaid with pale blue & plum, etched with mountains & trees; shade & base each with cameo signature; 23"H, 10"D shade; *$7,500 A.

Table lamp, domed shade & trumpet-form base, each of translucent red glass overlaid with dark amber, etched with grape leaves & clusters, both with cameo signatures; 15"H, 6¾"D shade, base rim chip; *$3,000 A.

Night light, gold ground with red Bleeding Heart flowers; adapted for American electricity; $1,350 D.

HAMPSHIRE POTTERY

Table lamp with Hampshire Art Nouveau base (having age crack), with crystal shade & prism; $195 D.

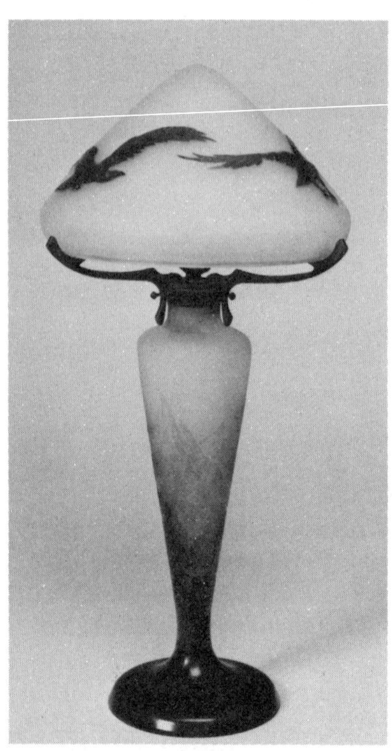

GALLE TABLE LAMP, triple overlay glass, bronze flower form base, c. 1900; *$7,500 A. (Christie's)

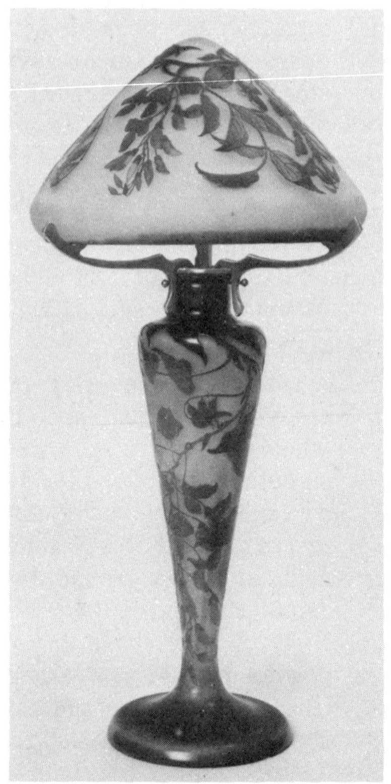

GALLE TABLE LAMP, silver overlay; *$7,500 A. (Christie's)

HANDEL

Table lamp, reverse-painted woodland scene on bronze base; $5,100 D.

Table lamp, scenic shade 18"D with "chipped ice" effect, bloody red; $2,500 D.

Table lamp, 14"D reverse-painted shade is signed, #d, & artist initialed; signed base; overall, 20"H, mint condition; $2,300 D.

Table lamp, shade decorated with 4 large white/green Lilies & 2 buds; on lily pad bronze base with dark patina; 16"H, 22"D; $1,950 D.

Boudoir lamp, floral decoration, 10"H; $1,250 D.

Table Lamp, scenic shade numbered 3164B and signed; on unsigned Art Nouveau base; $1,200 D.

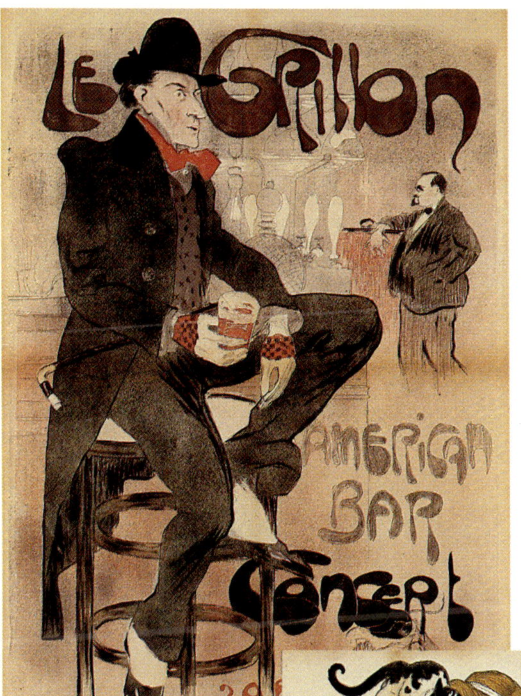

Left

Le Grillon poster, by Jacques Villon, c. 1899; 36½″x51″, slight staining at the fold & edges of the paper, framed; *$44,000 A.

Courtesy, Phillips New York

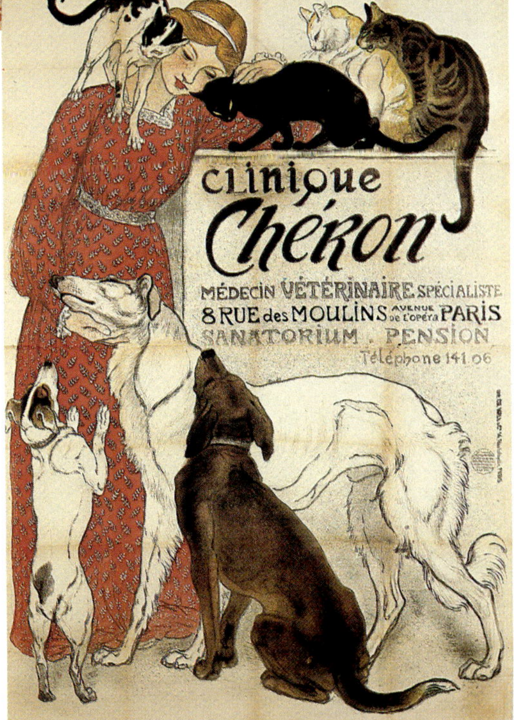

Right

Clinique Cheron poster, by Theophile Alexandre Steinlen; published by Ch. Wall, Paris, 1905; 53½″x76¾″, stains, tears, and some restorations, framed; *$10,000 A.

Courtesy, Phillips New York

*Auction Price

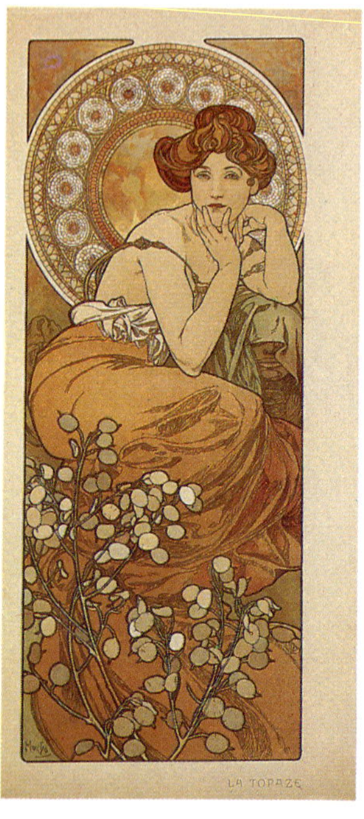

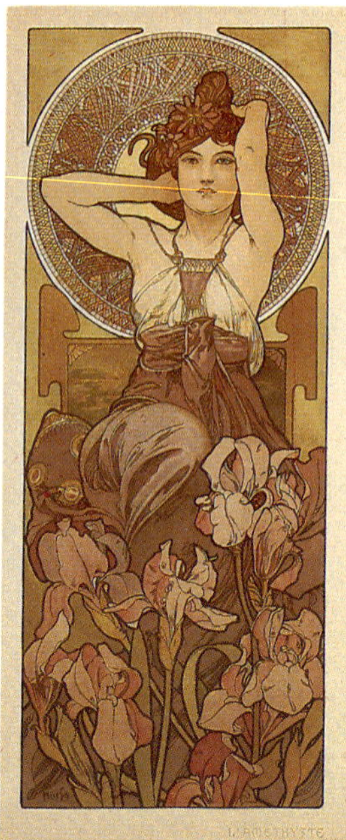

Set of four decorative panels by Alphonse Mucha, the ''Four Jewels'' (La Topaz, L'Amethyste, Le Rubis, and L'Emeraude); published by F. Champenois, Paris, 1900;

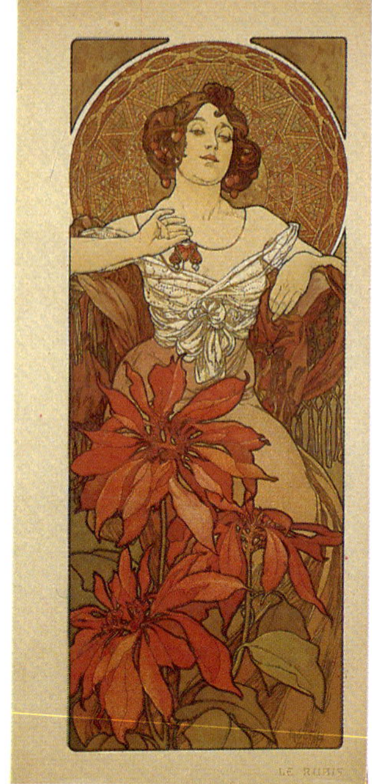

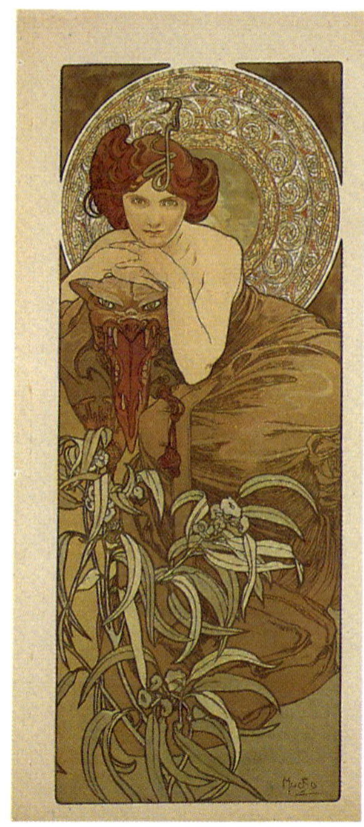

each panel 11⅞"x26½", excellent conditions, framed; the set, *$9,500 A.

Courtesy, Phillips New York

*Auction Price

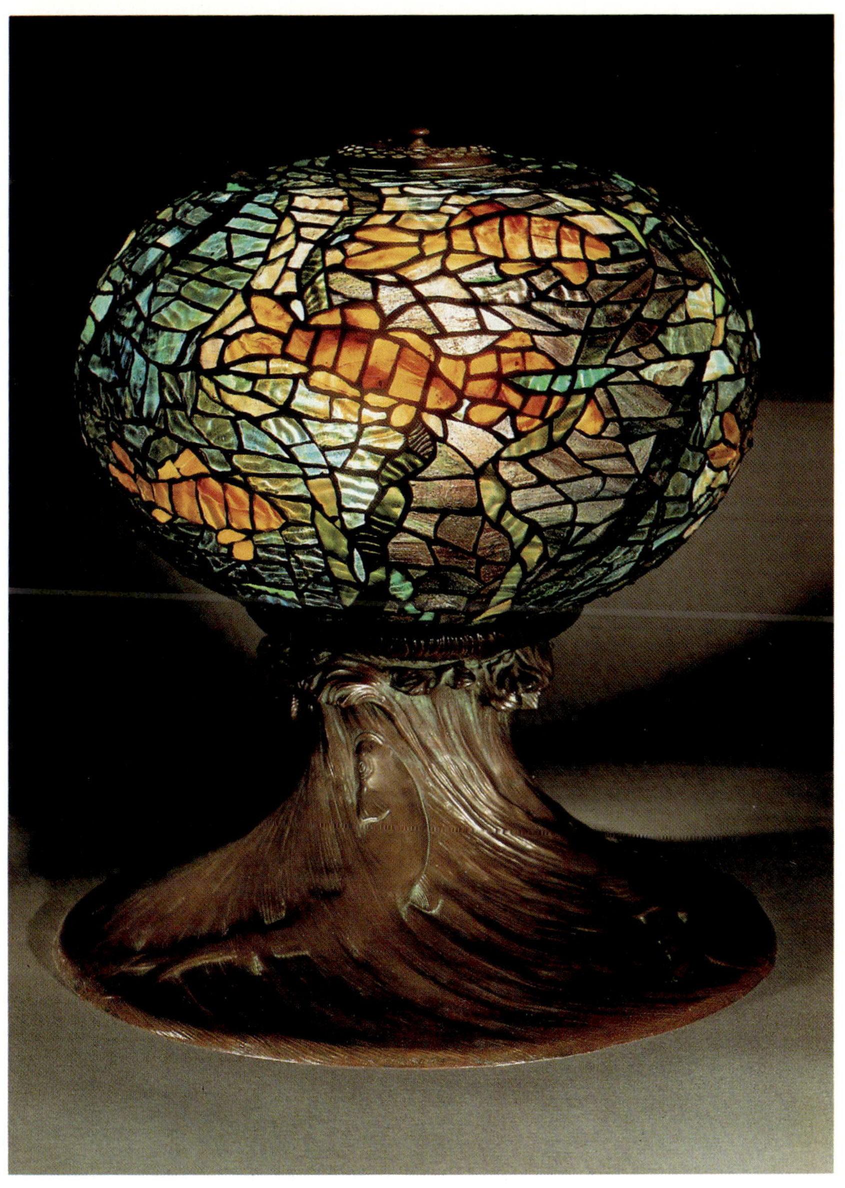

Fish Bowl-shaped
leaded glass and bronze table lamp,
from Tiffany Studios, New York, c. late 1890's; *$135,000 A.

Courtesy, Christie's, New York

*Auction Price

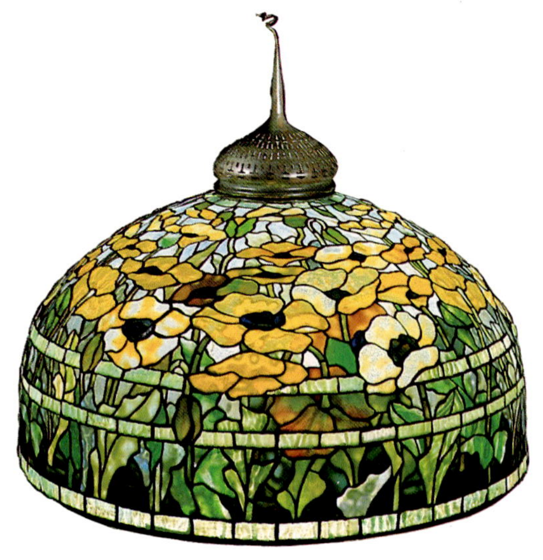

Above
Signed Oriental Poppy leaded glass and bronze floor lamp, from Tiffany Studios, New York; (only shade is shown) *$75,000 A.

Both photos courtesy, Christie's, New York

Below
A dragonfly leaded glass and bronze floor lamp (only shade is shown) Tiffany Studios; *$28,000 A.

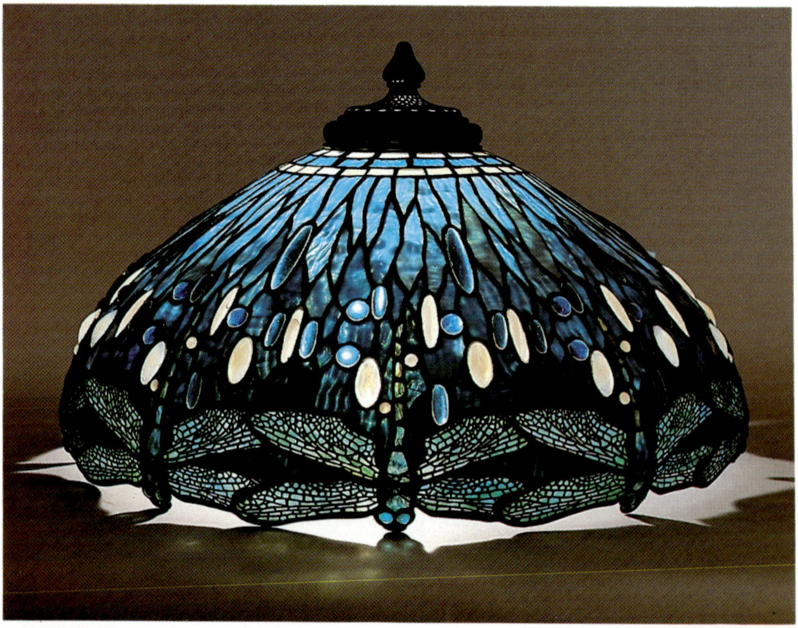

*Auction Price

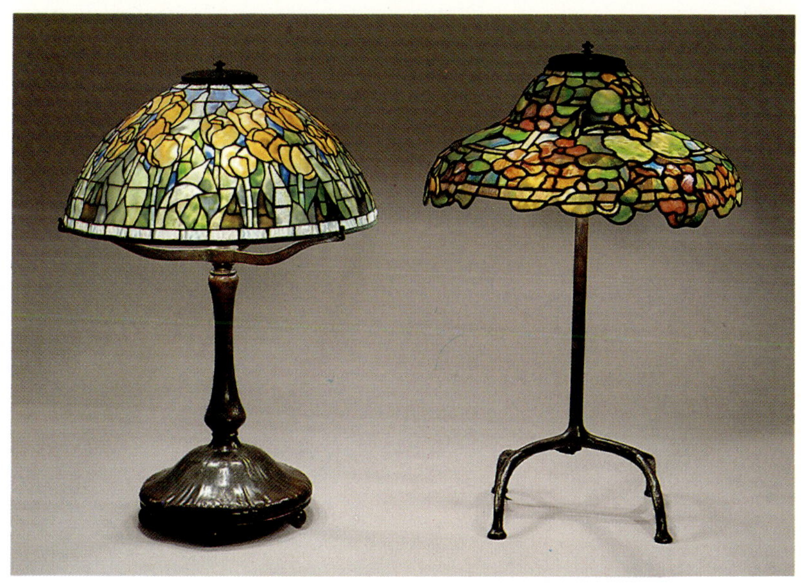

Above
Two signed lamps
from Tiffany Studios, New York, both early 20th century; (L) Nasturtium leaded glass and bronze shade, with bronze base; *$12,000 A. (R) Tulip leaded glass and bronze shade, on bronze base; *$19,000 A.

Both photos courtesy, Christie's, New York

Below
Five double overlay glass vases by Galle
(L to R) Yellow overlaid with red and crimson, *$3,000 A.; Chartreuse ground overlaid with pale blue and purple, *$2,000 A.; Translucent green overlaid with pale blue and purple, 18½" H., *$5,200 A.; Red and Blue streaked translucent yellow ground overlaid with amber and dark amber, *$4,000; Translucent pale blue ground overlaid with white and olive-green, *$4,200 A.

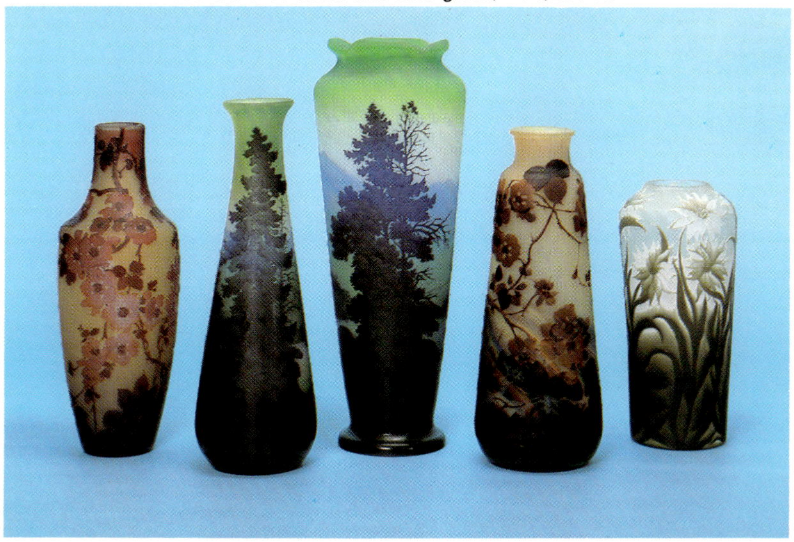

*Auction Price

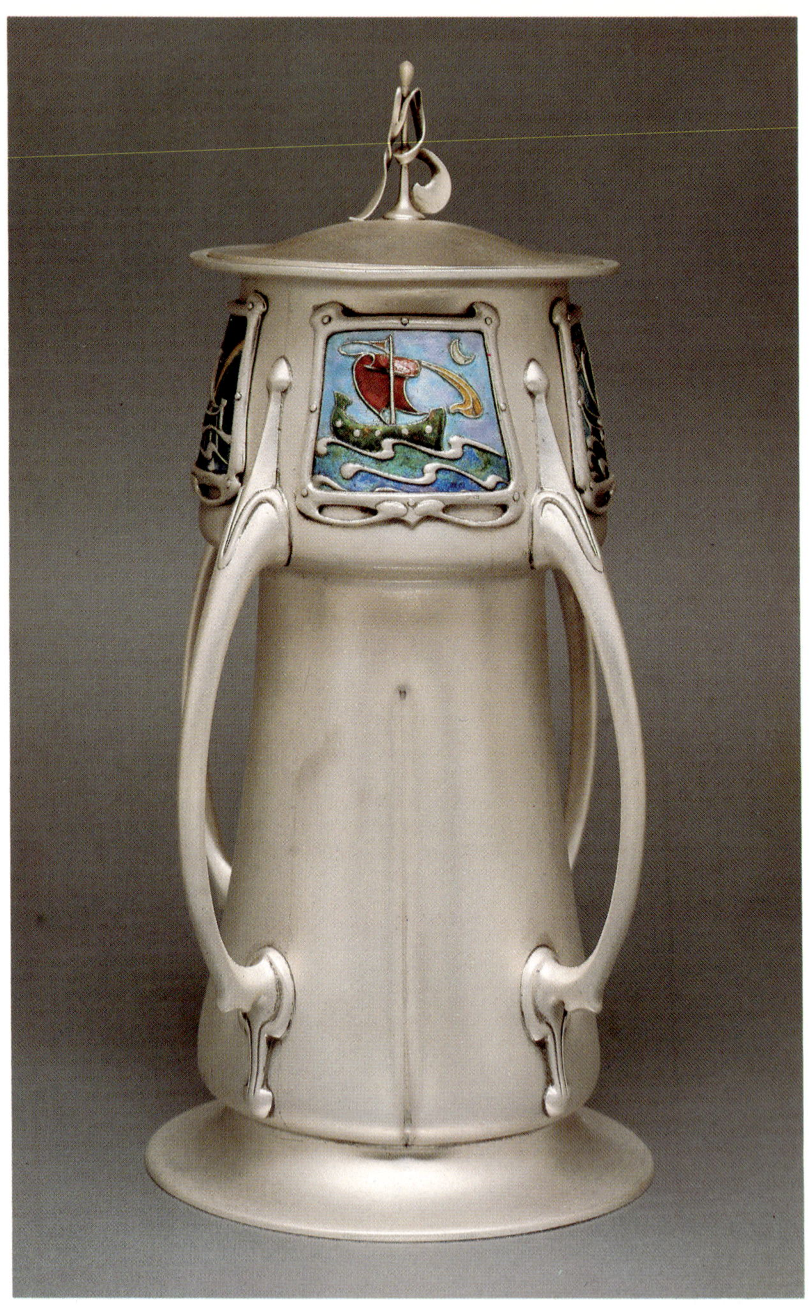

A "Cymbric"
enamelled silver covered presentation chalice,
c. 1901, *$5,200 A.,
from Liberty & Co.

Courtesy, Christie's, New York

*Auction Price

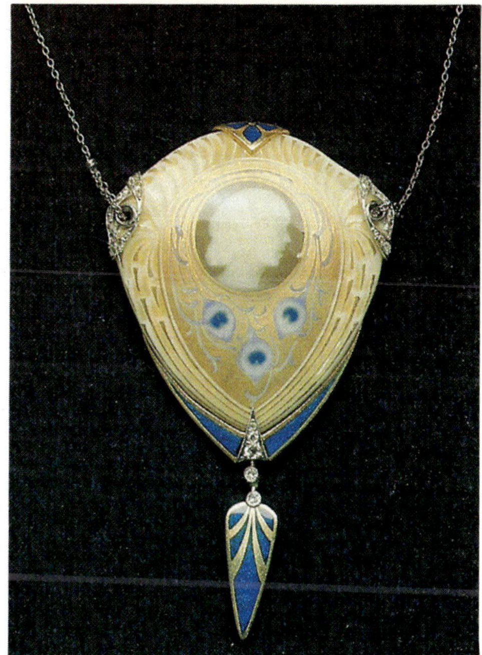

Top Left
Necklace, centered by brown and white pear-shaped porcelain cameo piece; yellow gold with royal blue enamel, with platinum and diamond-studded fillings, on platinum chain; in case, signed by Belloir, Paris; *$3,000 A.

Courtesy, Butterfield's

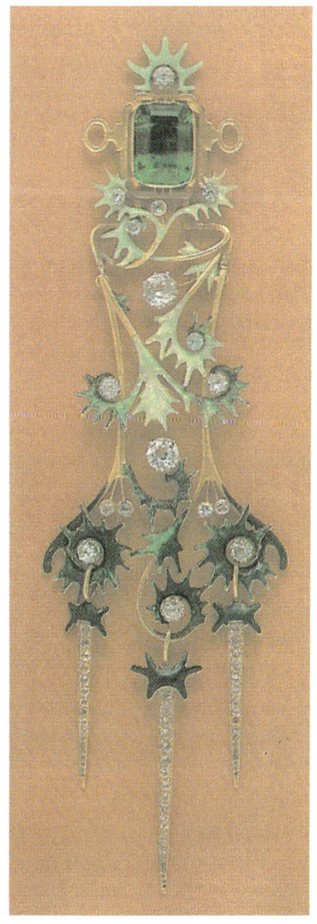

Right
Pendent, yellow gold with entrelac branches enameled in shades of green, designed by Rene Lalique, c. 1900, impressed LALIQUE; 7¼"L, set with paste (glass) brilliants to replace the original diamonds and emeralds, with some enamel restorations; *$20,000 A.

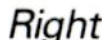

Courtesy, Sotheby's

Bottom Left
Plique-a-jour blue and green enamel wings center a golden sapphire enhanced by rose-cut diamonds accented by lavender/brown/white/green enamel work, topped by 2 European-cut diamonds, set in yellow gold mount, c. 1910, signed "L. Grautrails"; *$9,000 A.

Courtesy, Butterfield's

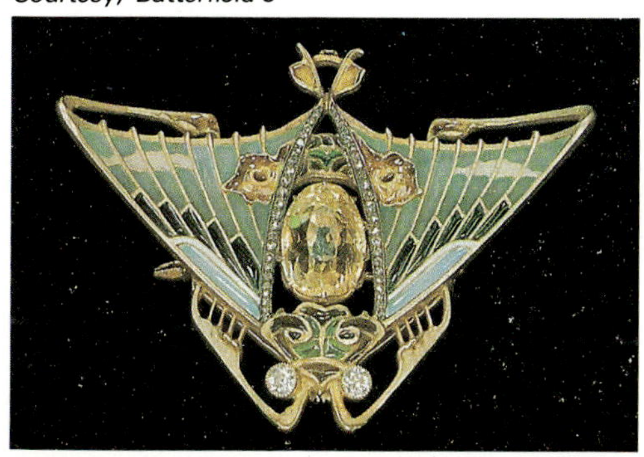

*Auction Price

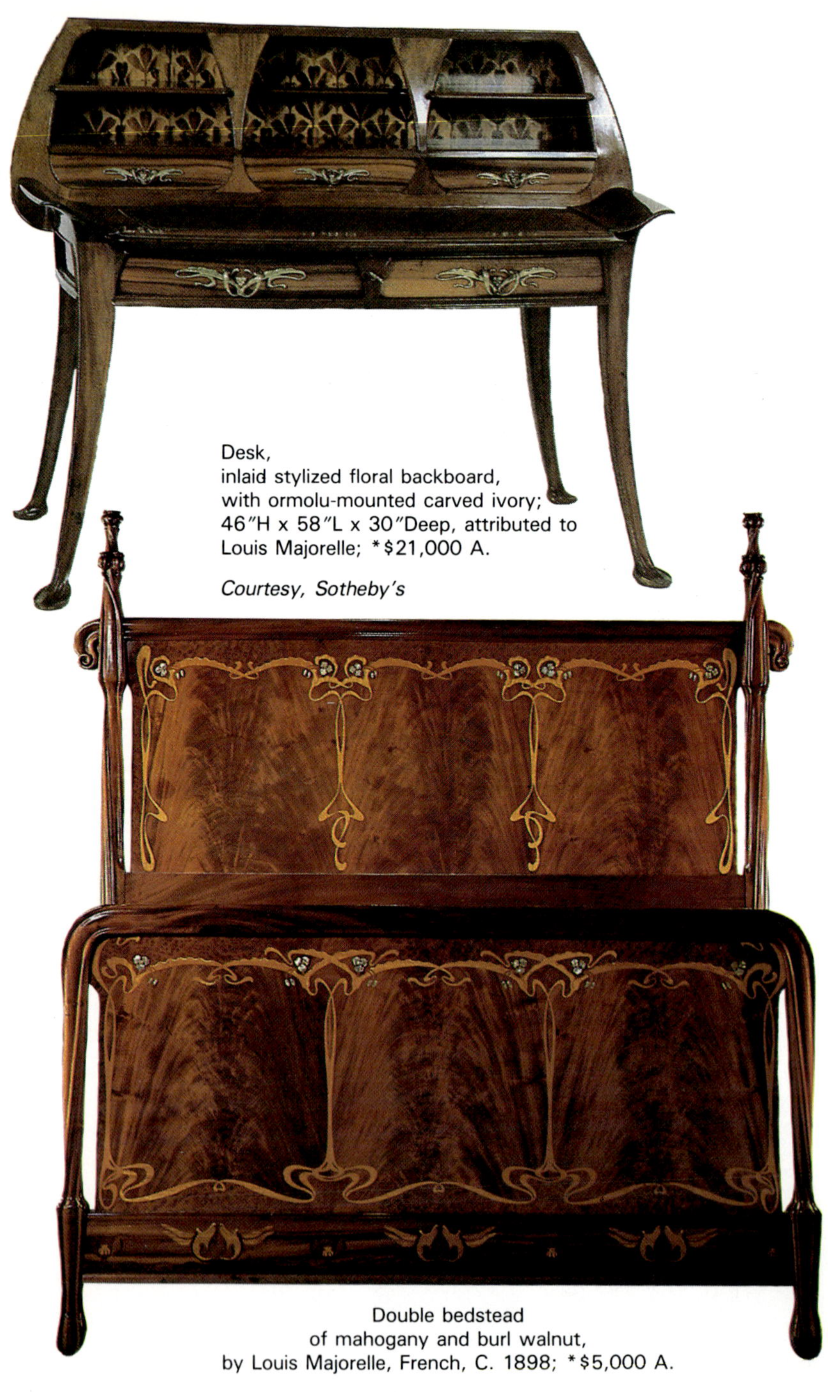

Desk,
inlaid stylized floral backboard,
with ormolu-mounted carved ivory;
46″H x 58″L x 30″Deep, attributed to
Louis Majorelle; *$21,000 A.

Courtesy, Sotheby's

Double bedstead
of mahogany and burl walnut,
by Louis Majorelle, French, C. 1898; *$5,000 A.

Courtesy, Christie's, New York

*Auction Price

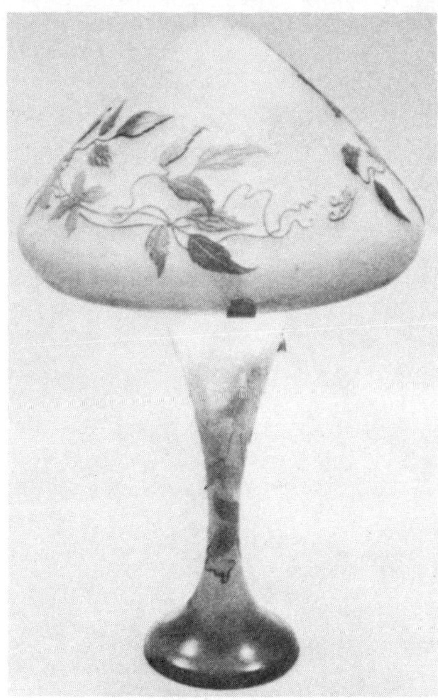

GALLE TABLE LAMP, matte amber ground overlaid with wine & blue blossoms /trails, the yellow/green standard with a similar decoration; both upper and lower parts signed "Galle" in cameo; 18"H; *$3,750 A. (Butterfield's)

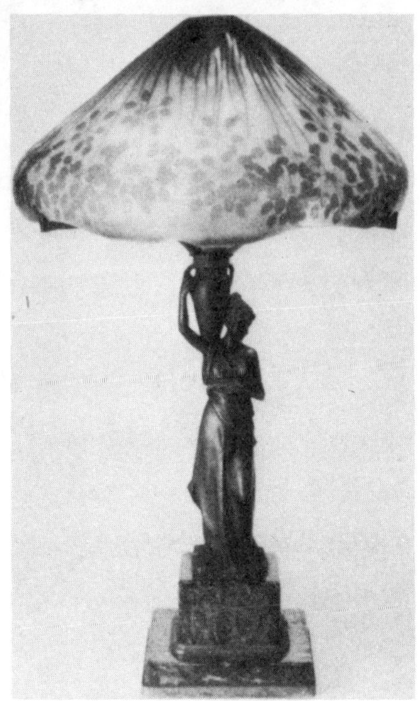

GALLE CAMEO "ANETH" SHADE on figural bronze base with marble plinth; shade opalescent glass overlaid in lime green shading to caramel, cut with Dill pods/leaves, fire polished, with cameo signature "Galle", the rim ground; 14½"H; *$2,600 A. (Sotheby's)

Desk lamp, gooseneck Lily, green/white petals, on bronze lily pad base, 14"H; $1,100 D.

Table lamp, reverse-painted domed shade with forest& landscape scene; tapered central standard graduated to trumpeted, fluted base; 24"H, 18"D; *$450 A.

Piano lamp, green leaded glass domed shade, signed; round bronze base with tapering support, signed; overall, 18½"H, shade 6¾"D; *$400 A.

Table lamp, domed glass shade overlaid with green, the lower border decorated with floral design; baluster central standard graduating to flattened circular signed base; 24"H, 19"D shade; *$375 A.

JEFFERSON

Table lamp, floral painted, brilliant colors, 18"; $1,775 D.

Table lamp, reverse painted woodland scene; $1,500 D.

MULLER FRERES

Table lamp, white & variegated blue satin shade 6"D, black iron base in Leaf & Grape pattern, overall 19"H; shade signed; $500 D.

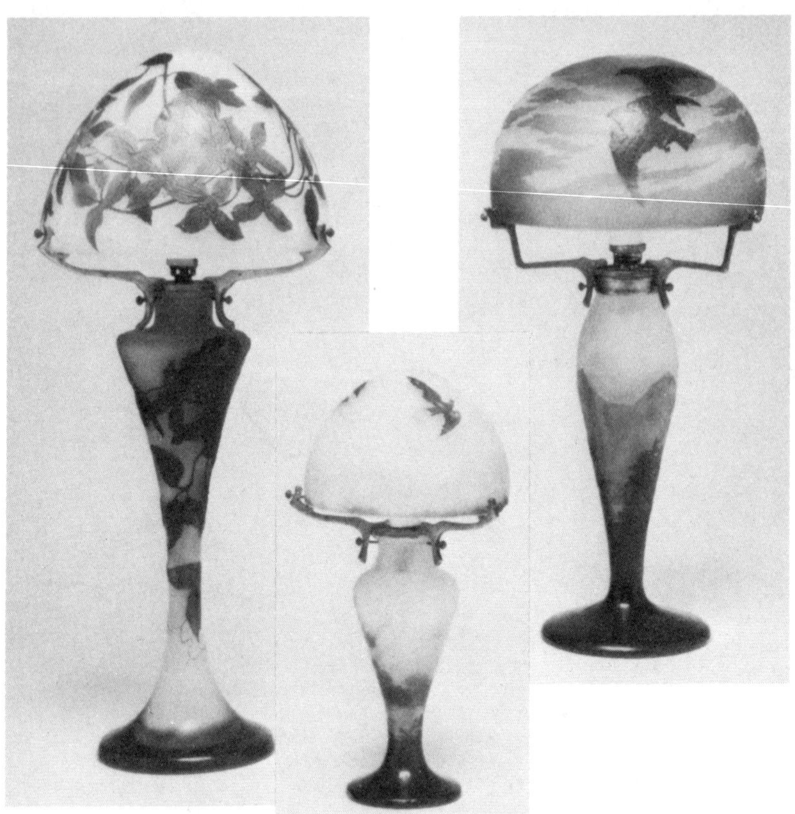

THREE GALLE GLASS AND BRONZE TABLE OR DESK LAMPS, all bases and shades being signed in cameo, c. 1900. (Left) opalescent gray overlaid in mauve-violet, cut with Clematis blossoms/vines, 17½"H, shade 7¼"D; *$2,800 A. (Center) pale lemon-yellow overlaid in blue-violet, the shade cut with birds soaring over clouds, the base cut with a wooded landscape and distant mountains; 11"H, shade 5 1/8"D; *$3,300 A. (Right) gray overlaid in blue/violet, the shade cut with 2 eagles flying against cloud-filled sky, the base cut with mountainous landscape & tall fir trees in foreground, partly fire-polished; 14½"H, shade 6¾"D; *$4,750 A. (Sotheby's)

PAIRPOINT

Table lamp, reverse-painted on glass shade is scene of sheep grazing, base & shade are signed; 13"H; $1,295 D.

Table lamp, "puffy" type in "Lotus" pattern; $2,400 A.

Table lamp, Venetian Harbor scenic, ships continue around shade in brilliant pastels/deep blues, 20"H; $2,650 D.

Table lamp, painted glass & patinated metal; colorful mountain lakeside with distant sailing boats on shade, stamped THE PAIRPOINT CORP'N at two spots; 2-handled base impressed PAIRPOINT D8034/MADE IN USA; 23½"H, 17¾"D shade; finial replaced, minor lower rim nicks; *$1,200 A.

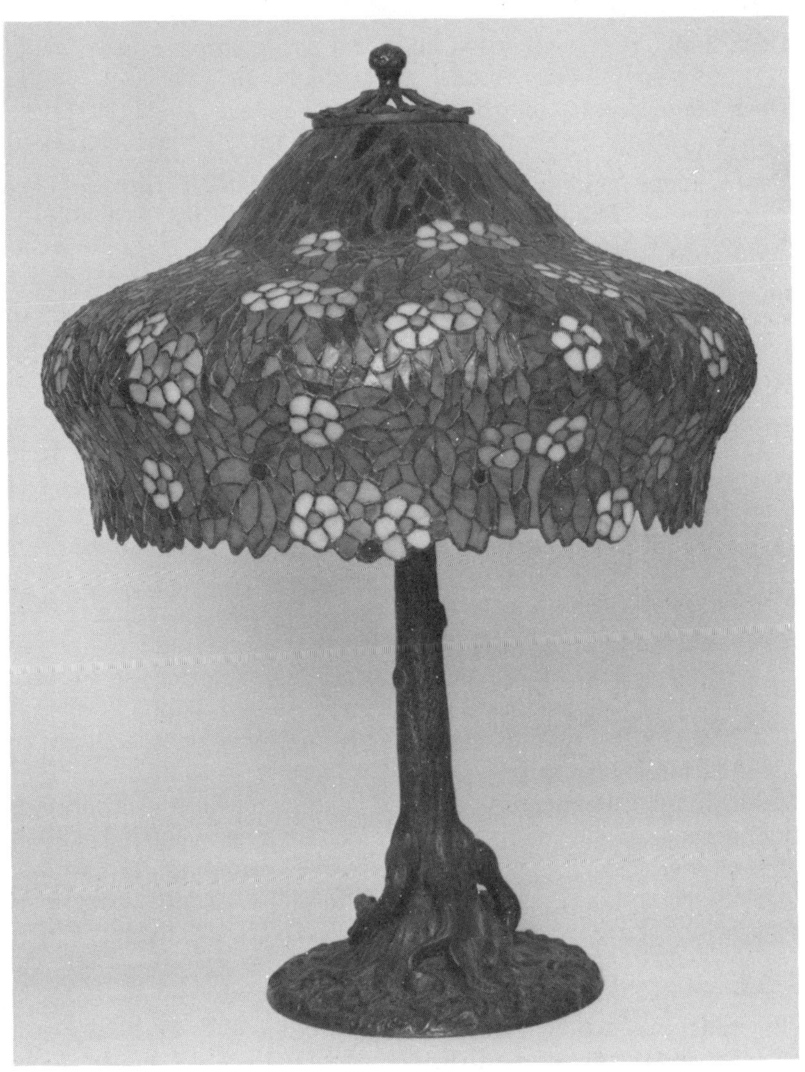

HANDEL TABLE LAMP, leaded glass "Cherry Blossom" pattern shade; *$8,800 A. (Christie's)

Desk lamp, painted glass & patinated metal; "Puffy" shade, interior painted mauve/yellow blossoms against beige/black ribboned lower border, upper section painted in brown with young trees against mottled blue ground; raised on silvered base which is molded. PAIRPOINT/C3064 around monogram; 14½"H, 9"D shade; *$1,100 A.

Table lamp, signed landscape decorated shade on silver patinated metal base, 22"H; *$850 A.

PITTSBURGH

Desk lamp, reverse-painted full floral shade, bronze base, acorn pull, early electric model, 12"D shade; $875 D.

Desk lamp, scenic, signed; $450 D.

QUEZAL

Table lamp, gold iridescent ribbed shade 10"H, bronze base marked "The Twilight #240" is footed pedestal; $1,500 D.

Night Light, opal with green/caramel decoration & gold metallic stringing on "Quezal"-signed shade, 6¼"H; on 4-footed base with roaring lions having serpent bodies, the base marked "E Pat Pending," overall 9½"H; $600 D.

RICHARD

Desk lamp, cameo base of turquiose/green ground with brown cameo; leaf-shaped foot with the underside of the base multicolored; dome a round oval of frosted grey with lily pad drops, gently scalloped bottom fitting neatly on supporting arms of base; base signed RICHARD; overall, 10"H; $725 D.

TIFFANY (Easily the most collected of the lamp manufacturers, Louis C. Tiffany's many variations in styles and colors can be confusing and even misleading if not accompanied with study of lamps themselves. First person study is always best, but be sure to see some of the fine references listed in the bibliography.)

Table lamp, "Laburnum" pattern leaded glass & gilt bronze; domed shade with irregular lower rim, mottled yellow clusters in green leaves on blue ground, having tag impressed TIFFANY STUDIOS NEW YORK 539; gilt-bronze base impressed TIFFANY STUDIOS NEW YORK 531; 30"H, 21"D shade; *$40,000 A.

Table lamp, "Peony" pattern, the shade with yellow-centered red/pink/mauve flowers among green leaves on blue/green ground, impressed TIFFANY STUDIOS NEW YORK 1505; base impressed TIFFANY STUDIOS NEW YORK 391; 28½"H, 22"D shade; *$38,000 A.

Table lamp, "Dragonfly" shade with green dragonflies having multi-colored red/green wings beneath gold glass jewels on greenish-yellow ground, impressed TIFFANY STUDIOS NEW YORK 1495; gold-patinated base impressed TIFFANY STUDIOS NEW YORK 532; 26"H, 20"D shade; *$13,650 A.

Table lamp, "Lotus" pattern shade, signed; 24"H, 25¼"D shade; *$13,000 A.

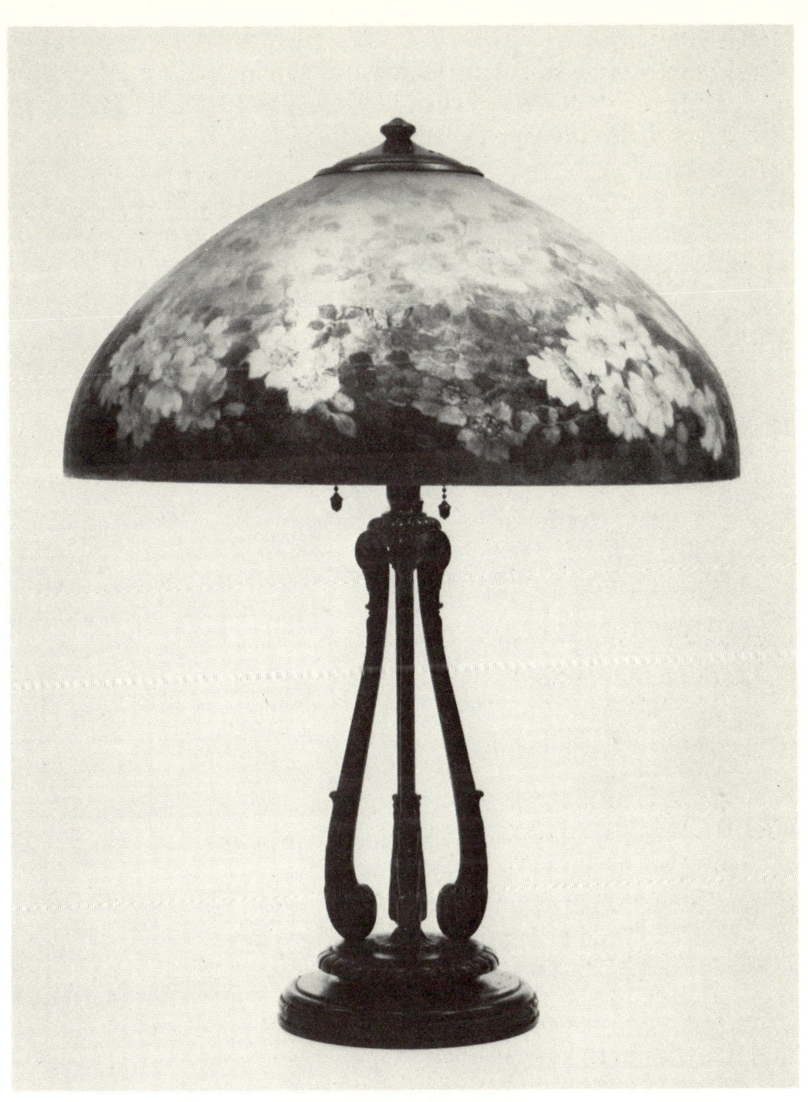

HANDEL REVERSE-PAINTED TABLE LAMP, the shade signed "Handel 6688," the base of patinated metal with original Handel paper label; 23¼"H, shade 17½"D; *$3,500 A. (C.G. Sloan)

Table lamp, "Dogwood" pattern shade on peacock base; shade with mottled white blossoms (some with pink tinges), all with yellow centers, against striated lavender-blue ground, impressed TIFFANY STUDIOS NEW YORK 1475-15; sockets, standard & switch replaced; 24"H, 18"D; *$13,000 A.

Table lamp, "Lotus" pattern shade, glass shading from bright green at top to white at lower rim, impressed TIFFANY STUDIOS NEW YORK; base impressed TIFFANY STUDIOS NEW YORK 28622; 26½"H, 26"D shade; *$12,000 A.

Table lamp, "Geranium" pattern shade; conical shade with flowering white blossoms in broad blue/green leaves on red-streaked green ground, with tag impressed TIFFANY STUDIOS NEW YORK 25880; on bronze base; 21½"H, 16"D shade; *$12,000 A.

Table lamp, "Alamander" pattern shade with bright yellow flowers having streaked brown centers, among variegated leaves on blue ground; base with blown yellow glass in chased bronze mount, impressed TIFFANY STUDIOS NEW YORK; 19¼"H, 18"D shade; *$12,000 A.

Table lamp, "Daffodil" pattern shade with deeply mottled yellow/orange flowers among green leaves on emerald ground, impressed TIFFANY STUDIOS NEW YORK 13613; base impressed TIFFANY STUDIOS NEW YORK 532; 26"H, 20"D shade; *$12,000 A.

Table lamp, 12-lily, amber iridescent shades (all marked); bronze base impressed TIFFANY STUDIOS/NEW/YORK/332; shades with minor upper rim chips, 1 with lower rim chip; 21½"H; *$11,500 A.

Table lamp, "Dragonfly" pattern shade with dragonflies having grey-blue bodies and rose/green wings against pale yellow ground; 22"H, 17"D shade; *$9,500 A.

Table lamp, "Fish Scale" type, shade with radiating bands of multi-colored blue-green panels above lower red/blue/green repeating border, impressed TIFFANY STUDIOS NEW YORK; base with canister, impressed TIFFANY STUDIOS NEW YORK 25779; 17¾"H, 13"D shade; *$9,000 A.

Table lamp with Favrile glass shade: striated gold feathers on cream, inscribed "S7894"; base a bronze mount housing green glass, impressed TIFFANY STUDIOS NEW YORK D856; 25"H, 12¾"D shade, one glass base panel repaired; *$9,000 A.

Table lamp, "Wild Rose" bordered shade, domed with band of amber/pink flowers among green leaves on green ground, with tag impressed TIFFANY STUDIOS NEW YORK 1997; bronze base impressed TIFFANY STUDIOS NEW YORK 533; 22"H, 16"D shade; *$9,000 A.

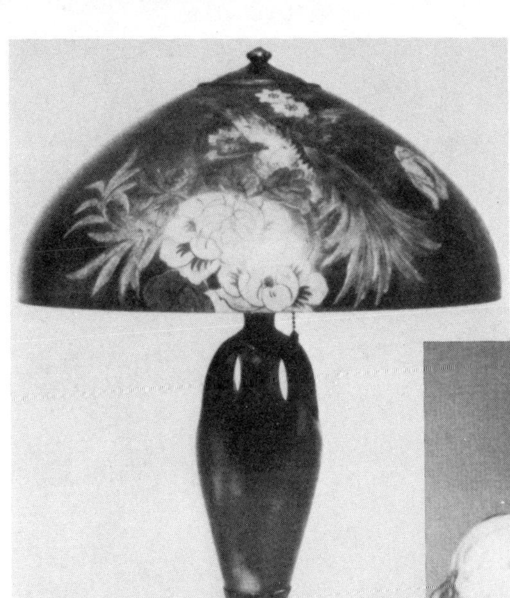

HANDEL TABLE LAMP, cameo & painted bird of paradise, shade & ring signed; 23½"H, shade 17¾"D; *$500 A. (Sotheby's)

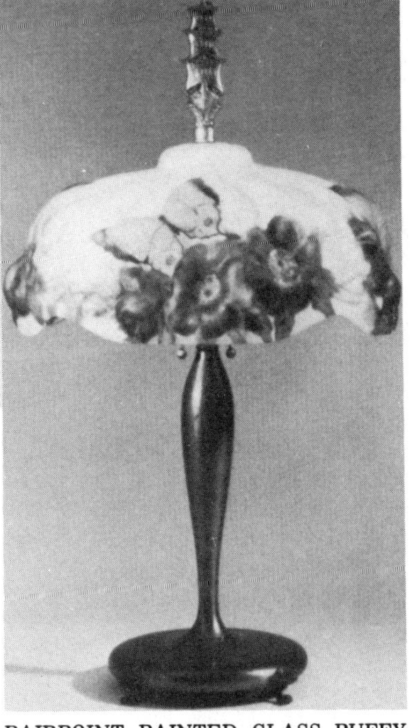

PAIRPOINT PAINTED GLASS PUFFY TABLE LAMP, shade signed, on patinated metal base with clipper ship finial; 24¾"H, shade 13¾"D) *$2,400 A. (Sotheby's)

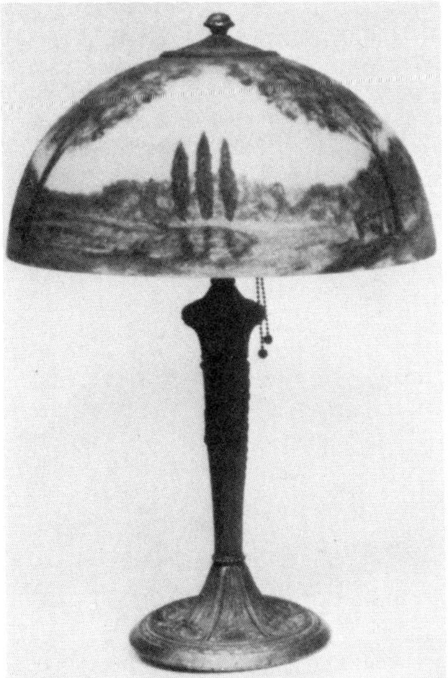

JEFFERSON TABLE LAMP, interior-painted with rural landscape, signed JEFFERSON AV, and 2807; 22½"H, shade 15½"D, slight lower rim wear; *$800 A. (Sotheby's)

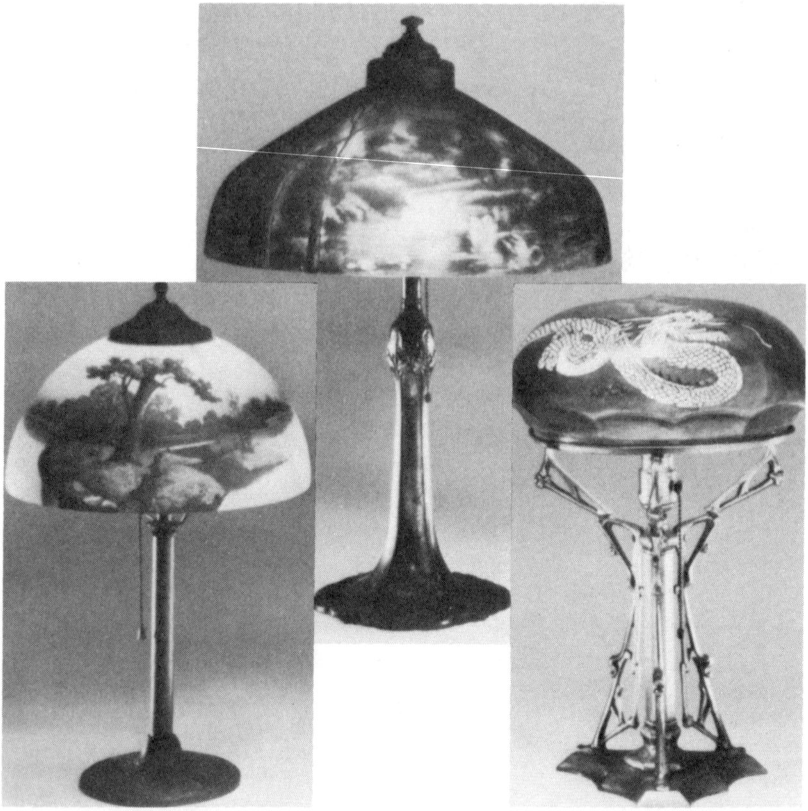

THREE AMERICAN PAINTED GLASS SHADE TABLE LAMPS, all early 20th century. (Left) lakeside forest scene in orange/ochre tones, with finial, enamel signed JEFFERSON 818, on patinated metal base (case #718); 19½"H, shade 12"D; *$500 A. (Center) swans in forest lake in green/brown, possibly attributable to Pittsburgh, on patinated metal base; 23"H, shade 16"D, upper rim chips; *$600 A. (Right) painted dragonfly & Sunflower on green ground, gilt-heightened, with paneled lower border, gilt Handel signature; base depatinated; 19"H, shade 12½"D; *$950 A. (Sotheby's)

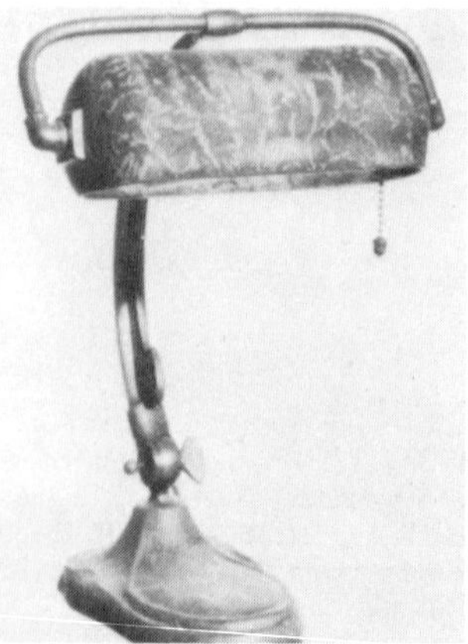

HANDEL STUDENT'S LAMP, trough-shaped shade of textured glass painted with moonlit lake scene surrounded by pines; signed HANDEL, numbered 65; curving bronze arm & foot; 13½"H, shade 8"L, *$500 A. (Phillips)

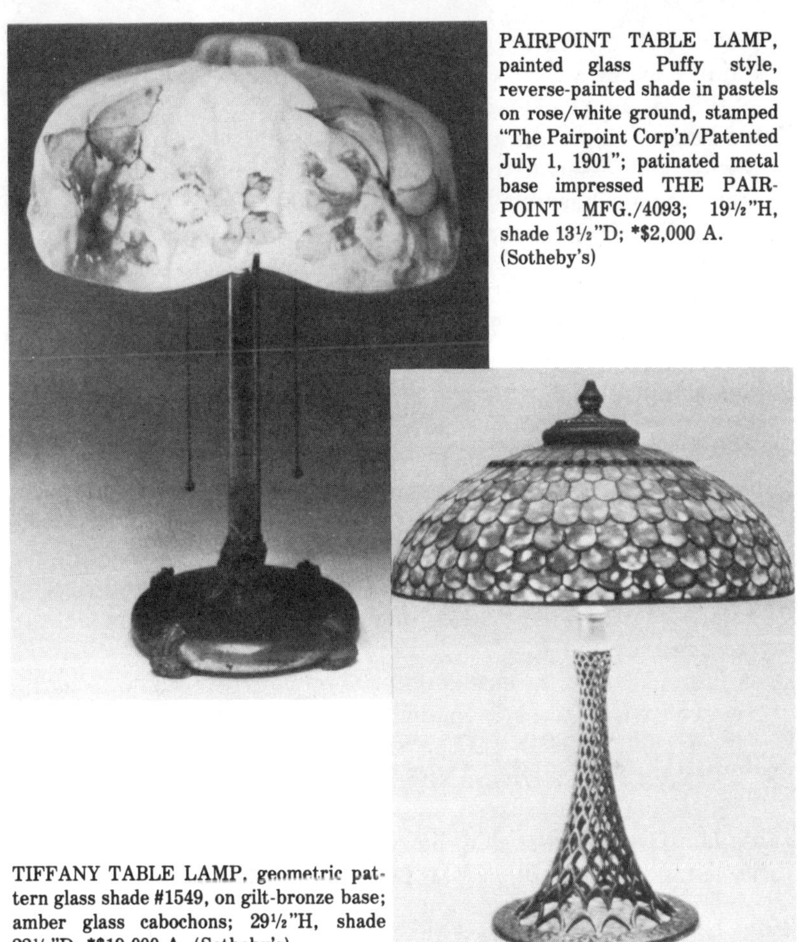

PAIRPOINT TABLE LAMP, painted glass Puffy style, reverse-painted shade in pastels on rose/white ground, stamped "The Pairpoint Corp'n/Patented July 1, 1901"; patinated metal base impressed THE PAIRPOINT MFG./4093; 19½"H, shade 13½"D; *$2,000 A. (Sotheby's)

TIFFANY TABLE LAMP, geometric pattern glass shade #1549, on gilt-bronze base; amber glass cabochons; 29½"H, shade 22¼"D; *$19,000 A. (Sotheby's)

Table lamp, 10-lily, with shades inscribed "L.C.T. Favrile"; bronze base impressed TIFFANY STUDIOS/NEW YORK/381; 20½"H, one shade with upper rim crack; *$8,500 A.

Table lamp, 10-lily, shades inscribed "L.C.T."; base impressed TIFFANY STUDIOS/NEW YORK/381; one shade with minor rim chip, 20"H; *$8,000 A.

Table lamp, "Daffodil" pattern shade; 20"H, 13¾"D; *$7,250 A.

Table lamp, green turtle-back, the shade with a central band of turtle-back tiles of mottled green, impressed TIFFANY STUDIOS NEW YORK 1482; base impressed TIFFANY STUDIOS NEW YORK 368; 24½"H, 18"D shade; *$7,000 A.

Table lamp, "Poinsettia" border shade with radiating bands of mottled olive glass with medial border of mottled &

opalescent crimson/ivory/green glass flowerheads, with finial, shade signed & #d 1556; base impressed name & #555; 20¼"H, 14"D shade; *$6,500 A.

Table lamp, 7-lily with amber iridescent shades, all signed; base with impressed mark & #1651; 20½"H, one shade restored upper rim, base drilled twice; *$6,000 A.

Table lamp, "Pomegranate" shade on bronze & turtle-back tile base; shade with band of yellow flowers on bright green, impressed TIFFANY STUDIOS NEW YORK; base with canister impressed TIFFANY STUDIOS NEW YORK 5135; 23½"H, 16"D shade; *$5,100 A.

Bridge lamp, shade with wavy iridescent striations in rose on ivory ground; both shade & bronze base signed; 55"H, 10¼"D shade; *$4,500 A.

Table lamp, "Whirling Leaf" pattern shade, 18"D; on metal base; $4,100 A.

Student lamp, 2-light, shades of iridescent olive edged in amber on pale green-tinged ivory ground, one shade inscribed "L.C.T."; 29½"H, 9¾"D, minute chip to upper rim on one shade; *$4,000 A.

Desk lamp, glass & bronze counterweight; green shade intaglio-carved with leaves & tendrils above decorated gold border, inscribed "2196G—L.C. Tiffany-Favrile"; base impressed TIFFANY STUDIOS NEW YORK; 15¾"H, 7"D shade; *$3,400 A.

Table lamp, 3-lily, shades & base signed; $3,250 D.

Table lamp, 10-panel linen fold; fabrique shade frosted, with each panel in 3 sections, & signed TIFFANY STUDIOS NY 1988; base gilt, signed TIFFANY STUDIOS NEW YORK 613; overall, 19"H; $3,200 D.

Desk lamp, turtle-back; ornate shade with 2 white turtle-back tiles, raised on twin arms supported by ribbed/domed gilt-bronze foot; impressed TIFFANY STUDIOS NEW YORK 9842; 17"H; *$3,200 A.

Desk lamp, counterweight gilt-bronze & Favrile, the iridescent gold glass inscribed "L.C.T. Favrile"; base impressed TIFFANY STUDIOS NEW YORK 468; 10½"D shade; *$2,800 A.

Desk lamp, turtle-back Zodiac style; 2 amber iridescent turtle-back glass tiles, each signed; Zodiac designs on base; 14½"H; *$2,700 A.

Desk lamp, counterbalance style of Favrile glass & bronze; ribbed domed shade of opalescent glass with iridescent gold

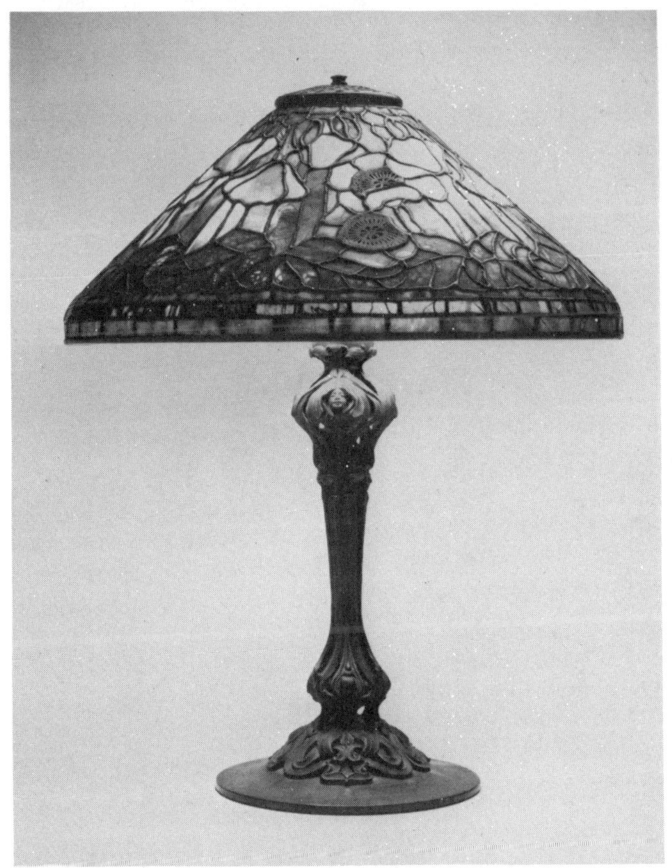

TIFFANY TABLE LAMP, "Orange Poppy" pattern shade signed (#1381), on unsigned metal base; shade 20"D; *$11,000 A. (C.G. Sloan)

waves on brown ground, engraved "L.C.T."; base of bronze, impressed TIFFANY STUDIOS NEW YORK 415; 15¼"H, 7"D shade, minor rim chips on top; *$2,700 A.

Desk lamp, turtle-back counterbalance style; shade with iridescent green turtle-back tiles supported by twin S-shape arms holding counterweight ball; bronze base, impressed TIFFANY STUDIOS NEW YORK; 16"H; *$2,500 A.

Desk lamp, counterweight glass & bronze style; green glass shade with 2 alternating bands of prunts at shoulder, inscribed "L.C.T."; base impressed TIFFANY STUDIOS NEW YORK 415; 16"H, 7"D shade; *$2,500 A.

Table lamp, 3-lily, with ruffled signed shades; bronze base signed & #320, with dark patina; $2,350 D.

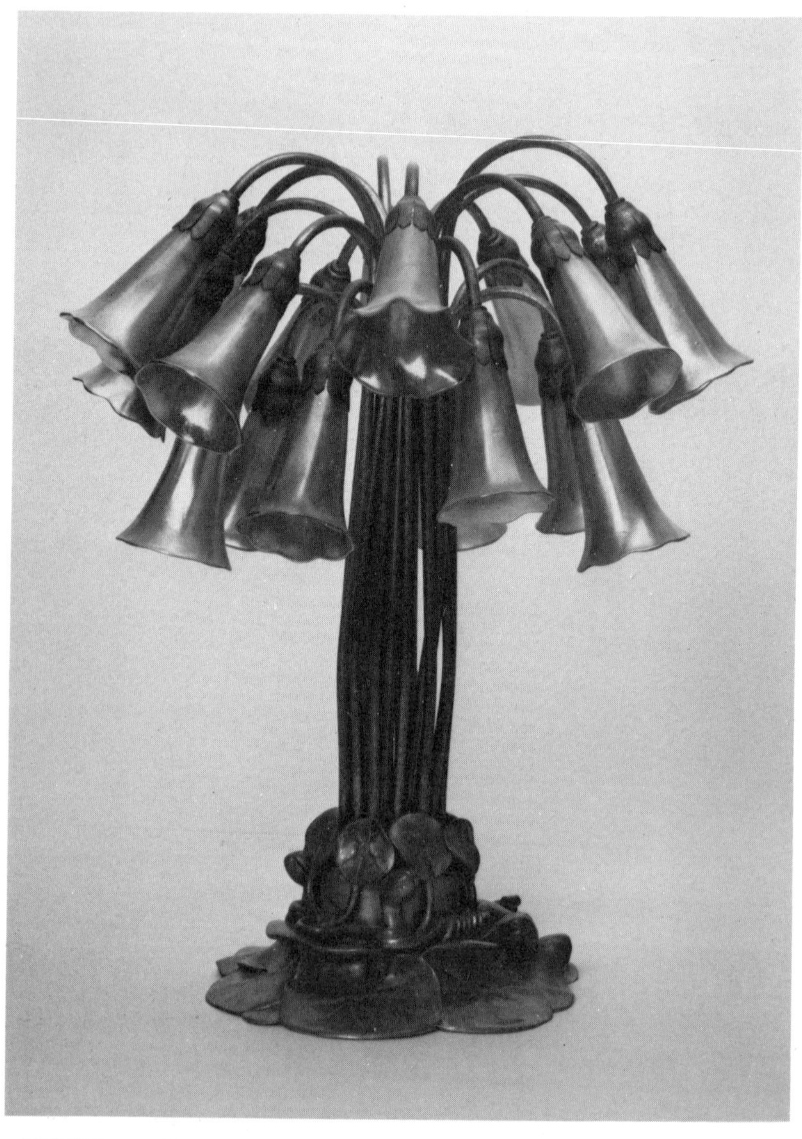

TIFFANY TABLE LAMP, 18-lily, gilt bronze with gold Favrile shades; *$17,000 A. (Christie's)

Desk lamp, turtle-back tile jeweled; 2 olive glass tiles tinged with amber iridescence; base set with silvery-blue iridescent glass "jewels," signed & #d 408; 14¼"H; *$2,300 A.

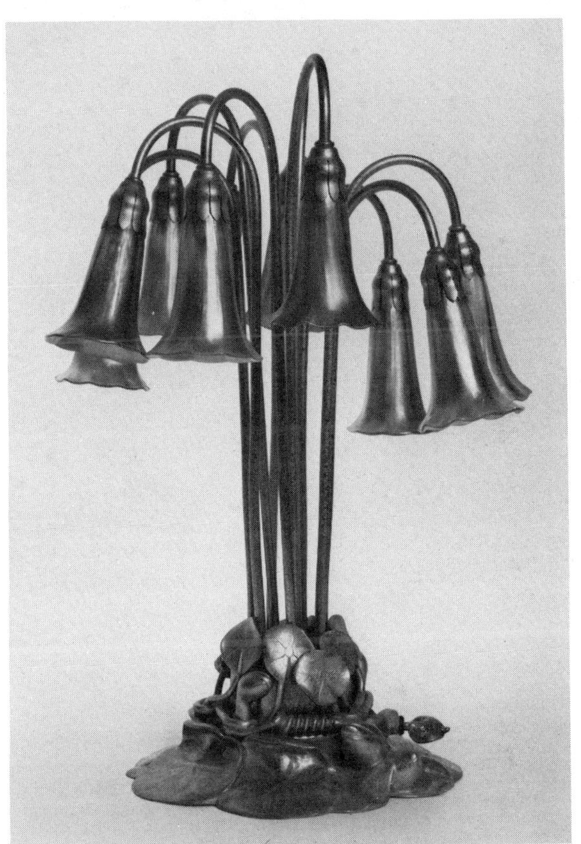

TIFFANY TABLE LAMP, 12-lily, bronze with gold Favrile shades; *$9,500 A. (Christie's)

Table lamp, brown shade with wavy appearance, signed; on columnar base with 3 arms, dark patinated bronze, pierced cap, shade & base signed; 21"H, 10"D shade; $2,250 D.

Piano lamp, long bent neck holding 3-panel shade with turtle-back tiles; marked TIFFANY STUDIOS NEW YORK 11180; $2,250 D.

Table lamp, hemispherical shade, opalescent with iridescent gold swirls on green ground, engraved "L.C.T. Favrile"; base impressed TIFFANY STUDIOS NEW YORK 436 S215; 18¼"H, 10"D shade; *$2,200 A.

Desk lamp, 3-light lily, glass & bronze; shades of opalescent white glass with striated green leaves, inscribed "L.C.T. Favrile"; bronze base with overhanging arms, handled column, ribbed domed foot, foot impressed TIFFANY STUDIOS NEW YORK 396; 16"H, 1 shade rim chipped; *$2,200 A.

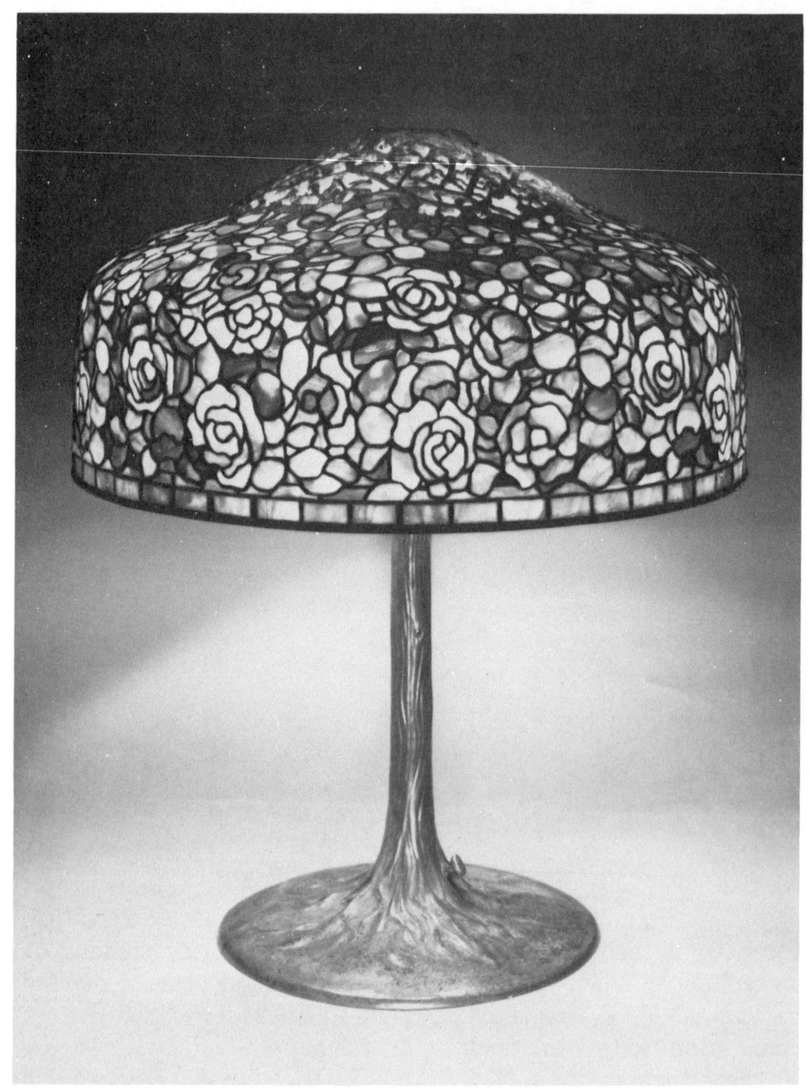

TIFFANY TABLE LAMP, "Rosebush" pattern leaded glass & bronze shade, bronze base; *$135,000 A. (Christie's)

Desk lamp, turtle-back tile style of Favrile glass & bronze; shade with iridescent green turtle-back tiles raised on twin arms supported by base set with green glass "jewels," impressed TIFFANY STUDIOS NEW YORK 28632; 14"H; *$2,100 A.

Desk lamp, ribbed amber domed shade with bands of iridescent gold waves, inscribed "L.C.T. Favrile"; bronze base cast in "Zodiac" pattern, impressed TIFFANY STUDIOS NEW YORK 864; 17"H, 7"D shade; *$1,700 A.

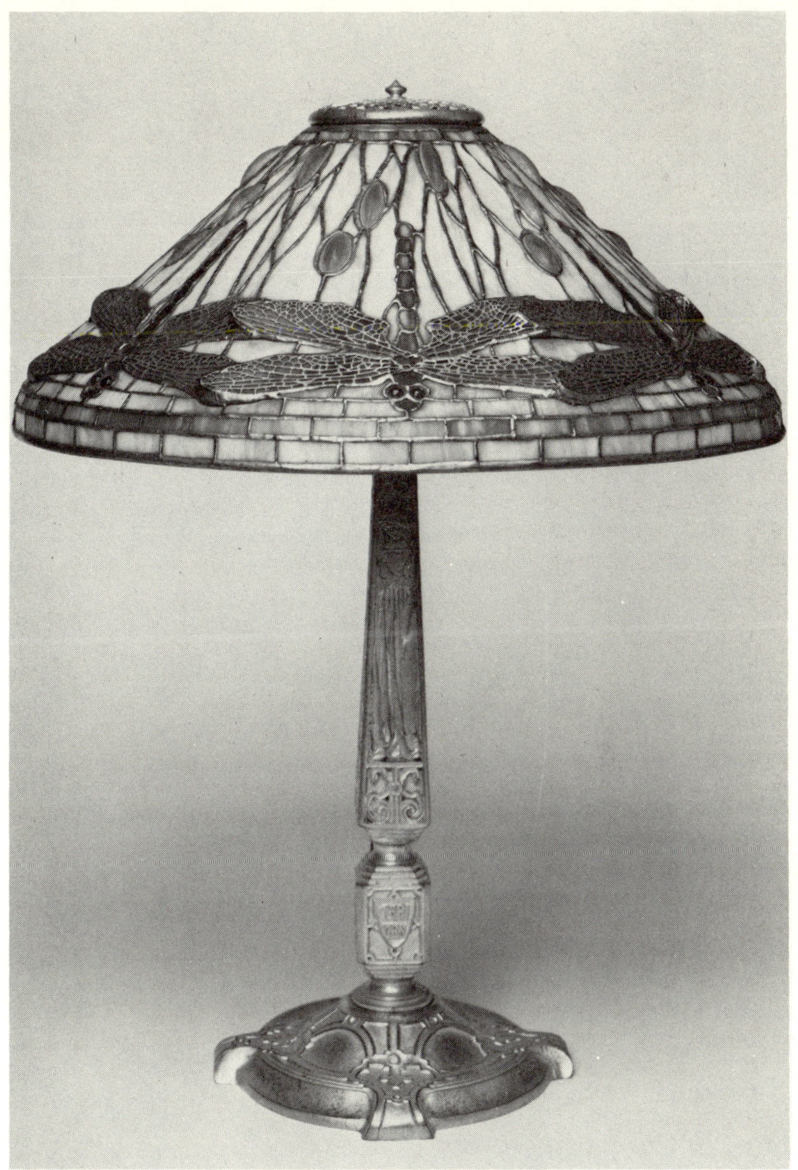

TIFFANY TABLE LAMP, "Dragonfly" pattern shade of leaded & stained glass, on gilt bronze base; *$13,500 A. (Christie's) (Compare with the other "Dragonfly" table lamp also sold through Christie's)

Desk lamp, 3-lily, domed leaf-moulded circular base supports short bulbous socket, continuing to scrolling carrying handle & 3rd supports, with iridescent amber shades; shades are inscribed, base inscribed & #d 320; 8¾"H; *$1,500 A.

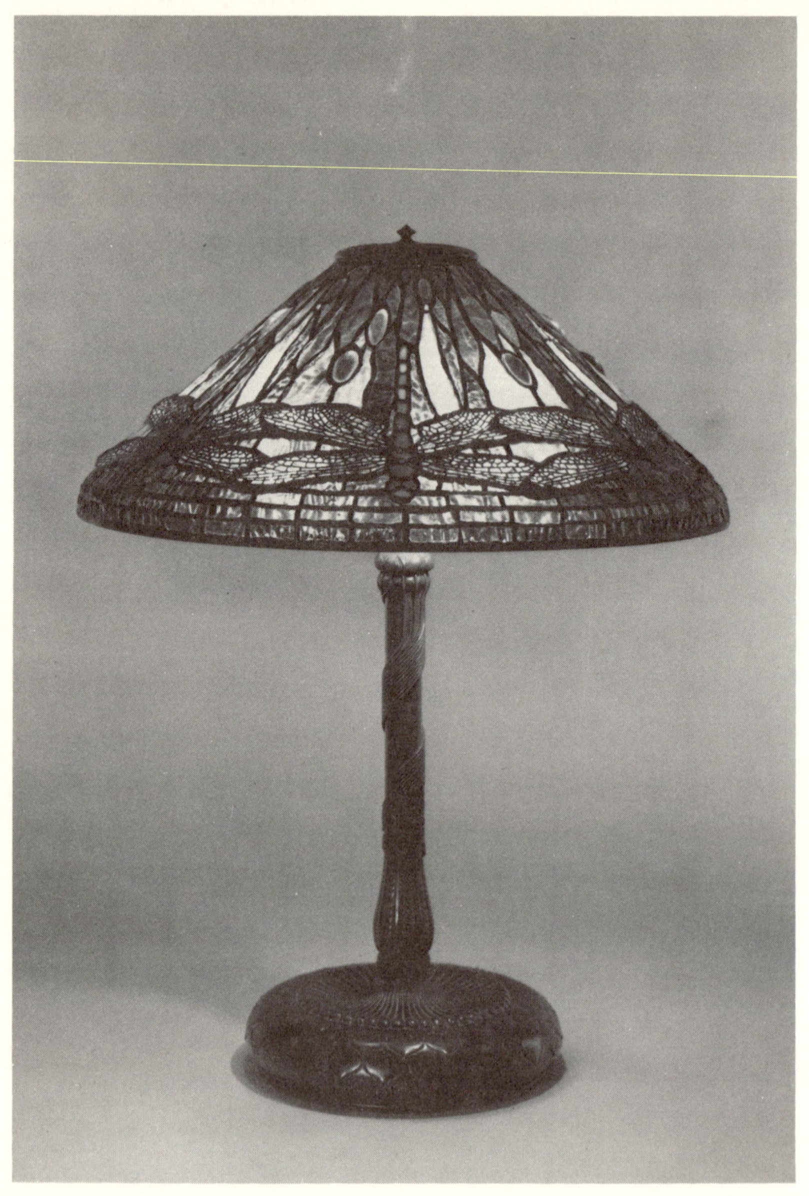

TIFFANY TABLE LAMP, "Dragonfly" pattern; *$14,000 A. (Christie's)

Desk lamp, glass & bronze; waisted bell-shaped shade of opalescent white striated with green leaves outlined in gold, inscribed "L.C.T."; bronze base with ribbed domed foot, impressed TIFFANY STUDIOS NEW YORK 424; 18"H, 5"D shade; *$1,400 A.

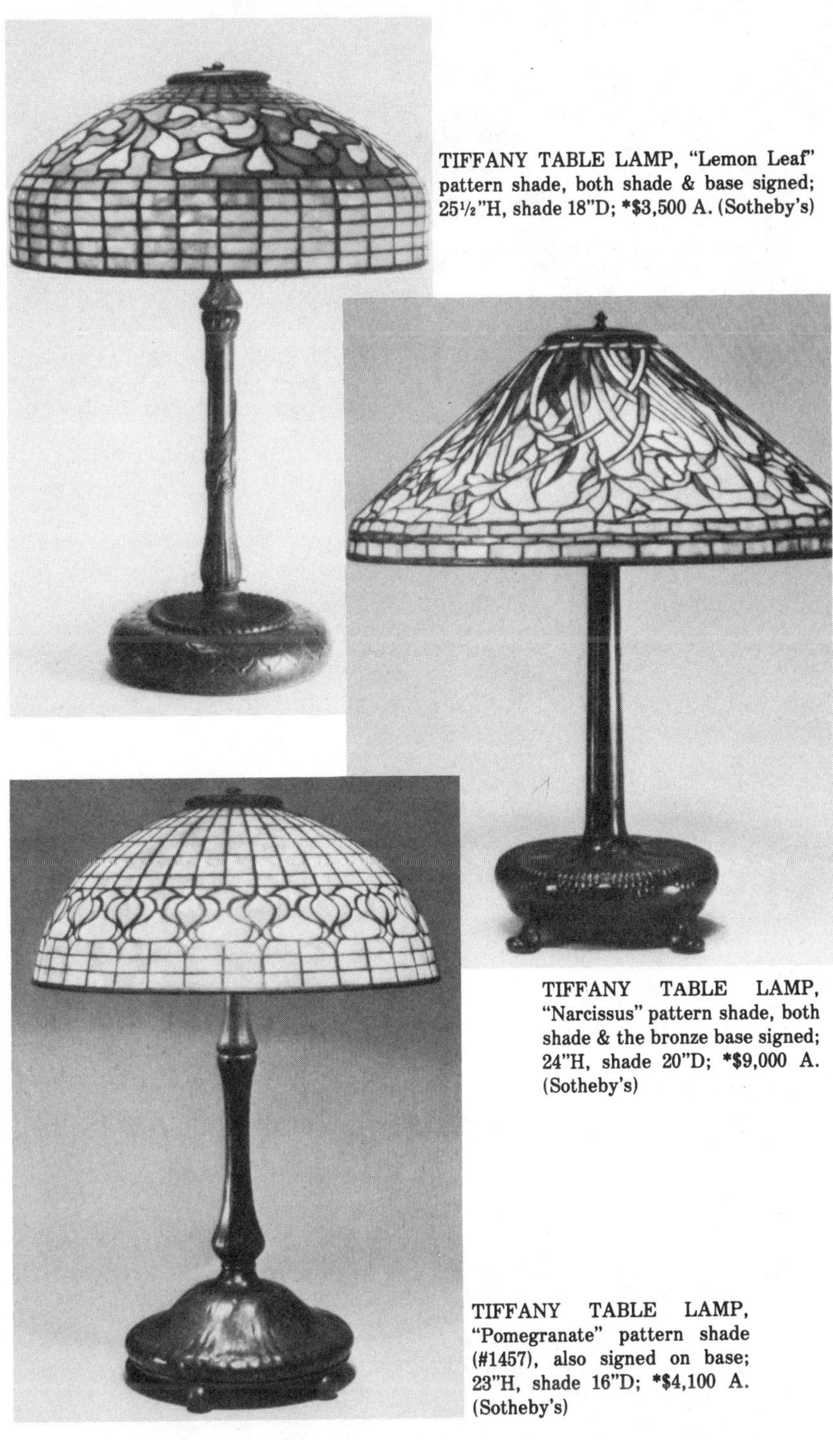

TIFFANY TABLE LAMP, "Lemon Leaf" pattern shade, both shade & base signed; 25½"H, shade 18"D; *$3,500 A. (Sotheby's)

TIFFANY TABLE LAMP, "Narcissus" pattern shade, both shade & the bronze base signed; 24"H, shade 20"D; *$9,000 A. (Sotheby's)

TIFFANY TABLE LAMP, "Pomegranate" pattern shade (#1457), also signed on base; 23"H, shade 16"D; *$4,100 A. (Sotheby's)

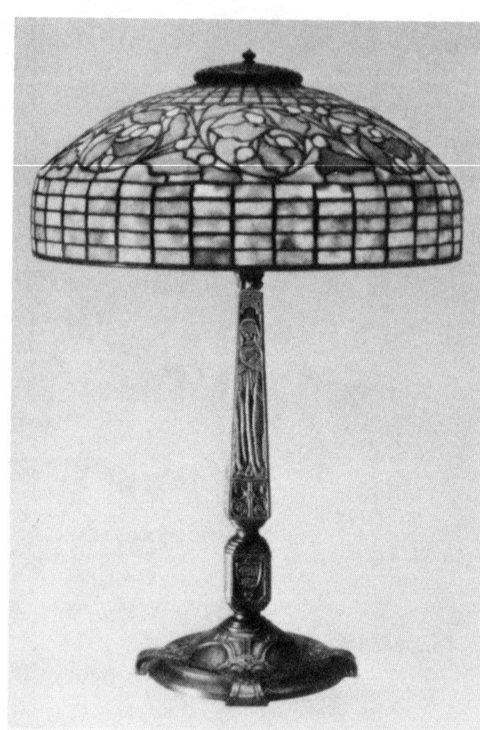

TIFFANY TABLE LAMP, "Acorn" pattern shade (#9467), on gilt-bronze "Four Virtues" base (#557); 25½"H, shade 18"D, replaced sockets; *$4,250 A. (Sotheby's)

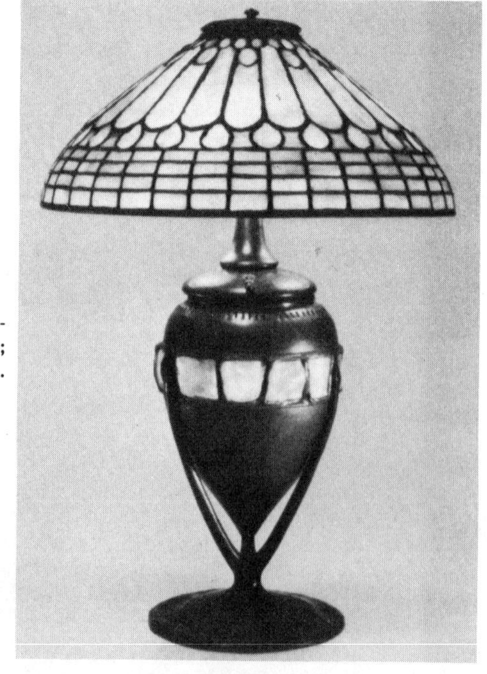

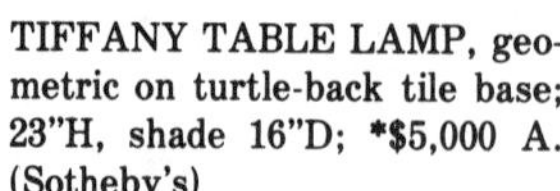

TIFFANY TABLE LAMP, geometric on turtle-back tile base; 23"H, shade 16"D; *$5,000 A. (Sotheby's)

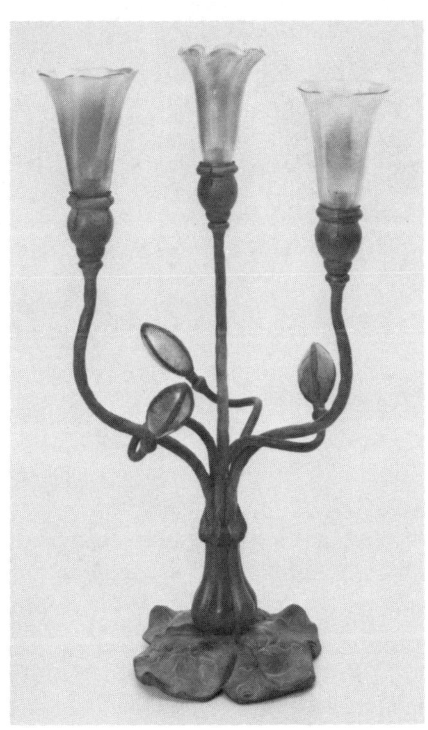

TIFFANY TABLE LAMP, 3-lily, Favrile glass & bronze; a pair, only one of which is illustrated; *$4,000 A. (Christie's)

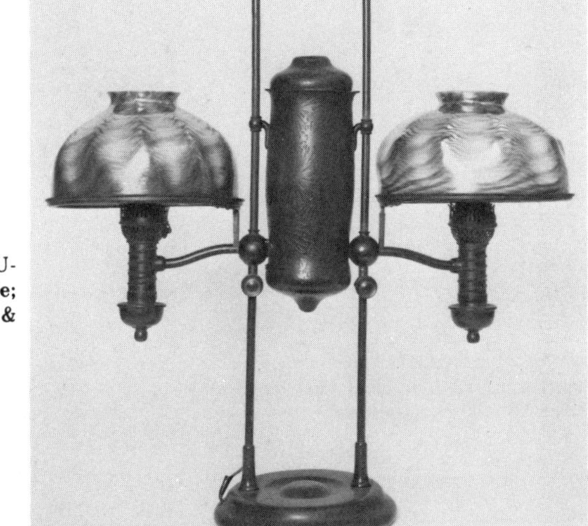

TIFFANY STUDENT Lamp, double; Favrile glass & bronze; *$4,200 A. (Christie's)

TIFFANY DESK LAMP, counter-balance, the shade of ivory cased in caramel, with iridescent golden-amber striations; base impressed with mark & #416; 14½"H extended, 7¼"D; *$2,200 A. (Sotheby's)

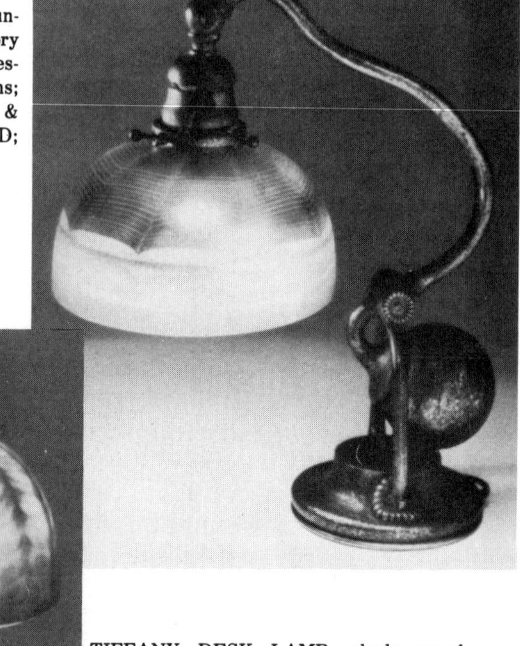

TIFFANY DESK LAMP, shade cased green to ochre at upper rim, signed; enameled domed foot on baluster standard, #15A; 15"H, shade 8"D; *$1,900 A. (Sotheby's)

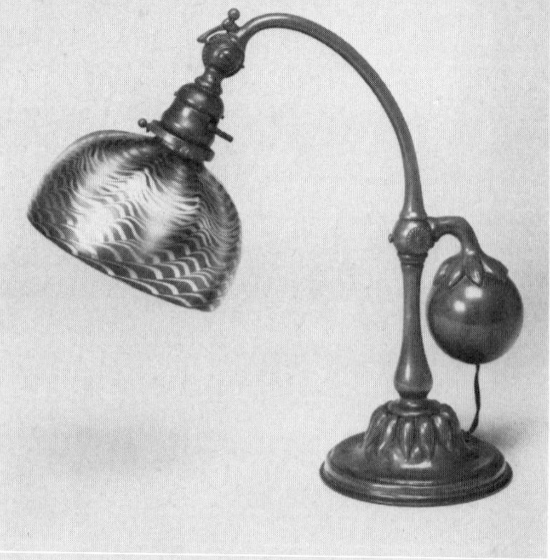

TIFFANY DESK LAMP, counter-balance, Favrile glass & bronze; *$2,700 A. (Christie's)

Table lamp, Favrile glass & bronze; shade with ruffled rim, of translucent pink with green-bordered gold leaves, unsigned; adjustable bronze base with 5 splayed feet, impressed TIFFANY STUDIOS NEW YORK 429A; 39"H; listed in 1906 price list as an adjustable hospital lamp; *$1,300 A.

Desk lamp, domed green shade with bands of iridescent gold waves, inscribed "L.C.T."; bronze base with etched finish, marked TIFFANY STUDIOS NEW YORK 424; 18"H, 7"D shade; missing 3 ball feet; *$1,300 A.

Desk lamp, Kava Shell & bronze harp; blue-tinted shade, base impressed TIFFANY STUDIOS NEW YORK 419; 13½"H; *$850 A.

WILKERSON

Table lamp, leaded glass shade set with "jewels"; ornate solid bronze base signed "Wilkerson, Brooklyn, N.Y."; $2,000 D.

Table lamp, leaded glass in red "Poppy" pattern, metal base, 20"H; $3,900 D.

MISCELLANEOUS & UNIDENTIFIED MAKERS: TABLE LAMPS, ETC.

Figural lamp, table type, bronze, after Adolf Josef Pohl; owl of brown patina, set with glass eyes; 19½"H, inscribed A.POHL/210/110; *$3,000 A.

Table lamp, American Arts & Crafts, peened finish, shallow domical shade with 6 ribbed dividers & mica panels; shade rests upon baluster form vase, with 3 handles modeled as elephant heads with attenuated trunks reaching to lower shoulder; 23"D shade; *$2,000 A.

Table lamp, figural, after Louis Potet; Art Nouveau girl on side, gilded bronze; artist's signature molded; $1,300 D.

Table lamp, figural after Charles Perron (molded signature), of woman, with founder's seal; lavender satin shade signed "Rethardes," c. 1900; 26½"H; $875 D.

Table lamp, figural of maiden standing on rocks in swirling drapery encircled by vine of fruiting grapes, after Auguste Moreau; issuing 4 orange-colored lights; covered circular plinth; 35"H; *$850 A.

Desk lamp, domed mosaic shade covered with 10 segments & jeweled panels; on reeded base with round foot; 16½"H; *$625 A.

Table lamp, figural of 21"H draped lady holding up 6" multi-color glass globe, atop 6"D base; overall, 30"H, white metal; $450 D.

Table lamp, paneled slag glass with filigree border, 20"H; $450 D.

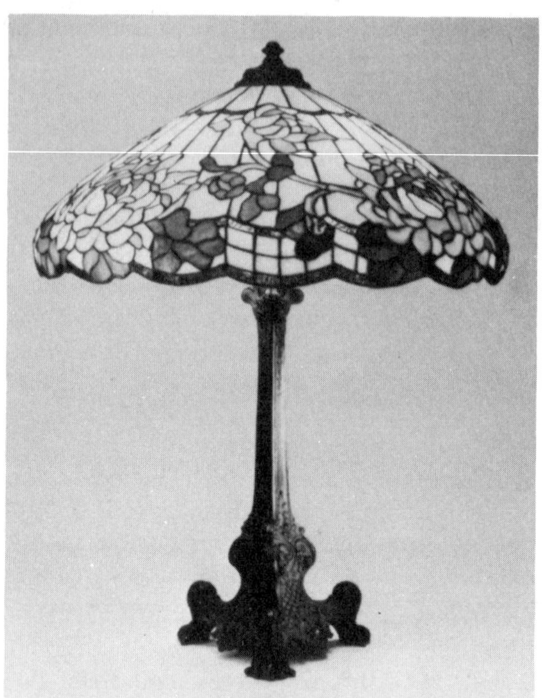

WILKINSON & CO. TABLE LAMP, "Peony" pattern leaded stained glass shade, patinated metal; 27¾"H, 22"D; *$2,400 A. (Sotheby's)

Table lamp, leaded umbrella shade of 18"D of white & butterscotch, slag scroll border; gilded Art Nouveau base with rams' heads & poppies in high relief; 23½"H; $395 D.

Table lamp, reverse-painted in Handel manner; foliate-shaped & leaf-decorated metal base, overall 20"H; *$375 A.

Table lamp, 6-panel curved caramel slag glass, lift-up shade, on ornate brass base; 24"H, 16½"D shade; $325 D.

Table lamp, figural of woman balancing 4 electric candlestick bulbs from S-curves rising above her head, plus single taller candlestick bulb; 22"H, polychromed white metal; $325 D.

Table lamp, leaded glass domed shade, 14"D; overall, 24"H; *$275 A.

Table lamp, blue slag glass domed shade with 8 panels; on fluted leaf-molded base, gilt metal, 22"H; *$225 A.

Table lamp, slag glass octagonal shade on scrollwork metal base, 27"H; *$225 A.

Table lamp, brown slag glass in domical paneled shade, on fluted metal base; 25"H; *$225 A.

Table lamp, brown slag glass & gilt metal domical shade, on baluster form stem with spreading foot; 24"H, c. 1910; *$225 A.

Desk lamp, iridescent gold single light with crimped base, 14"H; *$175 A.

Desk lamp, figural of reclining nude with 4-winged Cupid above, in white metal; "End-of-Day" glass shade with small diamond points; 14½"H, 11¼"L; $145 D.

Desk lamp, figural of reclining nude on sea lion, draped at hip, in white metal; "End-of-Day" glass shade with large diamond points; 19"H, 12"L; $135 D.

Desk lamp, bronzed with nude women front and back; marked "W.R.J. & A.G.F. Co. Pat. Appld. For," 6¼"H; $125 D.

Desk lamp, figural of seated long-haired nude holding pillar in lap, with double-rest ashtray extension; satinized shade in marbled pinks/blues; 11½"H, 8½"L, white metal; $90 D.

HANGING FIXTURES

Hanging shade, 8 leaded slag glass panels with bronze filigree, tropical sunset pattern, signed Handel, 23½"D; $2,495 D.

Ceiling fixture, ornate bronze with 5 gold iridescent shades, each signed Quezal and mint condition, each 5"H; $1,200 D.

Hanging shade, dark patinated brass with ornate embossed design, encompassing 8 deeply curved "Puffy" caramel slag glass bent panels, with crown & original beaded fringe, scalloped rim, ceiling fixture; $675 D.

Ceiling Dome shade; 8 curved caramel slag glass panels on top, 8 curved blue slag glass panels in apron; lions & other filigree designs over panels, one cracked but intact; 14"H, 21"D; $435 D.

Hanging glass shade, leaded geometric with red grape/leaf border, caramel slag glass ground; 24½"D; *$325 A.

Hanging shade, square body with pyramidal top; caramel-colored glass behind metal of floral & vining design; 6" x 5½"; $155 D.

SHADES (Individual lamp shades are here listed, following an alphabetical sequence of the makers' names. Unidentified and unmarked shades follow.)

DAUM NANCY

Mottled white to blue; $400 D.

FOSTORIA

Gold zipper over fine green pulled decoration on opal, gold lined; 7¼"H; $195 D.

FULPER

Unusual conical earthenware shade, chocolate-brown with inset sections of green & red-orange glass; impressed "5 23 59," attributed to Fulper although not carrying that name, 18"D at widest; *$800 A.

LUSTRE ART

Gold threading over green/gold leaves, set of 6; $750 D.

Green/gold hearts on opal with allover gold threading; gold lining, notched edge; 6¼"H, set of 3, one with small fitter chip; $330 D.

Bell-shaped, shaded green leaves on calcite ground with gold threading, gold lining, standard fitter; pair, $295 D.

Lily form, gold iridescent, fits Tiffany lily base; $250 D.

Gold webbing over green/gold leaves, opal glass with gold lining, 6"H; $115 D.

QUEZAL

Calcite diamond quilted center, pumpkin interior & exterior, 4½"H; set of 5, $875 D.

Floriform ribbed, engraved mark, 7¼"H; set of 5, *$550 A.

Gold applied threading on opal body, gold lined; random applied green/gold hearts, scalloped edge; set of 4, $475 D.

Gold spider webbing over green/gold leaves on opal glass, iridescent gold lining, rims notched; set of 3, $465 D.

Bell-form in ivory glass with amber iridescent interior, decorated with leaf-form iridescent/applied gold stringing, 5¼"D, inscribed QUEZAL; set of 4, *$400 A.

Bell-form, opalescent with white pulled feather design, inscribed "Quezal," 5½"H; set of 3, *$320 A.

Gold iridescent pulled feather design on calcite, gold iridescent interior; 6" x 4½", pair; $320 D.

Gold leaves on beige ground, iridescent gold interior, fitter size 2¼"; pair, $300 D.

Ribbed amber, engraved "Quezal," 6"H, 6¾"D at wide flaring mouth, regular 2½" fitter rim; $290 D.

Gold pulled feather on opal ground, pair; $250 D.

Trumpet form with iridescent pulled feather design, signed "Quezal" in silver pencil, 5¼"H, pair; *$240 A.

Lily pads & iridescent glass threads on white ground, scalloped rim, signed in silver pencil, 6"H, pair; *$220 A.

Green pulled feather design bordered in gold, on opal ribbed pattern ground, with gold lining; 5¼"D, 3½"H; $165 D.

White feather on gold iridesent ground; flake on inner fitter rim; $160 D.

Blue hearts & vines, engraved "Quezal"; $135 D.

STUEBEN

Gold drape on calcite, set of 3; $530 D.

Gold feather on opal, gold lined; pair, $250 D.

DESK LAMP, gilt bronze with mottled grey/orange shade; inscribed "C. Ranc.", 14½"H, somewhat rubbed; *$1,200 A. (Sotheby's)

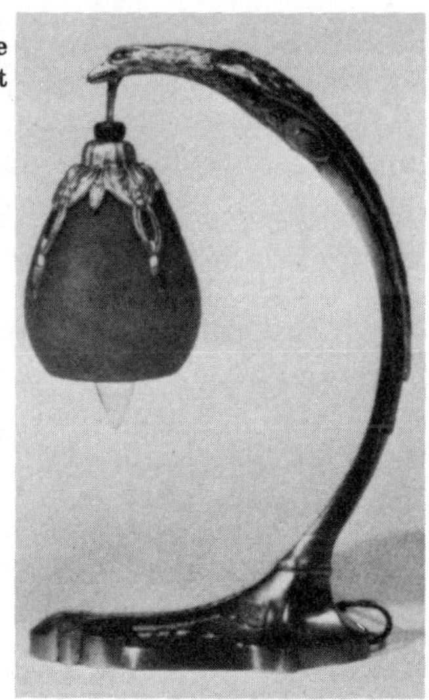

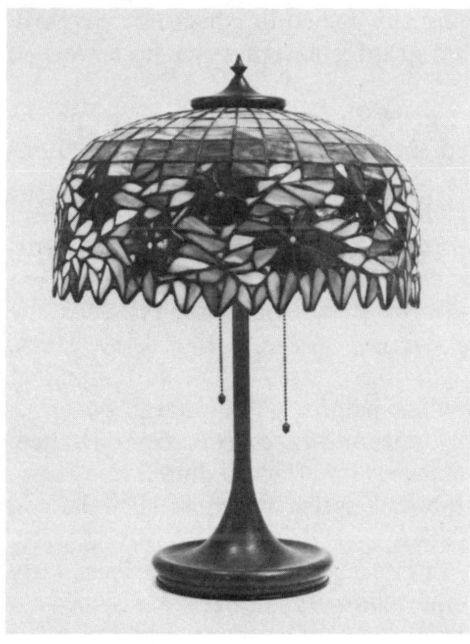

TABLE LAMP, leaded stained glass shade unsigned but attributed to Handel; 22"H, shade 16"D; *$1,400 A. (C.G. Sloan)

Green pulled feather design, gold iridescent lining with deep pink highlights; 6¼"H, signature with fleur de lis; $185 D.

Green drape with gold edge on opal ground, gold lined, ruffled edge; 4¾"H, 5½"D; $150 D.

Gold drape with gold hook border, gold lined; $135 D.

TIFFANY

Octagonal empire jewel lampshade, each panel with central jeweled white/pink flowered medallion on charcoal ground; impressed TIFFANY STUDIOS N.Y. 1953; 22"D; *$13,000 A.

Domed shade, opalescent with iridescent gold pulled feather design, inscribed "S7878," 12¾"D; *$950 A.

Diamond optic pattern in iridescent gold with blue/purple/green highlights; $250 D.

ASSORTED MAKERS

Acid cut-back Calcite domes, border decorated with stylized petal design above continuous Vetruvian scrollwork, 6"D; set of 3, *$200 A.

Flared-form with striated leaf design, iridescent interior, 5½"H; set of 4, *$200 A.

Lily form, gold iridescent, unsigned; $50 D.

POSTERS AND GRAPHICS

Graphic design experienced a tremendous spurt of growth immediately before and during the period in which Art Nouveau flourished. It's no wonder that graphic designers so often worked in the Art Nouveau styles.

A major art form which grew to fruition during this period was the poster. Developed in France (especially by Jules Cheret), the poster drew its original inspiration from Japanese woodcuts. The bright colors which characterized much of the Art Nouveau poster production present a bit of a predicament, though. Some of the most successful Art Nouveau posters were monochromatic or done only in black and white, such as those by the brilliant young British artist, Aubrey Beardsley. Flat, unshaded colors also were popular in this style, so looking at colors is simply insufficient when judging Art Nouveau posters.

Today's collector usually encounters posters from France, the home and nurturing culture for the medium, and from Belgium and the United States. English, German, Dutch, and Austrian posters, among others, are comparatively scarce. Fitting somewhere in between in scarcity are posters from Italy and Spain. Fortunately or unfortunately, posters are generally not collected by country of origin but by artist or subject.

Popular decorative motifs in poster design followed designs used in other media. The ever-present female was quite often presented as a nude; described by some writers as "sexless," she could often be quite alluring and bosomy. Other motifs were derived from nature, although certainly not copied from it: the seashell, the flower, a variety of insects (winged and otherwise), birds (swans, cranes, peacocks), and arboreal designs.

The poster was, and even today remains, a unique artistic medium. The poster was a commercial advertising device, produced to promote a particular firm, product, service, attraction, or vacation spot. To do this, it must: 1) grab the viewer's attention quickly, competing for it with other posters and visual stimuli; 2) quickly deliver the advertiser's intended message, for it may be seen only for a second or two by the passerby; 3) do both of the forementioned in an artistic, pleasing manner. It must be admitted that some of the more collectible posters fail to accomplish all three. Some, for instance, are filled with verbiage which is meaningless to the observer who only glances at the poster. Still, exceptions abound. The poster covered with wording **will** be read if the observer's interest can be held, making him a captive of the poster.

Lettering was one means of expressing the changing art scene in poster art. Lettering once remained discreetly segregated from the central image of the poster; with Art Nouveau design, lettering (frequently looking like it had been hand-drawn, which it of course had) descended into the image — or did the image ascend to obliterate part of the lettering? Whichever, the message, delivered in both picture and words, was to be taken as a whole rather than in its component parts.

One problem with posters is, the same poster can exist in several different states. A "state" in posters is a stage in the lithographic process (or chromolithographic process in most cases). Posters **can** and **are** found in various states prior to completion. Easiest to recognize is a poster seen with lettering which is later seen without lettering. Other states may be prior to the printing with a particular color; here, one should have access to good references regarding posters to judge whether or not the poster under consideration is in the "final state." (And a poster in a state other than the final state is NOT an undesirable poster!)

Another problem with posters is they are essentially ephemeral in nature — short-lived, fragile, not necessarily intended for preservation. That so many **have** been preserved is a tribute to the tastes of their former owners. True, many were released to the public as "art" posters, but the poster was fundamentally an advertising tool to which decorative art had been applied. For long-term preservation, the advertising tool had to be mounted on a linen backing or with what is known as a "mint" price for only a "fair" poster.

Few posters survive without some sort of damage. Most common are minor tears in the surrounding borders and damage (stains or tears) at folds. Although some collectors will insist upon only pristine, "mint" condition posters, most accept a poster with some minor damage. Let the condition be your guide as to what the price of a given poster should be; don't pay a "mint" price for only a "fair" poster.

Posters certainly weren't the only domain in which graphics designers worked in the Art Nouveau modes. The art lithograph grew in importance during this period. So did artistic post cards — designers such as Mucha often had their designs transferred from the poster medium to the smaller post cards.

A major area of growth which will not be covered in this book is that of book design. For many decades books have been collected as an end to themselves, not quite fitting into the "antiques" domain. Nevertheless, many Art Nouveau designers designed everything from bindings to type faces and illustrations.

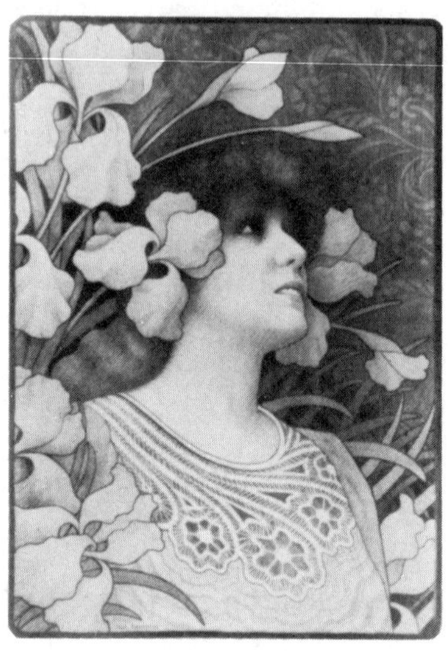

BERTHON, PAUL. "Sarah Bernhardt"; color lithograph by Bourgerie & Cie., Paris; 20" x 14¼", signed in block; *$1,200 A. (Phillips)

ANONYMOUS — Pan-American Exposition, Buffalo, May 1 - November 1, 1901; Niagara Falls anthropomorphized as "Niagara," a woman in diaphanous water; 25 3/8" x 48", printed by Gies & Co., Buffalo, NY; very fine, framed; *$1,450 A.

— To-Day Winter Number . . . Two Coloured Supplements. By Dudley Hardy & Hal Hurst; J. Weiner Ltd., London; 19 1/8" x 30¼", *$300 A.

— Paola del Monte Chanteuse Franco-Espagnole Folies-Bergere; Chaix, Paris, 1896; 34" x 48 1/8", slight staining & foxing at top right corner; *$250 A.

— Cree en 1865 / La Raphaelle Liqueur Bomal . . .; 60" x 48", dated 1908, pictures airplane; $200 D.

JANE ATCHE — "Job" cigarette papers, woman smoker in black cape; 41¾" x 57", printed by Imp. Cassan Fils, Toulouse Paris, c. 1896; very fine, framed; *$3,000 A.

C.B. — Cycles Gladiator 18, Boulevard Montmarte; female nude rider with orange hair against blue sky; printed by G. Massias, Paris, c. 1895; 53¾" x 38½", few unobtrusive tears, museum mounting; *$3,200 A.

FERNAND BAC — Tous Les Sois Scala Yvette Guilbert; printed Chaix, Paris, 1893; 32¾" x 84 3/8", very fine, one of 3 done by Bac for Guilbert; *$600 A.

LUCIEN BAYLAC — Creme Orientale Poudre & Savon Parfumerie Orientale . . .; eastern-looking woman, colorful; printed by Chaix, Paris, 1894; 33½" x 48", barely visible folds; *$250 A.

AUBREY BEARDSLEY — Keynote Series (10 items, beginning with Grant Allen's "The Woman Who Did"); printed by Forbes Co., Boston, 1896; 13½" x 19", very fine, framed; *$500 A.

— Sold Here. The Spinster's Scrip. Macmillan & Co.; black drawing with red text, 11¾" x 16¾", 4 corners tape-stained; *$300 A.

— For Sale Here The Yellow Book Volume VI July, 1895; 12 7/8" x 19", 4 corners tape-stained; *$300 A.

LOUIS BERGE — Ambassadeurs. Miette; printed by G. Bataile, Paris, c. 1898; 35¼" x 51½", slight staining at folds, bright colors; *$275 A.

PAUL BERTHON — Folies Bergere. Liane de Pougy; spider-web background behind woman with outstretched arms; printed by Lemercier, Paris; 23¾" x 61", framed, slight tears at folds, minor restoration; *$3,500 A.

— Le Livre de Magda; shapely nude with flowing blonde hair in woods among flowers & trees, feeding white doves flying about her head; 29" x 29½", custom framed, very fine condition; $1,250 D.

— Salon des 100, 17c exposition; 14 ¾" x 21½", printed by Typ. A. Davy, Paris, 1895; restorations: 3" x 4" upper right, 1 " x 2" upper left; framed; *$1,000 A.

— Eglantines; $750 D.

— Normandie Bretagne; 32" x 45¼", slight stain & a few marginal tears, museum mounting; printed by Chaix, Paris, 1897; *$450 A.

— Queen Wilhelmina; profile of queen against muted saffron ground showing Holland estuary, windmills; 38½" x 36", mint condition, 1901, on linen backing; $350 D.

— La Pointe de Bretteville; 25 7/8" x 13 1/8", lettering in margin only; 3 small border tears; 1899; *$150 A.

— Wilhelmina; 13½" x 15"; $100 D.

MAURICE BIAIS — Palais de Glace de Lyon; 29" x 44", slight tears & stains at folds; by Minot, Paris, 1902 (not shown on poster); *$400 A.

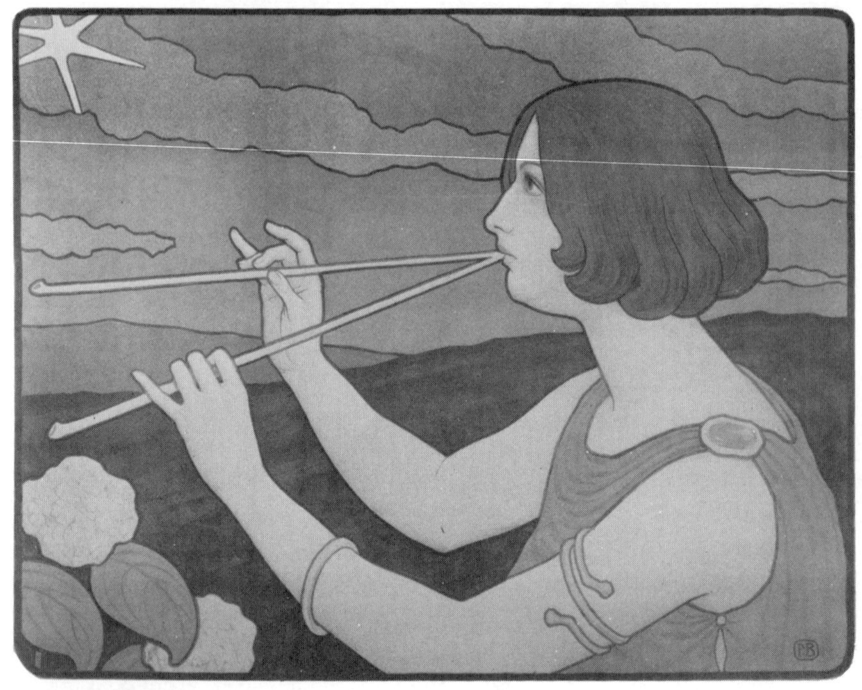

BERTHON, PAUL. "Girl with Pipes," decorative color lithographic panel, 1899; *$520 A. (Christie's)

ELISHA BROWN BIRD — The Chap Book; 1896; 13 1/8" x 18 3/8", slight tape stains at corners; *$275 A.

— The Century for March; lists contributions, including one by Woodrow Wilson; 13½" x 20½", by H.A. Thomas & Wylie Litho. Co., New York, 1896; horizontal fold shows slightly, 3 small tears bottom edge, 1 on left edge; *$150 A.

HENRI BOUTET — Exposition De Pastels Dessins et Gravures Henri Boutet . . .; by Lemercier, Paris, 1895; 15½" x 42", folds show, slight tear in midsection, framed; *$350 A.

WILL BRADLEY — Bradley — His Book; poster entitled "The Kiss", with fleur de lis border & peacock feather design; 28½" x 41", staining along folds, framed; an 1896 woodcut; *$3,400 A.

— Victor Bicycles; printed by J. Ottmann Lith., New York, 1895; 13 3/8" x 4¾", slight restorations along 4 horizontal folds, framed; *$2,200 A.

— When Hearts Are Trumps By Tom Hall; by Stone & Kimball, 1890; 14" x 17 1/8", border stains, 1 3-inch tear upper right corner, a 2-inch tear upper left corner; *$1,500 A.

— Whiting's Ledger Papers; woman kneels on grass, reaching out to touch poppy flowers about her; 9¼" x 19½", 1896; $1,200 D.

— Narcoti-Cure Price $5.00 Cures The Tobacco Habit in from 4 to 10 Days, The Narcoti Chemical Co., Springfield, Mass.; pictures St. George slaying the nicotine monster; 13¾" x 19 7/8", 1895, very fine, framed; *$1,100 A.

— Whiting's Ledger Papers; as noted above; on board with grommet hole at top; slight tape stains at 4 corners; *$900 A.

— Bradley — His Book Ten Cents For Sale Here June; (1896); 8 5/8" x 19 7/8", slight corner stains; *$900 A.

— The Chap Book; young girl kneels among many floating flowers; 1895, 22" x 16", laid on linen; some slight repairs upper corners, light yellow stain in one letter of wording; $750 D.

— Harper's Bazar Easter A.D. 1896; 11" x 16", slight border stains; *$650 A.

— Harper's Bazar Thanksgiving Number 1895; done in green & pink tones; 10¾" x 15¾", slight border stains; *$400 A.

— Field Flowers; announcing book of poems by the late poet; 1899; 10½" x 19½", 3-inch tear lower right, framed, *$400 A.

— Collier's Dramatic Number; 10½" x 14¾", slight stains & some creases at borders, 1901, 1½" tear bottom edge; *$200 A.

WILL CARQUEVILLE — Lippincott's August (1895); 12¼" x 18¾", slight edge stains; *$275 A.

— Lippincott's December (1894); Sober E. Carqueville Litho. Co., Chicago; 12¼" x 18 5/8", 4 corners tape-stained; *$275 A.

— Lippincott's February (1895); 12½" x 19", stains at 4 corners; *$250 A.

RAMON CASAS — Anis del Mono Vicente Bosch Barcelona Espana; 42 1/8" x 86 3/8", by Lith. Henrich & Ca., Barcelona, 1897; slight tears & restorations along folds & at top margin; *$500 A.

HENRI CASSIERS — Red Star Line Antwerpen - New York; delft tile design; O. de Rycker, Bruxelles, 1901; 43 5/8" x 61 1/8", very fine, framed; *$2,600 A.

— Coq Sur Mer; Affiches d'Art O. de Rycker & Mendel, Bruxelles, 1898; 60¼" x 44½", an 8-inch tear from lower right margin, center fold shows slightly; *$1,600 A.

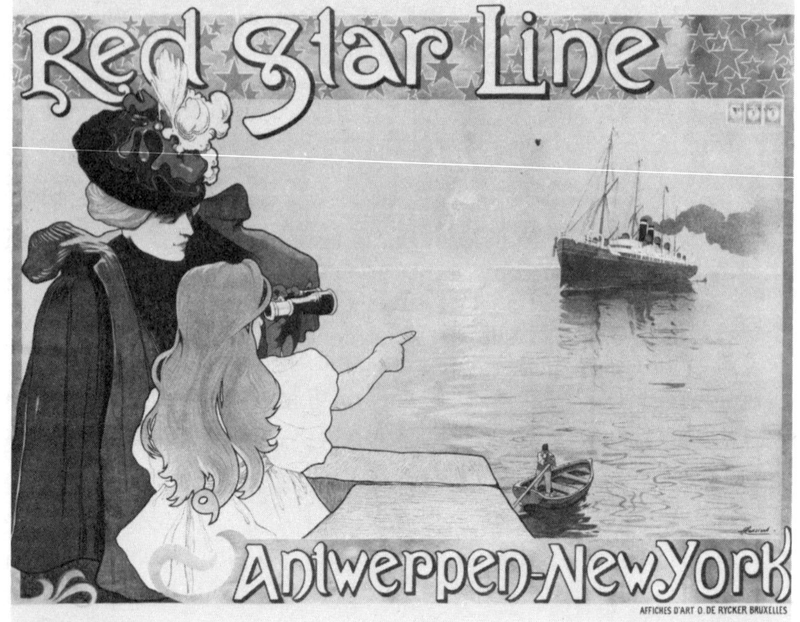

CASSIERS, HENRI. "Red Star Line. Antwerpen-New York"; color lithograph by Affiches d'Art O. de Rycker, Bruxelles, 1899; 48½" x 35 7/8", few barely visible border tears & a 10-inch tear from left; framed; *$5,000 A. (Phillips)

— Red Star Line Anvers-New York, Agence de Bruxelles; 2 seamen in skiff in foreground, with ship "Finland" approaching from background; by O. de Rycker & Mendel, Bruxelles, c. 1900; very fine, museum mounting; $900 A.

JULES CAYRON — Plus de Microbes, Le Sel Chabanal le Seal Desinfectant Aromatique . . . ; by E. Clement, Paris, c. 1898; 33 7/8" x 50", slight staining at folds; *$150 A.

MAURICE CHABAS — Exposition d'Art Decoratif . . .; by Lapina, Paris, 1917; exhibition was to raise funds for soldiers in the trenches; 30½" x 40", slight tears in lower image area & border; *$150 A.

JULES CHERET — Musee Grevin; clown plays mandolin in foregound, woman in yellow dress & wide-brim hat holds out skirt, center; followed by clown in red on brown horse, many people playing, windmill & moon in background; 52" x 38", linen backed, mint condition; $1,800 D.

— Saxoleine Petrole de Surete; lady in bright red dress with red hair holds up oil lamp with green shade, smiling happily, on blue ground; 49" x 35", linen-backed, 1900; mint condition; $1,200 D.

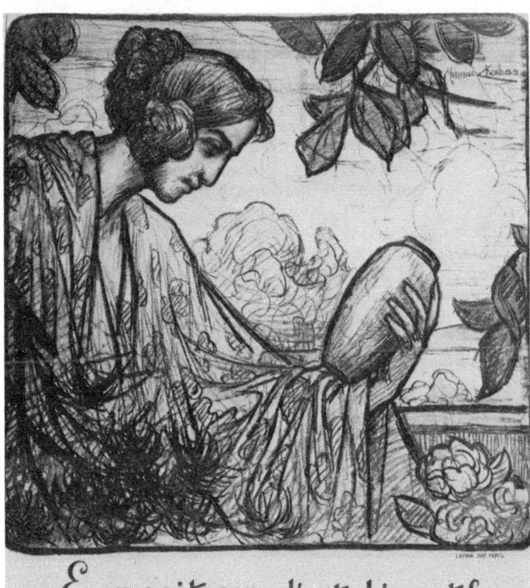

CHABAS, MAURICE. "Exposition d'Art Decoratif . . .", 1917; *$950 A. (Christie's)

— Saxoleine Petrole de Surete; woman facing right with one hand on lamp; by Chaix, Paris, 1894; 331/8" x 48½", folds show; *$1,100 A.

— Saxoleine Petrole de Surete; woman facing left with hands above a lamp; by Chaix, Paris, 1900; 33¼" x 48 1/8", slight stains at paper edge; *$900 A.

— L'Aureole du Midi Petrole du Surete; by Chaix, Paris, 1893; 33 3/8" x 48¼", one 5-inch tear at top not affecting image; *$900 A.

— Halle Aux Chapeau; printed by Imprimerie Chaix (ateliers Cheret), Paris, 1892; image size 46½" x 32¼", linen backed; *$750 A.

— Saxoleine Petrole du Surete; smiling lady in bright red dress/red hair holds up oil lamp with green shade against blue ground; 49" x 34½", linen backed, 1900; minor repairs upper left margin, one crease upper left extends into image; $650 D.

— Bal du Moulin Rouge, Place Blanche . . .; by Chaix, Paris, 1889; 34 1/8" x 48½", folds show, restoration & stains along left & top borders; museum mounting; *$600 A.

— Halle Aux Chapeau; two proofs, both 15 1/8" x 20", by Chaix, Paris, 1891; one missing buff and light blue touch-up, the other complete; *$350 A.

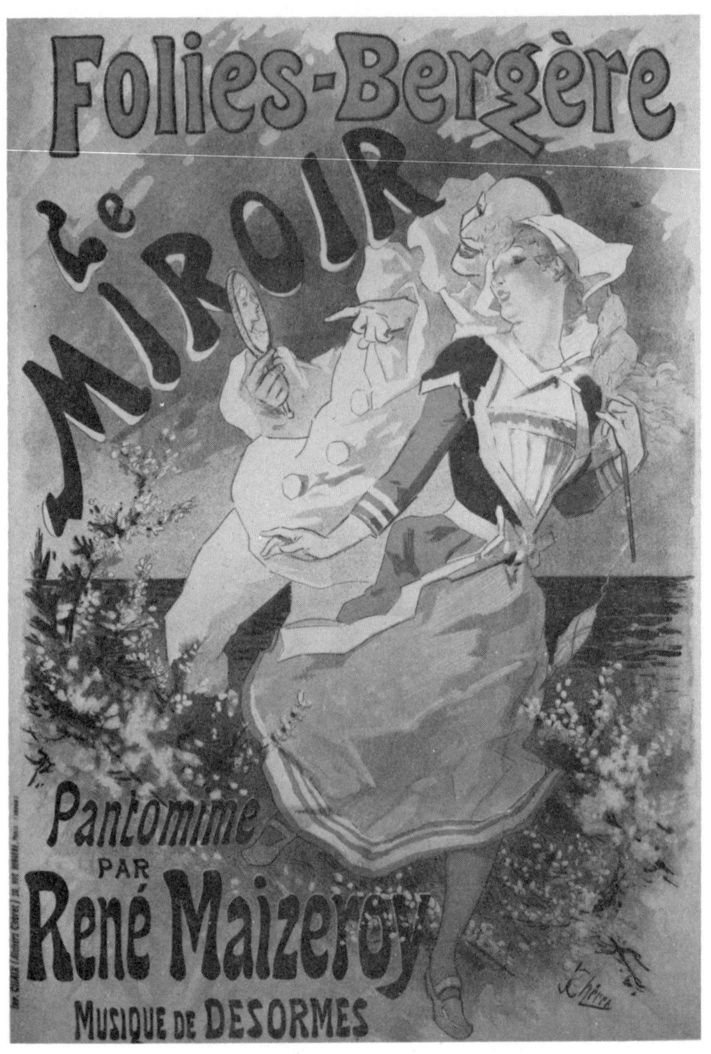

CHERET, JULES. "Folies Bergere. Le Miroir"; *$620 A. (Christie's)

— Halle Aux Chapeau; two proofs, both 15" x 20 5/8", Chaix, Paris, 1894; one missing 2 aqua tints at top & center text, the other complete; both very fine condition; *$350 A.

— Jardin de Paris; printed by Imprimerie Chaix (Ateliers Cheret), Paris, 1890; linen backed, sheet $32\frac{1}{2}$" x $21\frac{1}{4}$"; *$275 A.

ALFRED CHOUBRAC — Casino de Paris, Don Juan aux Enfers . . .; printed by Ateliers Choubrac a Colombes, Seine; 35 1/8" x 50 3/8", tears at folds & in top borders; *$200 A.

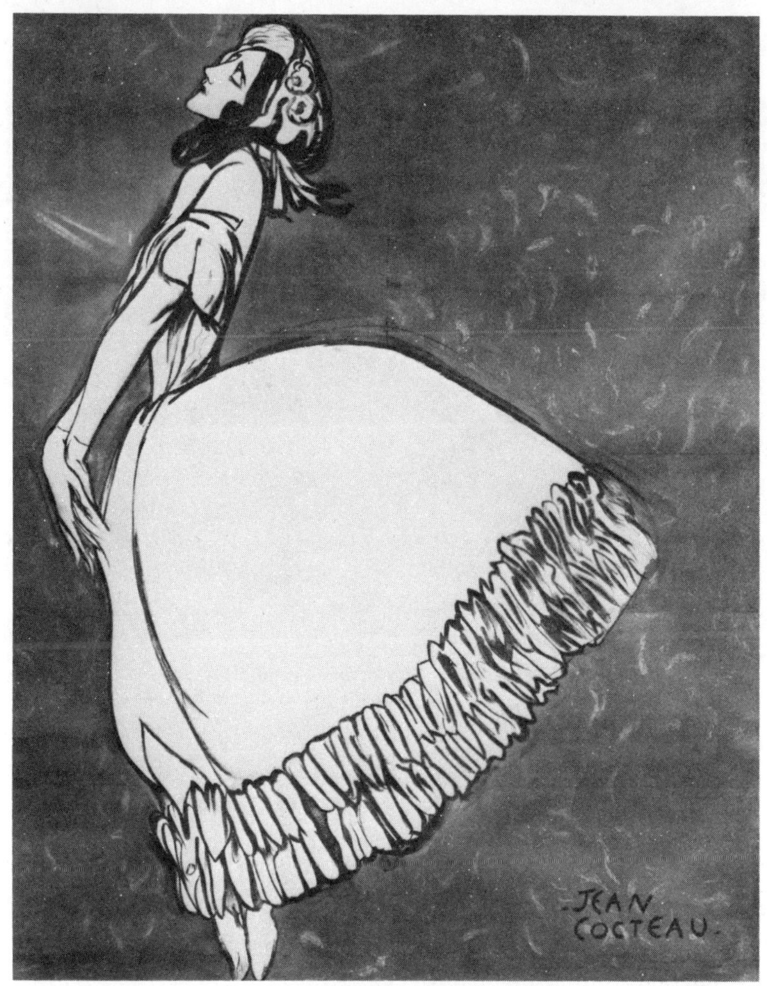

COCTEAU, JEAN. One of two posters (the other showing Nijinsky) originally done by the artist of the Ballet Russe, published by Eugene Verneau & Henri Chacoin, Paris, 1911; 48¾" x 68¼", the larger of two formats; restorations & slight background tears at folds; *$9,000 A. (Phillips)

FRANCISCO DE CIDON — Perfumeria Ladivfer . . .; by Font Reclams, Barcelona, 1903; 35 5/8" x 51 3/8", slight marginal tears, framed; *$1,000 A.

CLERICE FRERES (Victor & Francois) — Folies-Bergere, Le Timbre d'Or . . .; by Minot, Paris, 1900; 30¾" x 46", staining along folds; *$550 A.

AUGUSTE DONNAY — Imprimerie Liegeoise Henri Poncelot . .; printed by Henri Poncelot, Liege; 14 3/8" x 19 5/8", horizontal fold & slight creasing; *$225 A.

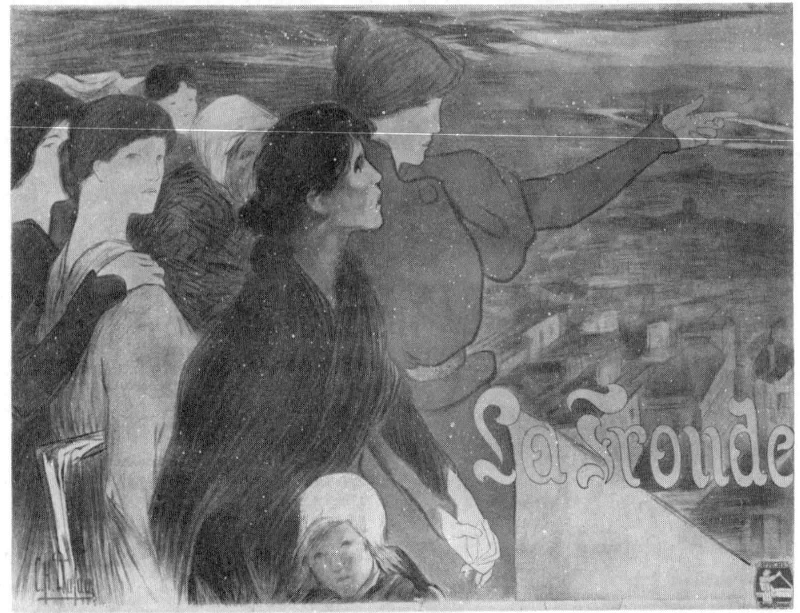

DUFAU, CLEMENTINE-HELENE. "La Fronde"; color lithograph by Impr. Charles Verneau, Paris, 1898; 52½" x 38", slight tears at bottom & left paper edge, framed; *$4,500 A. (Phillips)

L. DUPUY — Fetes de Charite; by L. Cassan, Toulouse; 36¾" x 40 3/8", tear from bottom to center; framed; *$800 A.

HENRY B. EDDY — The Criterion 10c A Copy; 1897, 13 7/8" x 21¾", staining left text border; *$200 A.

FARIA — Cecile Delagarde; by Fromstecher, Paris, c. 1897; 25 5/8" x 64", staining mainly marginal, some tears & folds; museum mounting, *$275 A.

GOERGES DE FEURE — Pierrefort; by Chaix, Paris, 1898; 32½" x 24 5/8", 2 slight tears at left border; fine frame; *$8,500 A.

— Paris-Almanach Edite par Sagot; printed by Bourgerie & Cie, Paris, 1894; 24" x 31", slight creases mid-section, framed; *$3,000 A.

— Comedie Parisienne La Loie Fuller . . . Salome; printed by P. Lemenil, Asnieres (Seine), 1895; 36½" x 50 5/8", some staining along folds & in margin; museum mounting; *$2,400 A.

— Salon des Cent; for the 5th exposition; by Bourgerie, Paris (not shown on poster), 1894; 15 3/8" x 23¾", restoration upper border; framed; *$1,200 A.

— Retour; from *L'Estampe Moderne;* 16½" x 20½", custom framed, mint condition; $450 D.
Retour; part of the *L'Estampe Moderne* series, with publisher's blind-stamp; image has very busy background with girl at right looking out at viewer; 14¼" x 10", good condition; *$200 A.

MAURICE DUFRENE — Rayon Des Soieres; 32" x 47½", linen backed, mint condition; $350 D.

HENRY GERBAULT — Chocolat Carpentier; by Courmont Freres, Paris, 1895; 36¼" x 50 7/8", foxing in background, stains along folds; *$350 A.

J. J. GOULD — Lippincott's March (1896); 11½" x 18 1/8", violet/maroon/yellow coloration; slight creases in image, border stains; *$250 A.
— How To Feed Children By Louise E. Hogan For Sale Here; 1896, 11" x 16 3/8", slight border stains; *$225 A.

EUGENE GRASSET — Marque Georges Richard Cycles & Automobiles; printed by Vaurigard G. de Malherbe, Paris, 1899; 58 7/8" x 43 7/8", minor tear at far left and far right margins; framed; *$3,000 A.
— Salondescent; woman with left arm encircling flowers, other holding book/pencil; 1894, printed on Japon, custom frame size 26" x 31"; $2,800 D.
— A New Life of Napoleon Magnificently Illustrated Is Now Beginning In The Century Magazine; central picture depicts Napoleon atop wooly-maned horse; 1894, 39 1/8" x 84 5/8", text areas top and bottom have been "recreated," framed; Grasset's first poster for *The Century;* *$2,800 A.
— Coquetterie; red-haired woman putting large orange flower in her hair, with ecru lace collar on green dress; 1897, 30" x 29", linen-backed, 1897; $2,500 D.
— Jalousie; circular portrait of draped woman with golden hair in lush garden with yellow flowers & dark blue trees; 1897, 39¼" x 29", linen backing, 1897; slight creases in image skillfully repaired; custom framed lithograph; $1,500 D.
— Grafton Glalery; beautiful woman looks down, holds stem of Iris in left hand, bowl of flowers in right arm; skin/dress color natural contrast with blue flowers & ground; 1893, 29" x 18", linen backed; minute tears top edge; $950 D.
— A La Place Clichy; by J. Minot, Paris, 1891; 45 3/8" x 62½", folds show slightly, 2 tears man's jacket on right side; Jack Rennert notes this may be a 1913 re-issue; *$800 A.

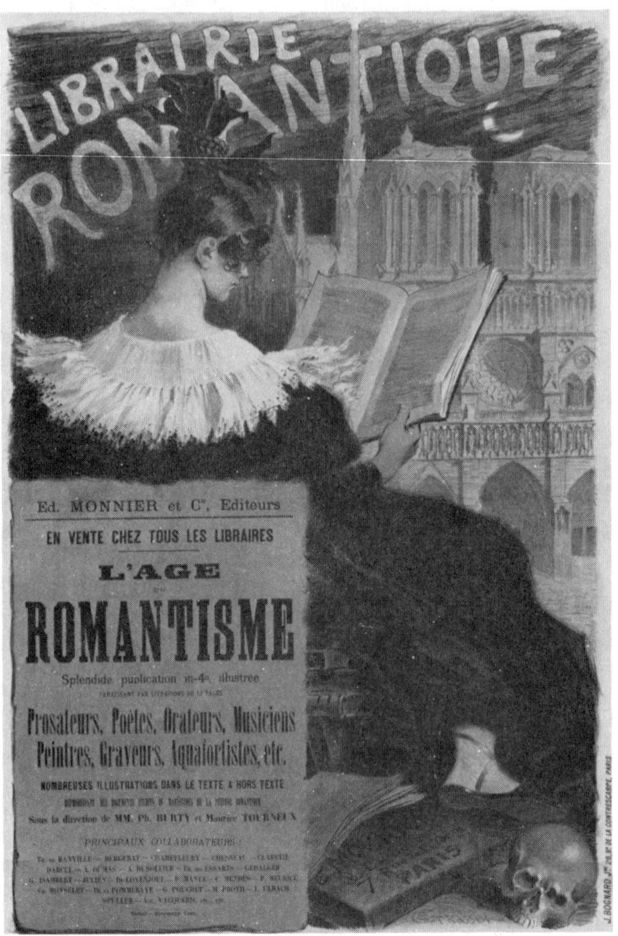

GRASSET, EUGENE. "Librairie Romantique . . .", color lithograph by J. Bognard, Paris, 1887; 34¾" x 50¾", slight stains at vertical fold, framed; *$3,800 A. (Phillips)

— Belle Jardiniere; red-haired woman reaches up to pluck blossom from tree; calendar is inserted lower left; 1894, 28" x 18", linen backed, mint condition, custom framed; $550 D.

— Nouveau Larousse Illustre; test band at bottom notes that, starting March, 1898, this publication will consist of 7 issues and cost 170 francs; by Vaugirard & de Malherbe, Paris, 1897; 14 7/8" x 22 1/8", slight marginal staining, framed; *$400 A.

— The June Century. Napoleon in Egypt; 1895, 14 5/8" x 20½", creases top and corners, stains bottom left paper edge; Grasset's second Century poster; *$400 A.

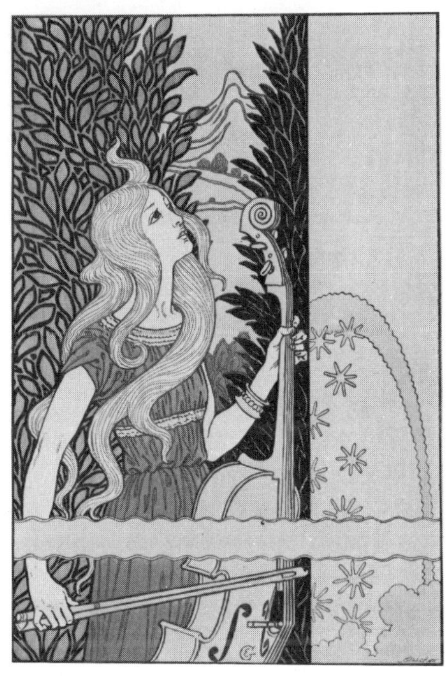

GRASSET, EUGENE. "Le Violencelliste," without lettering; *$100 A. (Christie's)

— Harper's Bazar Christmas Number 1891; shows Mary & child Jesus among Lilies; 11¼" x 16 1/8", 4 corners tape-stained; *$350 A.

— Harper's Magazine, Christmas, 1892; red-haired woman looks over shoulder as she blows a horn; dress a drab green, dark blue the predominant ground color; 16½" x 12", mint condition, custom framed with display placard; $275 D.

— Historie de France; woman sits on throne with book inscribed with names of France's heroes & French flag; 1894, 48" x 32½", linen backed, some small paper loss right margin; $275 D.

H. GRAY — Petrole Stella; printed by Courmont Freres, Paris, 1897; 37½" x 49¾", fine condition, framed; *$800 A.

JULES-ALEXANDRE GRUN — Concert de la Pepiniere; printed J. Thil, Paris, 1902; 37¼" x 51¼", restored tears upper right & left corner margins, framed; *$2,200 A.

— Moulin-Rouge, Theatre Concert; by J. Thil, Paris, c. 1898; 33¾" x 48 1/8", slight tear & restoration lower left margin; *$850 A.

— Cabaret artistique Le Carillon; by Formstecher, Paris, c. 1895; 24 1/8" x 31½", stains at top) *$300 A.

HENRI GUYDO — Amara Blanqui; by Camis, Paris, 1898; 44 44 7/8" x 76¾", very fine; *$500 A.

HAMNER — Delhaize Freres, Le Cafe; Lith. J. Goffart, Bruxelles, 1898; 26 7/8" x 50½", very fine, framed, *$750 A.

FRANK HAZENPLUG — The Emerson and Fisher Company Carriage Builders Cincinnati Ohio USA; printed by Stone & Kimball, Chicago, 1896; 14 1/8" x 19 5/8", folds are visible; *$600 A.

— Galloping Dick by H.B. Marriott Watson Published by Stone & Kimball; 1896; 14 1/8" x 21 1/8", slight restorations at 4 corners, 2-inch tear lower left corner; *$400 A.

— The Chap-Book (1896); woman in bentwood chair reading book or magazine propped against goblet; 13 7/8" x 21 1/8", tape stains at corners; *$400 A.

— The Chap-Book; 1895, 9 1/8" x 14¾", woman in red dress against black/white background; tape stains in corners; *$300 A.

PAUL HELLEU — Ed. Sagot; woman with hair up & bustled toward viewer looks at pictures, with red-chalk against peach coloring; 1901, 42" x 30", linen backed, mint condition; $300 D.

ARSENE HERBINIER — Salon des Cent; 1898, for January, 1899 exhibition; 16 7/8" x 14¾", slight tear 2/4" from top, framed; *$600 A.

A. HERPIN — Malo-Les-Bains pres Dunkerque; printed by L. Geisler aux Chatelles, 1898; 32 7/8" x 46", folds show, slight marginal tears; *$500 A.

HIGBY (?) — J. Manz & Co. 183-5-7 Monroe St. Chicago; pink & white lanterns hung like beaded curtain before lady; uses metallic gold/blue/green/red/black; 1896, 11½" x 18½", slight stain outer edges; *$650 A.

ARNOST HOFBAUER — Hana Kvapilova Recitace; 1899, 29 1/8" x 41 7/8", fine, framed; *$2,000 A.

ADOLF HOHENSTEIN — Cloisonne Artistic Glass; by Ricordi, Milano, 1899; 25" x 37¼", tears & restorations top & bottom, framed; *$600 A.

FRANZ VON HOLDER — Pour L'Art 1906 XIV Exposition Peinture, Sculpture, Musee Moderne . . .; by J.E. Goosens, Bruxelles, 1906; 19½" x 33¾", very fine; *$275 A.

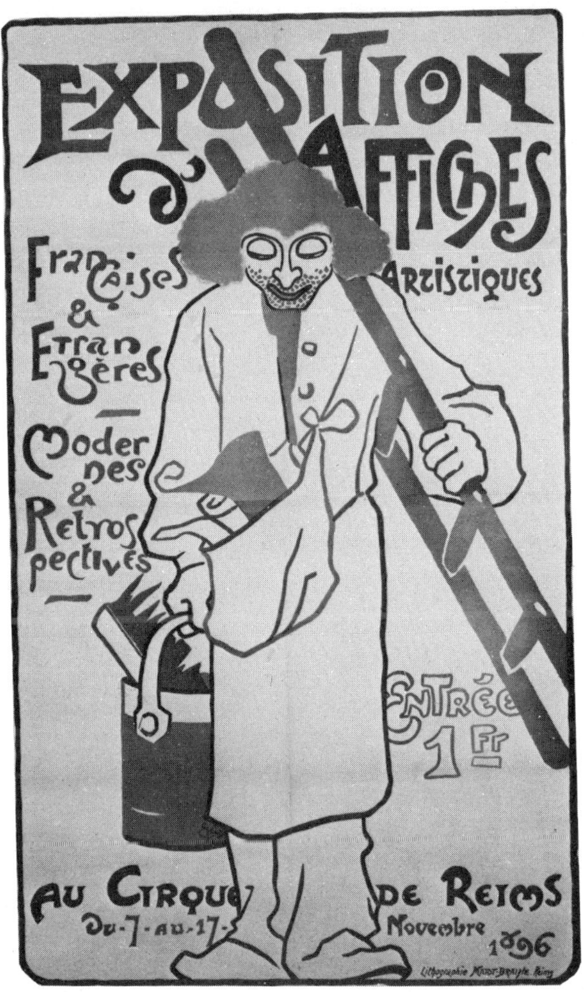

KALAS, ERNEST. "Exposition d'Affiches . . . de Reims"; color lithograph by Matot-Braine, Reims, 1896; 31½" x 54", folds show slightly, one of only two posters done by Kalas; *$2,200 A. (Phillips)

HENRI GABRIEL IBELS — Tous les Soits Irene Henry a l'Horloge; by G. Bataille, Paris, 1894; 35 1/8" x 50½", slight staining at folds; *$1,500 A.

— Salon des Cent, Salon de la Plume . . . ; by Eugene Verneau, Paris, 1893; 15¾" x 23½", folds barely visible; *$1,100 A.

GUSTAVE LORAIN — Art et Decoration . . .; by Lemercier, Paris, 1899; 17¼" x 24¾", very fine, museum mounted; seemingly derivative of Grasset; *$400 A.

E. CHARLES LUCAS — Peugeot Cycles; printed by Affiches Camis, Paris, 1897; 41¾" x 55", very fine; *$400 A.

FERDINAND LUNEL — Rouxel & Dubois Paris; pictures 2 bikers on tandem bicycle in space; printed by Charles Verneau, Paris, c. 1894; 54½" x 38¾", stains & slight restoration along folds; *$375 A.

METIVET — Eugenie Buffet; a Lautrec-like female stands before brick wall wearing orange scarf; 1896, custom framed on linen backing; $2,800 D.

GEORGES MEUNIER — Papier a Cigarettes JOB . . .; by Chaix, Paris, 1894; 2-sheet version, 33½" x 94 5/8", slight tears at folds; *$650 A.

— Theatre de L'Opera . . .; Chaix, Paris, 1895; 35 5/8" x 43¾", slight stains at top; *$600 A.

— Papier a Cigarettes JOB . . .; smaller version of above-cited poster, Chaix, Paris, 1894; 33 3/8" x 43½", fine frame; *$500 A.

— Pastilles au Miel Prunet; Chaix, Paris, 1894; 33 3/8" x 47¾", tears at folds; *$400 A.

— Excursions Normandie & Bretagne; Chaix, Paris, 1897; 29 5/8" x 41 1/8", slight tape stain lower left & right borders; *$400 A.

A. MICHELE — Chaudfontaine Gd. Establissement Thermal; for gambling establishment; by P. Lemenil, Asnieres, 1895; 29½" x 42 7/8", very slight stain far right paper edge; *$900 A.

MISTI — A Pygmalion . . . Blanc Toile Lingerie; printed by B. Servin, Toulouse-Paris, 1901; 4-sheet poster, 124¾" x 94¼", some stains along folds; *$1,000 A.

— Les Modern's . . .; by Lithographie Nouvelle, Asnieres, c. 1900; 30 1/8" x 45 1/8", slight border staining; *$375 A.

ETIENNE MOREAU-NELATON — Saint-Jean du Doigt . . .; by Charles Verneau, Paris, 1894; 38" x 52¾", 3 slight tears from bottom paper edge; *$100 A.

ALPHONSE MUCHA — Bieres de la Meuse; beautiful woman with large red flower in her hair leans forward facing viewer, holding tankard of ale in 1 hand, other hand propping head; by F. Champenois, Paris, 1897; linen-backed, no mention of size, very fine condition; $10,000 D.

— La Samaritaine; theater poster, decorated circle behind woman's head has Hebrew lettering, "Sarah Bernhardt"

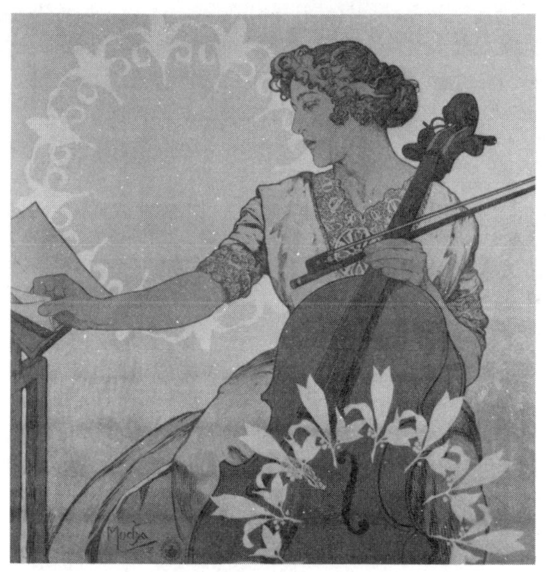

MUCHA, ALPHONSE. "Zdenka Cerny," 1913, no text; *$1,500 A. (Christie's)

printed in English; woman faces front, leans on large vase; 1897, 67½" x 22½", linen backed; $9,500 D.

— Moet & Chandon; 2 posters, each 9 7/8" x 25", framed; one for Grand Cremant Imperial, the other for Champagne White Star; *$9,500 A.

— Hamlet; another Bernhardt theatrical poster, showing Hamlet as a young blonde man holding sword, wearing cape; 1899, 78" x 28" on linen backing; $9,500 D.

— Bieres de la Meuse; same as above in design, 56" x 37" on linen backing, 1897; $8,000 D.

— Salon des Cent, 1896; by F. Champenois, Paris; 17 1/8" x 25 1/8", framed, flawless; *$8,000 A.

— JOB; purple background, golden macaroni curls; by F. Champenois, Paris, 1897; 18" x 26 1/8", very fine, framed; pencil signature; *$8,000 A.

— Amants; by Camis, Paris, 1895; 53" x 40 3/8", staining at midsection, slight tears & creases, fine frame; *$7,500 A.

— Pevecke Sdruzeni Ucitelu Moravskych; for Moravian Teachers' Choir; by V. Neubert, Smichov-Prague, 1911; 31¼" x 42¾", very fine, fine frame; *$6,000 A.

— Monaco. Monte-Carlo; by F. Champenois, Paris, 1897; 29¼" x 42½", very fine, framed; *$5,500 A.

Salon des Cent Juin 1897; by F. Champenois, Paris, 1897; 18 1/8" x 26 1/8", very fine, fine frame; *$5,000 A.

— JOB; woman sitting in circular motif; by F. Champenois, Paris, 1898; 38 5/8" x 58 3/8", very fine, framed. *$5,000 A.
— "Four Ages of Man"; set of 4 separate images, each 7½" x 7", unframed, very good condition; $4,500 D.
— Oesterreich . . . Paris 1900; created for Austrian Pavilion at the Paris World's Fair of 1900; by Kunstanstalt G. Czeiger, Wien, 1900; 26" x 40", linen backed, unframed; $4,500 D.
— Sarah Bernhardt American Tour Direction of Abbey, Schoeffel & Grau; by Strobridge Lithographers, Cincinnati, 1896; 29 1/8" x 77 5/8", very fine, framed; *$4,000 A.
— Champagne Ruinart; 21" x 43", gold leaf mat, triple matted, in Art Nouveau gold frame; few insignificant repairs; $4,000 D.
— Moet and Chandon, White Star; woman in flowing pink gown holds basket of grapes, surrounded by fields of flowers; 1899, linen backed, mint condition; $3,800 D.
— Nestle's Food for Infants; 19½" x 32½", original Art Nouveau frame with double material-covered mats, few slight repairs; $3,500 D.
— Biscuits Champagne Lefevre-Utile; shows 2 fashionably dressed women seated with standing man; by F. Champenois, Paris, 1897; all copies published on board with grommets; 13 5/8" x 20 1/8", very fine condition in fine frame; *$3,500 A.
— Biscuits Lefevre-Utile (date 1897 at bottom); by F. Champenois, Paris, 1896; pictures one woman; 17½" x 24¼"H, usual slight framing at bottom, framed; *$3,400 A.
— Biscuits Champagne Lefevre-Utile; 2 fashionable women seated at table with man standing; by F. Champenois, Paris, 1897; 13 5/8" x 20 1/8", 2 small ½-inch tears at top (where grommets were?), framed) *$3,000 A.
— Oesterreich . . . Paris 1900; by Kunstanstalt G. Czeiger, Wien, 1900; 28" x 39 5/8", very fine, framed; *$3,000 A.
— "Winter"; beautiful woman clad in green showing snow on bare tree branches; 1896, 31" x 51", custom framed on linen backing, minor scratches; $2,800 D.
— 1918-1928; for 10th anniversary of Czechoslovakian republic; by K. Kritz, Karlin-Prague; 33" x 47 5/8", very fine, museum mounting; *$2,700 A.
— unlettered specimen; shows 2 men, 1 with shirt, other without, in front of woman above with floral head dress; another version (not this) includes text banner at bottom; by

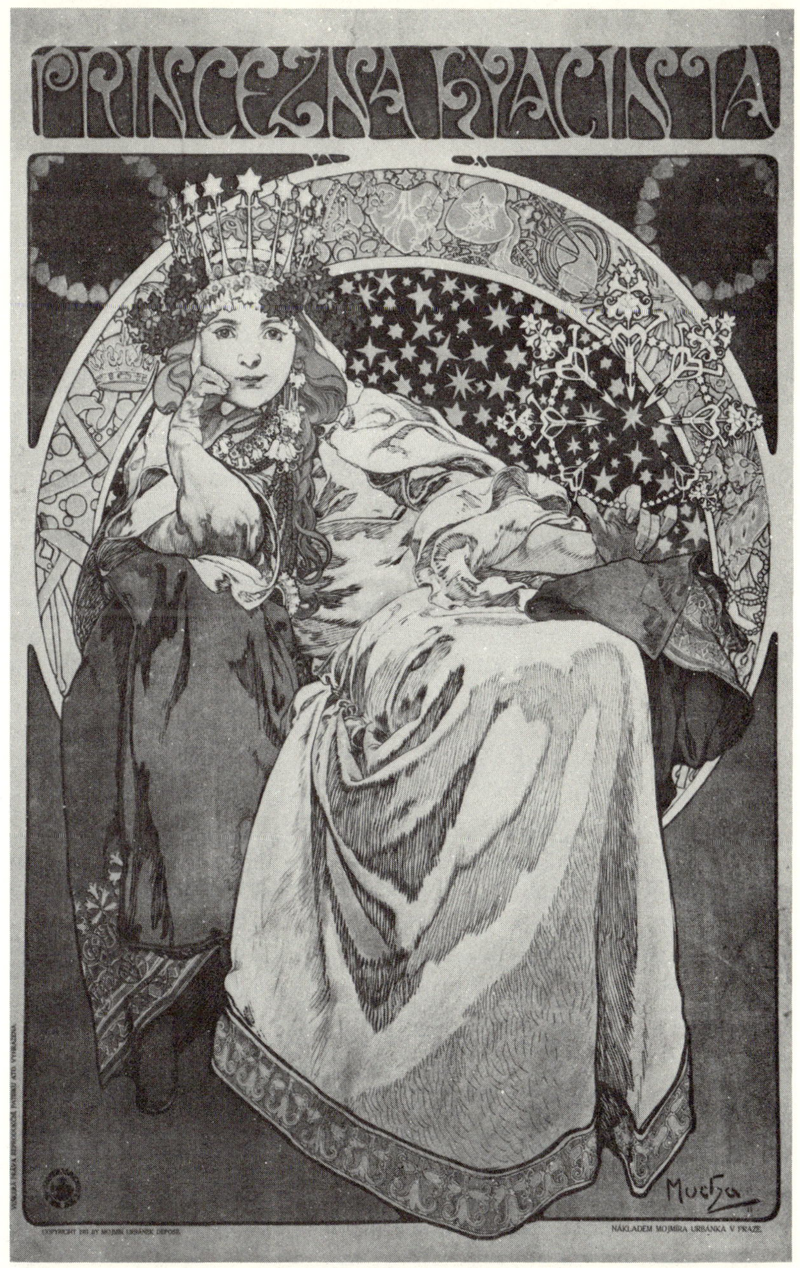

MUCHA, ALPHONSE. "Princezna Hyacinta," color lithograph published by V. Neubert, Smichov-Prague, 1911; 32 7/8" x 49½", 9" tear at top, 5" tear at bottom in a fine frame; use of gold & silver by Mucha on this one; *$9,400 A. (Phillips)

Jan Ziegloser, Prague, 1925; 32 5/8" x 48", very fine, museum mounting; *$2,700 A.

— Krajinska Vystava V Ivancicich; for a 1913 regional fair in Ivancice that may not have taken place; by V. Neubert, Smichov-Prague, 1912; 23 3/8" x 36 7/8", very fine, framed; *$2,700 A.

— Loterie Naronni Jenroty Pro Jihozxpanni Moravu Y Brne . . .; lottery for National Union for Southwest Moravia at Brno; by V. Neubert, Smichov-Prague, 1912; 39 3/8" x 74¼", text banners at top and bottom, slight tears top border, framed; *$2,700 A.

— Slavnosti; 11½" x 22", material-covered mat conforms to poster shape, in original Art Nouveau frame, fine condition; $2,600 D.

— Zdenka Czerny; framed, autographed by subject; $2,500 D.

— Flirt. Biscuits Lefevre-Utile; by F. Champenois, Paris; without mention of Grand Prix Paris 1900 at bottom; $2,250 D.

— Flirt. Biscuits Lefevre-Utile; by F. Champenois, Paris; 1900, 19" x 31½", custom-framed on linen backing; $1,600 D.

— Zdenka Czerny; 1913, 43" x 43¾", slight crease lower portion about 10"L, barely visible; no text; linen backing; $1,600 D.

— Flirt. Biscuits Lefevre-Utile; by F. Champenois, Paris, 1900; slight foxing in border is barely visible; with mention of Grand Prix Paris 1900; *$1,500 A.

— "The Harp Player"; lithograph, 21" x 15½"; *$900 A.

— Gismonda; from Maitres De L'Affiche; margin trimmed, otherwise excellent condition; double matted velvet & gold leaf framing; 14" x 22"; $900 D.

— La Samaritene; from Maitres De L'Affiche; trimmed margin, otherwise excellent; rust suede mat with wide semi-circular foil; 17" x 24½"; $850 D.

MANUEL ORAZI — La Maison Moderne; woman in shades of green/blue/orange; by J. Minot, Paris, 1900; 46" x 32 5/8", pronounced horizontal fold, framed; *$22,000 A.

— Palais de la Danse; designed for 1900 World's Fair in Paris; girls swirls around with dress flowing with cascading bubbles coming from glass in her hand; 61" x 22", linen backed, one small tear at bottom just entering image; $4,500 D.

— Lique Vinicole de France; by Charles Vernau, Paris, c. 1900; woman squeezing grapes hanging above bowl; 55" x 39 3/8", folds show slightly, framed; *$3,500 A.

BLANCHE OSTERTAG — Carson Pirie Scott & Co. January Undermuslin Sale; 17 7/8" x 19¼", c. 1905, very fine; *$850 A.

— Carson Pirie Scott & Co. January Linen and White Goods Sale; pictures mother & child; 13¼" x 19½", c. 1905, very fine; *$800 A.

— Carson Pirie Scott & Co. January Linens & White Goods Sale; 13 3/8" x 20"; c. 1905, folds show; (NOTE: this is different image from the similarly-titled poster above) *$650 A.

PAL — La Loie Fuller Folies-Bergere; state prior to use of final red plate; printed by Paul Dupont, Paris, c. 1895; 30 7/8" x 47 7/8", folds show, some slight upper marginal tears, framed; *$3,000 A.

— same as above; slight printer's creases, horizontal fold at top; museum mounting; *$2,800 A.

— Dentifrice Oriental . . .; Paul Dupont, Paris, 1893-1900 period; 57" x 48¾", folds show slightly, slight staining in top & bottom borders; *$700 A.

— Casino de Paris Programme. Tour les Soirs Blocksom and Burns . . .; Paul Dupont, Paris; 32¼" x 48½", slight stains at folds; *$600 A.

— Folies-Bergere. La Belle Guerrero; by Caby & Chardin, Paris; 32¼" x 47¾", slight staining at folds; *$600 A.

— Humber; man tipping hat to lady, both on bicycles; by Paul Dupont, Paris; 58 7/8" x 43 5/8", slight staining bottom paper edge, unobtrusive tears in right margin; *$550 A.

— Visitez Le Ralais Royal . . .; by Chardin, Paris; 40¾" x 52 3/8", restorations in several small areas; *$400 A.

— Ambassadeurs. Diamantine; by Paul Dupont, Paris, 1894; 30¾" x 47¾", restoration & staining at folds; *$300 A.

MAXFIELD PARRISH — Poster Show, Pennsylvania Academy of the Fine Arts, Phildelphia; by Ledger Show Printers, Philadelphia, 1896; 24½" x 34½", signed in pencil in lower right margin; printer's ink minor smudges lower right corner of impression; framed; white & brown tones; *$6,000 A.

— The Century Midsummer Holiday Number. August; by Thomas & Wylie Lithographic Co., 1897; 13½" x 19 7/8", staining & slight corner tears; *$900 A.

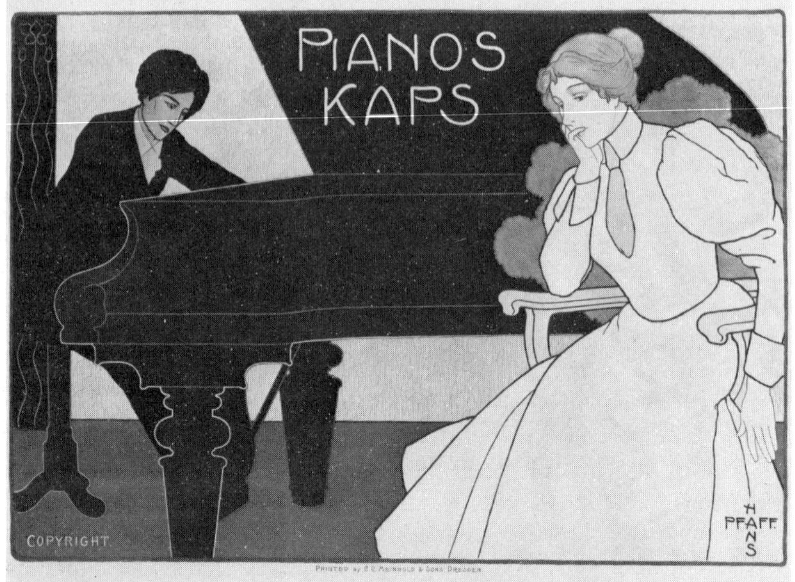

PFAFF, HANS. "Pianos Kaps," color lithograph by C.C. Meinhold & Sons, Dresden, 1897; 40 7/8" x 29¼", fine condition, framed; printed for the English-speaking market; *$3,600 A. (Phillips)

— Harper's Weekly National Authority on Amateur Sports; 15" x 20", c. 1896; slight staining at folds; *$650 A.

RENE PEAN — Montmarte Moulin de la Galette . . .; by Chaix, Paris, 1898; 42½" x 61½"; *$400 A.

— Winter Gardens. Blackpool. Les Montagnes Russes; by Chaix, Paris, 1904; 35" x 48¾", very fine; *$400 A.

— Le Fiance de Thylda; a French opera poster, with gaily costumed Parisiennes celebrating; 1900, 33" x 23", linen backing, very fine; $175 D.

EDWARD PENFIELD — Golf Calendar by Edward Penfield Published by R.H. Russell 1899; entire calendar: cover + 9 sheets, each representing one of 9 holes, covering entire year, as issued; each sheet 9 5/8" x 17 7/8", very fine, framed; *$5,000 A.

— same but cover only, 10" x 18", very fine; *$550 A.

— Harper's Christmas (1894); cat sits on lap of reading woman; 12 3/8" x 17¾", folds show; *$400 A.

— About Paris by Richard Harding Davis Illustrated by C.D. Gibson. Harper & Brothers, Publishers; 1895, 9 1/8" x 14½", slight corner stains; *$300 A.

— Three Gringos in Central America and Venezuela By Richard Harding Davis Illustrated Harper & Brothers, N.Y.; 1896, 11½" x 17½", slight restoration at folds; *$225 A.

— Perly-Cross A Novel by R.D. Blackmore. Harper & Brothers New York; 1894, 9¼" x 14", slight staining & creases at corners; *$125 A.

PRIVAT-LIVEMONT — Automobile Club de France. 5me Salon . . .; by J. Barreau, Paris, 1902; 39 1/8" x 50 7/8", staining & tears in margin barely visible, museum mounting; with side text; *$4,600 A.

— Automobile Club de France (in one line at top); by J. Barreau, Paris, 1903; 36¾" x 50¼", folds show slightly, museum mounting; *$4,500 .

— Bitter Oriental; by J.L. Goffart, Bruxelles, 1897; 31¾" x 43½", very fine, framed; *$3,500 A.

FREDERICK WINTHROP RAMSDELL — American Crescent Cylces; by Chaix, Paris, 1901; this is the larger of 2 formats; 40 7/8" x 61 3/8", slight tears in upper and lower borders; *$1,500 A.

ETHEL REED — The Penny Magazine Sold Here. 5 cts; printed by Hayes Bros., Philadelphia, 1896; 10¼" x 21 5/8", design in bright red & navy blue; very fine; *$600 A.

— The Boston Herald Every Lady Will Read Fashion Supplement March 24; 1894, 11 5/8" x 18 5/8", fold & corner stain shows; *$250 A.

LOUIS J. RHEAD — Poster Calendar by L. Prang & Co. Boston, U.S.A.; complete calendar, 13 lithographs, each sheet 11½" x 16½", professionally framed, very fine; *$1,700 A.

— Poster Calendar 1897; by L. Prang, Boston, 1896; cover + 4 sheets, 13¾" x 19 1/8", few marginal tears/stains, framed; *$1,200 A.

— Packer's Tar Soap Exquisite Cleanser, Soothing Antiseptic for the Hair and Skin; by J. Ottmann Lith. Co., New York, 1895; 13 7/8" x 19 7/8", slight crease far left, card stock, grommet hole at top, framed; *$900 A.

— The Century Magazine for June; pictures roses & woman; 1896, 10 7/8" x 21", slight tear lower right corner, fold shows; *$500 A.

— Poster Calendar by L. Prang & Co. Boston, U.S.A.; cover only, 1895, 11½" x 16 1/8", very fine; *$400 A.

— Scribners for Xmas; 1895, 13 1/8" x 19 3/8", horizontal fold shows, corner stains; *$400 A.

— St. Nicholas For Young Folks Edited By Mary Mapes Dodge August Holiday Number Now Ready The Century Co. New York; 1894, 10 5/8" x 13 7/8", folds show; *$250 D.

— The Century Christmas Number (other text mentions "The New Life of Napoleon"); 1894, smaller of 2 formats; 13" x 19 1/8", slight staining at 4 corners; *$250 A.

— The Evolution of Chruch Music by the Reverend Frank Landon Humphreys . . . Charles Scribner's Sons, Publishers, New York; 12¼" x 18 1/8", black & white linear design, tape stains 4 corners; *$75 A.

ALEJANDRO DE RIQUER E INGLADA — Ayuniamiento de Barcelona . . .; by J. Thomas, Barcelona, 1895; 59½" x 38 7/8", slight tears & stains border only, museum mounting; *$900 A.

GEORGES ROCHEGROSSE — Automobile Club de France 4me Exposition Internationale . . .; by L. Barreau, Paris, 1901; 37" x 50¼", folds barely visible, museum mounting; *$800 A.

HENRY M. ROSENBERG — The Century for September; woman facing left toward trees in upper left corner; by G.H. Buek & Co., Lithographers, New York, 1896; 14½" x 20 7/8", tape stains at 4 corners; *$200 A.

LEON VICTOR SOLON — The Studio . . .; 1896, 23 5/8" x 35¾", border stains; *$300 A.

THEOPHILE ALEXANDRE STEINLEN — Lait pur de la Vingeanne Sterilise; linen backed, mint condition; $13,500D.

— Tournee du Chat Noir; open-eyed black car stares forward; 1896, large version: 54" x 37", linen backed, slight creasing throughout but generally fine- $9,200 D.

— same as immediately prior, fully titled: Prochainement. Tournee du Chat Noir de Rodolphe Salis; by Charles Verneau, Paris, 1896; 38¾" x 54 7/8", a few unobtrusive tears & stains, fine frame; *$8,300 A.

— Le Journal . . . Grand Roman Inedit par Dubut de Laforest; by Charles Verneau, Paris, 1899; censored version, larger format: 49 1/8" x 73 7/8", full text banner; slight staining/creasing at top edge, framed; *$8,000 A.

— Ambassadeurs Yvette Guilbert Tous Les Soirs; by Charles Verneau, Paris, 1894; 30 5/8" x 70¼", slight tears along folds & in lower left background; *$7,500 A.

— Tournee du Chat Noir . . .; 52" x 37", 4-inch repair, framed; *$5,500 A.

— unlettered, picturing two cats, one dark, the other particolored; by Charles Verneau, Paris, 1894; was lithograph only version of Steinlen's "Exposition a la Bodiniere" poster; 20¾" x 23 7/8", very fine in fine frame; *$3,400 A.

— Mothu et Doria. Scenes Impressionnistes; by Pajol & Cie., Editeurs, Impressions Artistiques, Paris, 1893; 34¾" x 47 1/8", staining along folds & in background, framed; *$3,000 A.

— Arabian Racahout; mother spoon-feeds small child; 55½" x 20", linen backed, mint condition; $750 D.

TAMAGNO — L'Ete Ostende; by Affiches-Camis, Paris; 47 7/8" x 73¼", very fine; *$500 A.

— Terrot Bijon Motorcycles; by Lithographie Parisienne; 38¼" x 54 7/8", creases in right margin; *$375 A.

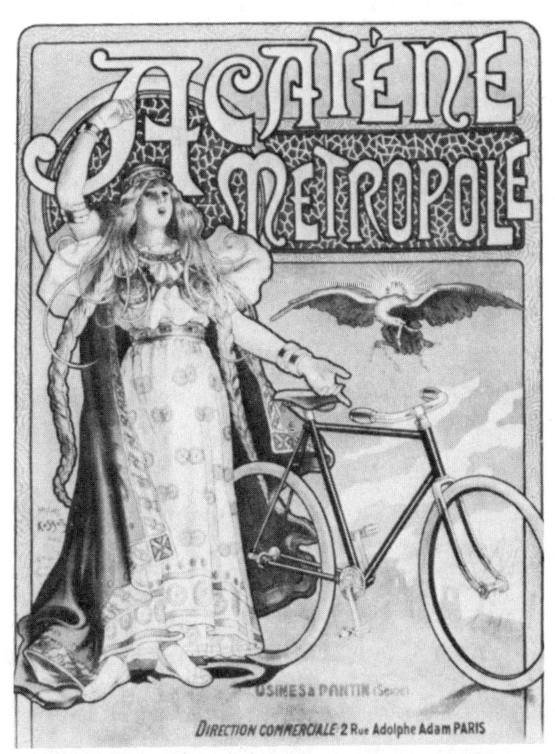

TICHON, CHARLES, after L. Baylac. "Acatene Metropole," color lithograph by Affiches Kossuth, Paris, c. 1898; sheet size 52½" x 41½", linen backed; *$525 A. (Morton's)

LOUIS TAUZIN — "Royan"; color lithograph printed by F. Champenois, Paris, c. 1895; sheet size 40¼" x 29", linen backed; *$475 A.

HENRY THIRIET — Omega Sans Chaine; bicycles, picturing winged woman walking bike, c. 1897; 38¼" x 55 1/8", some tears at folds & paper edge, slight ink offsetting, framed; *$1,800 A.

— same, one crease across upper bosom; 1895, 36" x 55", linen backed; $1,600 D.

HENRI DE TOULOUSE-LAUTREC — Caudieux; man in tuxedo minces about stage; 1893, 51¼" x 37½", linen backed, condition questionable, custom framed; $13,500 D.

— The Chap Book; bar scene; 1896, full margins, 16¼" x 23", linen backed; $10,500 D.

— May Milton; 1895, 23½" x 30¾", very fine, framed; reportedly limited to 100 copies; *$9,000 A.

— Catalogue d'Affiches A. Arnould . . .; 1896, 2nd state with lettering of poster used as catalog cover; 15 1/8" x 11", very fine in fine frame; *$6,750 A.

— La revue blanche . . .; by Edward Ancourt, Paris, 1895; 36¼" x 49¾", paper light-stained in background, framed; *$6,000 A.

— Lire Dans Le Matin . . .; by Chaix, Paris, 1893; 23 3/8" x 32 3/8", 2nd state with lettering at bottom; a few tears/restorations along folds & at corners; framed; *$1,700 A.

FERNAND TOUSSAINT — Cafe Jacqmotte Bruxelles; by Affiches d'Art O. de Rycker, Bruxelles, 1896; 33¾" x 45 3/8", slight tears/stains at folds, one 6-inch tear upper margin; framed; *$9,500 A.

ABEL TRUCHET — "Au Jardin du Tuilleries"; color lithograph, published Paris, c. 1895; image size 20½" x 28¼"; *$450 A.

MAURICE UTRILLO — Santiago Rusinol. Fulls de la Vida; Henrich y Ca., Barcelona; 28 3/8" x 40¼", slight tears left corners, framed; *$1,000 A.

GEORGES AUGUSTE VALLE — Fiancees Rivales Roman Inedit par Victor Chauvet . . .; by H. Herold, Paris; 2-sheet poster, 55 1/8" x 78 5/8", slight paper loss at top and bottom, folds show; *$300 A.

THEODORE VAN RYSSELBERGHE — La Libre esthetique; by Ve. Monnom, Bruxelles, 1896; 27 1/8" x 38¼", slight tears at paper edge, framed; *$6,000 A.

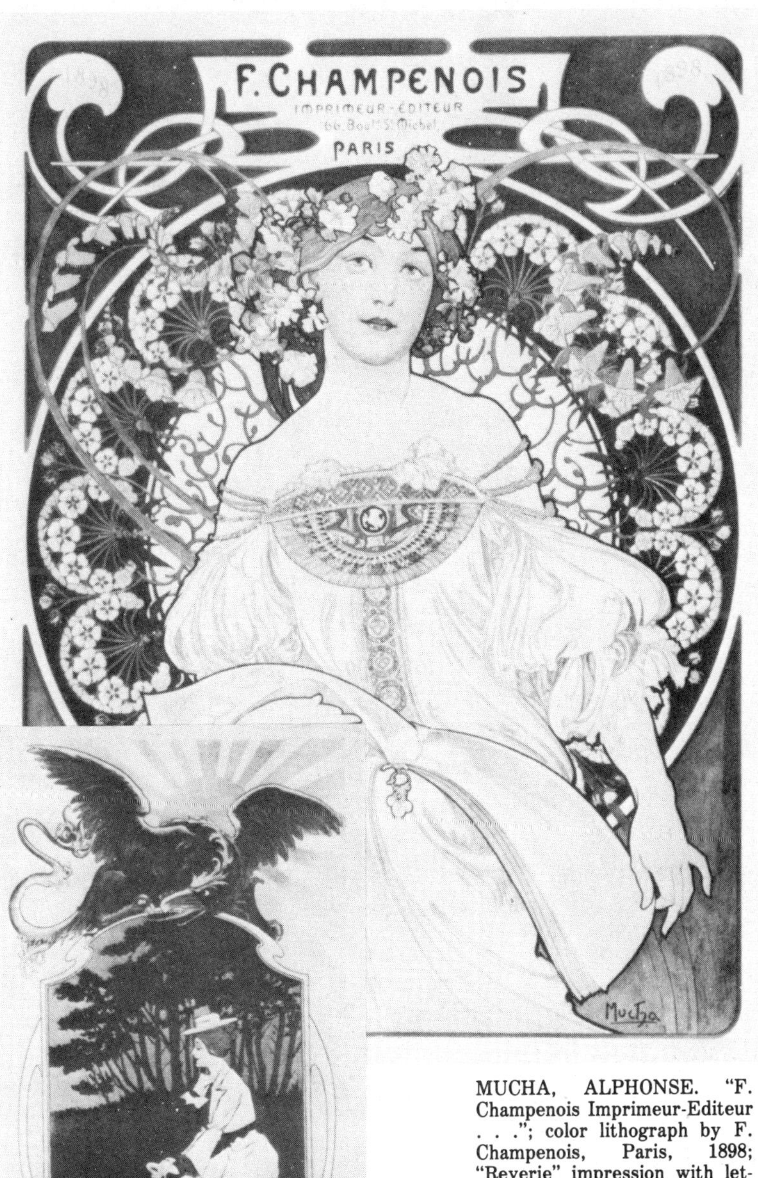

MUCHA, ALPHONSE. "F. Champenois Imprimeur-Editeur . . ."; color lithograph by F. Champenois, Paris, 1898; "Reverie" impression with lettering, a lighter hued variant; few creases, minor staining, linen backed, framed; 18 7/8" x 25 1/8"; *$4,000 A. (Sotheby's)

MISTI; "Cycles Griffon"; by Imprimerie du Griffon, Paris, 1900; color lithograph, a few minor defects but generally very good; linen-backed, 36" x 61¼"; *$300 A. (Sotheby's)

ANONYMOUS. "Filippo Haas & Figli Fornitori Della Reale Casa Genova · via Roma"; color lithograph, with margins; 44 1/8" x 32 5/8", some minor repairs, folds, marginal tears; linen backed; *$250 A. (Sotheby's)

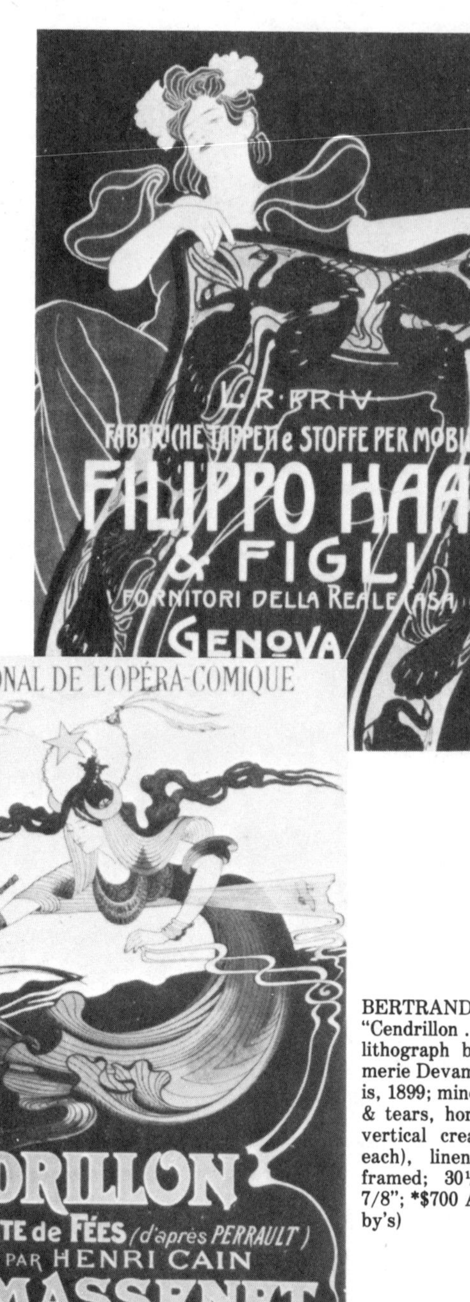

BERTRAND, EMILE. "Cendrillon . . ."; color lithograph by Impremerie Devambez, Paris, 1899; minor repairs & tears, horizontal & vertical creases (one each), linen backed, framed; 30¼" x 22 7/8"; *$700 A. (Sotheby's)

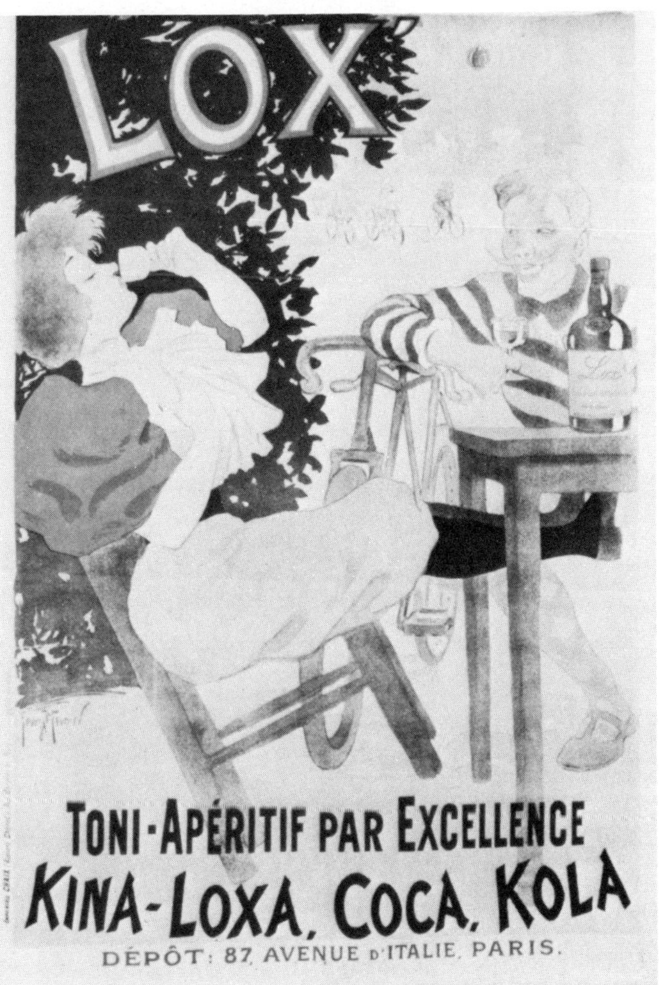

MEUNIER, GEORGES. "Lox. Toni-Apertif Par Excellence"; color lithograph by Impreimerie Chaix (Ateliers Cheret), Paris, 1895; minor folds & damage; linen backed, 59 7/8" x 34 5/8"; *$600 A. (Sotheby's)

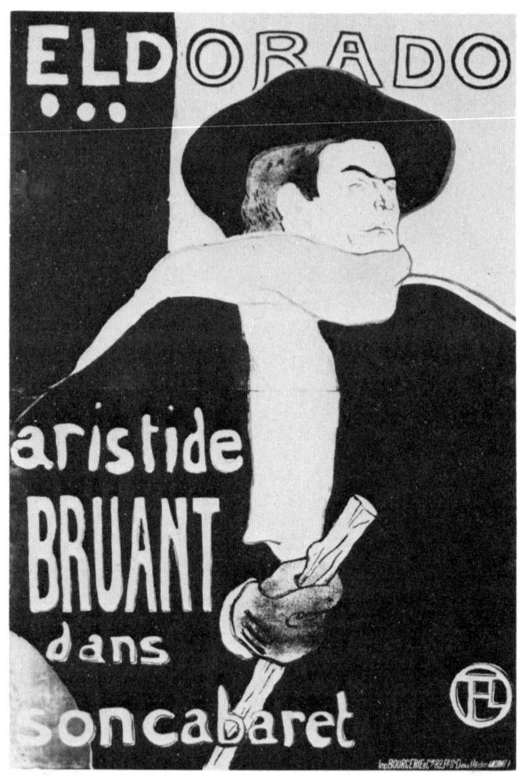

TOULOUSE-LAUTREC "Eldorado . . . ," color lithograph by Imp. Bourgerie, Paris, 1892; 38" x 57½", slight border creases, fine frame; *$18,000 A. (Phillips)

— N. Lembree, Avenue Louise 17, Bruxelles; by Ve. Monnom, Bruxelles; 18" x 25", very fine, framed; *$2,000 A.

ALEARDO VILLA — Caffaro; by Ricordi, Milano, c. 1897 (none of this information shown); 32 7/8" x 48¼", tears left & right margins, horizontal fold; NOTE: THIS POSTER IS UNSIGNED; *$250 A.

ADOLPHE LEON WILLETTE — Salle des Capucines . . .; by H. Sicard, Paris, c. 1890; 25 1/8" x 35 3/8", slight staining/ tears at paper edge; *$125 A.

CHARLES HERBERT WOODBURY — Boston Park Guide . . . By Sylvester Baxter; 1894, 12½" x 19¼", stains at outer edges; *$200 A.

DE YONGHE — The New York Times Sunday, March 1; Indian & tile background; by Liebler & Maass, New York, 1896; 18¼" x 28½", very fine; *$500 A.

FIGURES

The Victorian rage for figures cast in bronze continued through the Art Nouveau styles, although it was comparatively little affected by the movement. One would expect the Art Nouveau affection for symbolism to be manifested in cast figures, especially in allegorical figures. Such occurred but not with the frequency which would be expected.

One problem which cast figures present is that of time of production. Once an original model had been created by a sculptor, it could be copied for many years by independent foundries, both with and without the permission of the original artist. As a result, many figures were seen during the late 19th century and the very early 1900s which had their origins as much as a half-century earlier.

One group of sculptors which enjoyed renewed interest was "Les Animaliers," an unofficial categorization of sculptors who concentrated upon animal life. Their depictions of animals (either singly or in "groups" of two or more) were usually naturalistic or impressionistic. As Continental designers strove to find suitable inspirations from nature, Les Animaliers-sculpted figures gained new respectability.

Yet animals were certainly not the only objects depicted in Art Nouveau figures. The omnipresent Art Nouveau female was seen in her many guises: strictly European, Nubian, femme fatale, in states of reverie and despair, nude and clothed, young and mature, seated and standing, on termes and without being raised much above the bases, smiling and frowning — the possibilities must have seemed endless to the sculptors and to the buyers of the figures.

The metal in which most of these figures were cast was bronze. Later pieces in particular would often be cast in white metal, a less expensive substitute for bronze, and covered with a bronze plating or patination.

The subject of "patina" is one which still causes some consternation among collectors and dealers. Perhaps a difference should be noted between a natural patina, that created by the natural effects of weathering upon the outer surface of the figure, and the "manufactured patina" caused by chemically treating the surface at the time of manufacture. Whichever, most experts advise against attempting to remove that patina; the result would be an unnatural, "new"-appearing piece without the warm glow that older bronze acquires. Certainly one would never wish to remove any traces of gilding which might remain upon bronze. Still, one occasionally encounters objects which have been "depatinated," their patinas stripped from them for some reason. These are still collectible items, but most dealers would place a lower value upon them than upon comparable patinated figures.

Then there's the question of size. The same figure could be produced by two or more foundries, the major difference being in the size of the figure, or two or more sizes of one figure could be produced by a single foundry. It's not enough to know the sculptor, metal and subject; it's often necessary to note the name of the foundry (when possible) and the size of the figure to differentiate between two specimens.

All figures listed in this section are of bronze. They were products of the period of great growth of the French bronze foundries (during the second half of the 19th century, extending to about World War I) and the corresponding acceptance of the figures by aesthetes and collectors throughout the Western world. It can be noted that most of the figures were French, although foundries in other European countries and America began production just before the turn of the century.

For other examples of bronze sculpture, taken out of the realm of the purely decorative and applied to the so-called useful arts, see the chapters on lighting (for the metal bases) and metals.

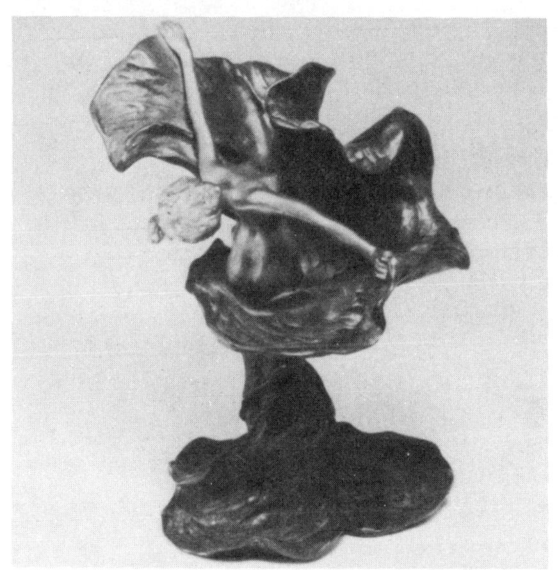

ANONYMOUS; parcel-gilt figure of Loie Fuller, brown patina, impressed LOUCHET under base; 8½"H, c. 1900; *$2,400 A. (Sotheby's)

ANONYMOUS — "Samurai on Horse," archer in full battle dress; inscribed "Exposition-Paris 1900," 17½"H x 13¼"L; $3,300 D.

— seated femal figure playing gilt lyre, on marble base, illegible signature, 7"H; $725 D.

— young female nude with draped length of fabric around waist leaning against rocky base; golden brown patina, marble base, overall 11"H; German, late 19th century, inscribed "V. Seyfert"; *$600 A.

BARYE, ANTOINE-LOUIS — large group of jaguar devouring hare; greenish-brown patina, 16"H x 39¾"L; inscribed A.L. BARYE and F. BARBEDIENNE, FONDEUR; *$6,000 A.

— jaguar devouring hare, medium patina, 8½"H x 21"L; *$5,000 A.

— walking lion, dark reddish-brown patina, 15 9/16"L, inscribed BARYE; *$1,700 A.

— Lion and Serpent, 14"H, marked signature; *$1,400 A.

— bear attacked by hounds, 10 5/8"H on separate red marble base, medium brown patina; inscribed BARYE and stamped FRANCE; *$800 A.

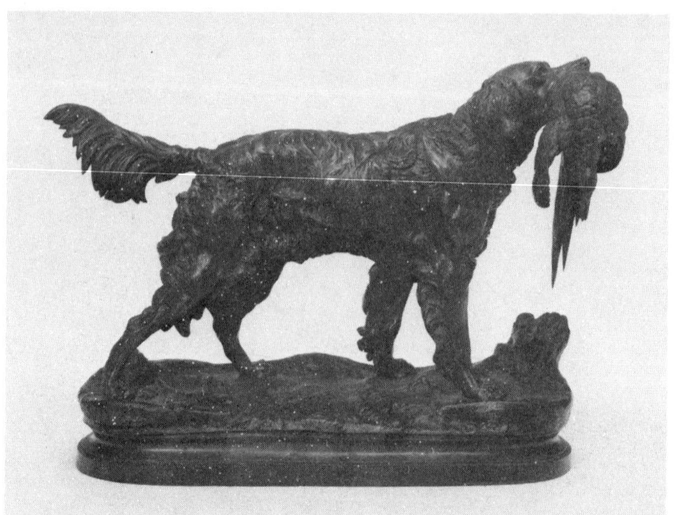

ANONYMOUS; setter softmouthing pheasant on naturalistic ground over marble base; *$1,600 A. (Christie's)

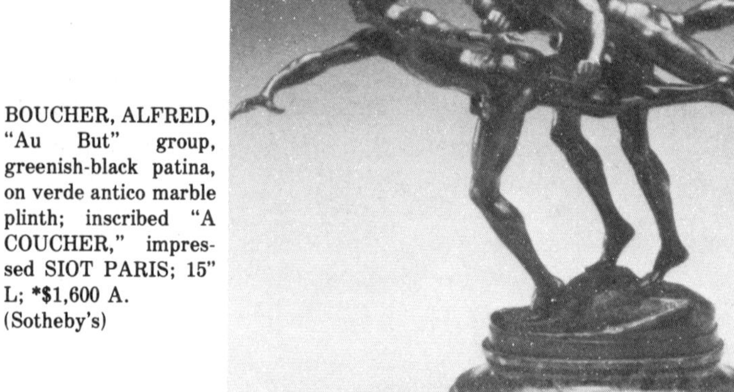

BOUCHER, ALFRED, "Au But" group, greenish-black patina, on verde antico marble plinth; inscribed "A COUCHER," impressed SIOT PARIS; 15" L; *$1,600 A. (Sotheby's)

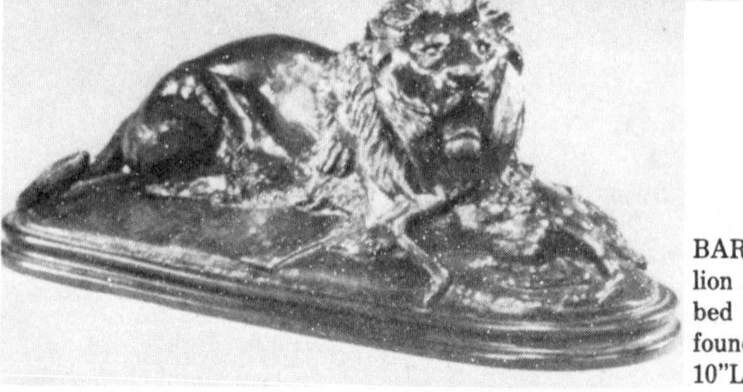

BARYE, ANTOINE-LOUIS; lion devouring antelope; inscribed signature, Barbedienne foundry, late 19th century; 10"L; *$550 A. (Morton's)

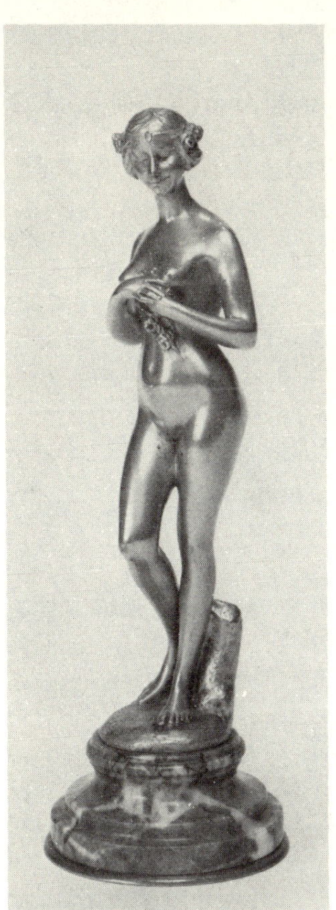

COUTAN, JULES FELIZ; smiling standing nymph, gilt-bronze, on waisted pink marble base; 9"H, inscribed "COUTAN-Montorgueil"; *$900 A. (Christie's)

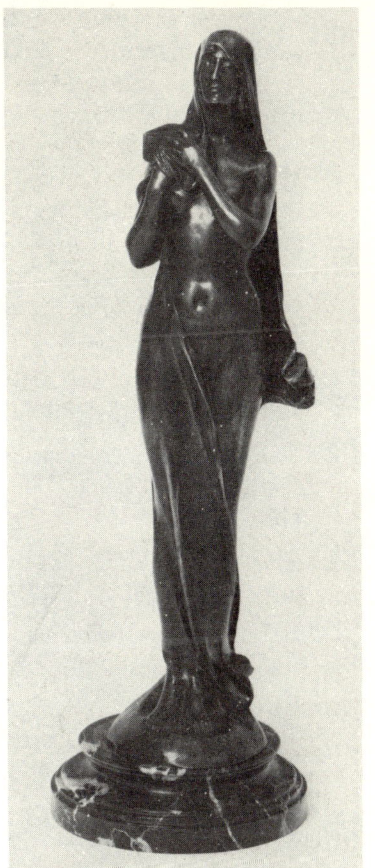

BOUVAL, MARUICE; "Le Secret," on rounded marble base *$2,700 A. (Christie's)

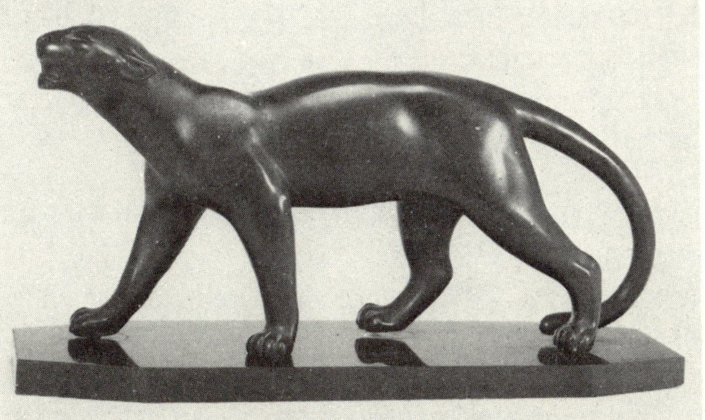

BRACQUEMONT; stalking panther, squared plinth, French, early 20th century; *$700 A. (Christie's)

— ocelot carrying off heron, dark olive patina, late 19th century, inscribed BARYE, 12"L; *$650 A.

— ratel stealing eggs, 4"H on green marble base, dark brown patina, inscribed BARYE; *$500 A.

— a stag, reddish-brown patina, 6¼"H, inscribed BARYE; *$450 A.

— tiger and crocodile, on green marble base; cast signature, marked 1836; 11"L; *$350 A.

— a stallion, 4¾"H; *$80 A.

— sculpted plaque of genet carrying off bird; brown patina, late 19th century; inscribed BARYE, 5"L; *$50 A.

BECK, EDMUND PHILIPP — female terme, medium brown patina, 4¼"H; inscribed as seal, "E. Beck 02"; *$260 A.

BESSERDICH — "La Lecture Gaie," reclining Art Nouveau lady reading large book; 7"L x 2½"H, marked "Vienna Bronze"; $160 D.

BEYRER, EDWARD (German, b. 1866) — a Collie; cast signature, with 1899 date, 7½"H; *$250 A.

BONHEUR, ISIDORE (French, 1827-1901) — horse & jockey, on marble base, signed, 8½"H; *$250 A.

BOUCHER, JEAN — figure of Victor Hugo in exile on Guernsey, greenish-brown patina with traces of verdigris, 27"H; inscribed "Jean Boucher 27-7-28 2" and "cire perdue R.C."; *$1,400 A.

BOURET, EUTROPE — classical lady, medium brown patina, inscribed BOURET, 19"H; *$650 A.

BRACONY — "Echo," an allegorical female figure, 26½"H, polychromed; French, late 19th century, inscribed "Bracony" and stamped TIFFANY & CO.; separate brass tag inscribed ECHO and SALON DES BEAUX ARTS; *$2,000 A.

BUGATTI, REMBRANDT — a pelican, 6"L; inscribed "R. Bugatti," impressed with rectangular foundry mark enclosing CIRE/PERDUE/AA. HEBRARD; underside impressed FRANCE; c. 1910; *$3,000 A.

CHERET, GUSTAVE-JOSEPH (French, 1839-1894) — putti with mask, 26"H, signed; *$1,500 A.

DAGONET, E. — dead doe, dark reddish-brown patina, on marble base; 8¾"L, c. 1900; *$350 A.

DALOU, AIME-JULES — "Le Baiser," couple embracing; 9¾"H, green marble base, dark brown patina with traces of verdigris; inscribed DALOU, impressed with Hebrard foundry seal; *$3,000 A.

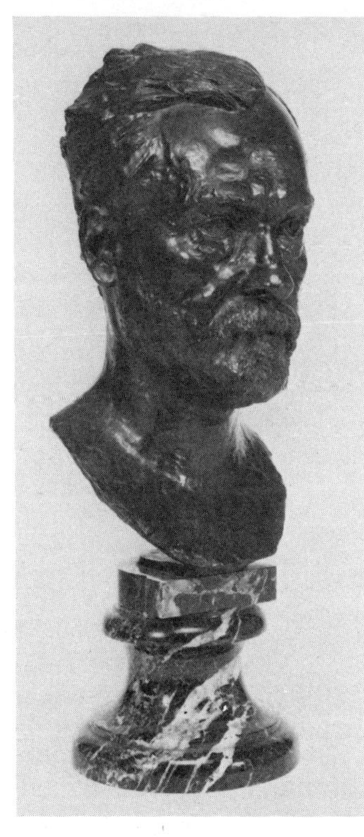

DUBOIS, PAUL; bust of Louis Pasteur, marble base; *$1,100 A. (Christie's)

DERENNE — leaping gazelle, greenish patina; 11½"H x 16 5/8"L, including stepped stone base; French, early 20th century; *$2,100 A.

DROUOT, EDOUART — gilt-bronze figure of nymph playing pipes, 26½"H; inscribed "E. Drouot"; *$1,400 A.

FOLLET (French, 19th-20th centuries) — enraptured nymph, nude, on naturalistic base; signed; *$525 A.

FRATIN, CHRISTOPHER — stallion, brown patina, 14½"H x 16½"L; impressed FRATIN and stamped NEDJED; *$1,800 A.

GARDET, GEORGES — group of 2 lionesses, brown patina, 20¼"L; inscribed G. GARDET, impressed with circular Siot-Decauville stamp; late 19th C; *$1,200 A.

— group, a buffalo attacked by puma, dark brown patina 8 3/8"H; inscribed G. GARDET, stamped TIFFANY & CO 6447, impressed with Siot-Decauville foundry stamp; *$700 A.

GARNIER, JEAN — young boy and frog, greenish brown patina, 14"H; *$800 A.

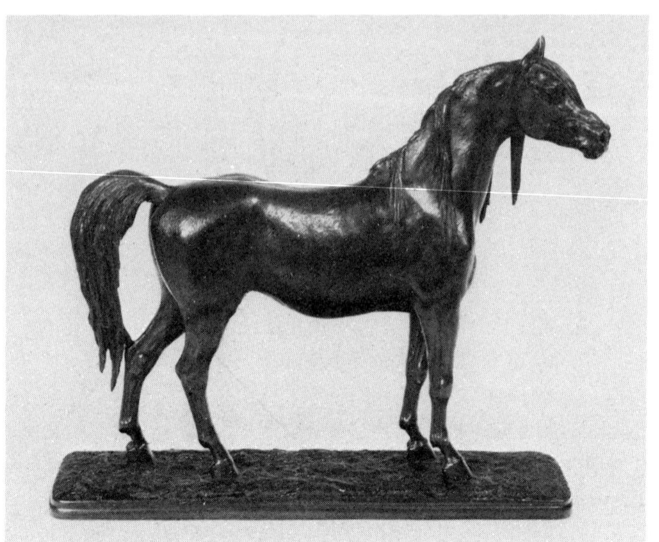

FRATIN, CHRISTOPHE; figure of stallion, late 19th century; *$1,800 A. (Christie's)

GAUDEZ, ADRIEN ETIENNE — "Tresors des Mers," figure of water nymph, reddish-brown patina, 41½"H; inscribed A. GAUDEZ; *$4,000 A.

GEROME, JEAN-LEON — "Victoire au Peplum," silvered & gilt-bronze figure of Nike; octagonal yellow marble base, 18¾"H, inscribed J.L. GEROME, stamped SIOT-PARIS Z 904; *$3,800 A.

— "Victoire," figure of Nike, gilt bronze; 21 7/8"H; inscribed J.L. GEROME, stamped SIOT 453B FRANCE; *$2,000 A.

GODET, HENRI — "Glaneuse," standing figure of young women with arms folded across bosom & leaning on her rake; roughly circular plinth inscribed "Glaneuse, partt. Godet, Salon des Beaux Arts," overall 9¼"H; *$200 A.

GREGOIRE, JEAN-LOUIS — allegorical gilt-bronze group, winged female and male on self-stand, 39¼"H; inscribed GREGOIRE; *$2,500 A.

KAUBA, CARL — bust of woman in elaborate evening dress with gilt rose blossoms at bodice; olive brown patina, flaring marble socle, overall 16"H, c. 1900, inscribed "C. Kauba"; *$950 A.

KOWALCZEWSKI, P.L. — figure of Diana, reddish-brown patina, on marble base; 12"H, inscribed "P.L. Kowalczewski"; *$600 A.

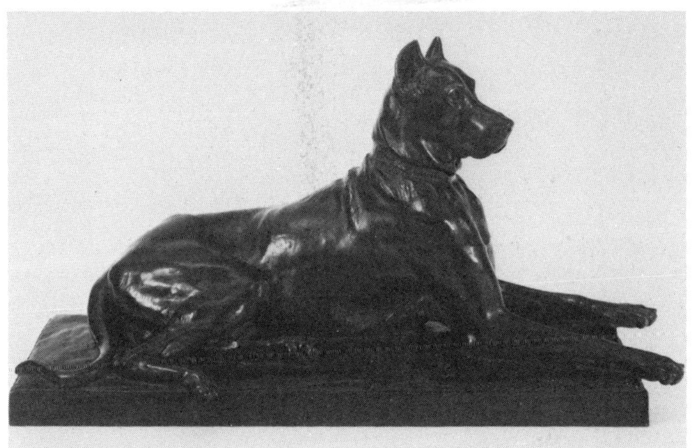

GARDET, GEORGES; reclining Great Dane; French, early 20th century; *$1,400 A. (Christie's)

LARCHE, RAOUL — mother & child, brown patina, 20¼"H; inscribed "Roul - Larche," stamped "8236," impressed Siot-Decauville foundry seal; late 19th C; *$5,200 A.

LE SOUDIER, JANA — 2 herons, brown patina, 20"H; inscribed "Jane/LeSoudier/2/10," impressed FRANCE, foundry mark SUSSE FRES/PARIS/CIRE PERDUE, and another SUSSE FRERES EDITEURS PARIS; early 20th Century; *$1,900 A.

LEVY, CHARLES-OCTAVE — "Faneur," a thresher, medium brown patina, 17"H; inscribed CH. LEVY and "faneur par CH. LEVY Salon des Beaux Arts," stamped "A1436," im pressed Bronze Guaranti seal; *$650 A.

LINDENBERG, M. — standing maiden, hair upswept revealing halter dress; brown & golden-brown patina, marble base, overall 10¼"H; inscribed "M. Lindenberg," and "Akt-Ges/vurm/H. Gladenbeck & Sohn"; c. 1900; *$500 A.

MARIOTON, EUGENE — nymph playing pipes, greenish-brown patina, 32 1/8"H; *$1,100 A.

MENE, PIERRE-JULES — bull & nest, 6" x 3½", inscribed mark; $550 D.

— "Tom, a pointer with tail curved inward & head raised, brown patina, 9¼"L; inscribed P.J.MENE/TOM:/MEDAILLE D'ARGENT/ADMIS AUX BEAUX ARTS; *$325 A.

MOIGNIEZ, J. — setter softmouthing pheasant, 17¼"H, inscribed signature, polychromed; *$1,600 A.

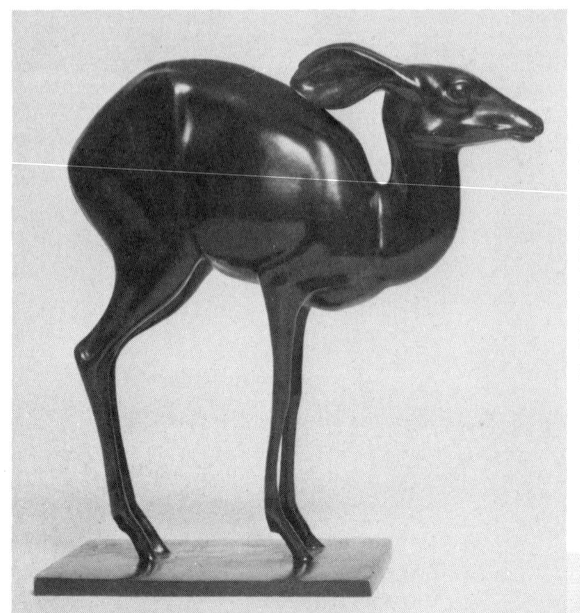

HATVANY, Christa-Winslow; frightened fawn, blackish-brown patina, 15"H; inscribed CHRISTA-WINSLOE HATVANY, and "Susse Fres Edts Paris,"; *$1,700 A. (Christie's)

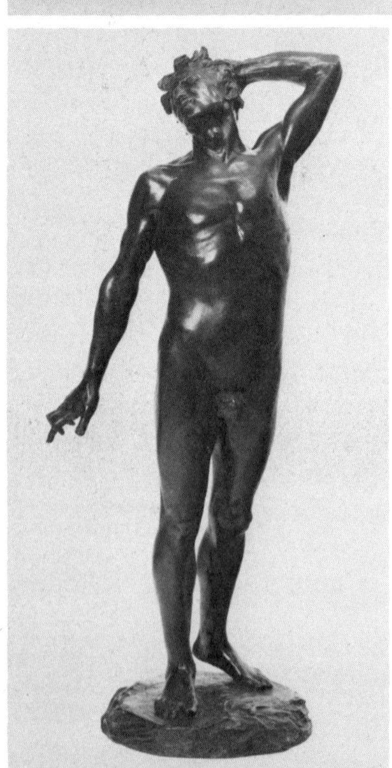

HUMPHRIES, CHARLES H.; male figure; American, early 20th century; *$1,000 A. (Christie's)

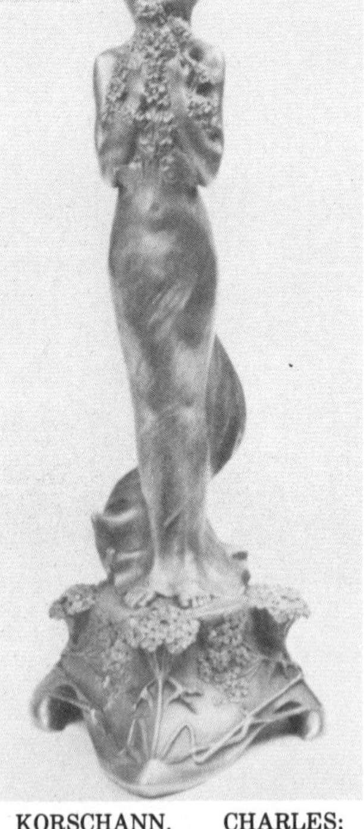

KORSCHANN, CHARLES; Ophelia, gilt-bronze, inscribed CH. KORSCHANN, with LOUCHET foundry mark, 13"H; *$1,700 A. (Phillips)

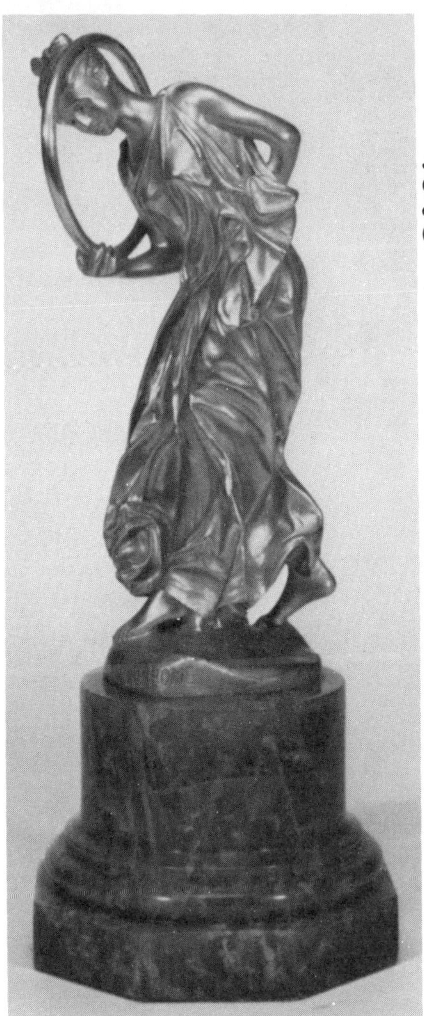

JEROME, J.-L.; "La Danseuse au Cerceau," gilt-bronze, French, late 19th century; on marble base; *$1,200 A. (Christie's)

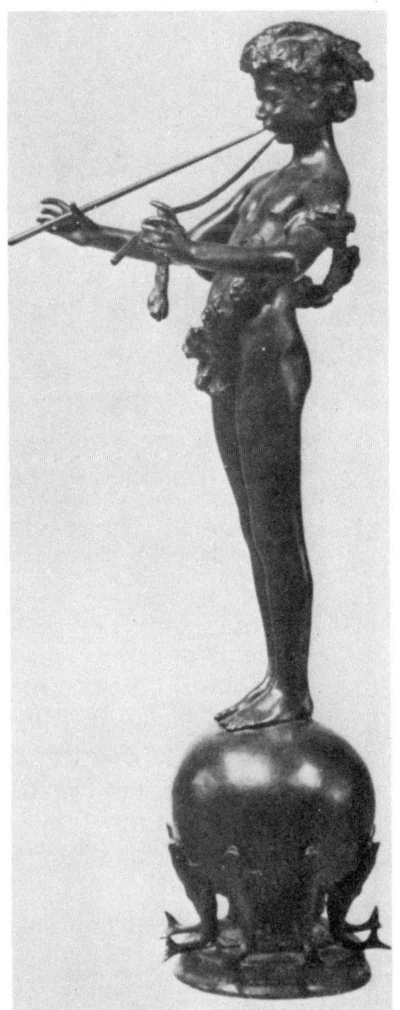

MacMONNIES, FREDERICK; figure of Pan; signed "Paris 1890, copyright 1894," the round base inscribed with title & "Roman Bronze Works New York," 29½"H; *$3,500 A. (Morton's)

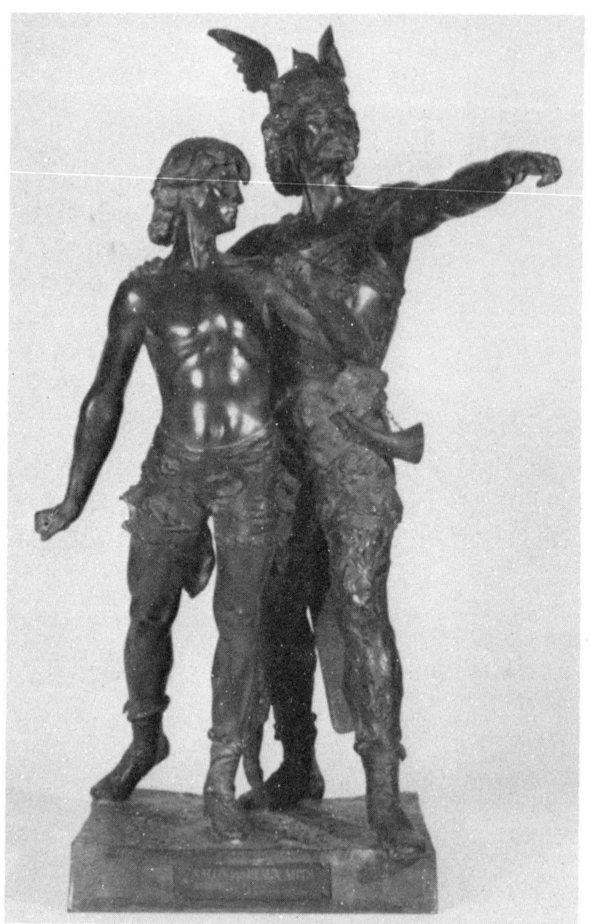

LAPORTE, EMILE; "Pro Patria," bronze allegorical group of 2 warriors; French, late 19th century; *$2,500 A. (Christie's)

— family of hares, brown patina, 11¼"H; *$1,200 A.

— 2 adult & 3 baby birds perched on rock; 7¼" x 4½" x 5"; inscribed signature; $700 D.

MOREAU, MATHEURIN — "La Libellule," allegorical female figure, sometimes known as "Nymph Fluviale," greenish-brown patina, 19"H; inscribed "Moreau Mathurin"; reduction of monument for a Paris fountain first exhibited at the Salon of 1873; *$700 A.

NELSON, ? — bust of young woman, 16"H; late 19th or early 29th centuries; *$450 A.

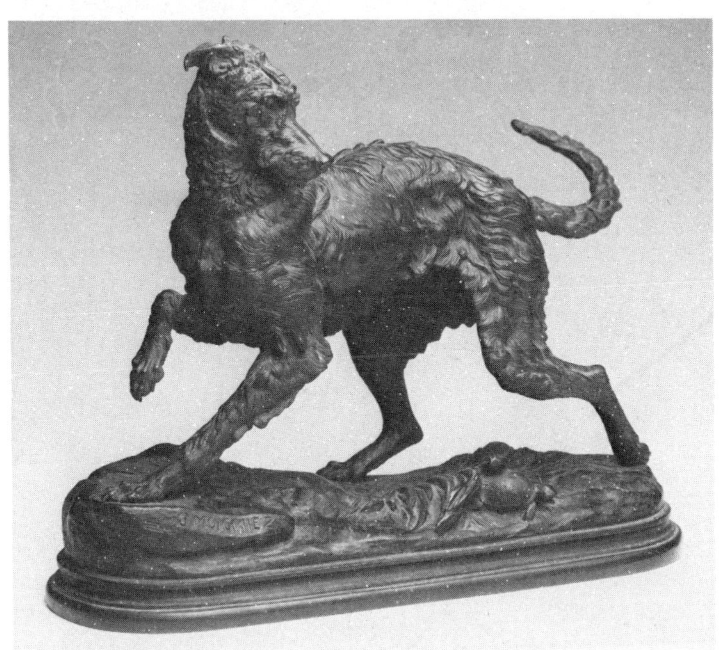

MOIGNIEZ, JULES; figure of wolfhound, 10"H; *$650 A. (C.G. Sloan)

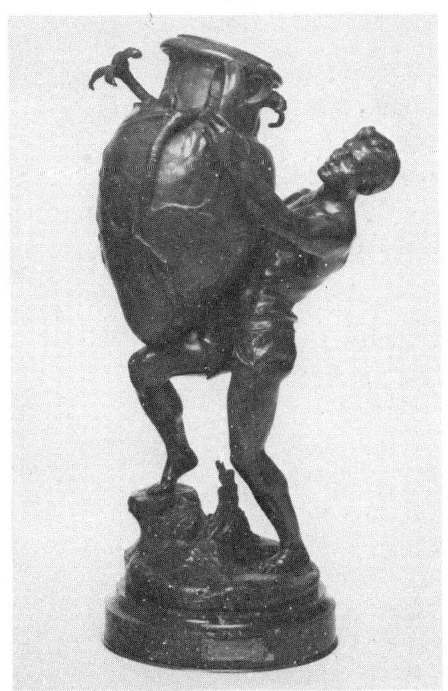

PEYROT; "Titan au Vase," man with amphora, French, late 19th century; *$2,400 A. (Christie's)

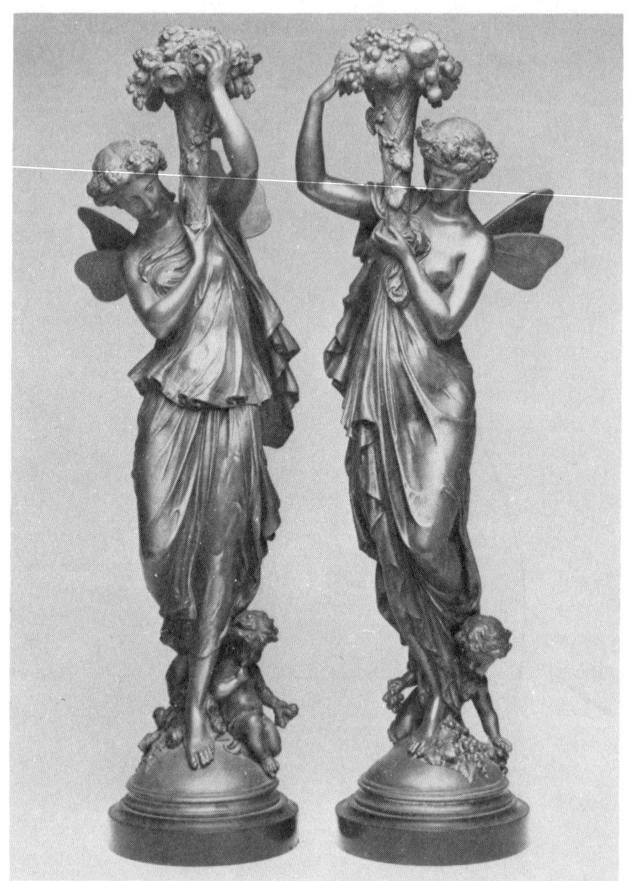

MOREAU, MATHURIN; pair of winged females supporting fruit- and flower-filled baskets, each on black marble bases; 23"H; *$1,250 A. (C.G. Sloan)

NOEL, ANTHONY PAUL — full figure of Oriental dancer, on self-bronze base incised with oriental motifs, overall 17¾"H; inscribed "Tony Neal," stamped "E487," with Siot-Decauville seal; *$2,400 A.

PAILLET, CHARLES — Irish wolfhound & kitten, green patina 5½"H; inscribed "ch Paillet," stamped BRONZE, impressed Barbedienne foundry seal; *$650 A.

PERRIN, JACQUES — "La Vague," figure of water numph, reddish-brown patina, 20½"H; inscribed J. PERRIN; separate brass tag inscribed LA VAGUE PAR JACQUES PERRIN HORS CONCOURS; *$900 A.

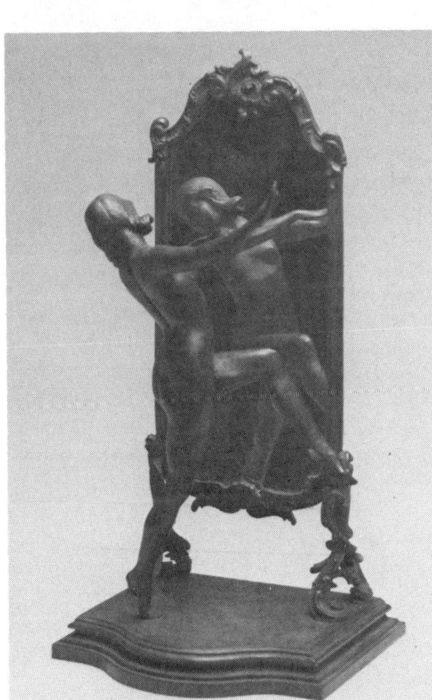

PINEDO, EMIL; female nude before mirror, 14"H; *$800 A. (C.G. Sloan)

Below, RENAUD, FRANCIS; "Loie Fuller," black patina, inscribed "Renaud 1901," 10½"H; *$2,400 A. (Phillips)

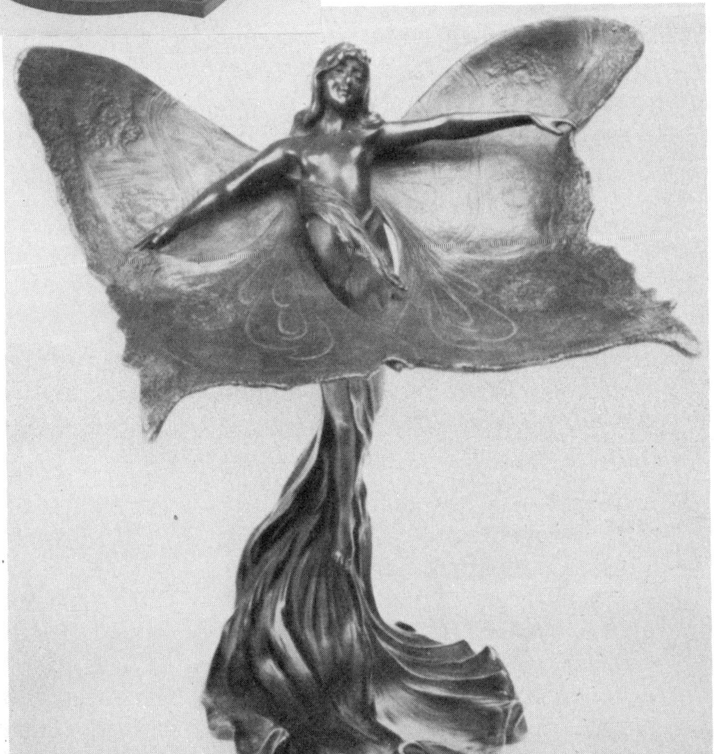

PICAULT, EMILE-LOUIS — medieval lady, dark brown patina, parcel gilt, 31 5/8"H; inscribed "E. Picault," stamped TIFFANY & CO, presentation inscription dated 1885; *$2,200 A.

— "Pro Jure," allegorical male figure, brownish-green patina, 18¾"H; inscribed E. PICAULT and PRO JURE; *$700 A.

— man in agriculture, "PAX LABOR," olive patina, 17¾"H; base cast with name of figure and "E. PICAULT," wheat stalk loose; *$650 A.

PREVOT, EDMOND — standing man, right arm upraised, snake around right ankle, nude on self-base; blackish-brown patina, 40¼"H, inscribed "E. Prevot 1892"; late 19th century; *$2,500 A.

RICHE, L. — reclining Alsatian dog, golden brown patina, 13½"H; inscribed signature, impressed with Jollet foundry seal, turn-of-the-century; *$700 A.

RIVET, A. — "La Vendange," inscribed on base "Recompensee Au Salon, 1888," 35"H; *$800 A.

SHATTER, S. FANFER — Dore bust of girl with draping gown, marble base, 8¾"H, foundry mark; $350 D.

SINDING, STEPHEN ABEL — "The Valkyrie" (equestrian group), brownish-black patina, 21¼"H; inscribed "Stephen Sinding," and ART. GES.GLADENBECK/BERLIN; *$800 A.

TOFANARI, SIRIO — an elephant, brown patina, 31"L; inscribed "Sirio Tofanari," early 20th century; *$2,200 A.

TROUBETSKOY, PRINCE PETER PAUL (Russian) — a Samoyed, 13 5/8"L, 3¼"H; *$800 A.

UNGER, HELLA — Art Nouveau dancing girl, 15"H; $1,500 D.

VALTON, CHARLES (French, 1851-1918) — recumbent lioness, 10½"L; *$225 A.

VILLANIS, E. — "Melodie," gilt-bronze allegorical female figure with stringed musical instrument, 29½"H; inscribed "E. Villanis" and MELODIE; *$2,800 A.

— "Deborah," figure of the prophetess, golden brown patina, 25"H; inscribed "E. Villanis" and DEBORAH; *$2,200 A.

— "Omphale," bust of young girl, dark reddish-brown patina, 20½"H; inscribed "E. Villanis" and OMPHALE, stamped "JP 1724," impressed with stamp of Societe des Bronzes de Paris seal; *$1,300 A.

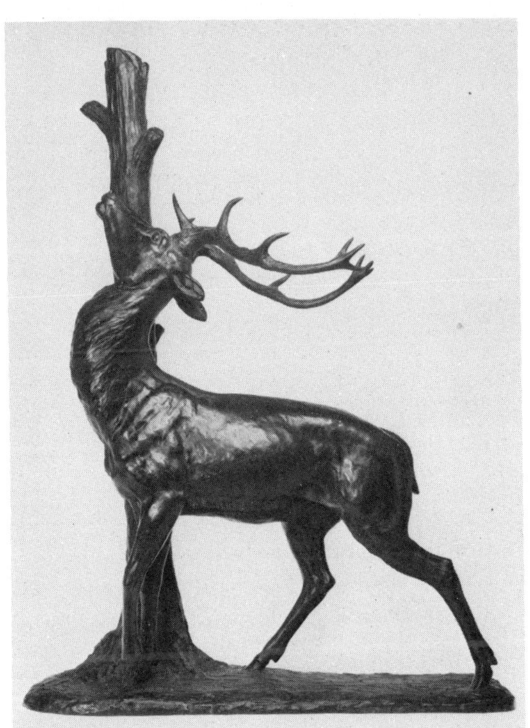

ROCHARD; stag at tree, 19th century, French; *$4,200 A. (Christie's)

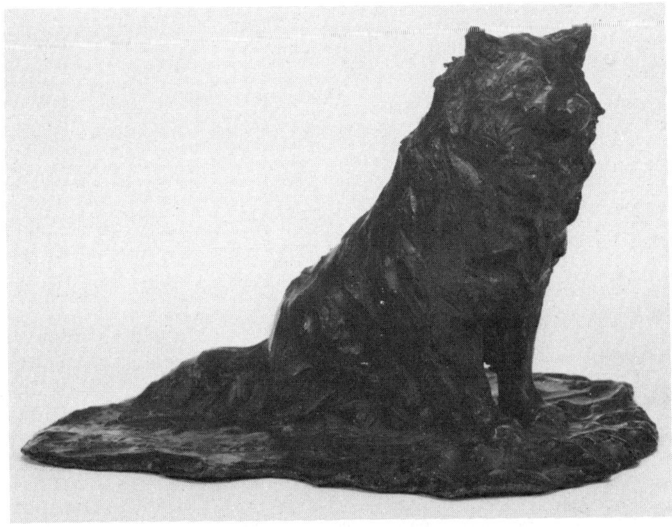

TROUBETSKY, PRINCE PETER PAUL; figure of Samoyed on naturalistic ground base; Russian, early 20th century; *$3,800 A. (Christie's)

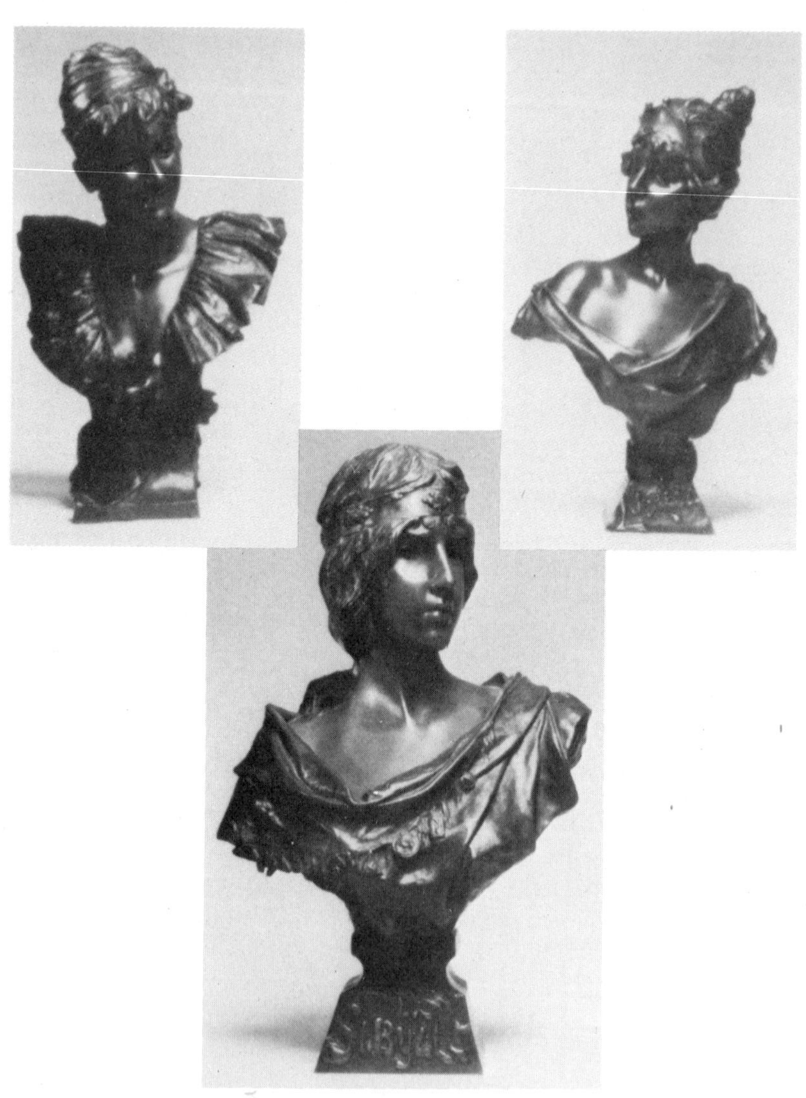

THREE BRONZE BUSTS OF WOMEN. (Left) "Fenna Mia," after George van der Straeten; 16"H, brown patina, inscribed "van der Straeten," impressed circular foundry mark enclosing SOCIETE DES BRONZES DE PARIS; *$800 A. (Center) "La Sibylle," after E. Villanis, 21"H, brown/gold/green patinated highlights; inscribed "F. Villanis," impressed circular foundry mark enclosing SOCIETE DES BRONZES DE PARIS, also impressed 4435L; *$1,100 A. (Right) "Lucrece," after Villanis; 14¾"H, brown & gilt patinas, inscribed "E. Villanis," impressed circular foundry mark enclosing H. HIRSCHWALD/BERLIN, numbered CB/3376; *$800 A. (Sotheby's)

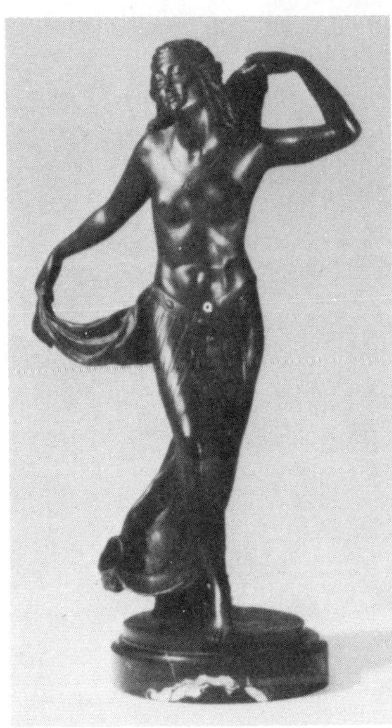

VALENTIEN, J.M.; figure of woman, brown patina, inscribed "M. Valentin"; on black marble pinth, 23½"H; *$1,300 A. (Sotheby's)

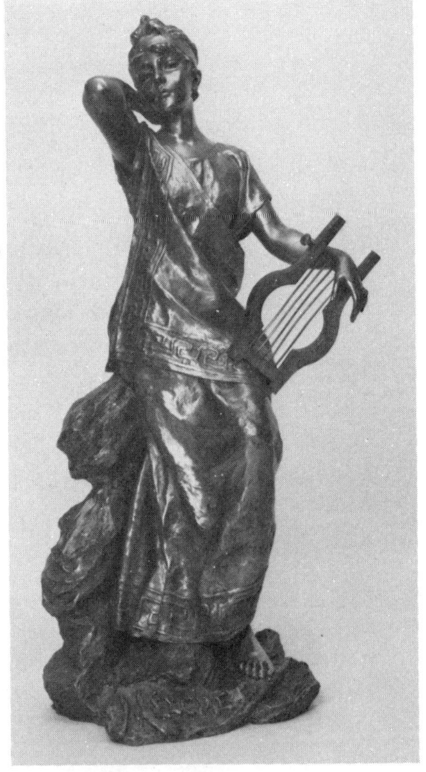

VILLANIS, E.; "Melodie," turn of the century, Italian; *$2,800 A. (Christie's)

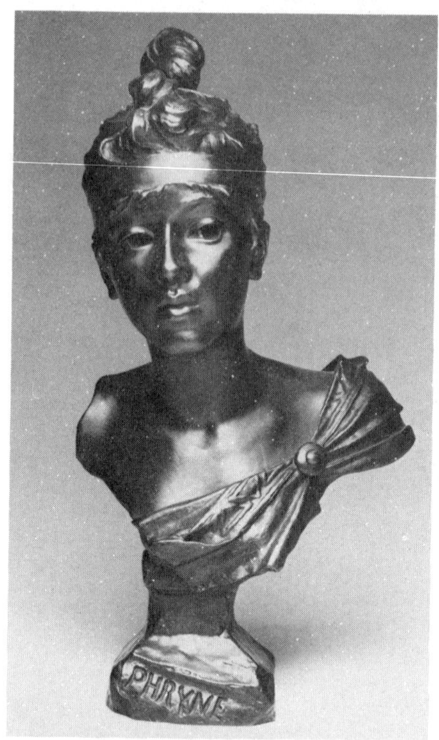

VILLANIS, E.; "Phryne," turn of the century, 24"H; *$950 A. (C.G. Sloan)

— "L'Histoire," 19"H, inscribed cast signature; *$950 A.
— "Saida," medium brown patina, 8 5/8"H includes red marble base; inscribed "E. Villanis" and SAIDA, stamped "C," impressed with Societe des Bronzes de Paris seal; *$600 A.
— "Nelly," bust of woman, dark brownish-green patina, square base, 10¼"H; inscribed "E. Villanis" and NELLY, stamped "5 7381," impressed with Bronze Guarantee seal; *$500 A.
— "Celia," 11"H; *$400 A.
— Cendrillon," head of an Art Nouveau maiden, 15"H; *$325 A.
— "Farfalla," bust of winged woman, greenish-brown patina, 5"H; inscribed "Villanis" and FARFALLA, stamped "LU 42," Italian-made c. 1900; *$200 A.

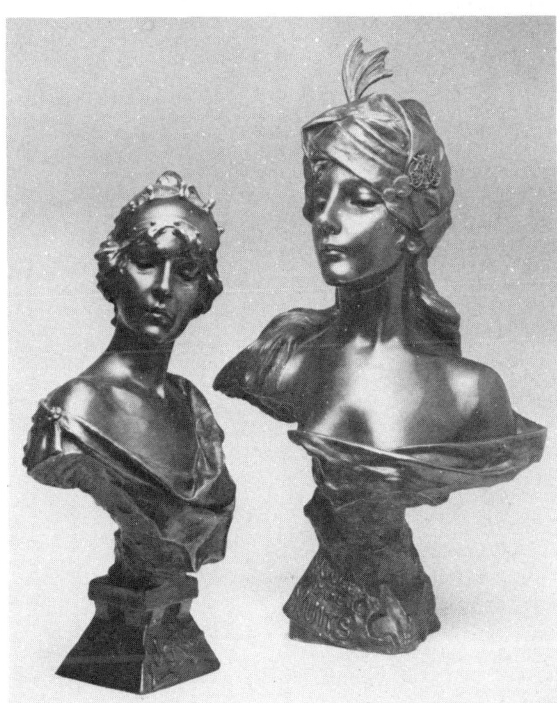

TWO BRONZES after Villanis. (Left) "Lucrece," 21"H; *$875 A. (Right) "Mille et une Nuits," 27"H; *$1,000 A. (C.G. Sloan)

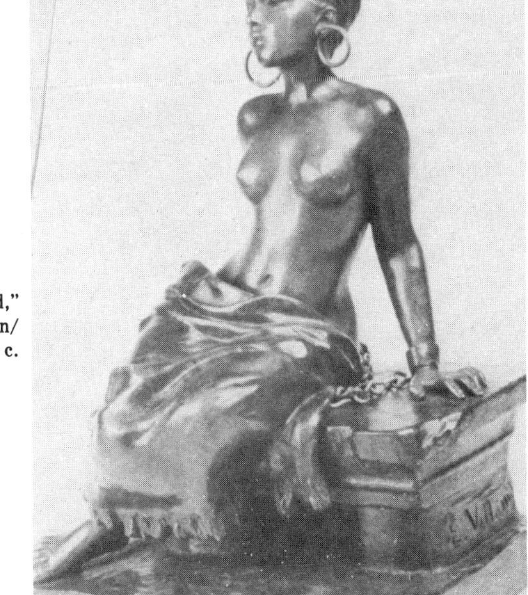

VILLANIS, E.; "Shackled," with removable skirt, green/brown patina, 15¾"H, signed, c. 1890; *$2,100 A. (Phillips)

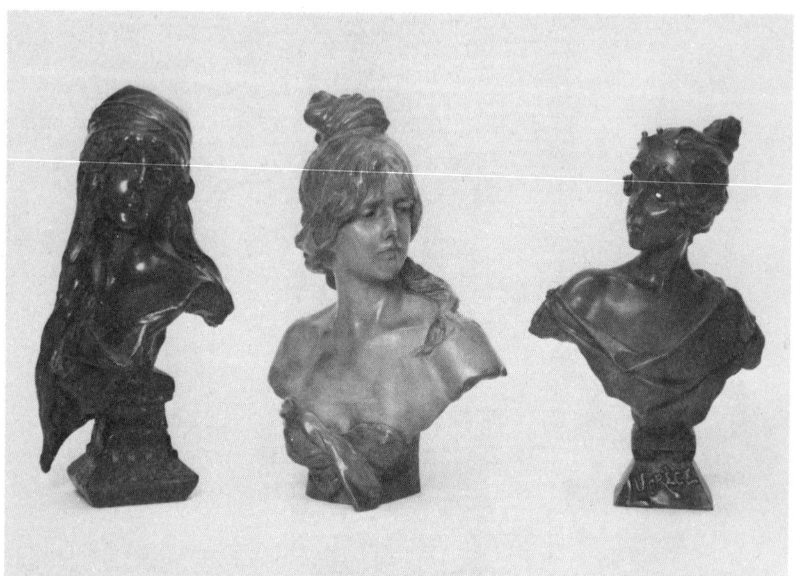

THREE BRONZE BUSTS OF WOMEN. (Left) "Sapphia," after E. Villanis, reddish-brown patina, 15 3/8"H, inscribed signature and "Sapphia," stamped K. K. KUNSTERZGIES-SEREI WEIN; *$850 A. (Center) after Alphonse Henri Nelson, mottled greenish-brown patina, 15 3/8"H, inscribed "A Nelson," with Goldscheider foundry seal; *$800 A. (Right) "Lucrece," after Villanis; 14 5/8"H, parcel-gilt, inscribed "E Villanis" and "LUCRECE," stamped "EW 5070," impressed seal Societe des Bronzes de Paris; *$850 A. (NOTE: This is the third "Lucrece" figure included, each, differing in size and other characteristics.) (Christie's)

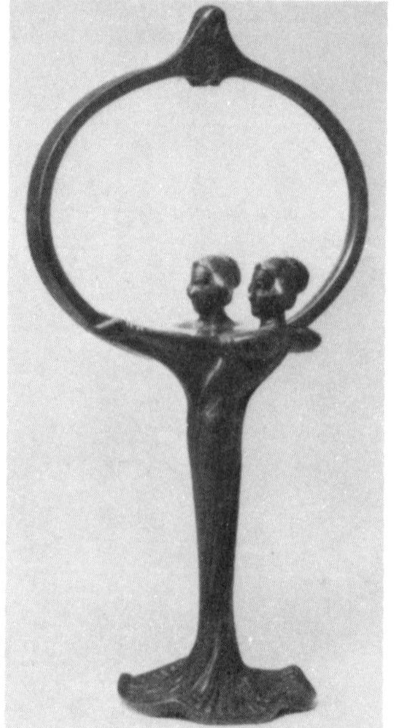

FIGURAL MIRROR, Austrian, brown patina, 12¼"H; *$2,000 A. (Sotheby's)

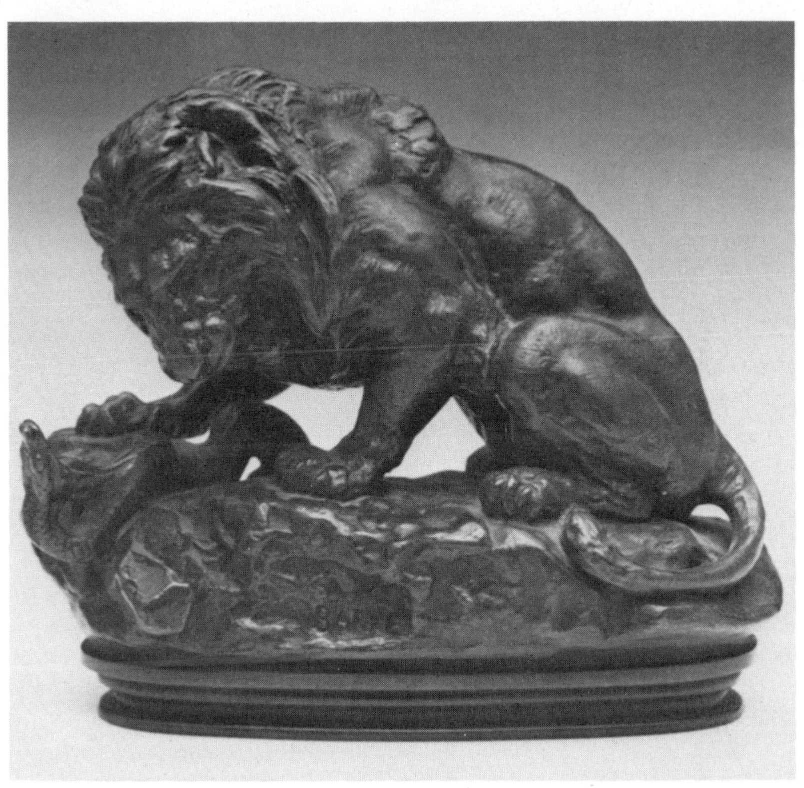

BARYE, ANTOINE LOUIS; lion & serpent, 6¾"H; *$1,350 A. (C.G. Sloan)

SILVER

Silver lent itself to the Art Nouveau designers well. Gold remained the most desirable fine metal for jewelry and objects de vertu, but silver became more widely used, especially if it was in harmony with stones used. In addition, the silver tableware, vases, and such could be made at much lower prices than comparable pieces made in gold. (See the chapter on Jewelry for silver jewelry items.)

The most popular design elements in silver were floral displays on table pieces, and female busts or heads on smaller, personal items. There were, of course, many variations and combinations of these and other elements, such as butterflies, peacocks, insects, berries and their vines, fish, animals, mermaids, and so forth.

It's hard to tell in all too many cases where neo-rococo repousse decoration leaves off and Art Nouveau design begins. In part this is because the same manufacturers often made both. In America, Unger Brothers, Whiting, and Gorham were some of the leading makers. Their silver items were much closer in style to the French floral heritage than to the later developments of Germany's Jugenstil. Extremes of stylization are practically unknown among American products.

Such isn't the case with European products, though. Austrian, German, and some English items were caricatures of flora and fauna, not merely in decoration but in overall shape. Such pieces generally date from the late 1890s into the 1900s. A direct correlation between these pieces and the later work of Art Deco designers can be drawn, particularly with the works of the Wiener Werkstatte.

All items listed in this chapter can be assumed to be Sterling silver unless otherwise stated. The exceptions will be plated items and those which were part of Gorham's "Martele" line (and related, similar objects).

Why single out Gorham? The answer is in the nature of silver itself and what Sterling silver is. Silver is a soft metal, too soft and susceptible to wear to be used in manufacturing in its so-called "pure" state. Technically, "pure" silver is a virtual impossibility; the chances of removing every last trace element which may be found in it is unlikely. As a result, silver, which is rated by its purity, is never shown as being 100% pure. The purity is shown in fineness, and absolute purity would be 1,000 parts fine. The normal "purity" for silver is shown as 999 parts per thousand, or occasionally, 999+ parts per thousand, or .999+ fine.

Sterling silver was, at the height of Art Nouveau fashion as well as today, a specified purity — 92.5 percent, 925 parts of silver with 75 parts of an alloyed metal, or .925 fine. High-quality vases and other objects, flatware, jewelry, and many more items were produced from sterling silver.

Gorham was a producer of sterling silver, but its Martele line was somewhat different. To outward appearances it looked identical to many of the sterling silver objects produced by Gorham and other firms. The differences were in the "snob appeal" advertising the line as a specialty, and the slightly higher silver content — actually only 2.7 percent higher. The "melt value" (value of the silver sold to be remelted into bullion) would be insignificantly higher; the value to collectors is much higher. Buyers today pay a premium for the Martele line and for any other line specified as having greater than the sterling norm — 92.5 percent silver.

So where is the value of silver from this period? Is it in the silver content, or is it in the intangible qualities which make up its collectibility? The answer depends upon the piece involved, but it probably depends a bit upon both factors. Even expensive pieces can fluctuate as the silver market changes, but their collectible value (the premium added to their intrinsic worth) remains relatively constant. Less desirable, poorly made pieces of sterling silver have very low premiums added to them and achieve almost all their value from their silver content. Exceptional pieces may be worth many times their silver content's value. Keep an eye on the silver market, and be prepared to **buy** if it shows a sudden jump; you may well catch some dealers whose prices haven't changed to reflect the higher silver market.

BAG, MESH — sterling, hvy frame has Viking face; 6½"L x 4"W; Blackinton; $325 D.

BAG, MESH (FRAME) — large gargoyle centered flanked by cherubs, 6"W; with matching gargoyle chatelaine hook, 3"W, signed Kerr; $295 D.

BASKET, CAKE — shallow oval, with everted rim and bail handle pierced & chased with foliate scrolls, similar interior chasing; Bailey Banks & Biddle, c. 1910; 11"L, 29 ozs.; *$550 A.

BASKET, MINIATURE — scroll open work swinging handle, 5"H to top; basket flares to 5¼"D; Bigelow & Kennard Co.; $145 D.

BOWLS — These popular forms were often decorated in the Art Nouveau manner, although many times the repousse decoration tended toward the neo-rococo. Chasings and raised decorations range from naturalistic to stylizations of nature-inspired motifs.

BOWL — large raised poppies around border, 24 ozs.; *$950 A.
— compressed hemispherical form embossed/chased with acorns/oak leaves over a hammered surface; Thune, Copenhagen, c. 1910; 5"D, 4 ozs.; *$100 A.
— sitting on 3-scroll feet with cork inserts on bottom, hvy applied Irises around edge, open work; 4"H x 10½"D; $85 D.
— pair of newer bowls in the Art Nouveau manner, 1¼"H x 2 5/8"D; $35 D.

BOWL, BERRY — floral design, Unger Bros., 13 ozs.; $450 D.

BOWL, CENTERPIECE — flaring oval set on conforming foot, hammered surface realistically embossed & chased with shells/coral/seaweed; blue crab legs applied at 3 points; Whiting Mfg. Co., c. 1900; 9½"L, 24 ozs. 10dwts.; *$1,200 A.

BOWL, FOOTED — shaped circular lobed with broad everted rim, chased with raspberry fruit/leaves/vines; set on 4 panel feet; Gorham, 1897; 11½"D, 34 ozs 12 dwts; *$850 A.

BOWL, FOOTED — undulating pierced and embossed rim & similarly decorated foot with stylized fruit/flowers; A.D. Hauptmann & Cie., Vienna, c. 1910; 5"H, 24 ozs 8 dwts; *$350 A.

BOWL, FRUIT — circular pierced with elaborate scrolling tendril motif, with glass liner; A.D. Hauptmann & Cie., Vienna, c. 1910; 8"D, 11 ozs 8 dwts without liner; *$150 A.

BOX — Martele line, lobed & shaped square section, surface embossed/chased with buds/foliage; interior set with later oval frame containing dried Edelweiss; Gorham, 8" square, 32 ozs gross; *$2,700 A.
— oval with hvy design of cherub on top, 3½"L; $195 D.
— round with AN decor, 4"D x 1¾"H, Unger Bros.; $175 D.

BOX, CIGARETTE — formal rustic legs with champleve panels of interlaced decor enameled Blue/green/mauve; with hallmarks of Liberty & Co.; design attributed to Rex Silver; 8"L; *$14,000 A.

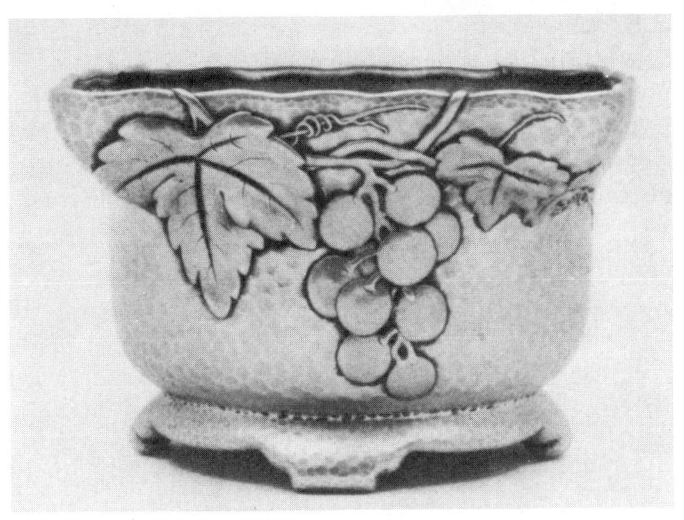

BOWL, TIFFANY & CO., c. 1885; 4½"H, 27 ozs.; *$1,100 A. (Sotheby's)

BOX, COLLAR BUTTON — lady's head with flowing hair, and poppies, in relief; Victor Silver Co., 2½"D; $48 D.
— another, similar, $38 D.

BOX, POWDER — large roses or poppies in relief, domed top; $37 D.

BOX, SNUFF — AN-style bird/tree engraving, dated; silver-plated, with some wear on plating; $25 D.

BREAD SERVER — AN style, $22 D.

BREAD TRAY — elliptical with pierced swept-back handles, body decorated with 3 realistically embossed/chased poppies; maker's mark "H et M" in rectangle, Vienna, c. 1905; 20½"L over handles, 25 ozs 16 dwts; *$700 A.
— shaped rim embossed/chased with Jack-in-the-pulpit flowers and long flowing stylized tendrils; Alois Pawliczek, Vienna, c. 1910; 16"L, 19 ozs 12 dwts; *$275 A.

BRUSH, CLOTHES — face with flowing hair surrounded by butterfly wings, poppies in repousse at each end; Unger Bros., #2175, monogrammed; $125 D.

BRUSH, HAIR — two in Art Nouveau commercial form, $24 D.
— pair with cherubs, one with damaged bristles; Derby Co.; $22 D.

BUCKLE PIN — heavy, Art Nouveau, 2¾" x 3¼"; $40 D.

BUTTER PAT — very ornate silverplate, 3" x 3"; $5 D.

BUTTONHOOK — maiden in flowing gown on scrolled handle, marked Sterling; 8½"L, some wear; $40 D.
— embossed floral handle, marked Unger Bros.; $30 D.
— embossed floral decor on hollow handle; $18 D.

CARD CASE — the card case/purse with chain, floral decor; possibly Unger; 3 ozs; $30 D.

CHALICE — "Cymric" with 4 curved handles, the top with 4 bright-colored enamel panels of Viking ships; matching cover has ornate finial; stamped hallmark Liberty & Co., London, 1901; 12¼"H, 58.5 ozs.; *$5,200 A.

CIGAR CUTTER — raised design, 1½"L; $29 D.

CIGARETTE HOLDER — tiered silver basket with stylized floral motif; designed by Joseph Hoffman, impressed with Wiener Werkstatte hallmark; 4"H; *$2,200 A.

COFFER — English Art Nouveau-style, stylized foliate design bas-relief 2 sides of winged maiden; 7¾"L x 4½"H; silverplated; *$260 A.

COMB, HAIR — 7½"L, $95 D.

COMPACT — hinged lid pierced & finely chased with 2 birds/flowers set with amethyst cabochon centers; fitted interior with mirror & powder box; some gold also; stamped BT No 875012 BOUCHERON PARIS; 3"L; *$500 A.

COMPOTE — broad bowl with lower band of scrolling grapeladen vines above spirally ribbed column; impressed hallmark George Jensen, 10¾"H; *$2,000 A.
— 2-handle, etched upper edge above applied band of interlocked floral medallions above similarly banded foot; Tiffany & Co., 6"H, 13 ozs.; *$175 A.

COOLER, CHAMPAGNE — Morning Glory vines around top, trimmed handles, monogram; silverplated, signed Southington, 10"H; $54 D.

CREAM PITCHER — Reed & Barton, AN-influenced; $85 D.

CREAMER AND SUGAR BOWL — cylindrical with wavy rims & twisted handles, sides etched with Morning Glory sprays, basket with swing handle; Whiting, retailed by Black, Starr & Frost, total 5 ozs. 10 dwts; *$125 A.

CROSS — Lily motif Bible marker, 2½"L; $25 D.

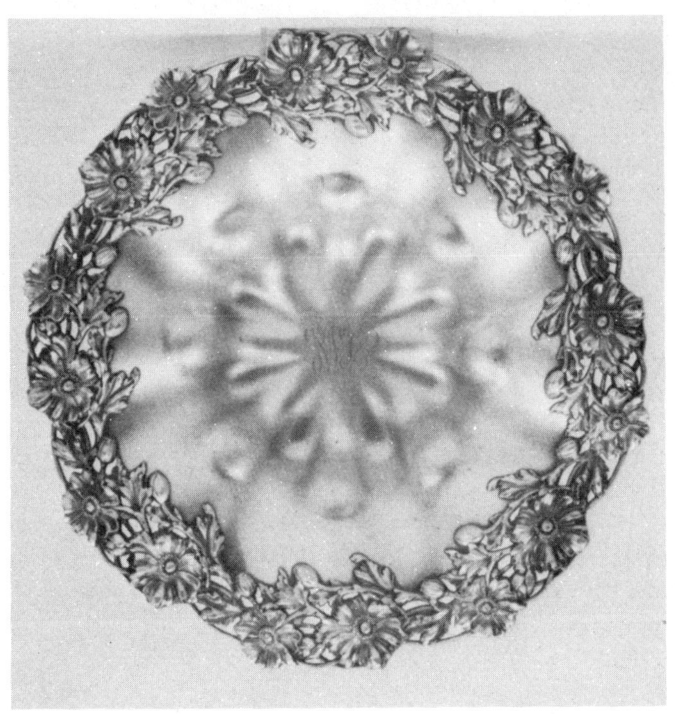

BOWL, UNGER BROS., Newark, NJ, c. 1900; broad rim, Poppy decoration; 9½"D, 7 ozs. 4 dwt.; *$275 A. (Sotheby's)

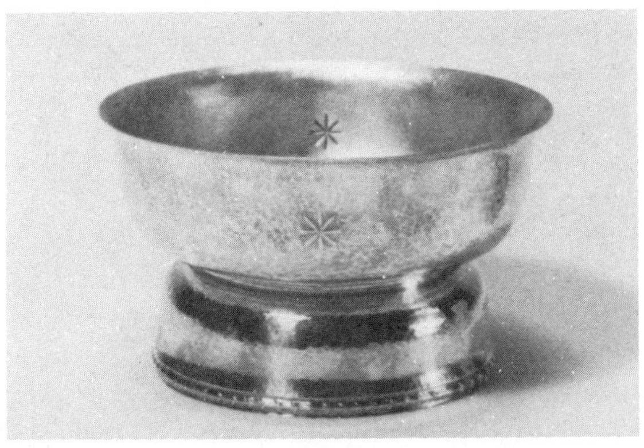

BOWL, DESIGNED BY JOSEF HOFFMANN, footed, domical form, hammered sides, repousse styled blossoms; 6½"D, 12 ozs.; *$1,700 A. (Sotheby's)

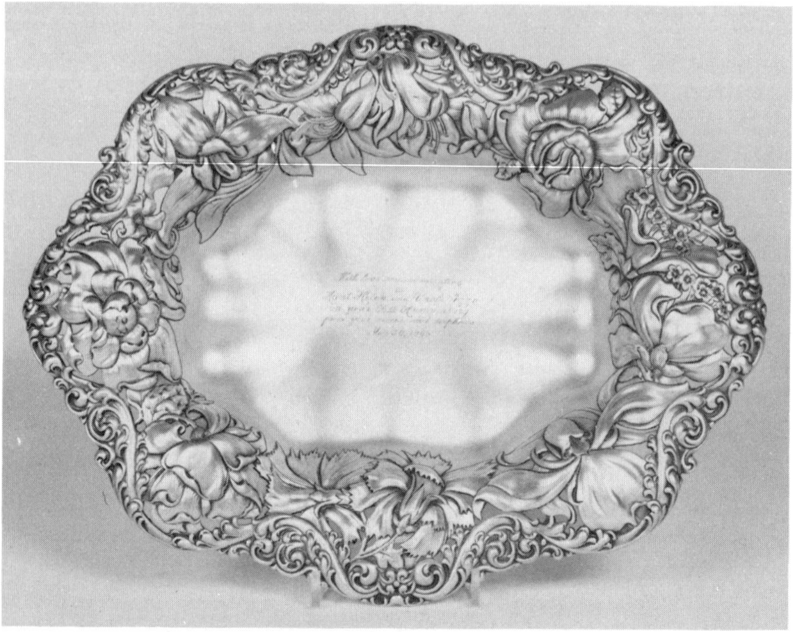

BOWL BY GORHAM, 1902; *$850 A. (Christie's East)

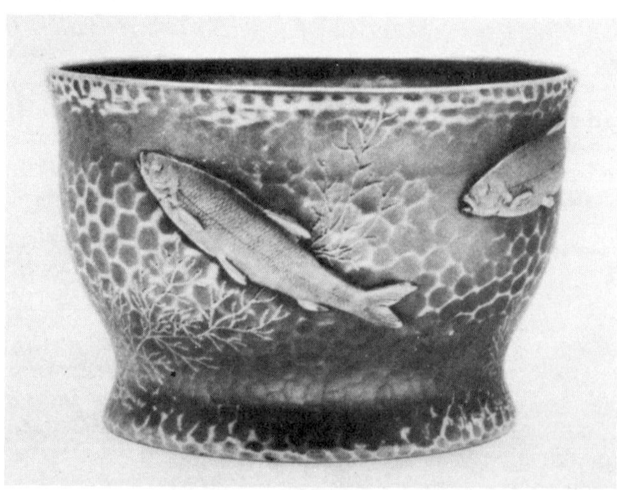

BOWL, TIFFANY & CO., NY, c. 1890; hammered surface with applied decor and traces of gilding; interior gilt washed; 6½"D, 17 ozs. 12 dwt.; *$1,200 A. (Sotheby's)

CRUMB SET — Flowing Iris raised design, free form open work handles, some sort of illegible signature; silverplated; $50 D.
— another, swirled decor raised, silverplated; $28 D.

CUP — Daffodils with long stems in relief around sides, rim slightly dented; 3"H; $110 D.

DESK SET, LADY'S — Water Lily pattern on letter/calendar holder, letter opener, inkwell, roll blotter, blotter holder; sterling on bronze; $320 D.

DISH — oval section, sides formed ribbed arches, handle a simple stylized tendril; marked H & M in rectangle, Vienna, c. 1910; 11"L, 15 ozs 8 dwts.; *$550 A.
— form of Poppy flowerhead; Wm. B. Durgin Co., c. 1928; 6"D, 7 ozs. 4 dwts.; *$325 A.
— oval, applied Carnation leaves/buds/vines form openwork around edge, puffed out sides; marked "Sterling" only but a product of Bixby Silver Co.; 10¾"L x 8¾"W, 13.5 troy ozs.; $275 D.
— oval, embossed/chased to resemble Jack-in-the-Pulpit leaf with blossom; International Silver Co., 11"L, 16 ozs.; *$200 A.
— broad pierced/embossed/chased rim decorated with profusion of Poppies in various stages of blooming, the center hand-hammered; on foot; 11½"D, prob. Austrian, c. 1890; silverplated; *$75 A.

DISH, NUT — floriform set of 10, silver-gilt, by Reed & Barton, c. 1900; 5 pair, each embossed/chased to represent Petunia, Cineraria, Clematis, Orchid, or Poppy; total weight 9 ozs.; *$300 A.

DRESSER SET — all-inclusive set includes toothbrush and crystal dresser box; design is female bust in high relief, flowing hair; *$1,450 A.
— 13-piece set includes hand mirror, hair brush, comb, buffer with tray, cuticle knife, file, buttonhook, nail scissors, 4 cut glass jars with silver tops (2 small, one powder jar, one hair receiver); circular and oval forms with engraved foliate borders, monogrammed; International Silver Co., early 20th Century; *$225 A.
— 5-piece Continental set: pin tray, brush lacking bristles, nail buffer, fitted tray, hand mirror; each piece decorated with peacock; *$225 A.
— 3-piece set: hair brush, hand mirror, and cut glass powder jar with silver top; plain forms with simple embossed floral details, monogrammed; by Watson; *$125 A.

— 2-piece set: mirror and brush; Cattails and Water Lilies in deep repousse; pistol handles; marked Anchor 600 X; by Hope Silver; $125 D.

— 3-piece set, silverplated: comb, hair brush, hand mirror, all with full body of Cupid; $85 D.

— 2-pieces: hand mirror and brush, embossed scrolls and lines; Homan Mfg., monogrammed; $65 D.

EYE GLASS CASE — scroll design on lid, monogrammed; purple velvet lining in lid & bottom; marked "Sterling", 4½" x 2¾"; $55 D.

FILE, MANICURE (NAIL) — sterling handle, 6½"L; $16 D.

FLASK — 2 mermaids on front, monogram & inscription on back; Unger Bros., one pint, 7¾" x 5"; $495 D.

— girl with flowing hair, high relief flowers; silverplated; $75 D.

— girl with flowing hair, high relief flowers; silverplated; $65 D.

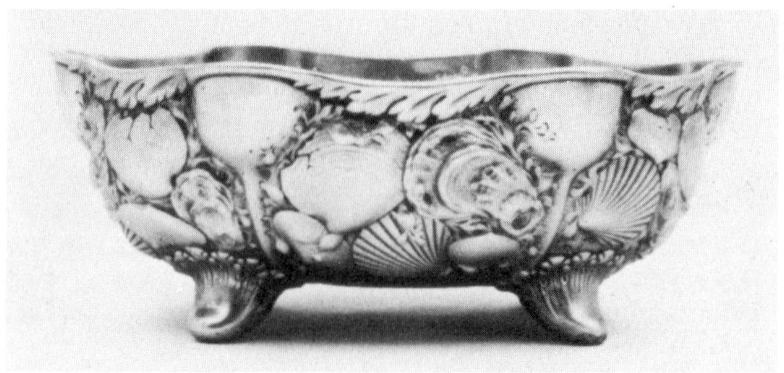

BOWL, CENTERPIECE, Whiting Mfg. Co., Providence, RI, c. 1885; embossed & chased with applied seaweed design lip, on 4 feet of foaming waves; 13½"L, 42 ozs. 12 dwt.; *$1,600 A. (Sotheby's)

FLATWARE: Silver flatware represents an outstanding collectible for the lover of Art Nouveau styling. The growth of a collection can be quite orderly as a table service for four grows to a service for six, eight, or even more. Added to the standard knives, forks, and spoons are a variety of specialty pieces that usually command higher collector interest and dollars. These are the serving pieces, the special-purpose sets of forks or spoons, and the like. In many cases collectors will assemble sets which contain similar patterns from more than one maker; just be sure you differentiate between silverplated and sterling silver in such cases.

—, ASSORTED — assembled service for 12: George W. Shiebler & Co., 1902, "Clematis" pattern; plus 48 pcs. Reed & Barton "Petunia" pattern, plus 2 carving sets & knife sharpener from Alvin Corporation, c. 1910; 180 pcs. or more, 226 ozs.; *$3,900 A.

—, ASSORTED — 125 pieces in the Secessionist taste, stylized strapwork/foliage, the reverse engraved with monogram; Heinrich Ecker, Vienna, c. 1905; 168 ozs.; *$2,500 A.

—, ASSORTED — serving fork and serving spoon each by Geo. W. Shiebler, New York, c. 1880; each in shape of clam shell applied with octopus, stem entwined with seaweed, finials as fish; total weight 8 ozs.; *$700 A.

—, ASSORTED — modified Morning Glory pattern, American, c. 1890; 63 pcs., 49 ozs.; *$950 A.

—, ASSORTED — specialty pieces from Tiffany & Co., c. 1900; Aspic Scoop, Ladle, and Fish Slice; stylized scrolling leaf pattern; 19 ozs.; *$650 A.

—, ASSORTED — serving pieces, mostly Durgin, Concord, NH; pair of Salad Servers, Sauce Ladle, Cheese Scoop, Butter Knife, all in entwined Daffodil/Iris pattern; 13 ozs.; *$350 A.

—, ASSORTED — 17 pcs. Tiffany & other flatware, total 22 ozs.; *$300 A.

—, ASSORTED — German, c. 1890, Coffin-edge shape chased with wavy tendrils; 13 pcs. composed of knives, forks, spoons, total 13 ozs.; *$150 A.

—, FORK, OYSTER — set of 12, hammered surfaces & variously applied insects & marine life in silver-gilt, tines gilt; total 6 ozs. 4 dwts.; Tiffany & Co., c. 1880; *$500 A.

—, FORK, PICKLE — Art Nouveau styling; $22 D.

—, SPOON — 9 enamel & silver gilt by Faberge; marked "Ruckert," Moscow, c. 1900; each 5¾"L; *$1,900 A.

—, SPOON — figural by Unger Bros., teaspoon size; $75 D.

—, SPOON — lady holding angel on handle, $55 D.

—, SPOON, BERRY — chased Strawberry on tip; interlaced vine handle, oyster shell shaped bowl; Tiffany & Co., 4 ozs. 4 dwt.; *$140 A.

FRAME, PICTURE — overall size 5 5/8" x 7 5/8"; frame 3/8" decorated with flowers/leaves with fine stippled background; unused monogram plaque; marked on back, "Tiffany and Co. Makers 3011 Sterling Silver 925-1000C"; *$275 A.

GLOVE STRETCHERS — $40 D.

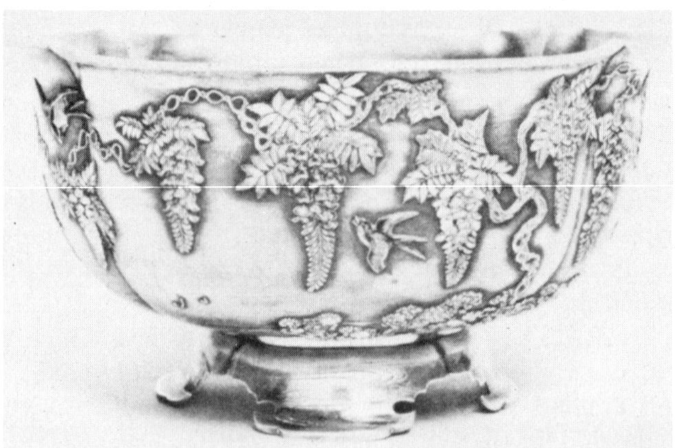

BOWL, CENTERPIECE, Japanese enameled in rounded quatrefoil form, with chased & applied decoration, on conforming base; 9½"L, 31 ozs.; *$550 A. (Butterfield's)

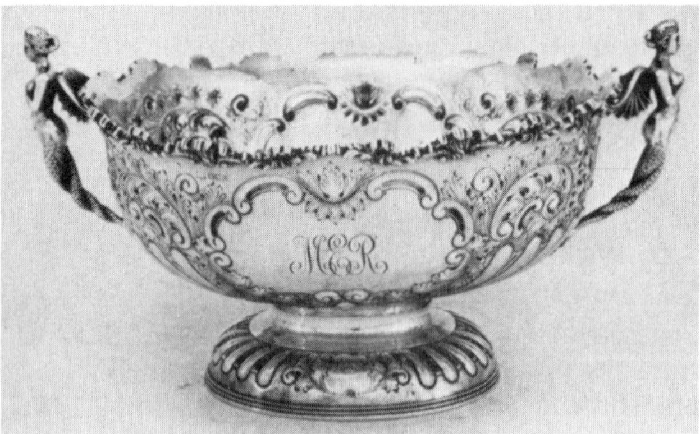

BOWL, CENTERPIECE, from Sheffield, 1901; 8¼"H x 16½"L, 74 ozs. 10 dwt.; *$3,250 A. (Morton's)

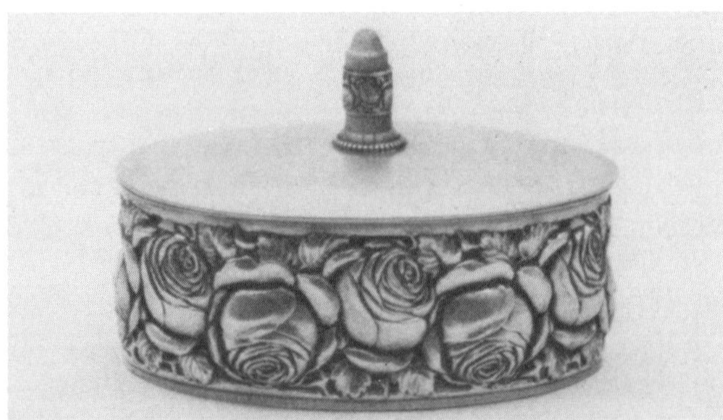

BOX, COVERED; in the Secessionist fashion by Struble & Sohn, Berlin, c. 1910; oval, embossed & chased with roses; ivory finial in beaded mount; plain hinged lid; 5"L, 8 ozs. 8 dwt.; *$375 A. (Sotheby's)

GOBLET — Medieval style, cup as a grape cluster applied with flower heads/leaves, on flared cylindrical foot chased with Latin inscription; foot rim chased/pierced with stylized foliate; prob. German, c. 1900, 13"H, 35.5 ozs.; *$475 A.

HAIR RECEIVER — floral decor in the Art Nouveau manner, by Van Bergh; silverplated; $48 D.

INKWELL — large figural hunting dog, inkwell inside tree trunk, 11"L; platform area somewhat grey but overall silverplating fine; $115 D.

—, DOUBLE — rectangular tray 12" x 6½", ornate edge, place for pens each side of 2 square cut glass bottles with matching tops; tops hinged, 2 dancing cherubs with tambourines in middle; Reed & Barton silverplated; $375 D.

LADLE — oval fluted vermeil bowl, treen handle; Tiffany & Co., 15½"L; *$150 A.

LETTER OPENER — floral decor, scrolling; silverplated; $19 D.

— moose head relief one side handle, pine cone/needles opposite; 8"L, c. 1900, silverplated; $17 D.

MATCH SAFE — nude woman with flowing hair in water, monogrammed; Unger Bros.; $275 D.

— full figure nude reclining on wind-swept waves, stork flying above, with highly embossed scrolls; 1¾" x 2¾"; $145 D.

— Art Nouveau tending toward rococo ornamentation; $100 D.

— full figure standing nude with flying scarf, mermaid beneath her feet, other elaborate decor; 1¾" x 2¾"; $95 D.

— embossed hanging bell flowers/vines/crawling snakes; marked A. Stowell & Co.; $65 D.

— floral design; $65 D.

MIRROR, DRESSER — lady's head, "Dawn," by Unger Bros.; $200 D.

MIRROR, HAND — reverse with repousse design of standing woman holding butterfly, stamped G. SILVER PAT. JUNE 13, 1905; American, c. 1910, 9¾"L; *$100 A.

— floral AN styling; several noted, $35 to $45 D.

— celluloid body, sterling reticulated back with floral motif; $18 D.

— floral decor, silverplated on brass, plating very worn; $15 D.

MIRROR HANDLE — American AN, engraved initial; 4 ozs. 7 dwts; *$50 A.

MUG, SHAVING — applied Croesus motif, decorated handle, re-silverplated; Derby, 1904; $42 D.

NAIL (MANICURE) BRUSH — decor of Cherub; $45 D.

NAIL (MANICURE) FILE CASE — engraved design, 3½"L; $15 D.

NAPKIN HOLDER — retailed by Marshall Field; $45 D.

NUT DISH SET — master plus 6 individual dishes, by Kerr; $150 D.

— 4 individual boat-shape dishes, floral rims, monogrammed; by Alvin; set, $76 D.

— 6 oval-shaped with raised floral borders, each 3½"D; marked Homan's Quadruple Plate; set, $48 D.

PITCHER, CREAM — "Athenic" pattern by Gorham, ivory & sterling; $1,600 D.

—, WATER — "Athenic" pattern by Gorham, design of Shasta Daisies; $1,750 D.

—, WATER— inverted pear form, applied/chased with Spring Daffodils about handle/body; set above domed circular foot; Towle Silversmiths, c. 1910, 9"H, 39 ozs. 8 dwts; *$700 A.

—, WATER — typical form, body embossed each side with stylized flower, handle applied with similar decor; Larsen & Co.,Copenhagen,1909; 9"H, 19 ozs. 3 dwts.; *$225 A.

PUNCH BOWL AND LADLE — "October Harvest" bowl with glass liner, 16½"H; $350 D.

PURSE — decor of lady's head; Whiting & Davis; $165 D.

— sterling handle & double chain, black knit with jet beads design on body; 5 winged cherubs, trees, flowers each side; Continental; $125 D.

SHOE HORN — floral design hollow handle; $20 D.

— another, same; $18 D.

SHOE HORN, BUTTON HOOK, & NAIL FILE SET — matched with hollow handles, floral relief designs; $40 D.

SILVER HOLLOW WARE SERVICE — 7-piece coffee & tea service: teapot, coffee pot, covered sugar bowl, waste bowl, kettle, warmer stand; each with chased repousse Poppies; hallmark of J.E. Caldwell & Co.; *$2,400 A.

TAZZA — circular plate inlaid with stylized pine trees in Japanese style forming central rosette, on raised circular splayed foot; stamped "TIFFANY & CO., MAKERS 16971 9703 Sterling and copper inlay", 8½"D; *$350 A.

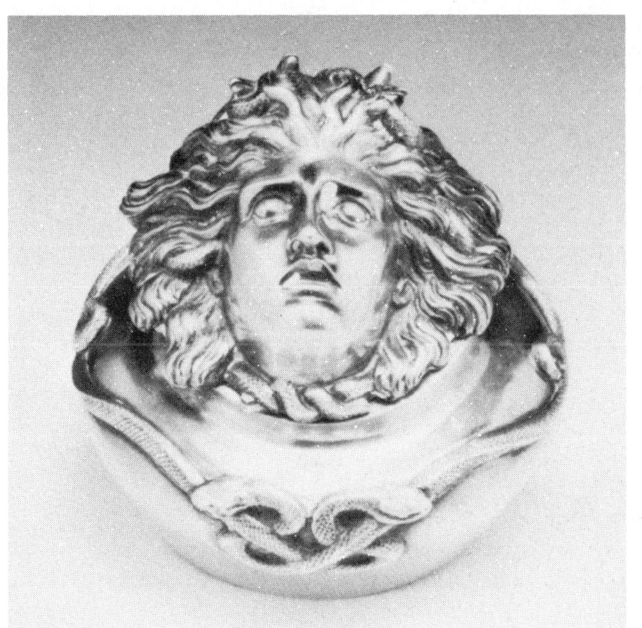

BOX, COVERED, silver-gilt with hinged cover in form of Medusa, snakes intertwined around box; Italian, c. 1900, 4"D, 8 ozs. 4 dwt.; *$800 A. (Sotheby's)

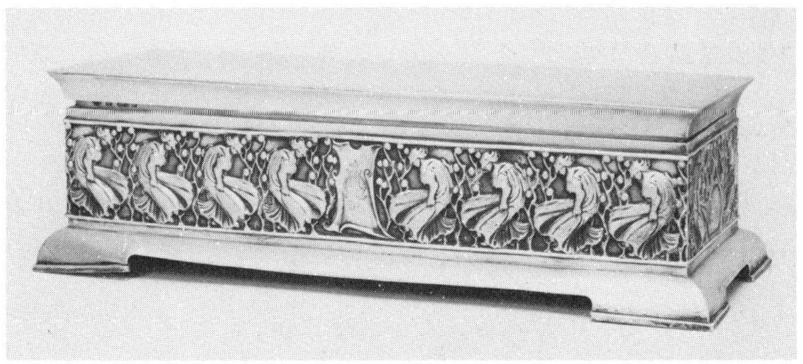

CASKET, SILVER, by William Hutton & Sons, England; *$1,500 A. (Christie's)

TEA BALL — embossed floral, hinged lid, chain; $135 D.

TEA CADDY — body with interlacing figure enameled blue/green/violet; cover with inset turquoise cabochon; hallmarks of Liberty & Co., 3½"H; *$900 A.

TOOTHBRUSH — fancy handle, clean bristles set in bone; $22D.
— high relief floral decor, hollow handle, bone with bristles; $20 D.

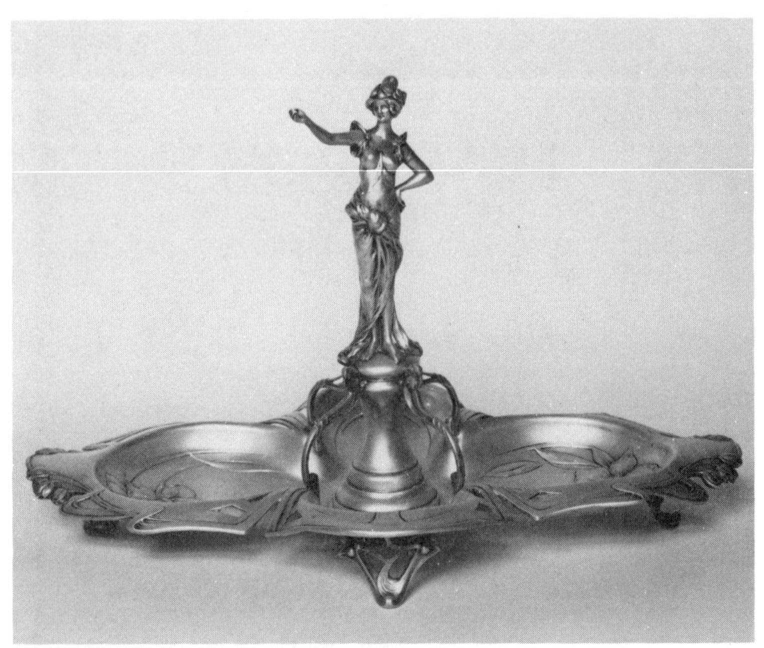

CENTERPIECE, AUSTRIAN, c. 1900; maker's mark "M.G."; *$1,400 A. (Christie's East)

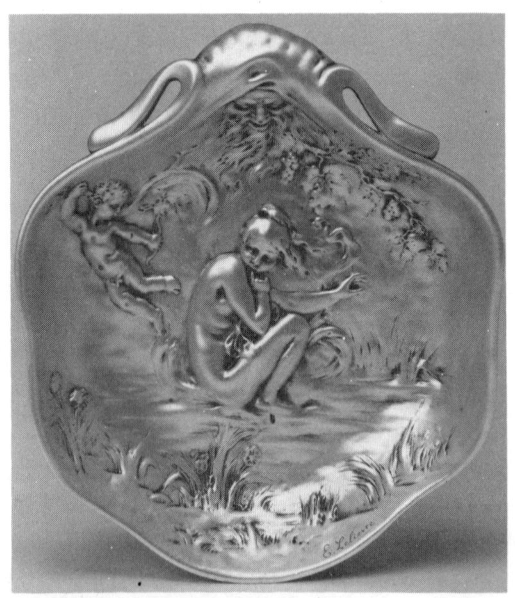

CENTERPIECE, FRENCH, by E. Lelievre; *$1,000 A. (Christie's)

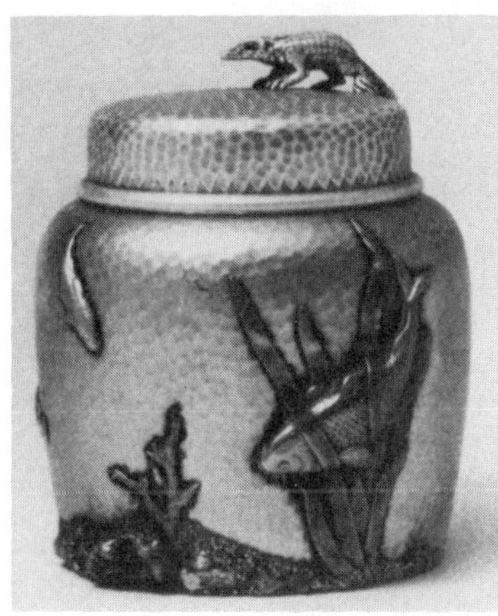

CANISTER, TEA, Gorham Mfg. Co.; in the Japanese style, hammered surface with applied decoration in silver, gold, copper; 3¾"H, 7 ozs.; *$2,000 A. (Sotheby's)

Below, COFFEE SET WITH HAMMERED SURFACE, each piece a lobed oviform on 4 ribbed & hooved feet; Coffee Pot, 6½"H; Tray, 13½"L; German, c. 1910; *$350 A. (Sotheby's)

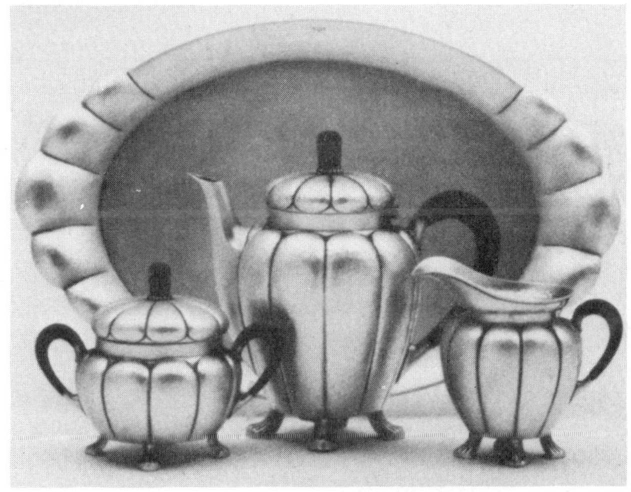

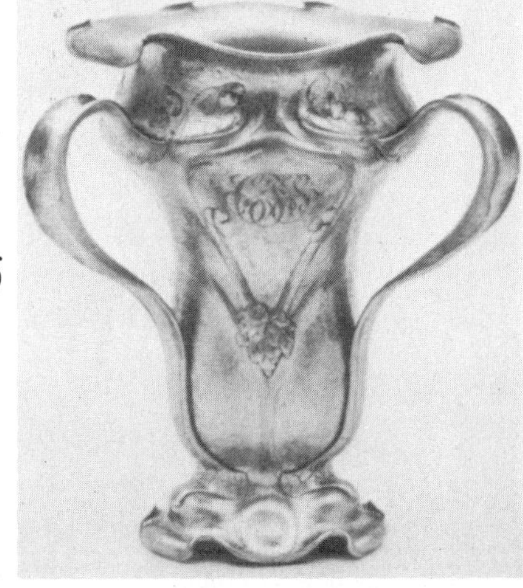

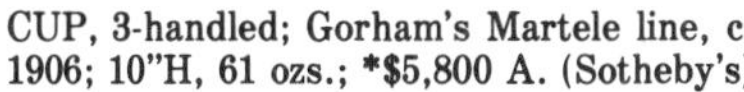

CUP, 3-handled; Gorham's Martele line, c. 1906; 10"H, 61 ozs.; *$5,800 A. (Sotheby's)

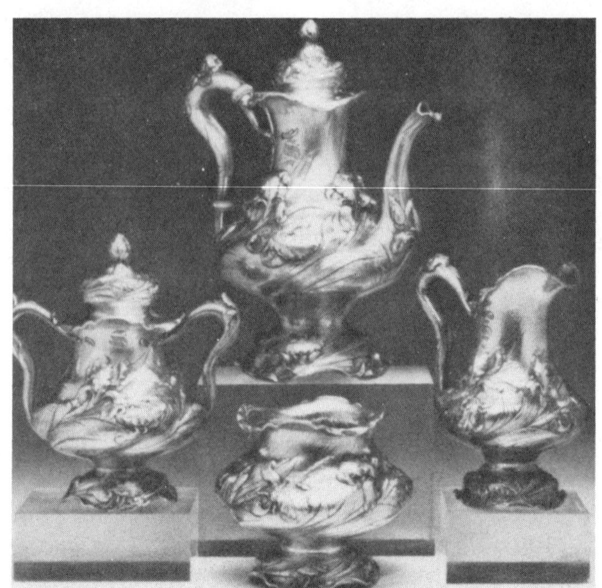

COFFEE SERVICE BY REED & BARTON; 4 pieces: coffee pot, covered sugar, creamer, waste bowl; pot, 10¾"H; total weight, 84 ozs. 4 dwt.; *$1,900 A. (C.G. Sloan)

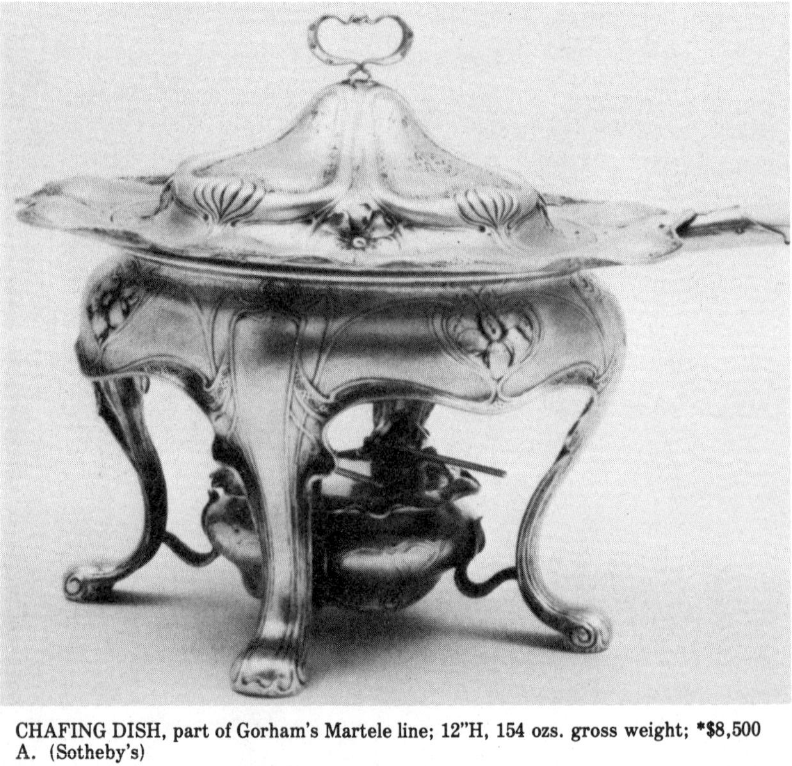

CHAFING DISH, part of Gorham's Martele line; 12"H, 154 ozs. gross weight; *$8,500 A. (Sotheby's)

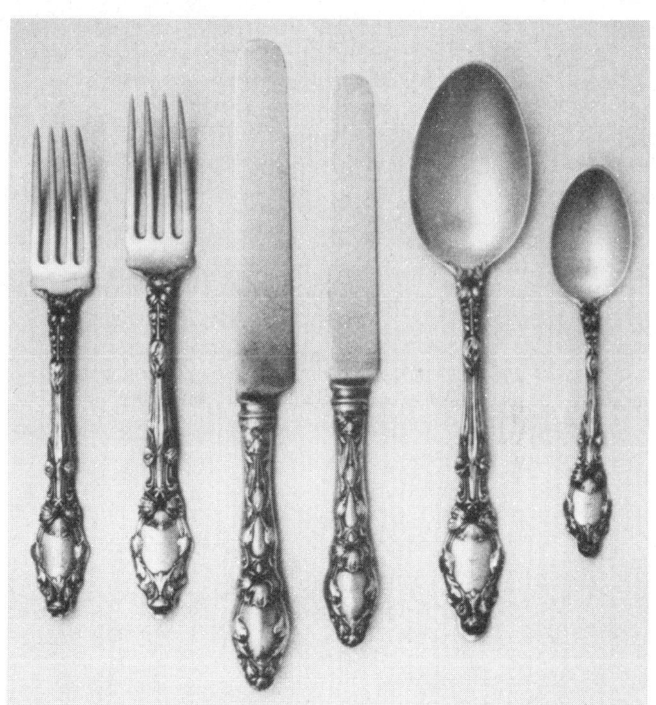

FLATWARE; representative pieces in Gorham's "Virginiana" pattern; in all, 84 pieces comprised of 12 Luncheon Forks, 12 Dinner Forks, 12 Soup Spoons, 12 Dinner Knives, 12 Luncheon Knives, 24 Teaspoons; 112 ozs. total weight; *$2,600 A. (Sotheby's)

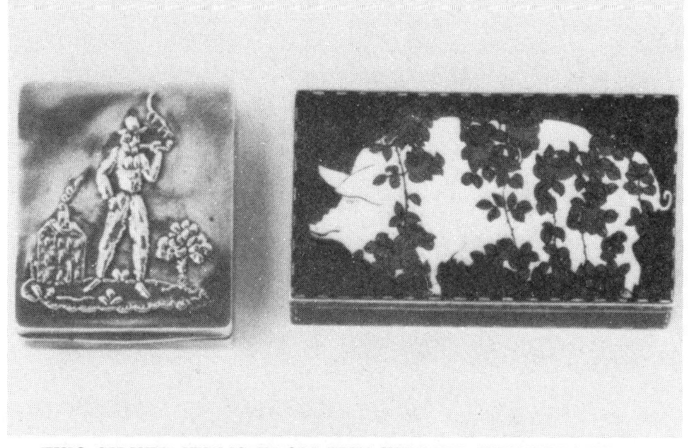

TWO SILVER ITEMS FROM THE WIENER WERKSTATTE, c. 1910. (Left) parcel-gilt compact, designed by Josef Hoffmann, gilt interior, 2¼"; *$450 A. (Right) box, covered, designed by Susi Singer, enameled with black & white checkered border, 3¾"L; *$2,200 A. (Sotheby's)

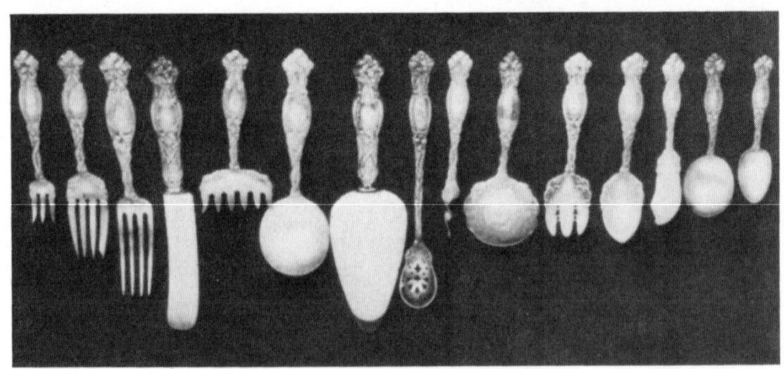

FLATWARE; representative pieces from service for 12 from Whiting Mfg. Co., including such items as Nut Picker, Sardine Fork, Pie Knife, etc.; 119.2 ozs. weighable silver content; *$3,250 A. (Phillips)

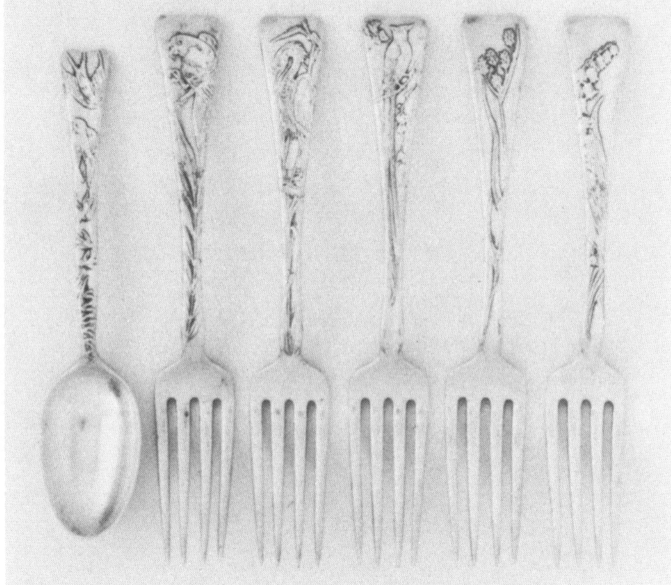

FLATWARE, TIFFANY & CO.'s "Lap Over Edge" pattern, c. 1885; each piece with different design; 6 pieces, 11 ozs.; *$325 A. (Sotheby's)

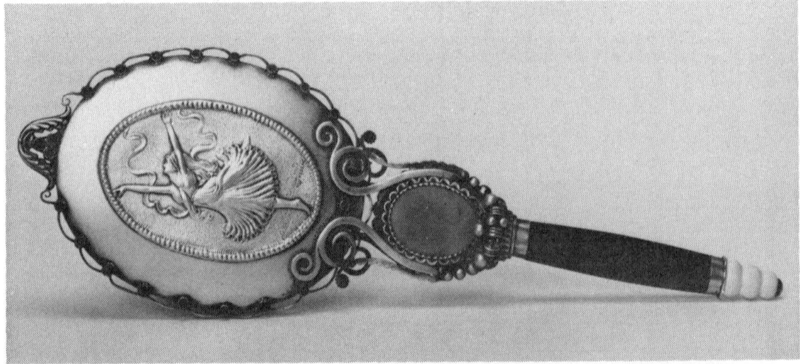

MIRROR, HAND; silver & ebony, by Paul Kiss; *$12,000 A. (Christie's)

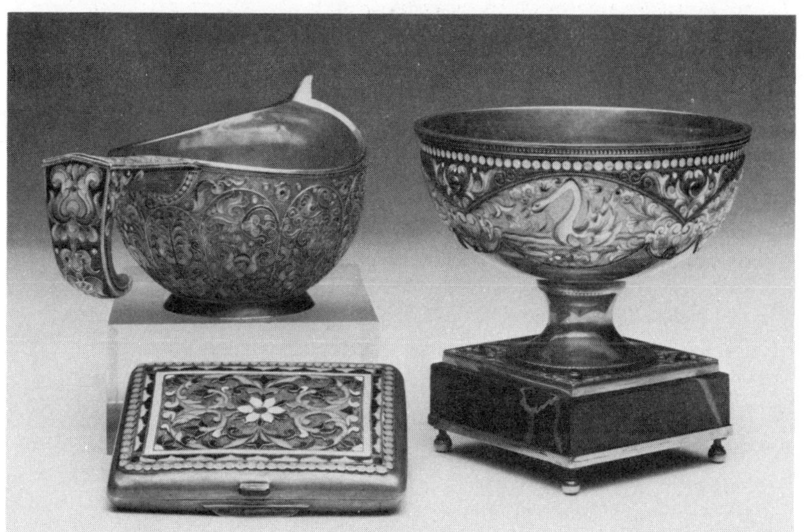

RUSSIAN SILVER AND ENAMEL PIECES. (Upper Left) Vermeil kovsh, marked "Khlebnikov," Moscow; *$3,300 A. (Lower Left) Cigarette case, 4"L; *$475 A. (Right) Vermeil footed bowl, marked "Gratchev," Moscow; square base set upon grey marble plinth on footed vermeil frame; 4¾"H x 4¾"D; *$2,500 A. (C.G. Sloan)

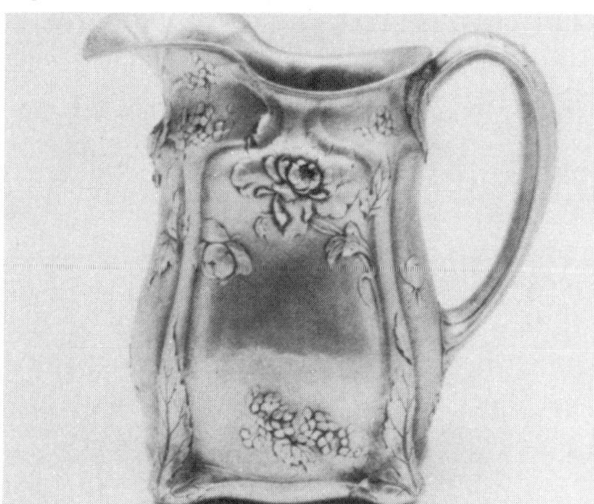

PITCHER, WATER; Gorham's Martele line, c. 1905; 8"H to lip, 40 ozs.; *$5,900 A. (Sotheby's)

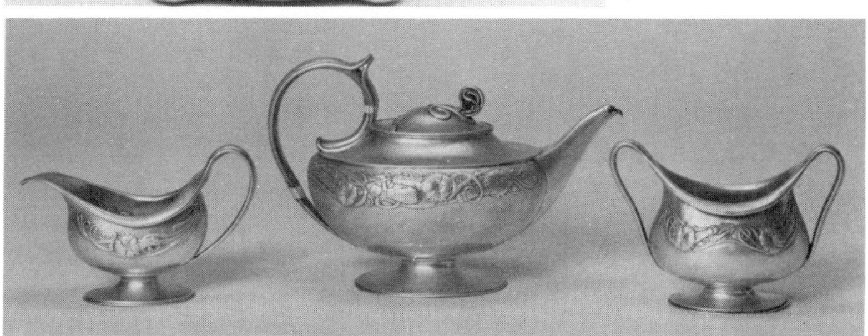

TEA SERVICE, 3 pieces by Omar Ramsden & Alwyn Carr, London, 1911; small pot, open sugar, open creamer; *$1,500 A. (Christie's)

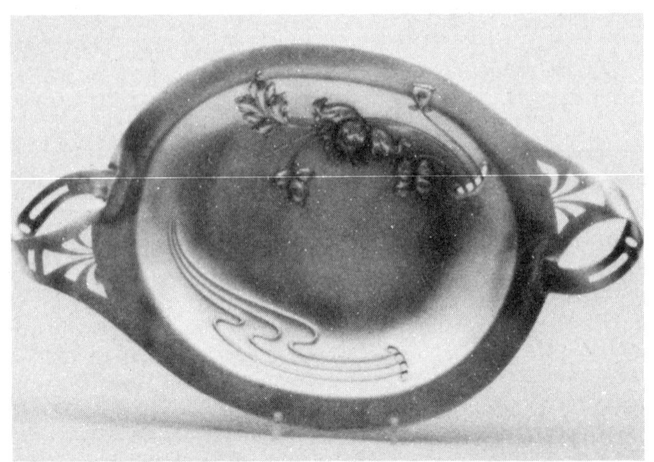

TRAY, BREAD; eliptical with Poppy motif; Austrian, marked "H et M" in rectangle, Vienna, c. 1905; 20½"L, 25 ozs. 16 dwt.; *$550 A. (Sotheby's)

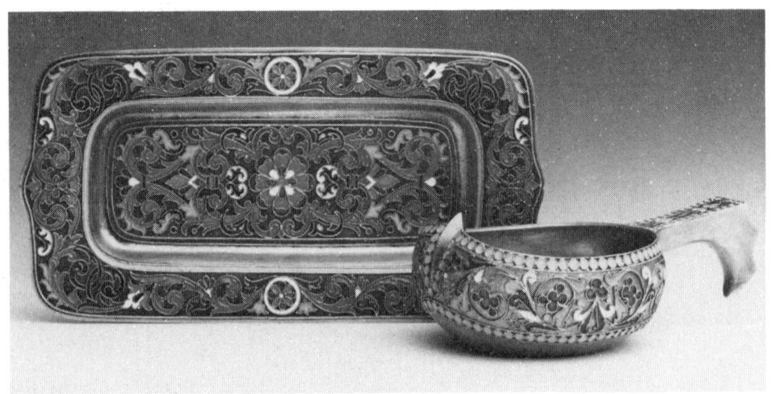

RUSSIAN SILVER & ENAMEL PIECES. (Left) Vermeil silver & enamel tray, Moscow, 1887, by Viktor Savinkov, retailed by Tiffany & Co., 6"L; *$500 A. (Right) Vermeil silver & enamel kvosh, made 1895, 4¼"L; *$750 A. (C.G. Sloan)

TOOTHPOWDER DISPENSER — cut glass jar, repousse floral lid; 4"H x 1½"D; $29 D.

TRAY — 28"L, 108 ozs. 3 dwts.; *$1,500 A.

— Chrysanthemums applied in high relief, scrolling each corner and connecting flowers as well, all on 3¼" border puffed out at random; 15" x 13", 51.2 troy ozs., attributed by mark to Bixby Silver Co.; $850 D.

— in the Secessionist manner, a shaped circular rim pierced/embossed with stylized foliate designs, surface cut with similar decor; Vienna, c. 1910; 13½"D, 17 ozs. 8 dwts.; *$550 A.

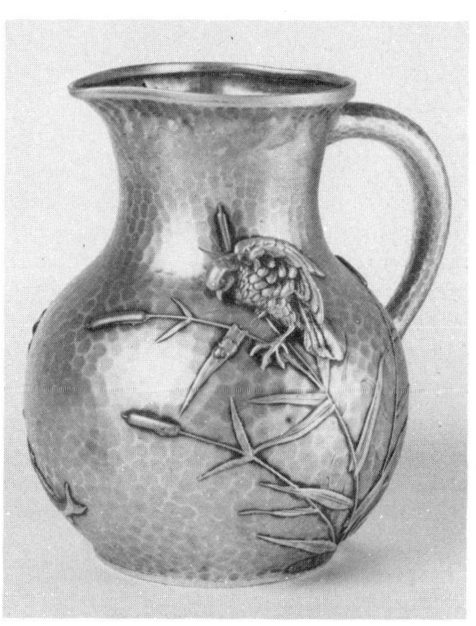

PITCHER, WATER; hammered silver, Arts & Crafts style, c. 1880; *$1,700 A. (Christie's East)

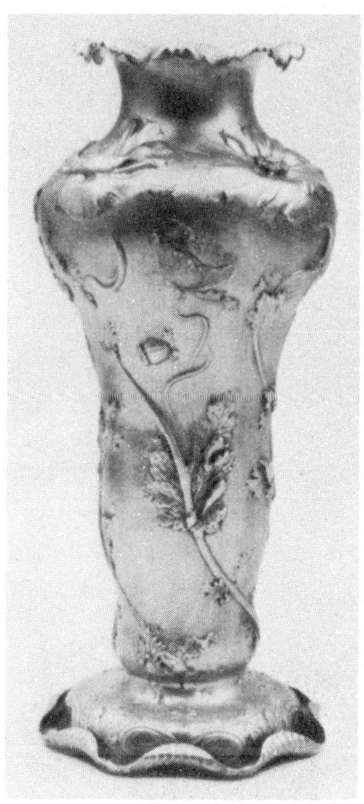

VASE, probably part of Gorham's Martele line, retailed by Black, Starr & Frost; stamped "950/1000 fine", 17½"H, 64 ozs.; *$1,750 A. (Sotheby's)

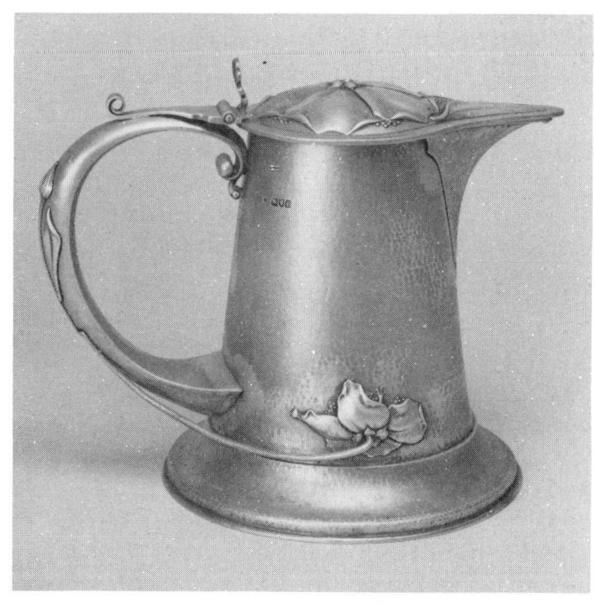

PITCHER, covered, by William Hutton & Sons, England; *$2,500 A. (Christie's)

— flat, 2 huge poppies, by Wallace, 13.5 ozs.; $435 D.

— set of 10 small trays in Art Nouveau manner, band of flowers in high relief on scalloped border, monogrammed; 3 1/8"D x ¾"H; $195 D.

TROPHY — 2-handled, 5½"H, 10.5 ozs.; *$275 A.

UMBRELLA — hickory shaft, L-shape silver handle enameled in green, stamped with Tiffany marks; 35½"L, some fabric tears; *$180 A.

UMBRELLA HANDLE — Art Nouveau manner; $45 D.

VASE — wide flared trumpet shape, lobed rim & partly fluted stem, above circle of beads over domed base; Tiffany & Co., 1907, 25½"H, 107 ozs.; *$2,000 A.

— elongated tulip form, top heavily applied/chased with Chrysanthemum blossoms, their stems/leaves flowing down body; all set above circular base with similar decor on 4 scrolling panel feet; Black, Starr & Frost, c. 1900, 20"H, 98 ozs.; *$1,750 A.

— swelling cylinder with broad everted lip, domed base, all embossed/chased/applied with Rose buds/vines/flowers; 2 undulating handles with conforming decor; Gorham Mfg. Co., c. 1905, 20"H, 86 ozs. 8 dwts.; *$1,400 A.

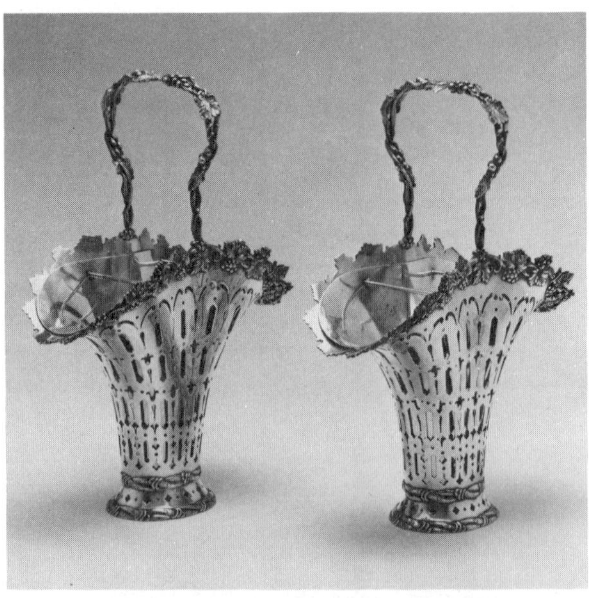

VASES, pair in basket form, applied grapevine borders/handles, pierced sides; baskets 13½"H, total 47 ozs. 16 dwt.; Tiffany & Co., NY; *$1,125 A. (C.G. Sloan)

— elongated gourd set on circular domed foot with broad crenulated edge; the entire vase embossed/chased with Poppy flowers/leaves; Black, Starr & Frost, c. 1905, although probably part of Gorham's Martele line; 14½"H, 39 ozs.; *$900 A.

— carved ivory body surrounded by silver mountings; French, 5¼"H; *$225 A.

— trumpet body pierced/embossed/chased with roses on vine set above domed circular foot similarly decorated; unmarked, c. 1900; lacks liner; 13"H, 16 ozs.; *$200 A.

— trumpet shape on round foot, foliate etched/pierced upper border, similarly decorated foot; 10½"H, 8 ozs. 2 dwts.; *$90 A.

— corset-shaped, Art Nouveau manner, 5½"H; silverplated; $12 D.

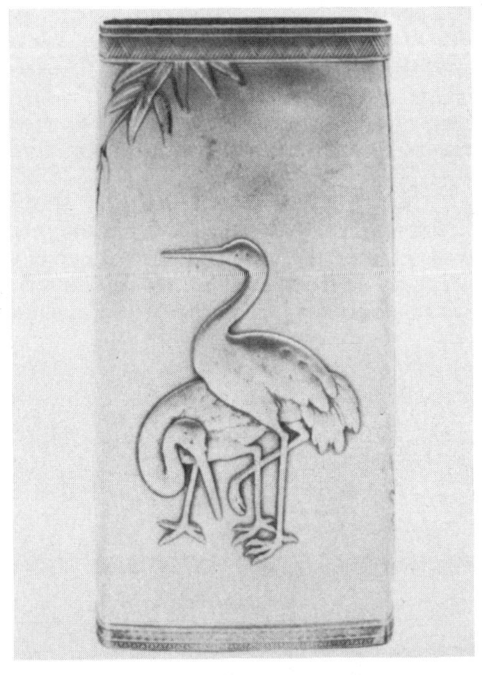

VASE IN JAPANESE FASHION, rectangular with applied cranes/swallows/bamboo/Cherry branch, the base & rim applied with bands of Oriental-inspired geometric motifs; Tiffany & Co., New York, c. 1875; 8½"H, 14 ozs. 12 dwt.; *$2,000 A. (Sotheby's)

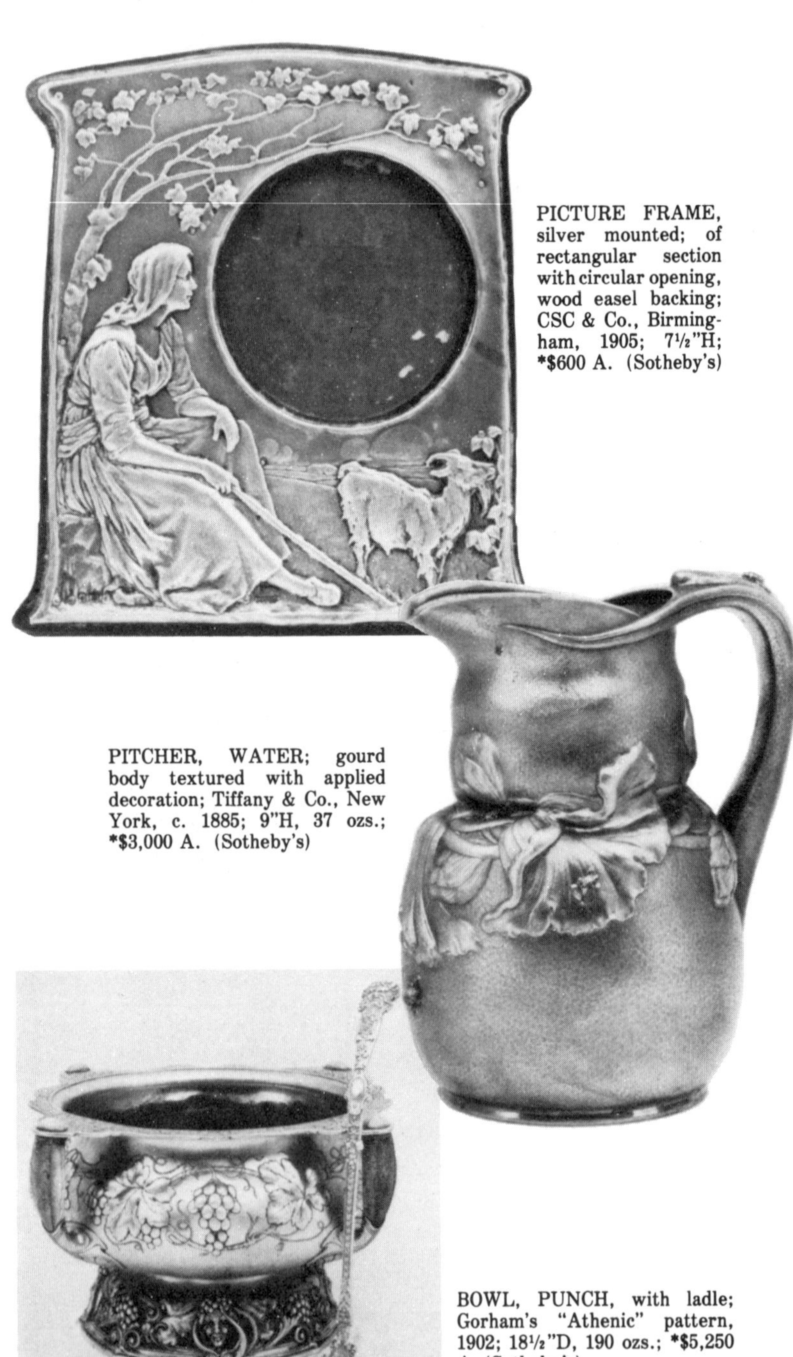

PICTURE FRAME, silver mounted; of rectangular section with circular opening, wood easel backing; CSC & Co., Birmingham, 1905; 7½"H; *$600 A. (Sotheby's)

PITCHER, WATER; gourd body textured with applied decoration; Tiffany & Co., New York, c. 1885; 9"H, 37 ozs.; *$3,000 A. (Sotheby's)

BOWL, PUNCH, with ladle; Gorham's "Athenic" pattern, 1902; 18½"D, 190 ozs.; *$5,250 A. (Sotheby's)

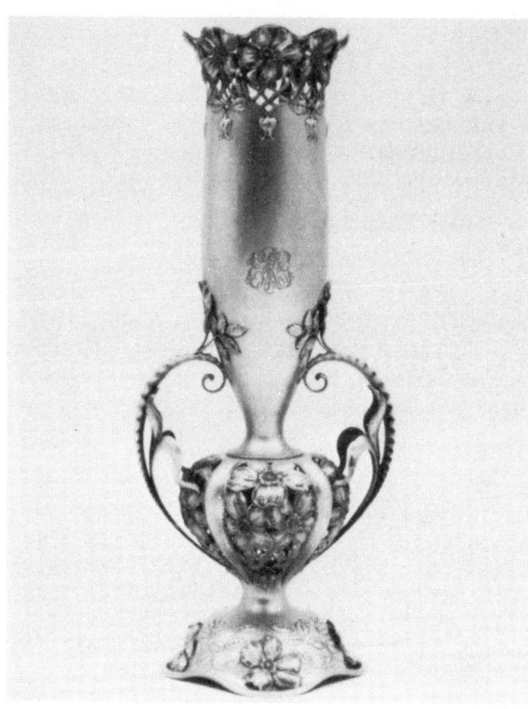

VASE WITH POPPY MOTIF, by Redlich & Co., New York, c. 1910; 22"H, 72 ozs. 8 dwt; *$1,600 A. (Sotheby's)

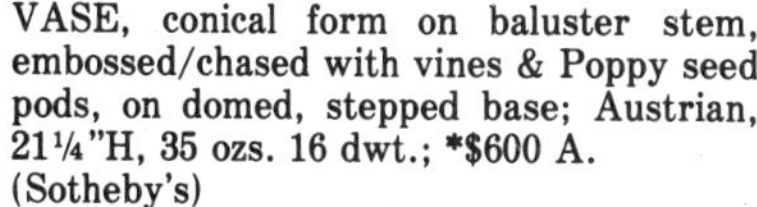

VASE, conical form on baluster stem, embossed/chased with vines & Poppy seed pods, on domed, stepped base; Austrian, 21¼"H, 35 ozs. 16 dwt.; *$600 A. (Sotheby's)

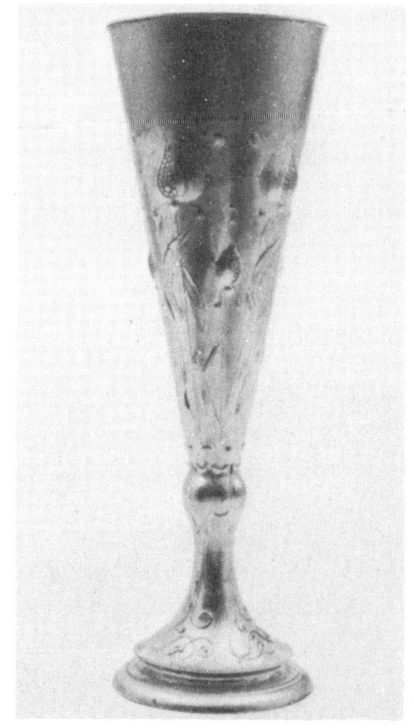

CAST METAL ITEMS

Gathered together in this chapter are a collection of both useful and decorative items cast from a variety of metals. The metals most commonly used were brass, iron, bronze, pewter, and that ambiguous term, "white metal." For other items made from these items, see chapters on Bronze Figures; Jewelry; and Lighting Devices.

Certain manufacturers were considered highly desirable at their times of productions, and many of those same firms' products are avidly collected today. Louis Comfort Tiffany's Tiffany Studios produced a wide variety of items, the primary metal used being bronze. J.P. Kayser & Sohn were known for their well-made, well-designed pewter products, marked with the firm trademark of "Kayserzinn." The Arts and Crafts fascination with copper as a design material was reflected in the many copper products, especially (in this country) by the Roycrofters. Yet many other well-made items were produced without any discernable markings or by small companies whose total output may only have run to a few different items.

Some of the most interesting items (due to their being relegated to the back rooms and out-of-the-way corners of some antique shops) are the cast iron pieces. In the Art Nouveau modes they are relatively few in number, tending toward the curvilinear styles rather than the later rectilinear types. Prices still tend to be relatively low due to little collector interest at the time; look for that to change in the future.

Collectors interested in collecting "sets" of objects should note the Tiffany desk set items. Once the perfect gift item for the upper middle class and others, such objects were easily added to at future holiday giftings — know which pieces the prospective receiver already has, and you'll know what pieces to buy them to help "fill out" the set. Today the collector can take advantage of this collecting factor by purchasing only a piece or two at a time, gradually filling out a set.

As desirable as the factor of being able to purchase a piece at a time to fill out a set may be, collectors should note the differences between various patterns. Some patterns have as many as 31 items in them, as Hugh McKean observed (in *The "Lost" Treasures of Louis Comfort Tiffany*); other patterns may have only a handful. To complicate things, there were many Tiffany-produced desk items which were not parts of sets, items produced individually and meant to be purchased as such.

Readers will notice reference to Dore finishes in the bronze items. The Dore finish was a gold patination applied to the bronze; when found today in a rubbed or otherwise damaged condition, it really should not be removed. Many of the smaller Tiffany items were produced with this finish, although some were apparently made both with and without it. Tiffany certainly wasn't the only manufacturer to adopt this gilding process, as it was extensively used in Europe, too.

Then there's the matter of "white metal." More properly, the term should be "white metals," for the name has been applied to a variety of alloyed metals, all of which share some common characteristics. Among these are britannia (or Britannia) metal, a tin-based alloy combined with copper and antimony, occasionally mixed with zinc and bismuth; spelter, a basically zinc alloy; pewter, a tin-based metal alloyed with copper, lead, and antimony; and several other related alloys. Their commonality is shown through their color, all being silvery-white in appearance (although some, such as pewter, tend toward the grey due to their lead contents).

As used in the context of this book, pewter is considered separately from the other white metals. As a group, white metal was an inexpensive, easy to work with substitute for other metals used in casting processes. As a result, it was used extensively in making such items as table lamp bases, some vases, and small decorative objects. When collectors find it today, it may be covered by a patina or gilding or enameling. Look at the bases of such pieces to determine the presence of the tell-tale silvery-white color, rather than the brownish look of bronze.

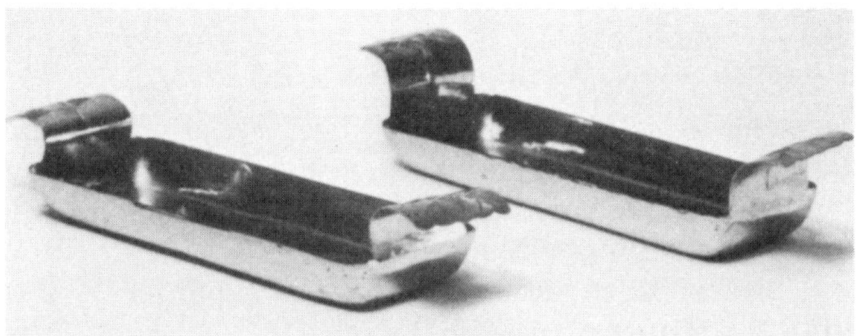

PAIR BRASS TRAYS, designed by Josef Hoffmann, c. 1910; by Wiener Werkstatte, each 10½"L; *$750 A. (Sotheby's)

BRASS ITEMS

Ashtray — nude, birds, & deer decoration; $52 D.
Blotter, Hand — girl's face in handle; $12 D.
Bookends — pair, extendable, Art Nouveau design; $60 D.
— pair, cast nude woman, small no-harm hole in base; $40 D.
Button — flowing hair woman, dime size; $8 D.
Desk Set — signed set by Bradley & Hubbard; blotter corners, letter holder, blotter, letter opener; $35 D.
Hearth Curb — Arts and Crafts style, inset with stylized lilies & square raised balustrading, implement rests either end; 53½"L; *$125 A.
Inkwell — round tray with standing lyre, clear glass bottle with matching brass lid; $97 D.
Inkwell/Pen Tray — Art Nouveau hair forms tray, large flower rotates for ink; some red patina, 9+"L; $90 D.
Letter Opener — Art Nouveau styling, cast iron handle; $18 D.
Mirror, Hand — brass frame, back with female color portrait on celluloid held in by brass openwork, 5 3/8"L; $30 D.
Planter — Arts and Crafts repousse with Moorish design; heraldic rampant lions & spread-wing eagle decor, lion loose-ring handles; 36"H, top 14" square; *$125 A.
Tray — Art Nouveau styling; $75 D.

BRONZE ITEMS: TIFFANY DESK SETS (these sets, available in about a dozen patterns, can be collected piece by piece, some with much greater availability than others. Once they were considered ideal gift items, only to go through a period of disenchantment and neglect. Once again they are being widely sought. Those pieces housing Tiffany's Favrile glass are especially desirable.)

Adams pattern — 2 pieces, pen holder and blotter; signed, #d 1778; both for $298 D.
— calendar, blotter holders, letter rack, with Dore finish; $275 D.
— picture frame, 9 x 12, signed & #d; $425 D.

American Indian pattern — 11-piece desk set, Dore finish; pair blotter ends, stationery rack, calendar frame, inkwell, stamp box, pen tray, notepad holder, spring clip, letter opener, magnifying glass; *$700 A.
— 4 pieces; large inkwell with insert, pen tray, 2-tiered letter box, paper clip; $450 D.
— rocker blotter, gold Dore finish; $99 D.
— calendar easel, gold Dore finish; $225 D.

— cigar box, Dore finish, patina, hinged lid & wood lining, 8"L x 5" deep, x 2¾"H; $335 D.
— inkwell, large tapered, with insert; $288 D.
— inkwell, same as above; $225 D.
— letter opener, signed Tiffany Studios & #d; $170 D.
— same letter opener as above, tip nicked; $45 D.
— letter rack, large with closed sides; $425 D.
— pad holder; $190 D.

— stamp box, with 3-section tray; $239 D.

Aztec pattern — 4 pieces: pen tray, inkwell, 2 blotter ends; *$275 A.

Bookmark pattern — inkwell, Dore finish, 3¼"W; *$225 A.
— letter opener, Dore finish; $65 D.

Chinese pattern — humidor, 8 x 5, marked Tiffany Studios; $600 D.
— letter opener; $115 D.
— memo pad, signed & #d; $110 D.

Classic pattern — 9 pieces, Dore finish: 2 blotter ends, pen tray, paper knife, memo pad, inkstand, calendar, rocker blotter, paper rack; each impressed TIFFANY STUDIOS NEW YORK, with #; *$1,200 A.

Grapevine pattern — 12 pieces, panels of glass cracked; *$900 A.
— 6 pieces, each impressed with mark, minor cracks to glass contained; inkwell with contemporary glass liner, rocker blotter, footed pen tray, letter opener, 2 blotter powder containers; *$700 A.
— inkwell, green glass liner, 4¼" square; $295 D.
— inkwell, green slag glass liner; $280 D.
— jewel box, amber glass, velvet lined lid; $400 D.
— jewel box, amber glass, Dore finish; $395 D.
— letter holder, 3-section, 6 x 10, #1008, Dore finish; $369 D.

Nautical pattern — letter holder, 2-section, dolphins playing among waves, sea shell center piece, Dore finish; $375 D.

Pine Needle pattern — 12 pieces, each impressed with TIFFANY STUDIOS NEW YORK and serial number: 4 blotter corners, rocker blotter, letter scale, stamp box, pen tray, small square inkstand, small paper rack, pen holder & pen brush; *$1,300 A.

— 8 pieces, each impressed with company marks and serial number: 2 blotter ends, cigar humidor box, book rack, utility box (missing 1 ball foot), small square inkstand, large round inkstand, large paper rack; *$700 A.

— 4 pieces, each marked with firm mark and serial numbers (#844 and #1004): pair blotter ends, pen tray, inkwell, pen; pierced green patinated bronze over green glass; *$250 A.

— blotter ends & paper clip; each stamped TIFFANY STUDIOS NEW YORK, Dore finish; blotter ends numbered 999 on ends; paper clip numbered 1190; *$150 A.

— inkwell, ball feet, original green mottled glass insert, #845; $359 D.

— tobacco jar, covered; separate liner & interior lid, 6¾"H, unsigned; *$300 A.

— twine holder, impressed mark; lid missing hinge; $190 D.

— utility box, on 4 bun feet, frame enclosing glass impressed with mark, & #813; 6½ x 3 7/8; *$275 A.

Venetian pattern — 5 pieces, each in Dore finish (rubbed), impressed mark & #d: letter rack, rocker blotter, covered box, table clock, calendar holder; *$950 A.

— blotter ends, pair, 19"; $210 D.

— letter opener; $175 D.

— letter rack, closed sides, Dore finish; $400 D.

Zodiac pattern — 12 pieces, each with impressed mark, Dore finish: 4 blotter ends, small stamp box, larger box, postal scale, letter opener, letter holder, calendar holder, inkwell, rocking blotter; $1,750 D.

— 9 pieces, brown patina; $1,465 D.

— 9 pieces, brown patina; $1,295 D.

— 5 pieces, Dore finish: pair blotter ends, paper knife, memo pad, large letter rack; all impressed mark with serial numbers; *$700 A.

— 6 pieces, each impressed with mark and #: large picture frame, covered box, letter rack, pen tray, 2 short blotter ends; *$700 A.

— 7 pieces, Dore finish, each impressed with mark and #: pen tray, inkstand, calendar, ashtray, small paper rack, stamp box, postal scale; *$580 A.

— 8 pieces, each marked and #d: letter rack, 4 blotter corners, pen tray, utility box, inkstand with liner; *$550 A.

— 5 assorted pieces, Dore finish; *$350 A.

— pair blotter ends; $150 D.

— bookends, Dore finish, signed & #d; pair, $320 D.

— bookends, same as above; pair, $275 D.
— box, handkerchief; Dore finish, 6¼" square; $225 D.
— inkwell, octagonal, in segmented tray, green-brown patina, glass liner; stamped TIFFANY STUDIOS NEW YORK 1076; 10¾"W; $400 A.
— inkwell, as above; *$300 A.
— inkwell cover; $50 D.
— letter rack, 2-section; $175 D.
— letter rack, 2-section, green patina; $175 D.
— magnifying glass; $325 D.
— matchbox holder, 4½"; $150 D.
— paperweight, patinated; $152 D.
— pen tray, shallow rectangular cast at ends with Pisces & Scorpio signs; Dore finish, #D100, 10"L; $190 D.
— picture frame, 7 x 8, for 4 x 5 photo; $325 D.
— postal scale; $275 D.
— postal scale, brown patina; $250 D.

BRONZE ITEMS: MISCELLANEOUS

Ashtray — shell form, 5"D, signature of Jennings Brothers, gilt; $150 D.
— Art Nouveau styling, 6½"L; *$100 A.
Bowl — Lily pad form, frog on rim; $80 D.
Box — enamel flower on cover, Dore finish, hinged, 4" x 4"; $65 D.

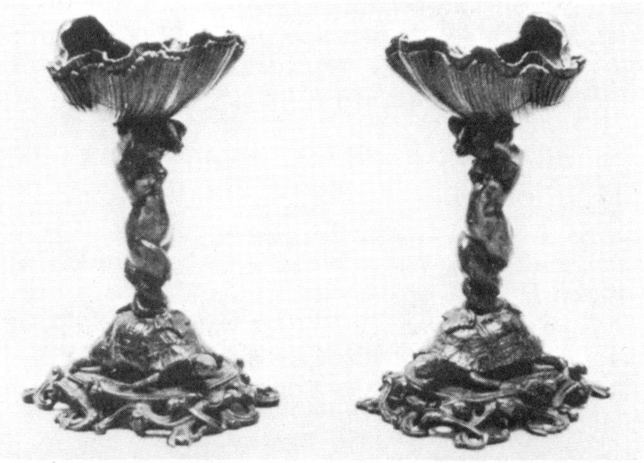

BRONZE CENTERPIECES, PAIR; patinated Nautilus style, French, late 19th century, 9"H; *$650 A. (Butterfield's)

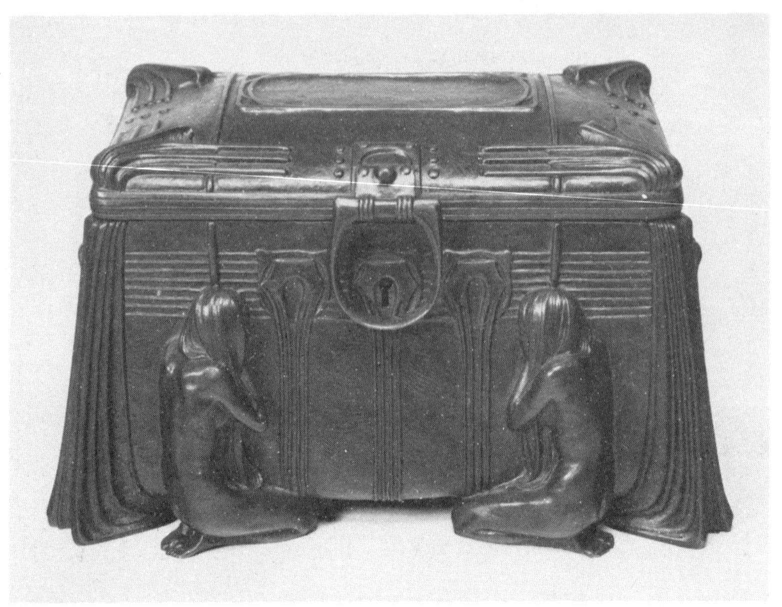

BRONZE CASKET, designed by Gustave Gurschner, Austrian, early 20th century; *$12,500 A. (Christie's)

Centerpiece — gilt-bronze & blackish-green marble, early 20th century; circular marble basin set within parcel-gilt bronze stepped rim cast with 3 walking polar bears; indistinguishable stamp on underside; 15"D; *$1,000 A.

Charger — Abalone patter, Dore finish, by Tiffany Studios, 14"D; $200 D.

Compote — Tiffany Studios, #1724; $225 D.

Dish — fern dish, cast with frieze of classical women; impressed S113 TIFFANY STUDIOS FROM THE ANTIQUE 1612; regilt, 4"H; *$460 A.

— figural shell, Dore finish on interior with kneeling nude in relief on wave with many fish; footed underside is silverclad with 2 makers' marks, "Susse Fres," and artist signature "Ledru"; 7½" x 6¾"; $375 D.

Knife Sharpener — stylized bird, Art Nouveau, 6½"L; $35 D.

Paperweight — Bulldog, by Tiffany Studios; $150 D.

— letters "BTEA" conjoined, marked "Dinner, March 1905," from Tiffany Studios; $135 D.

Pen Tray — crouching nude maiden behind elongated pod-form tray, brown patina, inscribed "V.W." & "H.B.S." as monogramming; probably Austrian, c. 1910, 12"L; *$500 A.

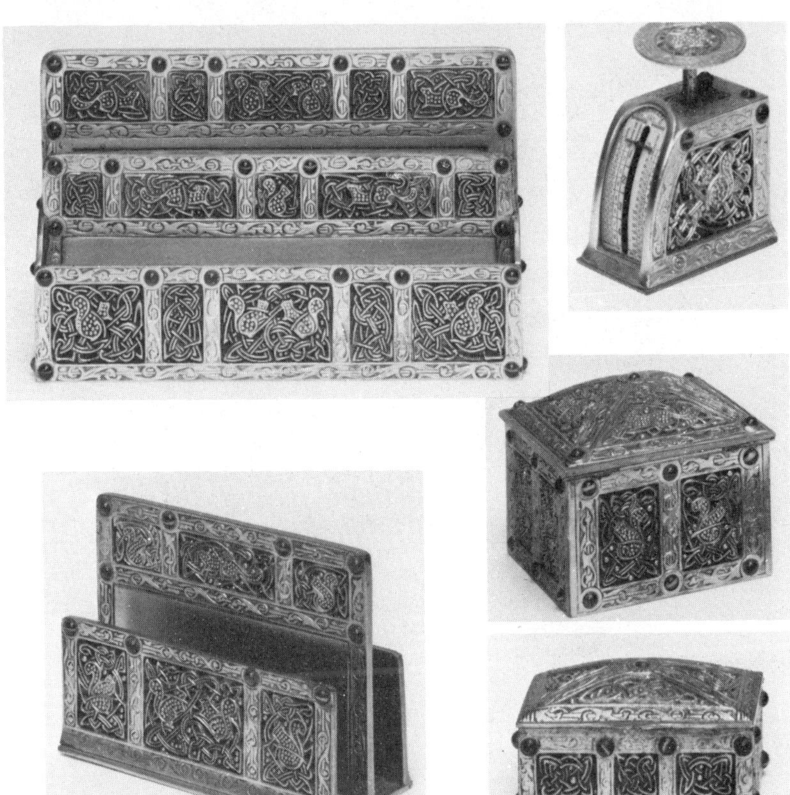

BRONZE DESK SET BY TIFFANY STUDIOS, New York, in the "9th Century" pattern, gilt, 14 pieces; *$2,200 A. (Christie's)

Picture Frame — Favrile glass and bronze frame (rectangular) with oval center bordered by heavily iridized & crackled blue glass; impressed TIFFANY FURNACES 56; 10½"H; *$850 A.

Plaque — bust of woman, 9½ x 13, mark unreadable; $245 D.

Plate — Greek border design, Dore finish, 9"D, from Tiffany Studios; $85 D.

— Tiffany Studios, #1708; $75 D.

Standish — Art Nouveau styling, 10½"L; *$50 A.

Surtouts de Table — from models by Raoul Larche; pair, composed of two centerpieces designed as putti frolicking at pond banks, both inscribed RAOUL LARCHE; 11¼"H, wired for electricity; *$4,000 A.

Tazza — maiden as support for leaf/vine-covered dish, 9"H; $200 D.

BRONZE DINNER BELL, after a model by E.M. Sandez; French, early 20th century; *$600 A. (Christie's)

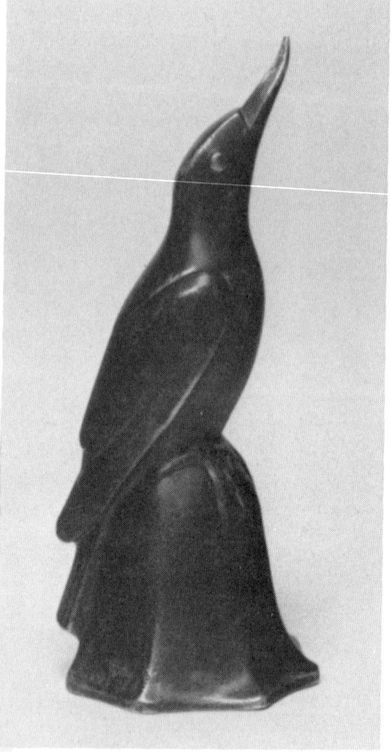

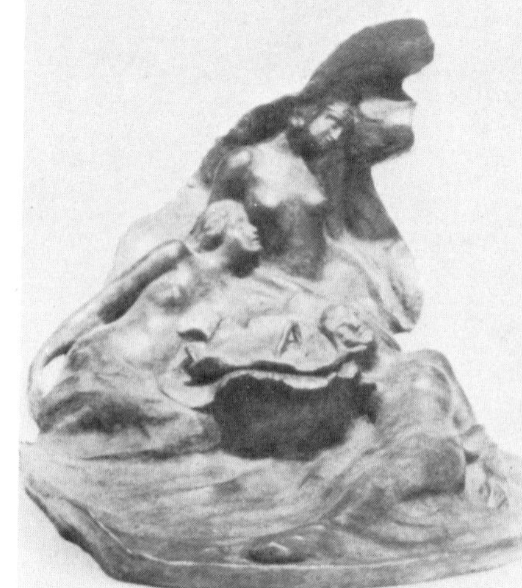

BRONZE FIGURAL INKWELL by Clara Hill, signed "Clara Hill," 8¾"H x 10¼"W; *$1,200 A. (Phillips)

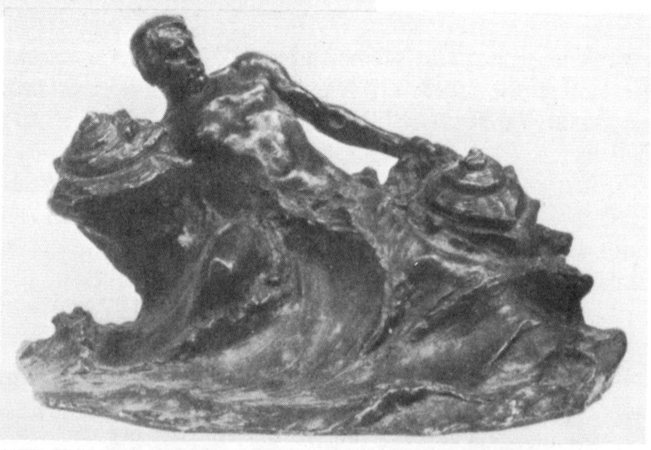

BRONZE FIGURAL DOUBLE INKSTAND, after Hans Muller, c. 1900; greenish-brown patina, inscribed "H. Muller," 14½"L, lacks one glass liner; *$800 A. (Sotheby's)

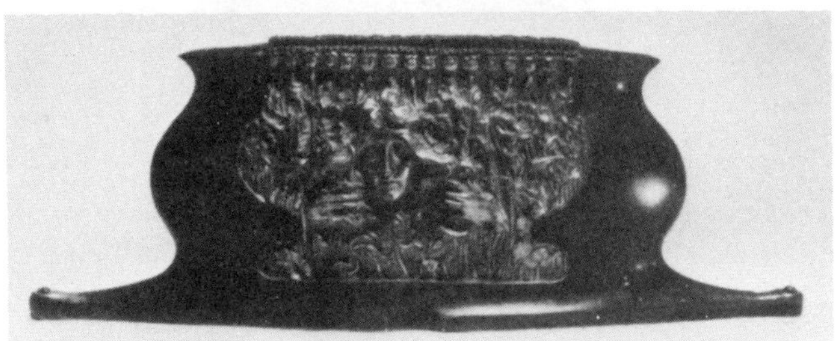

BRONZE JARDINIERE, parcel-gilt, after Charles Korschann, reverse cast panel of a field of Poppies; inscribed "Charles Korschann Paris," underside impressed LOUCHET; 15¾"L; *$1,300 A. (Sotheby's)

Tray — from model by A. Villien; formed as eagle with outspread wings perching on rocks, rim formed as entwined oak boughs; twice inscribed "A. Villien," gilt, 10½"H; **$750 A.

— enameled rectangular, gilt-bronze with etched finish & enameled border in green/blue/yellow; impressed LOUIS C. TIFFANY FURNACES INC. 305; 13¾"L; *$420 A.

— full female figure in relief; $100 D.

— Tiffany Studios #1859, 2½ x 4"; $65 D.

Triptych — left & right panels depict maiden in profile with Alsace & Lorraine above head; Center panel, draped goddess hovers above sleeping woman on ground; outer panels signed "G. PRUD'HOMME," center panel signature appears to be "H. ALLAUCRY"; 6½"L x 2¾"H; $395 D.

Trivet — iridescent tesserae tiles showing dragonfly with streaked wings; stamped mark of Tiffany Studios, 6¾"D; *$900 A.

Vase — from model by Auguste Ledru; baluster form, body cast with mask of Poseidon & figures of Nereids frolicking in sea; a Nereid climbs along side of vase, grasping rim; strap handle; inscribed "Ledru" and "Epreuve originale," impressed twice "Thiebaut Frers" foundry seal; brown patina, 17 3/8"H; *$2,000 A.

— after Joseph-Maria-Thomas Lambeaux, known as "Jef"; silvered bronze, rubbed, c. 1900; 21"H, inscribed JEF LAMBEAUX; *$1,000 A.

— after Jeanne Jozon; baluster form, body decorated with profile of woman & thistle plants; side handle formed as thistle; inscribed J. JOZON and "Salon des Beaux-Arts," underside stamped "13" and "7831" and impressed with Bronze Guaranti seal; brown patina, 9"H; *$900 A.

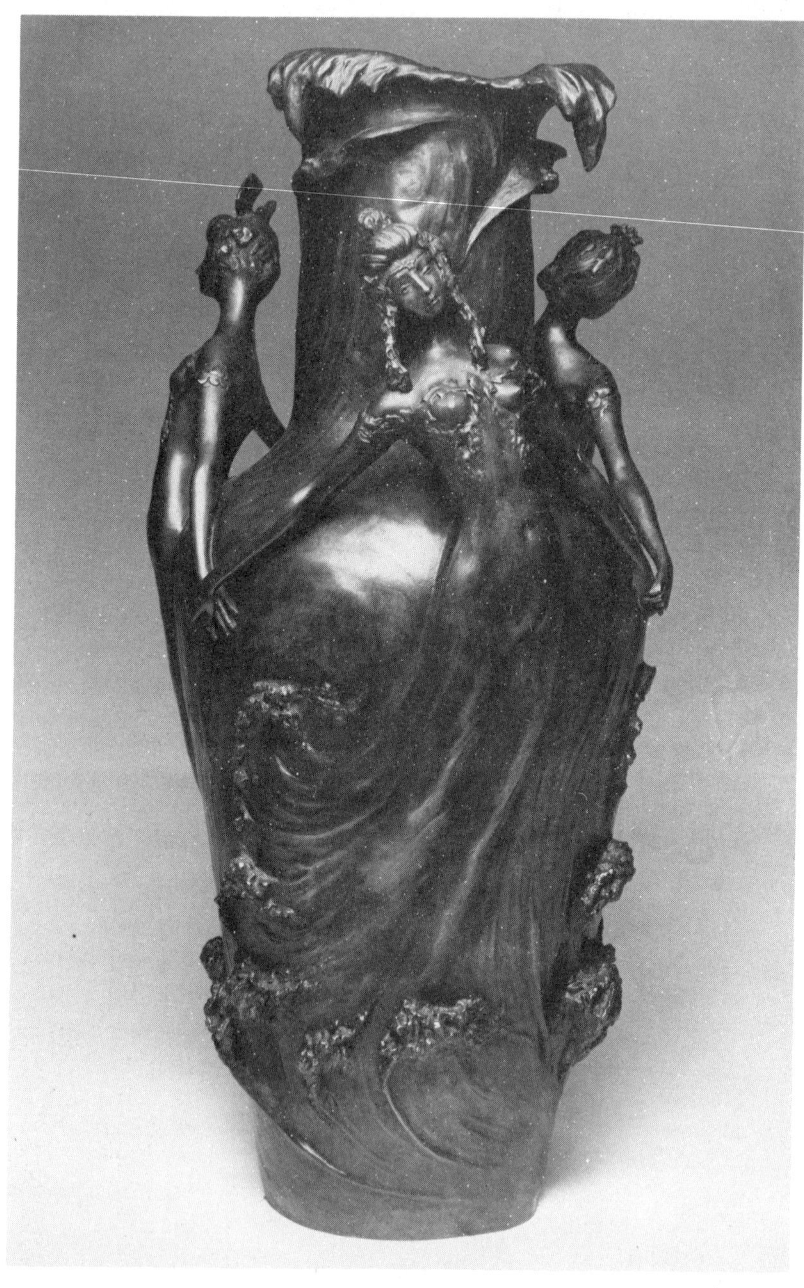

BRONZE VASE, after Louis Chalon; "Les Filles de la Mer," 25"H; *$2,000 A. (C.G. Sloan)

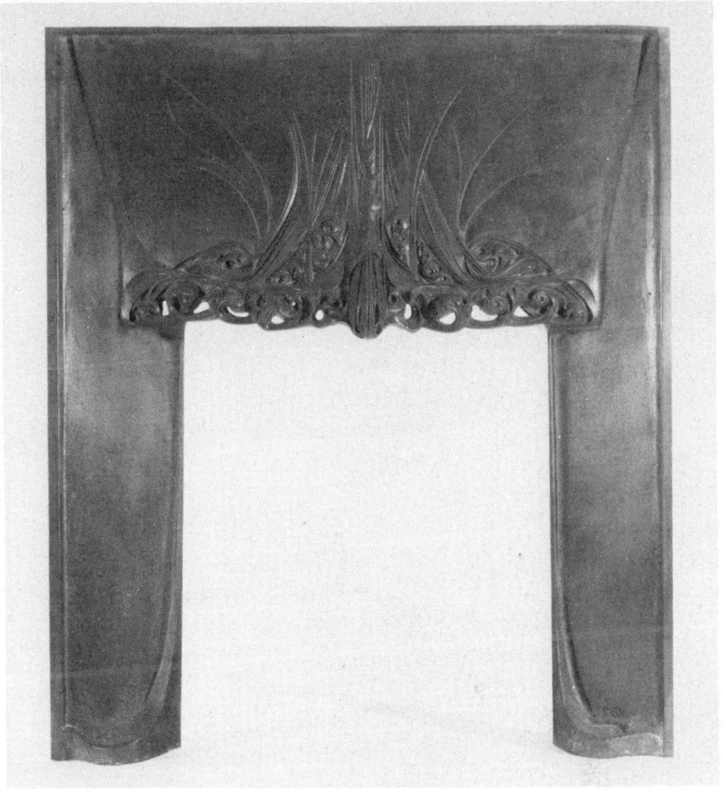

IRON FIREPLACE HEARTH, designed by Hector Guimard; *$5,000 A. (Christie's)

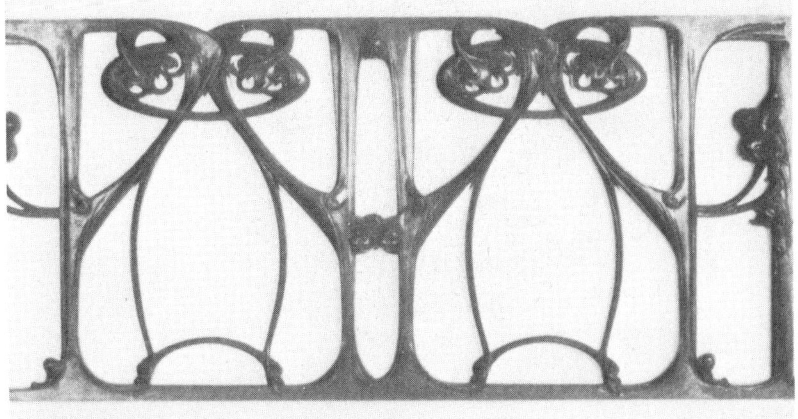

IRON GRILLE, designed by Hector Guimard, impressed "GD.1.10"; 52"L, minor crack; *$5,000 A. (Sotheby's)

— after Suzanne Bizard; relief of winged maiden & insects; French, early 20th century, 6½"H; *$350 A.

— bunches of grapes in high relief, Dore finish, dark patina, 10"H; $250 D.

— pair cabinet vases, matched; one with little girl looking up at bird on tree branch; other with girl rubbing eyes crying, looking at broken jug on ground; the pair, $200 D.

— Dore finish, blue enameling at base, marked Louis C. Tiffany Furnaces 166A, 11"H; $175 D.

COPPER ITEMS

Ashtray — 4½"D, with glass insert; by Roycroft; $20 D.

Bookends — pair, woman with flowing hair; $148 D.

— domed, heavy hand-hammered with crimped edges, by Roycroft; 3½"H x 4¼" base; $45 D.

— same; $40 D.

— same; $33 D.

Bowl — 4"D x 2½"H; by Roycroft; $38 D.

Box — enamel-on-copper, grape-laden vines in naturalistic colors in repousse, covered; inscribed "L.C. Tiffany SC 327," 5¾"D, minor restoration; *$3,000 A.

— enamel-on-copper, polychrome octopus-like designs, circular & covered; inscribed "Louis C. Tiffany" & "904110," 4"D; *$1,000 A.

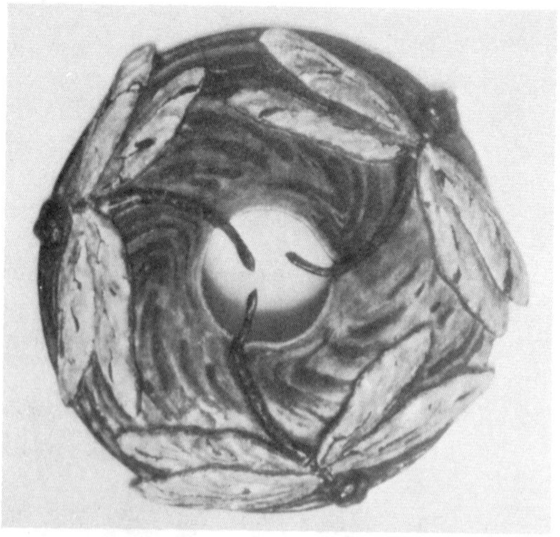

COPPER-BODIED BOX COVER by Tiffany Studios; enamel-on-copper, dragonflies with salmon-colored wings & deep blue bodies against mottled copper & yellow ground; 8"D, c. 1912, some losses of enamel; *$425 A. (Sotheby's)

Inkwell — reindeer decoration, copper on pewter; $49 D.

Jewel Casket — enameled copper, the hinged top & sides with interlacing green champleve enameled scrolls heightened with red/white on hammered ground; from The Art Crafts Shop, Buffalo, New York; 7"L x 4"H; *$110 A.

Ladle — Mission style; $15 D.

Powder Flask — berries/scrolls design; from G. & J.W. Hawksley, Sheffield; $75 D.

Service Plates — 6 hand-hammered Arts & Crafts type, each 12"D; set, *$25 A.

Vase — enamel-on-copper, 4 panels of arcs shading from purple to pink; gilt signature of C. Faure, 5¾"H; *$800 A.

— enamel-on-copper oviform with bottle neck and everted rim; body with red foiled ground decorated in high relief with blue/gold floriforms; by C. Faure, Limoges, 10"H; *$250 A.

CAST IRON ITEMS

Bookends — expandable to 15", Art Nouveau pierced ends; $35 D.

Mirror, Dressing — ornate gilt-painted with animals/nudes/heads, 18"H; original mirror with silvering flaking away; $77 D.

Picture Frame — gilded on folding stand, oval, openwork scrolls/leaves as decoration; 10½" x 8, 1 brass hinge missing; $35 D.

Plate — decorated with cupids, 13"D; $30 D.

Tieback — Art Nouveau-styled Morning Glory, 100% original paint; $65 D.

Tray — animal figure (lion?) in relief; $30 D.

PEWTER ITEMS

Bowl — Water Lily & Dragonflies, fruit bowl, 10"D; marked Kayserzinn; $165 D.

— Poppies in high relief, loop handles, 4 small pointed feet, 14" across handles; bowl 6½"D x 2¼"H; marked "Germany"; $75 D.

Dish — Chrysanthemums on leaf form, handled, footed; 10"L, marked Kayserzinn; $110 D.

— Turnip design on celery dish, some pitting; $55 D.

— berries decoration, handled; by Orvit (Arts & Crafts); $35 D.

Jewel Box — hinged, traces of original brass plating visible, oblong, 7 x 4 x 3; $49 D.

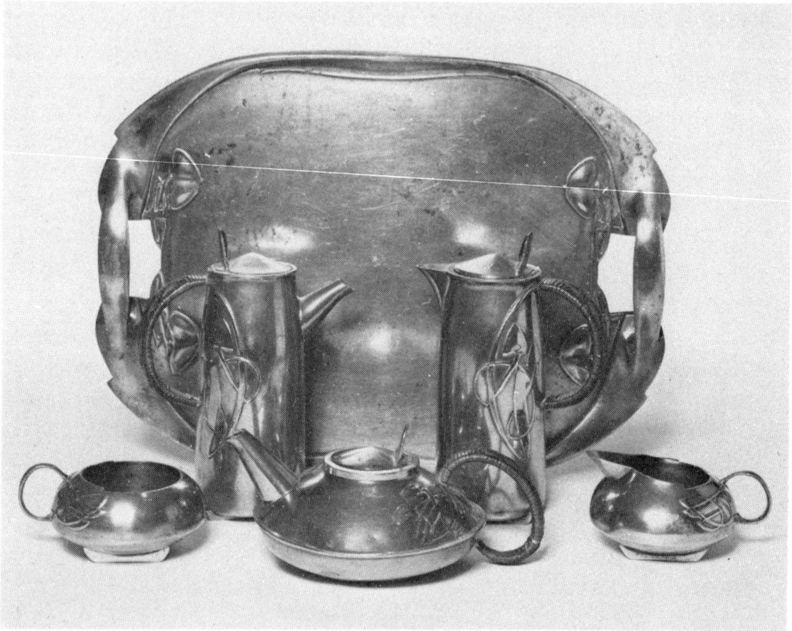

PEWTER COFFEE & TEA SERVICE, part of Liberty & Co.'s "Tudric" line, designed by Archibald Knox; *$1,100 A. (Christie's)

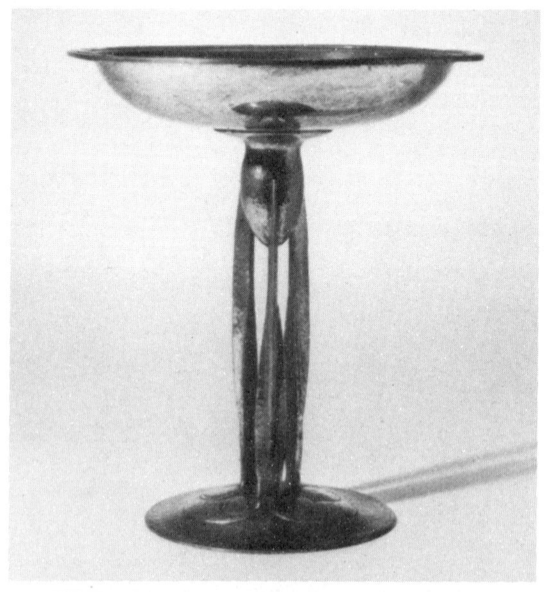

PEWTER TAZZA, part of Liberty & Co.'s "Tudric" line, made for them by Solkets; 11"H; *$275 A. (Sotheby's)

Knife Rest — dog shape; signed Kayserzinn; $45 D.

Knife Sharpener — repousse pewter covering steel forms a stylized bird, 6½"L; $30 D.

Matchbox Holder — floral Art Nouveau decroation; $20 D.

Pitcher — design of Mephistopheles, marked Kayserzinn; $250 D.

Platter — pond design showing fish in low relief among softly scrolled water swirls, border design of dragonflies & Water Lilies; marked KAYSERZINN on reverse; 24½"L x 11"W; $165 D.

Sugar Bowl — Art Nouveau floral relief, open type, oval, 4 x 2¼; $20 D.

Teapot — Fuschsia flowers in relief; 5½"H, 7¾"L spout to handle; marked Kayserzinn; $90 D.

— rooster & chickens in relief; 7¾"H, 6½"L spout to handle; 2 minor dents; marked Kayserzinn; $80 D.

— Art Nouveau floral in relief; 6¼"H, 7"L spout to handle; marked Kayserzinn; $75 D.

Tray — crayfish & other shellfish in relief, marked Kayserzinn & #d, 13"L; $225 D.

— 3-compartment Russian, handmade by Count Nekrassoff, 11" x 11½"; $95 D.

— large Dahlia flowers & dragonfly in relief, 12½ x 9½; marked Kayserzinn; $70 D.

— leaf tray, handmade by Count Nemeroff's studio, Russia; $69 D.

Vase — Poppies/leaves in high relief, 8"H; $180 D.

— flowers in relief, 3 fancy reticulated handles, overall gold finish; by Orvit; $70 D.

WHITE METAL ITEMS (Despite the constraints of chemical composition, some dealers lump all "spelter" items, be they Britannia metal or some forms of pewter, under this general classification. Basically, it was an inexpensive substitute for other metals, usually covered with a plated or painted coating.)

Inkwell — double inkwell, brown finish with pressed clear bottles and matching caps; pen rack holds 3 pens; calendar has day/date/month knobs; 9 x 6; $165 D.

— nude with long flowing hair, flowers; flowered lid, glass insert; $55 D.

Tea & Coffee Service — coffee pot, tea pot, hot water pot, covered sugar, creamer; all embossed with florid Art Nouveau strapwork, each impressed OSIRIS and numbered between 581 and 585; German, c. 1900; coffee pot, 8"H; *$250 A.

Tray — nude female kneeling before detailed open clam shell, her hair knotted at back of her head; she is 5½"H, the clam measuring 7½ x 8¾; $95 D.

Vase — pitcher type, nude lady in Art Nouveau fashion, advertising the I.C. Newman Diamond Shop, Chicago; 6"H; $95 D.

MISCELLANEOUS ART NOUVEAU

In the ideal arrangement of things, there would be no need for a "miscellaneous" chapter. Such a chapter often winds up being just a dumping ground for those pieces which don't fit neatly into other classifications.

That, for the most part, is what this chapter is. It's an accumulation of odds and ends, a composite of some pretty fair items which just don't fit the organizational structure I set up. Wooden marquetry trays by Galle, though they might be structurally similar to furniture by Galle, are just not pieces of furniture. Clocks — be they ceramic or white metal — just don't fit the categories for those items; clocks are a different sort of animal, and horologists could convincingly argue that they deserve a chapter of their own.

Certainly tossing in one or two items for this chapter doesn't do them justice. Perhaps in future editions there will be enough prices reported to extend and enlarge several of the types of items into chapters of their own. Until then, this will serve to round out the world of Art Nouveau, pointing out the tremendous variety found within the Art Nouveau styles.

MISCELLANEOUS

BELT BUCKLE — of gutta percha, 1" x 2", needs catch repair; $45 D.

BOOK — Vedder, Elihu (illustrator), *The Rubaiyat of Omar Khayam,* translated by Edward Fitzgerald. Boston: Houghton, Mifflin & Co., 1886; $65 D.

BOOKLET — 1915 Majestic Theatre, with Art Nouveau cover; $7 D.

BOOK MARK — Rand McNally & Co., nickel plating over brass, 4½"L; $7 D.

BUTTONHOOK/SHOEHORN — folding combination model, patented 1917; $10 D.

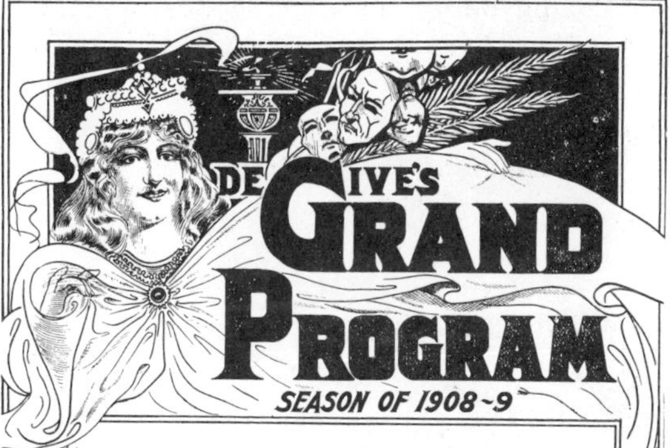

OPERA PROGRAM, designed by G. Haynes; 7½ x 10¼"; $1.50 D. (Private collection)

And Ready to Wear

The costly, yet simple elegance and the subtle atmosphere of high breeding of this shop will appeal to those who have been patronizing fashionable tailors.

The superi
the tailor
ion.

CLOU

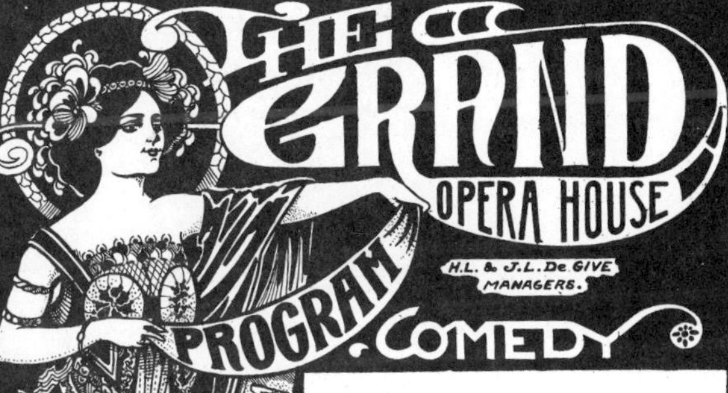

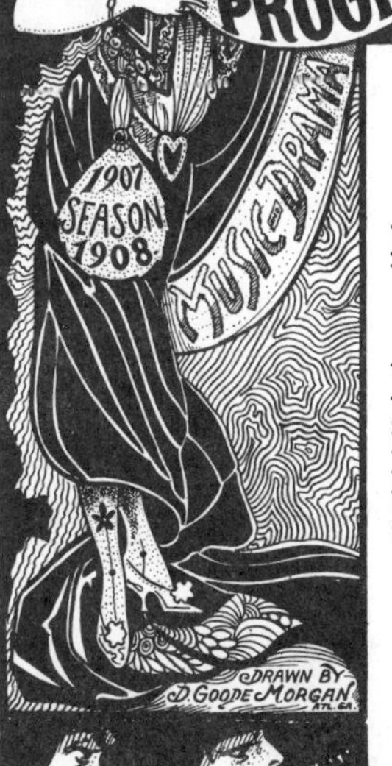

"Correct Clothes for Men"

Fall Suits Now Ready

$18.50, $20.00,
$25.00 to $45.00

Workmanship that is never under any circumstances slighted.

Styles adapted to the requirements of men of critical taste.

Prices as low as are usually demanded elsewhere for ordinary clothes.

These garments are the products of Alfred Benjamin & Co.'s expert organization and made expressly to meet our needs.

ESSIG BROS.,
"Correct Clothes for Men,"
26 Whitehall St.

OPERA PROGRAM, designed by D. Goode Morgan, of Atlanta; 7¾ x 10¾"; $1.50 D. (Private collection)

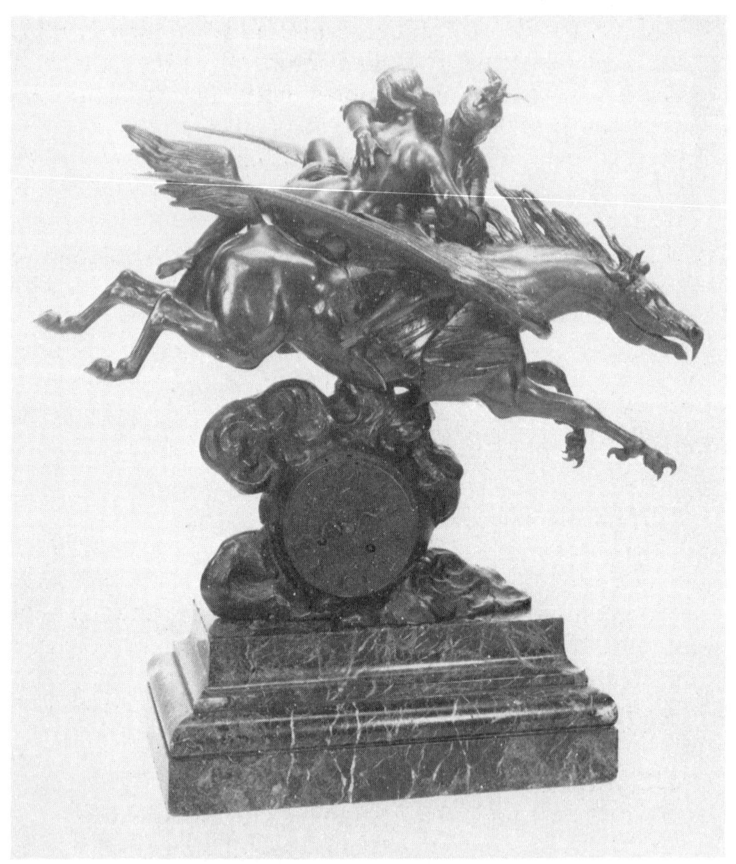

CLOCK, after a model by A.-L. Barye, of Roger & Angelica borne by the Hippogriff; French, early 20th century; bronze, on marble base; *$4,000 A. (Christie's)

CANDY TIN — "Gold Pheasant," San Francisco, 8"D x 1¼"H; $18 D.

— "Salmagundi," in the style of Mucha, by Whitman's Chocolates; $25 D.

— "Salmagundi," as above; $15 D.

CATALOG — Tiffany Studios, *Lamps and Fixtures*. NY: Allied Arts Co., 1900; *$520 A.

CIGAR HOLDER — bare-breasted Art Nouveau woman holding drape above head; amber stem; $80 D.

— woman with flowing dress; no stem; $70 D.

CIGARETTE CASE — graduated pink-to-blue hues in plique-a-jour web motif, with applied diamond spider, the body & eyes set with synthetic rubies with natural ruby thumb-piece, set in yellow gold case; *$4,500 A.

CLOCK, BONN — "Trustee" case, Ansonia movement; 10"W x 10½"H, deep pink with gold & floral touches, Art Nouveau-influenced; $265 D.

CLOCK, GRANDFATHER'S — Mission style, leaded glass door, chimes, with Waterbury movement; 76½"H x 18¼"W x 13½" deep; $850 D.

CLOCK, LAMP — decorated metal base with Aurene shade, the clock suspended from the lamp stem; $550 D.

CLOCK, MANTEL — Weller Louwelsa, floral, electric, 10" x 11"; $950 D.

— Weller Louwelsa, 11" x 11"; $950 D.

— Weller Louwelsa, 7"H x 5"W; $500 D.

CLOCK, MANTEL — ornate Art Nouveau style cast iron with gilt wash; movement from the Vermont Clock Co., platform escapement, strikes on half-hour, cleaned, running; $600 D.

CLOCK, MANTEL — chalkware female figural, Art Nouveau, 24"H, c. 1902; $425 D.

CLOCK, WALL — Sessions Mission-style oak, running; $70 D.

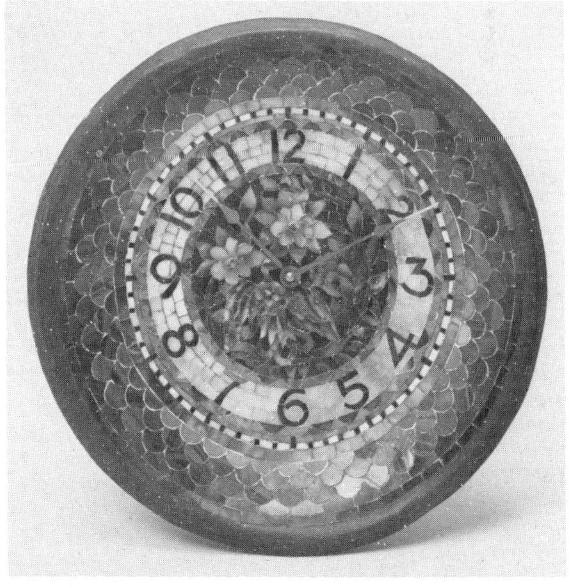

CLOCK, MOSAIC FAVRILE GLASS, by Tiffany Studios, early 20th century; *$2,700 A. (Christie's)

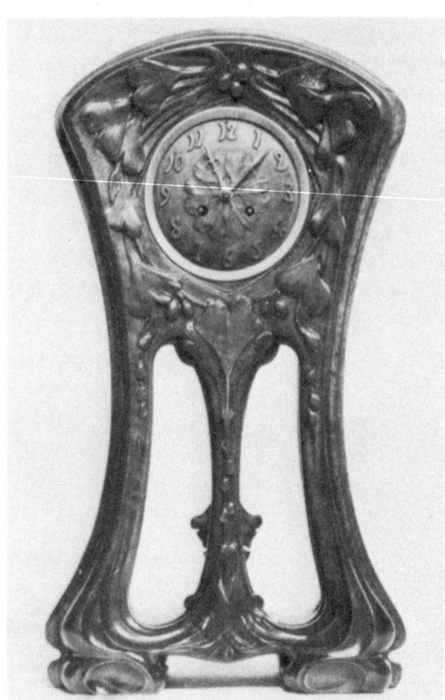

CLOCK, MANTEL; carved fruitwood with Gingko berries/ leaves, the face also carved with leaves; circular face ring inscribed LAVA NANCY; 22"H, French, c. 1900; *$2,400 A. (Sotheby's)

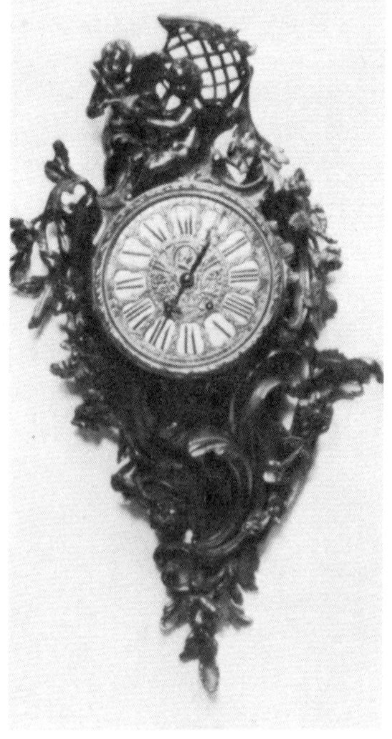

CLOCK, CARTEL; gilt-bronze, blue numerals against white ground, 30"H, French, c. 1900; *$600 A. (Sotheby's)

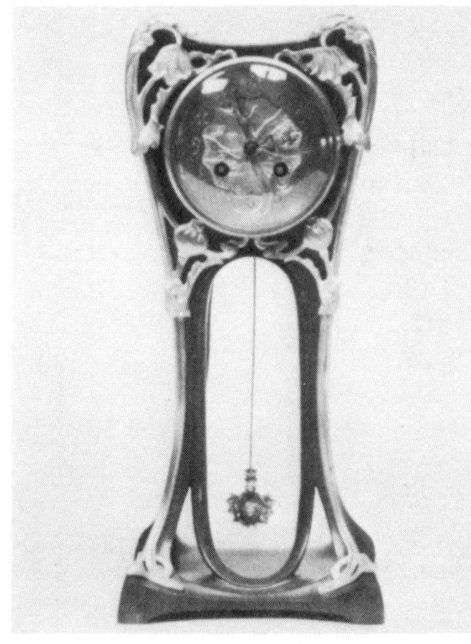

CLOCK, TABLE; gilt-bronze mounted carved fruitwood, attributed to Majorelle, 14½"H; *$4,000 A. (Sotheby's)

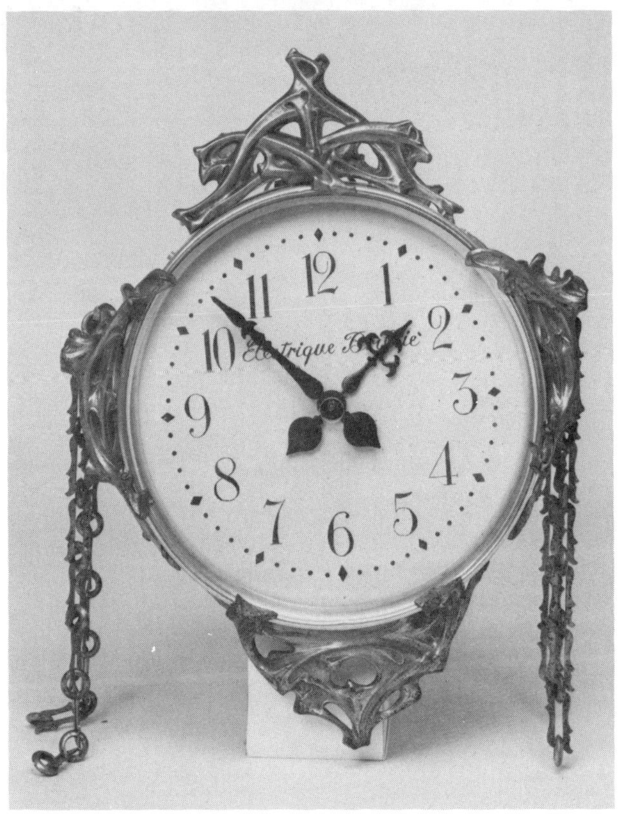

CLOCK, HANGING; double dial, gilt-bronze, by Hector Guimard; *$6,500 A. (Christie's)

CLOCK, WIND-UP — white metal case, Art Nouveau; $35 D.

DRESSER PIECES — amber-colored celluloid hand mirror & dresser box; $49 D.

EYE GLASS CASE — black lacquered with gold Art Nouveau scrolling designs, purple cloth lining; 6" x 1½"; $18 D.
— same, but 7" x 1½"; $18 D.

FAN, ADVERTISING — B.P.O.E., Art Nouveau style, 1909; $28 D.

FAUCETS — pair fancy Art Nouveau nickel plated, one needing brazing at base; $47 D.

FIGURE — anonymous sculptor; dancing female figure; bronzed white metal on white marble base; 10"H; $45 D.
— after Franz Barwig; "Stag at Rest," reclining figure of stag; inscribed "FB", brass, 8¼"H; made in 1914; *$1,000 A.

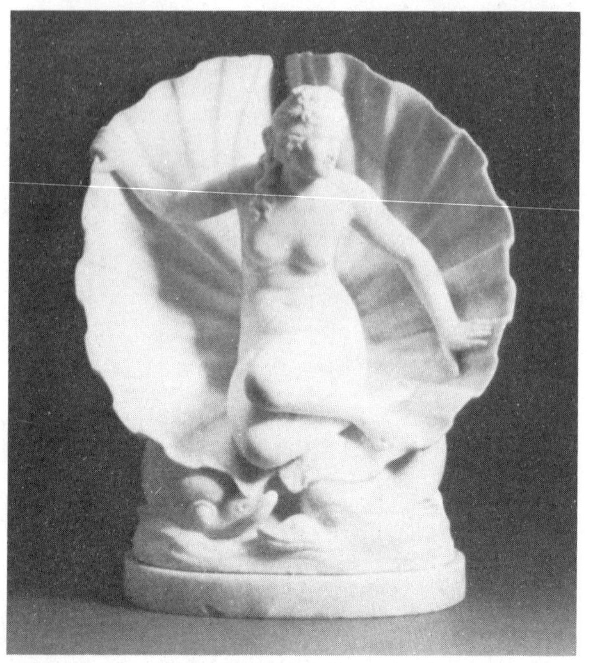

SOAPSTONE, CARVED FIGURE; Venus Anadyomene, Italian, late 19th or early 20th centuries; 17"H; *$600 A. (Sotheby's)

— after Antonio Canova; seated child writing on tablet; inscribed A. CANOVA; late 19th or early 20th century, soapstone, 15¾"H; *$300 A.

— after Rodolf Kaesbach; figure of woman, her garment stained brown; inscribed "Kaesbach," 18¼"H, late 19th or early 20th century, on veined marble socle; made of alabaster; *$900 A.

— after Auguste Moreau; "L'Amour au Papillion," white metal on molded verde antico plinth, 21"H; *$180 A.

INKWELL, FIGURAL — figural dog and tree trunk, the trunk holding the inkwell, with hinged lid; 11"L; $98 D.

LAMP/BANK/CLOCK — Art Nouveau combination, the style taken to its commercial extreme; $175 D.

MIRROR, DRESSING — gilt metal, full female figural, the flowing robe supporting the mirror, with floriform lights, 21" x 14"; signed "Pfeiffer"; $550 D.

MIRROR, HAND — celluloid with floral motif on back; $14 D.

MIRROR, TRAVELING — figure of woman on tree limb with cherub flying above, on embossed ivory-colored celluloid; beveled outside, trifold, each panel 10" x 10", with chain for hanging; $150 D.

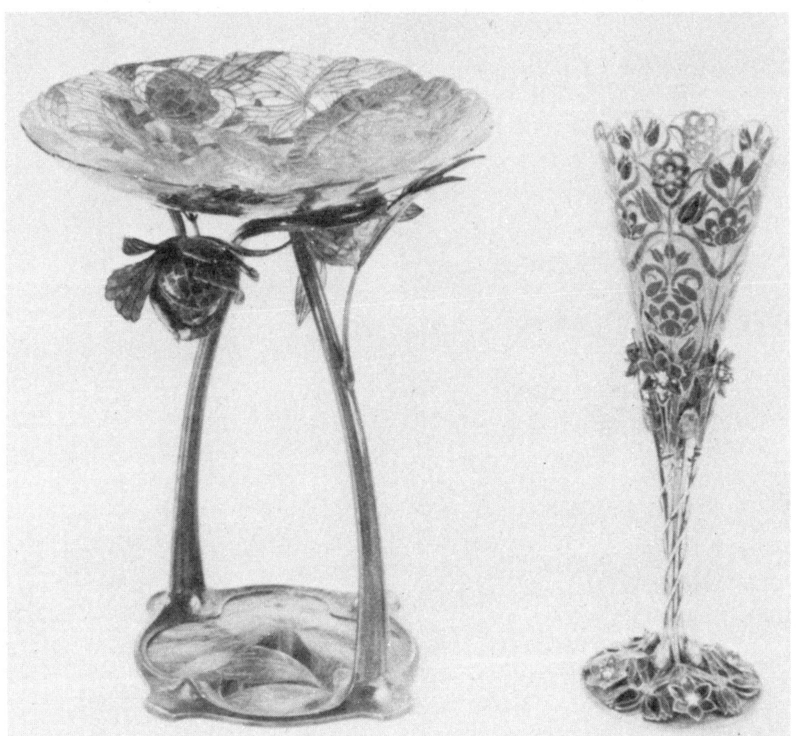

TWO FINE PLIQUE A JOUR ENAMEL PIECES, each 9"H. (Left) tazza, Swedish, the shallow bowl decorated with Peonies, resting upon supporting tendrils arising from similar quatrefoil base; *$6,500 A. (Right) vase by Mark Hammer, impressed on base with the Hammer touch-mark; *$2,400 A. (Phillips)

PAPER — original design for wall hanging by Koloman Moser: Die Riefenzit, from *Die Zuelle*, 1901; 9" x 10¾"; *$300 A.

PERIODICAL — *The Fra*, group of four, including Vol. I, #1; published by the Roycrofters; $32 D.

— *The Studio*, 25 leather-bound volumes from 1905-1914 (#34-51, and #55-61); *$2,200 A.

PERIODICAL COVER — *L'Estampe Moderne*, from woodcut by Alphonse Mucha, 16" x 11¼"; *$550 A.

— *L'Estampe Moderne*, by Alphonse Mucha, November, 1899; $400 D.

— *L'Estampe Moderne*, by Alphonse Mucha, October, 1897; 12¼" x 16¼"; $75 D.

— *L'Habitation Pratique*, May, 1910; fresh impression, matted & shrink-wrapped; 13" x 11¾"; *$50 A.

— *L'Habitation Pratique*, by Mucha; suede matt with special wood trim and oak frame; 21" x 26"; Mint; $325 D.

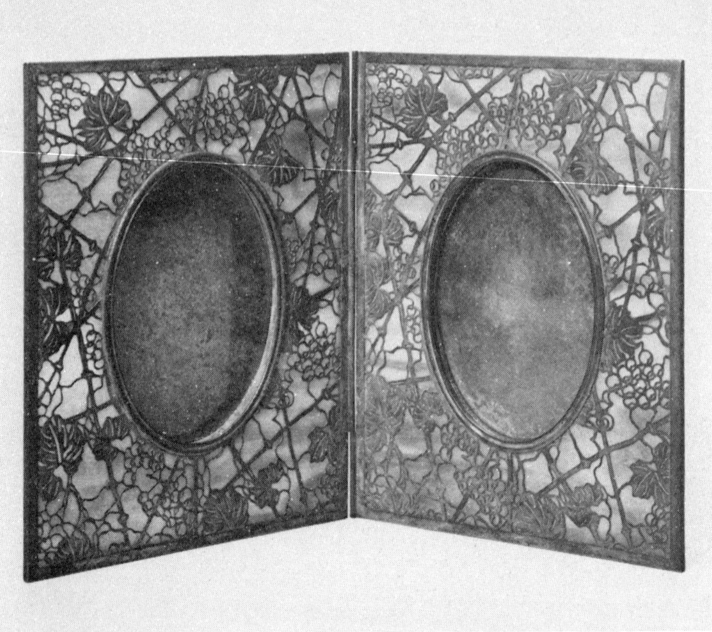

PICTURE FRAME, double-sided, of Favrile glass & metal, by Tiffany Studios; *$1,200 A. (Christie's)

— *Hearst's International,* 1922; by Mucha; small repair upper right corner; Art Nouveau frame with gold pie corners, material matting, foil filet; 13" x 17½"; $250 D.

— *Literary Digest,* May 2, 1908; by Alphonse Mucha; small area upper left corner missing, otherwise good; 11½" x 8¼"; *$60 A.

— *Literary Digest,* by Mucha; framed in material-covered mat & antique silver frame, 14" x 19"; $250 D.

— *La Plume,* by Alphonse Mucha; double silk covered mats & antique frame, 12½" x 14"; Mint; $250 D.

PICTURE FRAME — Abalone pattern by Tiffany; 7" x 9", for 4" x 5½" picture; $235 D.

PILLOW — oilcloth, feather stuffed, with Art Nouveau-styled women front and back; in dark greens, black, red; $50 D.

— same; $45 D.

PITCHER — chalkware, lady with flowing hair in high moulded relief, in soft green & gold; $150 D.

POST CARDS — P.F.B. Co., 5-lot set from series #7227; *$217 A.

— P.F.B. Co., 6-lot set from series #8120, with a nymph and shell in cameo style; $300 A.

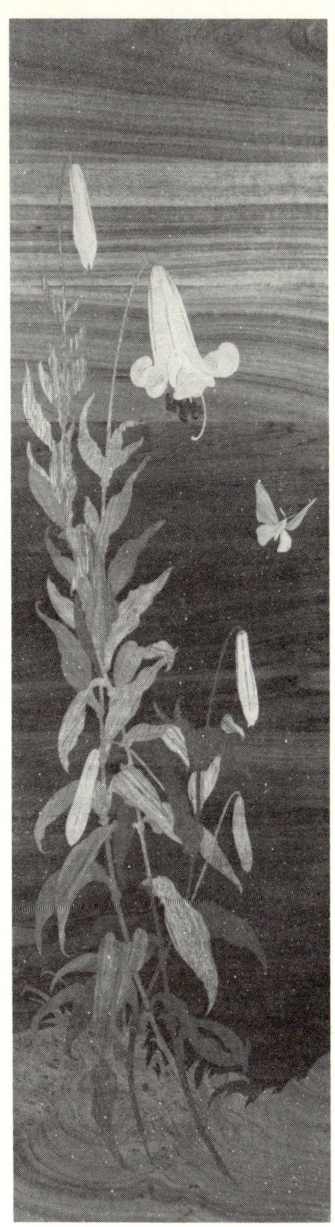

PANEL, one of a pair of inlaid mahogany by Louis Majorelle; *$2,000 A. (Christie's)

PURSE, BEADED — Art Nouveau; $16 D.

SHEET MUSIC — suitable for framing; 35 for $150, or each $6 D.

— Art Nouveau & Gibson girls, early 1900s; 18 for $75 D.

TEA CADDY — bronze, copper & silver; swollen rectangular form, the surface with marbleized brass/copper patination; the silver cover & lid etched with Oriental-style flowers, with a knop of netsuke of Foo dog form; by Tiffany & Co., c. 1885, 5"L; *$1,400 A.

TRAY — fruitwood marquetry, 2-handled, now set with glass top; 24"L across handles; c. 1900; signed in marquetry, Galle"; *$1,300 A.

— floral marquetry oval galleried, the shaped gallery with sterling mounts; 19½"L; signed Emile Galle; *$650 A.

— octagonal 2-handled, burl maple veneer (plus rosewood & fruitwoods), depicting a ruined castle among trees; inlaid mahogany, marquetry signature of Emile Galle; 17¼"W; *$650 A.

— lacquered wood, carved all over with bud handles & ruffled/pinched edges, 11" x 24"; $85 D.

WALL PLAQUE — inlaid mahogany, depicting riverscape with silhouetted rooftops & grazing sheep, veneered in burl maple/oak/fruitwoods; marquetry Galle signature, the frame with an upper frieze of carved prunts; 21" x 27¾"; *$1,900 A.

WATCH, POCKET — Swiss, approximately 14s silveroid, OF SS; case as maiden's head in high relief on front cover; silver-toned dial; $62 D.

— Elgin 17-jewel, sterling silver medallion in face; $105 D.

ARTISTS, ARTISANS, AND THEORETICIANS: A GUIDE

The chapter which follows is a quick, concise, but certainly not complete index of some of the major and minor artists, craftspersons, educators, writers, practitioners, manufacturers, and others who helped make Art Nouveau the many-faceted movement it became. Such a listing could never be complete. Many thousands of artists and artisans worked in these styles in the late 19th and early 20th centuries — and that doesn't even take into consideration those who preceded the informal movement, those who may have adapted some minor parts of it into their designs, and so on.

Spellings of names vary from source to source. Indeed, the owners of these names sometimes spelled the names differently on their signed works. Hyphenated surnames are always alphabetized under the first letter of the first part of the surname.

Dates, too, have a maddening way of being reported differently from source to source. I ask readers to rely upon the dates given, but only as general references. In some cases, three different dates of death have been seen for a particular artist, and I've considered it better in such cases to simply report the date of birth. In other cases, dates of activity in the Art Nouveau modes will be given.

Many workers in Art Nouveau lived into the 1950s and 1960s. For the most part, they had abandoned the Art Nouveau approaches many years before their deaths. Therefore, I considered it most important to show generally when they were working in the Art Nouveau styles. This doesn't imply that their artistic or crafts activities ceased when they abandoned the style, as many remained quite active in decorative arts.

Finally, the length of, presence or absence of, or listings under an artist or artisan should not be compared to another to determine comparative importance. Some longer entries are such because the information was more readily available.

A

Andre, Emile (French, 1871-1933) — leading architect at Nancy who was also a furniture designer; his earlier period was strongly neo-rococo influenced, although after 1900 his designs grew more simplified.

Angst, Charles Albert (Swiss, b. 1875) — sculptor, artist-craftsman.

Anquetin, Louis (French ?, 1861-1932) — posterist; his first poster done in 1894.

Argy-Rousseau, G. (French, b. 1885) — glass worker best known for his work in pate-de-verre, he became associated more with the Art Deco movement.

Ashbee, Charles R. (English, 1863-1942) — influenced by William Morris, Ashbee sought to utilize the machine in applied art; founder of the Guild and School of Handicraft, London, 1888; founder, School of Arts and Crafts, 1904 (which continued until 1914); served as a major influence upon the Austrian Secessionists, especially the Darmstadt school; worked in metals.

Audiger & Meyer — firm in Krefeld, Germany, making textiles c. 1908.

Auriol, Georges — his publication in 1892 of *Le Livre des Monogrammes* in Paris demonstrated the influence of Japonism upon French Art Nouveau.

B

Bac, Fernand (French, 1859-1952) — posterist, did series of 3 for Yvette Guilbert.

Barlach, Ernst (German, 1870-1938) — sculptor and printmaker, educated in Hamburg, Dresden and Paris; a contributor to *Jugend* 1897-1902 who first worked in the German Jugendstil, later changing after a trip to Russia in 1906. Mainly Expressionistic, his works have been noted in ceramics, too.

Barwig, Franz (Austrian, b. 1868) — originally a carver of Gothic-styled religious figures; after moving to Vienna and associating with Secessionists in the early 1900s he concentrated on nudes and animals; was a colleague of Josef Urban after World War I.

Barye, Antoine-Louis (French, 1796-1875) — a forerunner of the Art Nouveau influences in sculpting; he was foremost of the group called "Les Animaliers," sculptors concentrating upon animal-inspired subjects.

Basile, Ernesto — Italian architect and furniture designer for the Palermo firm of Ducrot, active in early 1900s.

Baumann, Ludwig (Austrian, 1853-1936) — Viennese interior and industrial designer, active in the very early 1900s.

de Bazel, Karel Petrus Cornelis (Dutch, 1869-1923) — architect, designer, and graphic artist, he was one of the shapers of the Dutch Art Nouveau movement; his book illustrations show an Egyptian influence.

Beardsley, Aubrey Vincent (English, 1872-1898) — noted graphic artist and illustrator, originally influenced by the pre-Raphaelites and William Morris; served as art director for *The Yellow Book* and later *Savoy;* his early death and his foreknowledge of it may have inspired some of his work.

Becker, Edmond Henri (French, b. 1871) — craftsman, wood-carver, medalist; worked with the Paris firm of Boucheron in jewelry, active turn-of-the-century.

Beetz-Charpentier, Eliza — Dutch-born sculptor who worked in statues, portraits and medals; a pupil of and later married to Alexander Charpentier.

Behmer, Marcus (German, b. 1879) — book designer specializing in fantasy-style book-plate, book and card design.

Behrens, Peter (German, 1868-1940) — originally a painter, he was a graphic designer in the 1890s; a founder of the Munich Secession in 1893, a member of the Mathildehohe artist' colony at Darmstadt, 1889-1903, headed the Dusseldorf Kunstgewerbeschule, 1903-1907; later taught architecture in Vienna and Berlin, his pupils including Le Corbusier, Gropius, and Mies van der Rohe; a designer of furniture, architecture, and the well-rounded artist-craftsman which was so common during this period, he adhered to the rigorous functionalism of the Germanic late Art Nouveau.

Bellery-Desfontaines, Henri-Jules Ferdinand (French, 1867-1910) — painter, craftsman, lithographer and illustrator.

Beville, Eugene (French, 1868-1931) — worked in leather and metals at turn of century.

Benson, W.A.S. (English, 1854-1924) — at one time associated with William Morris, he was a designer for the Birmingham Guild of Handicrafts, working mainly in base metals but also in silver, sometimes decorated with precious stones.

Berge, Henri (French) — modeler for Almaric Walter in pate-de-verre glass.

Berlepsch-Valendas, Hans Eduard von (Swiss, 1849-1921) — architect, painter, craftsman who designed books, buildings, and furniture; influenced by the English Arts and Crafts Movement, especially by William Morris.

Berthon, Paul (French, 1872-1909) — painter and posterist, noted for his use of pastel colors and his somewhat ethereal females; did about 15 posters and 60 decorative panels.

Besnard, Paul Albert (French, 1849-1934) — painter and print-maker who studied at the Ecole des Beaux-Arts.

Bigaux, Louis Felix (French) — painter and decorator, designer of wallpaper and tapestry.

Bindesboll, Thorvald (Danish, 1846-1908) — architect, graphic artist, designer who was active in furniture design, ceramics, metals, embroidery and bookbinding.

Binet, Rene (French, 1866-1911) — architect and painter, best known for his design for the main entrance to the Paris World's Fair, 1900.

Bing, S. (German, establishing fame in France) — a native of Hamburg, Bing opened a Paris shop specializing in the importation of Oriental decorative items; the store was reorganized and reopened in 1895 under the name of "Maison L'Art Nouveau," still carrying Oriental goods but specializing in the "new art" of Europe and America. The store, at 22 rue de Provence, stayed open until 1902, giving its name to the art movement.

Bird, Elisha Brown (American, 1867-1943) — posterist for many literary journals.

Bizard, Suzanne (French, 1876-1963) — designer in bronzes and other fields.

Bonnard, Pierre (French, 1867-1947) — primarily a painter, he also did lithographs and sculpture; a contributor to *Revue Blanche*, 1893.

Bonvallet, Lucien (French, b. 1861) — artist-craftsman, specializing in metals after 1895; created mountings for some work by Galle and Dalpayrat.

Bosselt, Rudolf (German, 1871-1938) — sculptor and professor, 1904-1931; mainly worked in small metal pieces but did larger works as well.

Bottee, Louis Alexandre (French, 1852-1941) — sculptor and engraver of medals.

Boucheron, Frederic (French, 1830-1902) — founder of a jewelry firm in Paris, 1858; displayed at the Philadelphia Exhibition; son Louis managed firm after his death.

Bouval, Maruice (French, d. 1920) — stayed with early period motifs of young girls and flowers in his bronzes.

Bradley, Will (American, b. 1868) — posterist and illustrator, graphic designer, typographer; founded Wayside Press in Springfield, Mass., 1895, publishing 7 issues of *Bradley: His Book*; press moved to Cambridge 1898 to become part of University Press; was art director of *Century Magazine*, art editor for *Collier's*, art director for *Good Housekeeping*, supervising art director for Hearst Publications.

Bradley & Hubbard Mfg. Co. — Meriden, Connecticut; produced metal ware and lamps in late 1800s and early 1900s.

Brandt, Edgar W. (French, b. 1880) — metal designer, better known for Art Deco designs.

Brangwyn, Frank (English, 1867-1943) — apprentice to William Morris' workshops; was a designer of furniture, textiles, carpets, as well as a printmaker and painter.

Brouwer, William Coenraad (Dutch, 1877-1933) — potter and sculptor who founded own pottery in Leiderdorp, 1901.

Bugatti, Carlo (Italian, b. c. 1855) — an extreme Orientalist who blended Mid-Eastern influences with folk designs, often seen in his parchment chairs.

Burne-Jones, Edward (English, 1833-1898) — a second generation Pre-Raphaelite painter, friend of Dante Gabriel Rosetti and William Morris, admirer of Blake; served as an influence upon the French Symbolist movement, and was greatly admired by Beardsley.

C

Carder, Frederick (orig. English, 1863-1963) — the guiding force behind the Steuben Glass products, he trained at several fine English factories; one of the most inventive of glass designers practicing in the United States.

Carqueville, Will (American, 1871-1946) — painter and posterist, his series of posters for *Lippincott's* was done before he traveled to Paris for art study in the 1890s.

Carriere, Eugene (French, 1849-1906) — painter and lithographer, a founding member of Societe Nationale des Beaux Arts, 1890; used fog-like transparent envelopings for his figures; an exhibitor at Bing's L'Art Nouveau.

Casas, Ramon (Spanish, 1866-1932) — posterist.

Cassiers, Henri (Dutch ?, 1858-1944) — as a posterist, specialized in ships, sailors, and Dutch peasants.

Cayron, Jules (French, 1868-1940) — posterist.

Ceramic Art Company, Trenton, New Jersey — an early producer of American Belleek, established 1879 by J. Coxon and W. Lenox; a forerunner of Lenox china.

Chabas, Maurice (French, 1862-1947) — posterist.

Chaplet, Ernest (French, 1835-1909) — potter in stoneware and porcelain; worked at Sevres and managed the Haviland factory (Limoges); after 1884 produced ceramics under own name, collaborating with Gauguin in 1886.

Charpentier, Alexandre (French, 1856-1909) — sculptor, designer in graphics, metals, ceramics, leather; his early furniture reflects an English Arts and Crafts influence, later taking on a more Continental Art Nouveau flavor with the occasional addition of carved relief nudes; his furniture often was in pale blonde wood with gilt bronze plaques; very active in the 1890s in the applied arts.

Chelsea Keramic Art Works (Chelsea, Massachusetts) — established by Alexander W. Robertson in 1872; closed in 1889, reorganizing as Chelsea Pottery U.S. in 1891; became the Dedham Pottery, Dedham, Massachusetts, in 1895.

Cheret, Joseph (French, d. 1894) — sculptor, became director of modeling studio at the Manufactory of Sevres; did bronze designs not quite divorced from the Classical traditions; some of his works issued posthumously by the Parisian founder Soleau in 1900 and 1904.

Cheret, Jules (French, 1836-1932) — posterist, considered the father of the modern color poster; established own press 1866; during 1893-1900 period was strongly influenced by Toulouse-Lautrec, later adopting a more mid-Impressionistic style.

Chini, Galileo (Italian) — ceramicist working at Florence, often utilizing faience; active in late 1890s and early 1900s.

Choubrac, Alfred (French, 1853-1902) — posterist; noted for doing the first poster for American dancer Loie Fuller.

Christian, Desire (French, 1846-1907) — glassmaker, employed by Burgun, Schverer & Co. at Meisenthal, Alsace-Lorraine; some of the glassware attributed to Galle is undoubtedly from his plant, produced under secret contract.

Cocteau, Jean (French, 1889-1963) — artist and posterist, whose early posters (often connected with dance) show some transitional signs of Art Nouveau.

Colenbrander, Theodorus A.C. (Dutch, 1941-1930) — ceramics and textile designer, employed by the Rozenburg firm at The Hague; his textile styles especially were derived from the bold colors and lines of the Javanese batiks; headed the Amersfoorter wallpaper factory, 1895.

Colonna, Edward (Eugene) (French, 1862-1948) — French designer of furniture, glass, ceramics, jewelry, textiles; worked briefly with Associated Artists, New York; lived mainly in Paris and worked for S. Bing in 1890s; was in the Secession exhibit, Munich, 1899 and Turin International exhibit, 1902.

Cometti, Giacomo (Italian) — furniture designer in the first decade of the 20th century, possibly at Turin.

Coudyser, Jules (French) — decorator-artist specializing in lace and embroidery, active at the turn of the century.

Couty, Edme (French, d. 1917) — painter-decorator who designed tapestries, furniture, book covers, ceramics; employed by Sevres factory; active at turn of the century.

Crane, Walter (English, 1845-1915) — painter, illustrator, book designer, and writer; a Pre-Raphaelite who was a major influence on English Art Nouveau; co-founder of the Century Guild, 1882; his early emphasis was upon stylized flora; would later renounce Art Nouveau as decadent.

D

Dalpayrat, Adrien Pierre (French, 1844) — potter specializing in glaze effects on porcelain and stoneware; the firm Dalpayrat et Lesbros (with Adele Lesbros) in Bourg-la-Reine specialized in glazed sculptured wares; worked at one time for La Maison Moderne, collaborated also with Voisin Delacroix; an award winner at the 1893 World Columbian Exposition, Chicago.

Dampt, Jean-Auguste (French, 1853-1946) — sculptor, engraver, craftsman, best-known for his plant form-inspired light fixtures; active at the turn of the century.

Daum, August (French, 1854-1909) — glass manufacturer at Nancy with brother Antonin; studied with Galle, although his commercial productions were generally more restrained and refined than those of Galle.

Davidson, Peter Wyler (English, d. 1933) — jewelry designer, early 1900s.

Decoeur, Emile (French, 1876-1953) — potter first working in faience, later in stoneware; apprenticed to and later a collaborator with Edmond Lachenal.

Degue — signature on glass similar to that of Schneider production.

Delaherche, Auguste (French, 1857-1940) — an important potter, buying and operating Ernest Chaplet's shop 1887-1894; occasionally associated with S. Bing; after 1904, made only unique pieces, usually in stoneware; a lover of Chinese and Japanese earthenware, perhaps influenced by them.

Delatte, Andre (French) — cameo glass maker at Nancy, beginning his own firm in 1921; products similar to the commercial late production of Galle, as well as those of Daum and Mueller; handles often formed by shearing stems along length and pushing them back toward body.

DeMorgan, William (English) — artist whose interest turned to ceramic design and decoration, especially using designs derived from 17th and 18th century Spanish-Moorish earthenware; a friend of William Morris.

Deraisme, Georges Pierre (French, b. 1865) — sculptor, member Societe Centrale des Arts Decoratifs; active at turn of the century.

De Vez — mark found on some French cameo glass from Cristallerie de Pantin, late 1890s and early 1900s.

Dijsselhof, Gerrit W. (Dutch, 1866-1924) — painter, textile and furniture designer; furniture of 1890s often utilized medieval motifs, an apparent influence of the English Arts and Crafts Movement; textile design, like much of that from Holland, was influenced by Javanese batiks; a leader of the Dutch Art Nouveau movement.

Donnay, Auguste (French, 1862-1921) — posterist.

Defau, Clementine-Helene (French, 1869-1937) — posterist, book illustrator, post card designer.

Dufrene, Maurice (French, 1876-1925) — designer of furniture, rugs, jewelry, wallpaper, book bindings; after 1899 was craftsman at La Maison Moderne; would later renounce Art Nouveau in favor of industrial design techniques.

Dumont, Henri (French, b. 1859) — painter and printmaker; from 1893 concentrated almost exclusively on floral still lifes; occasionally signed first name "Henry."

Dunand, Jean (Swiss, 1877-1942) — sculptor and metal designer, studied with Jean Dampt; experimented with beaten metal after 1900; although his first vases were definitely Art Nouveau, he later turned to more geometric Art Deco types.

Durand, Victor (French) — glassmaker moving to the United States in late 1800s; most of his well-known iridescent glass was produced at the Durand Art Glass Works, Vineland, New Jersey, in the 1912-1924 period; operation of the factory was assumed by Victor Durand Jr., after the death of his father in 1924, and the factory closed operations in 1931.

E

Eckmann, Otto (German, 1865-1902) — painter, designer of type faces, stained glass, furniture, rugs, wallpaper, metal objects, tapestries, textiles; gave up painting in 1894 to devote time to decorative arts; designed for the magazines *Jugend* and *Pan*; his adoption of the Japanese floral art styles influenced his work, making him a leader in the German "floral style" and influencing other German artists;

his book of the alphabet became famous among the Jugendstil group, and in 1897 he became a teacher at the Kunstgewerbeschule, Berlin.

Ekberg, J. (Swedish) — ceramicist, at the Gustafsberg factory, c. 1897-1899.

Endell, August (German, 1871-1925) — architect and designer, self-taught as an artist; influenced by Obrist at Munich; member of the Jugendstil group, he also designed jewelry, furniture and textiles.

F

Faberge, Peter Carl (Russian, b. 1846) — jeweler and jewelry designer; took over his father's jewelry firm in St. Petersburg, Russia, educated at times in Germany, England and France; awarded Royal Warrant by Czar Alexander III, 1880s; continued supplied royal family until Russian revolution.

de Falke, Gisela (Austrian) — designer and worker in glass, ceramics, and metals; studied with Joseph Hoffmann; worked in Vienna, turn of the century.

Feuillatre, Eugene (French, 1870-1916) — sculptor, goldsmith, enamel craftsman; worked for Rene Lalique before establishing own workshop and, like Lalique, also worked in glass.

de Feure, Georges (pseudonym for Georges Joseph van Sluijters, 1868-1928) — painter, printmaker, posterist, designer of ceramics, furniture, tapestries, book ornaments, glass; Paris-born son of a Dutch father and French mother, student of Jules Cheret, influenced by Grasset; worked for Bing's L'Art Nouveau, designed for Porcelaines GDA; a professor of decorative arts at Ecole Nationale des Beaux Arts.

Finch, Alfred William (Belgian, 1854-1930) — painter, printmaker, and ceramicist; he brought back the new Arts and Crafts Movement influence after a visit to England, influencing van de Velde and others; later set up ceramics shop and craft school in Finland.

Fischer, Moritz (Hungarian) — founder of porcelain works at Herend, Hungary, in 1839, which remained active into the 20th century; products sometimes referred to as "Herend porcelain."

Fisher, Alexander (English, 1864-1936) — painter, goldsmith, sculptor, enamelist; studied under Dalpayrat in Paris, later setting up London workshop; popularized enamel work in

England, often incorporating Celtic influences in that and his gold work; placed in charge of enameling department, Central School of Arts and Crafts, 1896.

Follot, Paul (French, 1877-1911) — designer of furniture and table settings; student of Grasset, worked for Bing at L'Art Nouveau, Meier-Graefe at La Maison Moderne.

Fostoria Glass — Ohio firm formed 1899; first glass produced 1901, in 1912 registered "Iris" trademark for iridescent ware similar to Tiffany's; closed 1917.

Fouquet, Georges (French, 1862-1957) — operator of jewelry firm established by his father in 1860; worked in gold and plique-a-jour.

Fry, Laura Ann (American, 1857-1943) — ceramicist, designer; a leader of Cincinnati's womens art movement, the first employee at Rookwood; later a decorator for Lonhuda Pottery, Steubenville, 1891-1894.

Fulper — mark used by the American Pottery Co., Flemington, New Jersey; successor company to firm established 1805; art pottery produced 1910-1929, at which time it became Stangl Pottery.

Fumagalli, Celestino (Italian) — sculptor and goldsmith, studio in Turin, active at the turn of the century.

G

Gaillard, Eugene (French, 1862-1933) — architect, furniture and fabric designer; one of the foremost furniture designers at the turn of the century.

Gaillard, Lucien (French, b. 1861) — jeweler and operator of jewelry firm established by family; used insect and flower forms; participated, Glasgow International Exhibition, 1901.

Galle, Emile (French, 1846-1904) — best known for his glassware; also designed furniture, ceramics; early training in pottery occurred at his father works at Saint Clement; strongly influenced by Symbolists; his production of glassware at Nancy originally concentrated upon realistic, dimensional floral stylings, later changing to a more stylized representation; in his furniture, use of inlays common; founder of an association of craftsmen at Nancy although such a group had been around him there informally since about 1890; glass production continued until 1935, although some of that produced after his death carries a star before his name in the signature.

Gaudi, Antonio (Spanish, 1852-1926) — dominating influence in Spanish Art Nouveau; the son of a coppersmith, he often used metalwork in architecture, as well as designing furniture; was particularly fond of zoomorphic design styles.

Gaudin, Felix (French) — designer of stained glass, active at turn of the century.

Gerbault, Henry (French, 1863-1930) — posterist.

Germain, Louise (French, 1880) — watercolorist; specialist in leather and book covers, active at the turn of the century.

Glatigny — French *atelier*, an artists' colony in Glatigny, near Versailles, established in the 1890s and active at the turn of the century; porcelain production noted.

Godet, Henri (French, b. 1863) — sculptor and artist.

Goldsmiths and Silversmiths Co., Ltd. — British firm producing household objects in gold and silver, established 1890s.

Gouda — in addition to its fame for cheese, this town in Holland has a 300-year-old pottery tradition; many companies have worked there; the Zenith Pottery and the Zuid-Hollandsche pottery there marked their brightly colored Art Nouveau pieces "Gouda" during the 1890-1940 period; some pieces signed only "Royal Zuid."

Grasset, Eugene (Swiss-born, 1841-1917) — fame established in France; trained as architect, published *Ornements Typographiques* in 1870s; major factor in poster design as well as designing mosaics, jewelry, ceramics, stained glass windows; work often nature-derived, his illustrations influenced both by Celts and Japanese.

Gray, H. (pseudonym for Henri Boulanger, 1858-1924) — highly productive French posterist.

Gruber, Jacques (French, b. 1870) — painter, designer of glass, jewelry, furniture, textiles; studied in Paris under Symbolist painter Gustave Moureau; joined Daum firm in Nancy as decorator in 1894, setting up own shop in 1897 which produced mostly glass panels but also textiles and furniture similar to that of Eugene Vallin.

Grueby, William H. (American) — established pottery 1894, most pieces using heavy shapes with either floral or geometric designs; business incorporated 1897; in 1908 it was divided into The Grueby Pottery Company, and Grueby Faience & Tile Co.; in business at Boston until 1920.

Gruel, Leon (French) — bookbinder often utilizing stylized plant forms as decorative devices, active turn of the century.

Grun, Jules-Alexandre (French, 1868-1934) — posterist.

Guimard, Hector (French, 1867-1942) — the major Parisian Art Nouveau furniture designer, using naturalistic themes; a follower of Horta, but also influenced by English architecture and naturalistic themes; as an architect made extensive use of cast iron; also a sculptor; most active in 1895-1905 period.

Gurschner, Gustav (Austrian ?) — sculptor, lighting designer, displayed with Viennese Secession group in 1898; often used 2 separate motifs: women and seashells.

Guydo, Henri (French, b. 1870) — posterist.

H

Habert-Dys, Jules Auguste (French, b. 1850) — painter, engraver, designer of glass and ceramics; his ceramics work Oriental-influenced; designer for Sevres porcelain; developed a relief-type glass often using metal trails on surface.

Habich, Ludwig (Germany, 1972-1949) — sculptor and medalist; 1900-1906, member of the Darmstadt artists' colony; from 1910, professor at Academy of Fine Arts, Stuttgart.

Hamner (pseudonym of Herman Richir, 1866-1942) — Belgian (?) posterist.

Handel, Philip (American, 1866-1914) — glass decorator and lamp designer; partnership with Adolph Eyden (Eyden & Handel), Meriden, Connecticut, 1885, as decorating firm; bought out Eyden 1893, eventually moved firm to New York City by 1900 with name changed to Handel & Company; patented his "chipped glass" technique 1904, utilizing sandblasting to produce a frosted finish; produced metalwork for his lamps as well; upon his death, widow Fanny took over; factory closed 1936, firm formally ended 1941.

Hankar, Paul (Belgian, 1859-1901) — architect, furniture designer, ironworker; influenced by English Arts and Crafts Movement and Oriental art; style tended toward the rectilinear; active 1890s.

Hazenplug, Frank (b. 1873) — posterist, active 1890s.

Hansen-Jacobsen, Niels (Danish, b. 1861) — sculptor and ceramicist, active at turn of the century.

Harvey, Agnes Bankier — metal and jewelry designer, worker in enamels; member, Glasgow School of Art; active very early 1900s.

Hoentschel, Georges (French, 1855-1915) — architect, sculptor, and ceramicist; inspired by nature and Japanese art; active at turn of the century.

Hofbauer, Arnost (Czech, 1869-1944) — posterist active in Vienna Secession, influenced by Japanese graphic arts.

Hoffman, Joseph (Austrian, 1870-1955) — architect, illustrator, designer, theoretician; placed design under strict geometric rules, denying direct connection with Nature; headed the "Viennese Secession" movement of the Jugendstil; established the Vienna Werkstatte in 1903 with Koloman Moser; a repeated characteristic was the use of the checkerboard pattern; work paralleled that of Glasgow's Mackintosh.

Hoffmann, Julius — decorative arts designer; publisher, *Dekorative Vorbilder.*

Hohenstein, Adolf (b. 1854) — posterist, did much work for Ricordi, Milan, c. 1889-1914.

Hohlwein, Ludwig (German, 1874-1949) — architect, painter, designer of furnishings, ceramics, posters, books; active at turn of the century.

von Holder, Franz (Belgian, 1822-1919) — artist and posterist whose later production was in the Art Nouveau manner.

Homar, Gaspar (Spanish) — cabinetmaker, adherent to Horta's ideas, turn of the century.

Honesdale Decorating Company — set up 1901 by glass manufacturer C. Dorflinger & Sons at Honesdale, Pennsylvania; Dorflinger supplied the firm with lead crystal blanks; after sale to Carl Francis Prosch (1864-1937), lime glass blanks were bought from such firms as Heisey and Fostoria; most common mark: "Honesdale" in gold script; after Porsch's purchase, used "P" in shield; firm ended 1932.

Horta, Victor (Belgian, 1861-1947) — architect, theoretician, designer of furniture; studied Paris and Brussels; his Hotel Tassel, Brussels, was first unified major building in the Art Nouveau mode; used exposed metal, glass and ornamentation, seeing the projects as wholes rather than assimilated pieces; common to his work was baroque form and plant motifs; furniture was naturalistic; abandoned Art Nouveau style c. 1905.

Husson, Henri (French, 1852-1914) — goldsmith, jewelry and silverware designer; active at turn of the century.

I

Ibels, Henri Gabriel (French, 1867-1936) — posterist.

J

Jacobus, Pauline (American (?), 1840-1930) — ceramist, founder of the Pauline Pottery, Chicago, Illinois; active c. 1880-1911.

Jallot, Leon (French) — furniture designer employed by S. Bing, active c. 1895-c. 1910.

Jean, Auguste (French) — potter, ceramist, glass maker; glass freeform vases often had his signature on an applied pastille, but it was also found in gilt script.

Jones, Owen (English, 1809-1874) — direct predecessor to England's Arts and Crafts and Art Nouveau movements; designer of textiles, wallpapers, etc., active in the late mid-19th century.

K

Kayser, J.P., & Sohn — German pewter firm which developed a new mixture of copper and antimony, giving their products greater brightness and durability; signed works are marked "KAYSERZINN," and were produced in the late 1800s and very early 1900s.

Kenton & Co. — English firm at Bloomsbury, active 1890-1892, formed by Ernest Gimson, Mervyn McCartney, W.R. Lethaby, and R. Blomfield, each a designer supervising the construction of their own furniture designs.

King, Jessie Marion (Scottish, 1875-1949) — illustrator, watercolorist, bookbinder, fabric and costume designer, batik artist, jewelry and wallpaper designer; educated at Glasgow Art School; gold medal winner for book cover design, Turin, 1902; married E.A. Taylor, 1908; remained active in design and arts until her death.

Klimt, Gustav (Austrian, 1862-1918) — painter, muralist, posterist; internationally famous as a portrait and landscape artist at the turn of the century; co-founder, Vienna Secession, 1897, and its first president; chief proponent of Art Nouveau painting in Vienna; seceded from the Secession in 1908 and formed a new group, "Kunstschau."

Knox, Archibald (English) — silver, pewter, and enamel designer, especially for Liberty and Company.

Koehler, Florence (American, 1861-1944) — lived and worked in Chicago; from 1900 her jewelry designs showed Art Nouveau stylings.

Koepping, Karl (German, 1848-1914) — painter, printmaker, glass designer; Japanese influence seen in his floriform use, from c. 1895; an editor of *Pan* from 1896; transferred the Japanese technique of using multi-colored glazes fused to the surfaces of earthenware to his own glass designs.

L

Lafitte, G. (French) — jewelry designer, active turn of the century.

Lalique, Rene (French, 1860-1945) — jeweler, jewelry designer, and glassmaker/designer; apprenticed to goldsmith Louis Aucoc and had his own Parisian workshop, 1885; his jewelry designs of the last two decades of the 19th century, and the very early 20th century, hailed as major Art Nouveau designs, with their asymmetrical designs taken from nature; became interested in glass about 1900; began cire-perdue casting in 1902; originally made glass perfume bottles for Francois Coty, but later made models for firms such as Forvil, Morabito, Worth, Orsay, Roger & Gallet, and Vigny; glassware particularly popular in 1920s; most of his glass was more geometrical and closer to Art Deco designs, although his uses of maidens and mermaids especially can be considered a continuation of his Art Nouveau heritage.

Lambert, Theodore (French, b. 1857) — architect, designer of furniture, jewelry and lighting fixtures; active at the turn of the century.

Laporte-Blairsy, Leo (French, 1865-1922) — sculptor, printmaker, and specialist in the design of lighting fixtures; active from the 1890s until his death.

Larche, Raoul-Francois (French, 1860-1912) — sculptor, painter, designer of lamps and table sets; many of his sculptures and other metal designs were released by Siot of Paris.

Lauger, Max (German, 1864-1952) — architect and ceramist; used simplified traditional Oriental vase forms with color and plant motifs; both studied and taught at the Kunstgewerbeschule; signed pieces "MLK."

Lebeau, Joris Johannes Christiaan (Dutch, c. 1877-1946) — printmaker, posterist, designer of glass and textiles; active early 1900s.

Legras, Auguste (French) — founder of glasshouse, St. Denis, France, 1864; took over nearby Vidie works in Pantin, 1867; rt glass production begun c. 1900 under management of Francois-Theodore Legras, who was in charge of production at both plants; among production: "Mont Joye" line, usually featuring a frosted transparent body, or pastel bodies with floral designs and gilding; usual signature on regular line was "Legras SD" or "Sargel SD"; August retired 1909, and was succeded by son Charles; the glassworks closed in 1914 due to the war, reopening in 1919; 1920: formal merger with the Pantin works, becoming "Verreries et Cristalleries de St. Denis et de Pantin Reunies"; 1920s production included acid-mottled surfaces which were then enameled to look like cameo glass.

Lelievre, Eugene (French, b. 1856) — sculptor, founder of Artistes Decorateurs; active at turn of the century.

Lemmen, Georges (Belgian, 1865-1916) — painter, graphic artist, designer of jewelry, tapestry, bookbindings, and metal fittings; in painting, was influenced by Seurat; 1894-1897; associated with van de Velde in Brussels.

Lenox China — made Trenton, New Jersey, after 1906; see Ceramic Art Company

Leveille, Ernest Michel (French) — acquired Rousseau's glass-house in 1885 and continued its Japanese-inspired traditions; also produced porcelain; still active at the turn of the century.

Lhuer, Victor (French) — painter, designer of fabrics, active at turn of the century.

Liberty, Arthur Lasenby (English, b. 1843) — founder of the firm Liberty and Company, London, in 1875, which would later spread the Art Nouveau gospel to other European nations; own lines of silver and pewter were made, as well as production in furniture, ceramics, textiles, wallpaper, etc.; many of their products were made for them by other companies.

Lienard, Paul (French, 1849-1900) — sculptor and jewelry designer.

Lobmeyr, J. & L. — glassworks stemming from one opened in Vienna in 1823 by Josef Lobmeyr, who died 1855; his son Josef took over, joined in 1859 by brother Ludwig; firm name changed to J. & L. Lobmeyr, 1860; Josef, Jr. died 1864, leaving Ludwig to head the firm until 1902; a pioneer firm in the manufacture of cameo glass and iridescent styles as well, exerting a direct influence on other major makers (including Tiffany); went on to design glassware for the Wiener Werkstatte and Vienna Secession.

Loetz (or Lotz) (or Joh. Lotz Witwe) — iridescent Art Nouveau glassware produced at the factory in Klostermuhle, Bohemia; Johann Loetz acquired the glasshouse in 1840 and died 1848; widow Susanne took over, calling firm Glasfabrik Johann Loetz Witwe; Johann's grandson, Max Ritter von Spaun, took over 1879; bankruptcy declared 1911, firm reorganized as limited company 1913; went public after World War I, closing during World War II; a major producer of iridescent glass.

Low, J. & J.G., Art Tile Works — Chelsea, Massachusetts, 1877-1902.

Lustre Art Glass Co. — founded on Long Island, New York, in 1920 by Conrad Vahlsing and Paul Franks, making shades and globes similar to that produced by Quezal (q.v.); iridescent glass.

M

Macbeth, Ann (Scottish (?), 1875-1948) — designer and maker of embroidery; trained at Glasgow and taught embroidery there from 1900.

MacDonald, Frances (Scottish, 1874-1921) — designer and teacher of enameling and metal work; married Herbert MacNair and collaborated with him after; taught at the Glasgow School from 1907; one of the Scottish "Big Four".

MacDonald, Margaret (Scottish, 1865-1933) — worker in metal, stained glass, and (later) gesso panels; married Charles Rennie Mackintosh; one of the "Big Four" at Glasgow.

Mackintosh, Charles Rennie (Scottish, 1868-1928) — architect, watercolorist, interior designer, designer of furniture and lighting fixtures; major British Isles architect of the 1880s; founder and director (with wife, Margaret MacDonald) of Glasgow Art School; furniture design generally post-1900; designs drew opposition in England, but were influential in Germany and Austria; one of the "Big Four."

Mackmurdo, Arthur Heygate (English, 1851-1942) — forerunner of the Art Nouveau movement; architect, designer, editor; co-founder of the Century Guild and active in the English Arts and Crafts Movement; from 1884, edited *The Hobby Horse* for The Century Guild, the forerunner to the Kelmscott Press and Dove Press work; gave up architecture and turned to economics about 1900.

MacNair, Herbert (Scottish, b. 1870) — architect, designer; one of the "Big Four" of Scottish Art Nouveau.

Maillol, Aristide (French, 1861-1944) — painter and tapestry designer; operated workshop for tapestries, 1893-1895; devoted self to sculpture, especially bronzes, from 1898.

Maison Cardeilhac — French silver firm, established 1804 making flatware and cutlery; Ernest Cardeilhac (1854-1904) expanded it to gold and silversmithing.

Maison Moderne, La — Paris shop specializing in Art Nouveau items, founded 1897 by German art critic Meier-Graefe.

Maison Vever — French jewelry firm established by Ernest Vever, who retired 1880; sons Paul (1851-1915) and Henri (1854-1942) took over; usually used naturalistic motifs; second only to Lalique in importance in French Art Nouveau jewelry.

Majorelle, Louis (French, 1859-1929) — best-known as furniture designer, also associated with ceramics and lamp design; raised in Nancy, educated Paris, returned to Nancy to take over father's furniture manufactory and ceramics factory; early designs show strong rococo influence; as Galle's influence upon him grew, his use of structural plant forms, dynamic lines, and feelings of movement in his furniture increased, c. 1897; a member of the Nancy school, he watched it decline after Galle's death, and his designs tended again toward the classical.

Martin, Camille (French, 1861-1898) — painter and decorative artist at Nancy.

Massier, Clement (French) — ceramist/manufacturer, Golfe-Juane, France, late 19th and early 20th centuries; characterized by iridescent and metallic lustre glazes; when signed, mark may read, "J. Massier Fils."

Mazzucotelli, Allessandro (Italian) — iron craftsman, active early 20th century.

McLaughlin, Mary Louise (American, 1847-1939) — ceramist; studied at Cincinnati School of Design, 1873-1877; organizer of Women's Pottery Club, Cincinnati, 1879.

Meheut, Mathurin (French, 1882-1958) — painter, wood engraver, book illustrator, lace and tapestry designer, ceramist, draftsman; active turn of the century, especially early 1900s.

Meier, Emil (Austrian, b. 1877) — sculptor and ceramic artist working at Vienna, active early 20th century.

Meunier, Georges (French, 1869-1939) — posterist; first poster done 1894.

Michel, Eugene (French) — born Luneville; joined F.E. Rousseau as engraver, 1867; stayed when Leveille took over; believed to have died before 1915; signatures on glass engraved in script "E. Michel."

Minne, George (Belgian, 1866-1941) — sculptor and draftsman; worked in Art Nouveau in 1890s, later returning to his classical style.

Misti (pseudonym for Ferdinand Mifliez, 1865-1923) — posterist; lived in France.

Moigniez, Jules (French (?), 1835-1894) — bronze sculptor.

Molenaar, H. (Dutch ?) — artist employed by Dutch ceramic firm of N.V. Plateelbakkerij Schoonhoven, which started production of wares similar to those of Gouda just before 1920.

Moorcroft, William (English, d. 1945) — manager of art pottery department for James MacIntyre & Co., England, 1898-1913; began Moorcroft Pottery at Burslem, 1913; production continued after his death by son Walter.

Moreau-Nelaton, Etienne (French, 1859-1927) — posterist.

Moretti, Gaetano (Italian) — designer for the firm of Ceruti, in Milan; active at time of the Turin exhibition, 1902.

Morris, William (English, 1834-1896) — painter, designer, decorator, and theoretician, also a socialist, who was the major factor behind the English Arts and Crafts Movement; also, founder of the Kelmscott Press.

Moser, Koloman (Austrian, 1868-1918) — painter, printmaker, teacher; encouraged the Austrian Arts and Crafts move through his works, books, and teaching; a founder of the Vienna Secession in 1897; co-founder, Wienere Werkstatte, with Hoffmann and Warndorfer, on handicraft shop idea.

Moser, Ludwig (Czech, 1833-1916) — founder of glasshouse at Karlsbad, Bohemia, in 1857; business incorporated (Ludwig Moser and Sohne) in 1900; Art Nouveau and other iridescent glass made up a portion of their output.

Mucha, Alphonse Maria (Czech, 1860-1939) — Moravian-born, studied in Munich, Vienna, and Paris; worked as graphic designer, book illustrator, designer of jewelry, textiles, and furniture while in Paris; major fame accompanied his entrance into poster field in 1895; later returned to Czechoslovakia where he concentrated on his great painting masterpiece, The Slav Epic.

Muller Freres — French glasshouse, at Luneville, later locating at Croismare; operated very early 1900s until 1930s.

Munch, Edvard (Norwegian, 1863-1944) — painter and printmaker; began exhibiting in Germany in 1892 and became a major influence upon German Expressionist painting; his works carried by S. Bing's L'Art Nouveau, 1896.

N

Nash, Arthur (English, 1849-1934) — English born and trained glassmaker, receiving his early glass education at (among others) Webb's; came to the United States 1893 to operate Tiffany's Corona, New York glasshouse; left Tiffany 1919 (although Tiffany glass continued being made another nine years) and established his own firm; sons A. Douglas and Leslie worked for him, Douglas later going to Libbey Glass, Toledo, as designer.

Nash, A. Douglas, Corp. — A. Douglas Nash, son of Arthur (above), managed Tiffany's Corona shop after his father left there, 1919-1928; setting up own shop, he signed early works "A.D.N.A." (A. Douglas Nash Associates); after 1929 incorporation, "Nash" signature used; works closed 1931; A.D. Nash went with Libbey Glass in Toledo until 1935, dying 1940.

Neven, G. (Dutch ?) — artist employed by Dutch ceramic firm of N.V. Plateelbakkerij Schoonhoven from c. 1920.

Newcomb Pottery — New Orleans, Louisiana concern connected with Sophie Newcomb College; the pottery founded by Ellsworth and William Woodward, 1896; work continued there through 1940s, with decoration done by female students; usual mark: N within larger C.

Nieuwenhuis, Th. (Dutch, 1866-1951) — graphic artist, ceramicist, designer, active in Dutch Art Nouveau movement; influenced by the English Arts and Crafts Movement, Japanese art, and Javanese batiks; emphasized lines using coiled snakes, peacock feathers, and other elements derived from nature; designed pottery for the De Distel earthenware factory, Amsterdam, 1895-1923.

Noritake — trade name for porcelain made in Japan after 1904 by Nippon Toki Kaisha.

Northwood, John (English, 1836-1902) — glassmaker; art director for Stevens & Williams, 1882-1902; responsible for many of the innovative glass techniques which led to S & W's glass being internationally acclaimed.

O

Obrist, Hermann (Swiss, 1863-1927) — applied art designer/craftsman, sculptor; embroidery workshop established Florence, Italy, 1892, which he moved to Munich in 1894; closely allied with the Jugendstil group, deriving motifs from nature with inventive stylizations.

Ohr, George E. (American, 1857-1918) — raised and trained in Biloxi, Mississippi, as a blacksmith, Ohr would become known as "the Mad Potter of Biloxi" for his eccentric appearance, actions, and products; trained in pottery under Joseph Meyer starting c. 1885; established own pottery Biloxi late 1880s; stayed in pottery until 1909, becoming a Cadillac dealer.

Olbrich, Joseph (Austrian, 1867-1908) — architect, illustrator, draftsman, designer; leader in the Viennese Secession, became leader of the "Darmstadt colony" of artists and craftsmen; opened school in Weimar that would gain international acclaim later as the Bauhaus; denied connections of his creations with Nature, imposing strict adherence to geometric patterns.

Orazi, Manuel (1860-1934) — worked in Paris as painter, illustrator; produced only a few posters.

P

Pairpoint — originated 1880 as silverplating firm, Pairpoint Manufacturing Co.; merged with Mt. Washington Glass Co., 1894, as Pairpoint Corporation, producing glass and metal decorative and utilitarian products.

PAL (Pseudonym of Jean de Paleologue, 1860-1942) — Rumanian-born, worked in England as illustrator under name Julius Price before settling in Paris; his Paris period, 1893-1900, was most productive in terms of posters; moved to United States 1900.

Pankok, Bernhard (German, 1872-1943) — designer and graphic artist; transposed organic form to furniture and ornaments; contributor to *Jugend;* after 1902, active in Stuttgart; see Paul, Bruno.

Parrish, Maxfield (American, 1870-1966) — painter, illustrator, graphic designer; his early works show some Art Nouveau influence.

Paul, Bruno (German, b. 1874) — painter, printmaker, educator, decorative artist; contributor to *Jugend;* founded the Vereinigte Werkstatten fur Kunst, Munich, 1897; would become director of Vereinigte Staatsschule fur freie und anglewandte Kunst, Berlin, 1924-1932.

Pean, Rene (French, b. 1875) — posterist; student of Cheret.

Penfield, Edward (American, 1866-1925) — famed posterist and artist; art director for Harper's, 1891-1901.

Perry, Mary Chase (American, 1868-1961) — founder, Pewabic Pottery, Detroit, c. 1903.

Pfaff, Hans (German (?), b. 1875) — painter, designer, magazine and book illustrator; contributor to *Jugend.*

Pickard, Wilder — founder of ceramic decorating firm, Pickard China, in 1894, the firm still active at Antioch, Illinois; all blanks from the Art Nouveau period were obtained from other companies.

Plumet, Charles (French, 1861-1928) — architect, calligrapher, furniture designer; was architect-in-chief, Paris World's Fair, 1900.

Poillon, Clara L. (American, 1850-1936) — co-founder, Poillon Pottery, Woodbridge, New Jersey, c. 1901.

Powell, James, & Sons — English glassmaking firm commissioned to produce table glass by William Morris; after 1880, was operated by Harry J. Powell, who stayed with the company until World War I.

Prevot, Edmond (French) — sculptor, active late 19th century.

Prevot, Gabriel (French) — designer of lace and embroidery; active turn of the century, especially early 20th century.

Privat-Livemont (Belgian, 1861-1935) — the outstanding Belgian posterist, did first poster in 1890; by 1900 had completed 30 posters.

Prouve, Victor Emile (French, 1858-1943) — sculptor, painter, medalist, printmaker, designer of glass, ceramics, lace, jewelry, book bindings, embroidery, marquetry; studied and worked with Galle and Majorelle; later, was director, Ecole des Beaux Arts, Nancy.

Q

Quarti, Eugenio (Italian) — furniture designer, Milan, early 20th century.

Quezal — glass made 1901-1920 by Martin Bach, Sr., with iridescence and shapes similar to that produced by Tiffany.

R

Ramsdell, Frederick Winthrop (Winthrop (English (?), 1865-1915) — posterist; studied in Paris, his art reflecting influence of Grasset.

Ranson, Paul Elie (French, c. 1863-1909) — painter, printmaker, designer of ceramics and tapestries; active 1890s and very early 1900s.

Rathbone, Richard Llewelyn Benson (English) — jewelry designer active at turn of century.

Reed, Ethel (American, b. 1876) — posterist and painter, active 1890s and very early 20th century.

Rhead, Frederick Hurthen — ceramicist employed by several American pottery firms; established Rhead Pottery, Santa Barbara, California, in business 1913-1917.

Rhead, Louis J. (English-born, 1857-1926) — posterist, artist; influenced by Grasset; moved to United States 1883.

de Ribaucourt, Georges (French, 1881-1907) — jewelry designer, sculptor, decorator.

Richard — mark found on French acid-etched cameo glass, 1920s, in Lorraine; produced bowls, lamps, night lights, vases, etc., with cameo script signature.

Ricketts, Charles (Swiss-born, 1866-1931) — painter, sculptor, printmaker, decorative designer, editor; Geneva-born, grew up in France, moved to England; founded Vale Press, 1896, illustrating most books from that firm in following years; his graphics stem from William Morris and the Pre-Raphaelites, sculpture followed Rodin, and his painting was after Delacroix; editor, *The Dial,* 1889-1897; designed jewelry and small bronzes; member, Royal Academy, 1922.

Riemerschmid, Richard (German, 1868-1957) — architect, designer of furniture and silver; designs tended toward the functional and simple; taught, Nuremburg Art School, 1902-1905.

de Riquer e Inglada, Alejandro (Spanish, 1856-1920) — leader in the Spanish Art Nouveau poster movement.

Rivaud, Charles (French, 1859-1923) — decorator and designer of metal jewelry, active 1890s and early 20th century.

Robert, Emile (French, 1860-1924) — ironwork designer, active early 1900s.

Roblin Art Pottery — established San Francisco, California, by Alexander W. Robertson and Linna Irelan; active 1896-1906.

Roche, Pierre (French, 1855-1922) — sculptor, medalist, and ceramicist; studied with Rodin and others; received silver medal, Exposition Universelle, 1900.

Rochegrosse, Georges (French, 1859-1938) — posterist.

Rookwood Pottery — established 1880 at Cincinnati, Ohio, by Maria Longworth Nichols (Storer); strong Oriental influences in many works, partially derived from 1876 Philadelphia World's Fair displays of Oriental works.

Rorstrand Faience — firm founded 1726 at Great Rorstrand, near Stockholm, Sweden; still in business; works developed Art Nouveau influences about 1900.

Rousseau, F. Eugene (French, 1827-1891) — designer working first in ceramics, then in glass; with Galle, was one of the most influential French craftsmen working in the Japanese style; one important type of glass he produced was a cased glass with designs engraved on a colorful outer layer to reveal a translucent inner layer.

Royal Bayreuth — ceramics company established 1794 at Tettau, Bavaria; after 1919 their mark usually doesn't mention Bavaria.

Royal Bonn — ceramic manufacturer, established 1755, as Bonn China Manufactory; Royal Bonn was a trade name adopted in the 19th century.

Royal Crown Derby — ceramics manufacturer in England, established in mid-19th century; sometimes referred to as Crown Derby.

Royal Dux — trade name for porcelain from Duxer Porzellanmanufaktur, established 1860 in Dux, Bohemia (now Czechoslovakia); reproductions abound!

Rozenburg (Haagsche Plateelbakkerij Rozenburg) — Dutch ceramics firm established in last quarter of 19th century, The Hague; T.A.C. Colenbrander (q.v.) was most responsible for designs in 1880s; J. Jurian Kok introduced own Art Nouveau style later; production in porcelain and earthenware until at least 1916.

S

Saint-Louis, Compagnie des Verreries et Cristalleries de — glass firm originally in France, located in Prussian-controlled territory after Franco-Prussian War, finally back in French hands; one of the signatures used on glassware was "D'Argental."

Sauvage, Henri (French, 1873-1932) — sculptor, painter, architect, furniture designer; worked at Nancy turn of the century.

Schaffer & Vater — German ceramic firm, active 1890-1918; best-remembered now for their small curiosity and whimsy Pieces.

Scharvogel, Julius Johann (German, 1854-1938) — ceramicist, influenced by Oriental ceramics; prosperous workshop at Munich; experimented with underglaze painting.

Scheidecker, Paul Frank (English-born) — painter, silver designer; worked in France, active early 1900s.

Schmuz-Baudisz, Theodor Hermann (German, 1859-1942) — painter, ceramicist; director, Staatliche Porzellan Manufactur, Berlin, 1908-1926.

Schneckendorf, Josef Emil (Austrian, b. 1865) — Romanian-born, studied at Munich, was sculptor, designer and craftsman; about 1898 manufactured glassware; from 1907, director, Grossherzoglich Hessische Edelglasmanufaktur, Darmstadt, founded by the Grand Duke of Hesse.

Schneider Glassworks — art glass maker at Epinay-sur-Seine, France, operated 1903-1930 by Charles (1881-1962) and Ernest Schneider; signatures attributed include "Charder" and "Le Verre Francais."

von Schnellenbuhel, Gertraud (German, b. 1878) — painter, designer of metals; studied painting at Munich, turned to applied art c. 1902, taking a metals course at the Debschitz school; joined workshop of Adalbert Kinzinger, silversmith, 1911.

Schoonhoven — mark used by N.V. Plateelbakkerij firm, across river from Gouda, Holland.

Seguin, Pierre (French, b. 1872) — sculptor and designer; studied and later taught at Ecole Superieure des Arts Decoratifs; active turn of the century.

Seguy, E.A. (French) — artist and designer; several design portfolios printed Paris, 1900-1931 period.

Selmersheim, Pierre (French, b. 1869) — decorator and craftsman, brother of Tony.

Selmersheim, Tony (French, b. 1871) — painter and craftsman; member of "Les Cinq," which was later known as "Les Six."

Serrurier-Bovy, Gustave (Belgian, 1858-1910) — architect, interior designer, furniture designer; influenced by Willaim Morris and Horta.

Shaw, E. & Sons — English Arts and Crafts furniture makers at Bradford.

Sherrebek — tapestry firm in Schleswig-Holstein-Jacobsen, begun by pastor who wished to revive historical local rug-making industry; among leading artists/designers there were Ockmann and Hans Thoma.

Sika, Jutta (Austrian, 1877-1964) — painter, designer in ceramics, glass, furniture; she studied with Moser and Roller at the Kungstgewerbeschule in Vienna; designed for the Bock firm, and for the Wiener Werkstatte; she helped found Wiener Kunst im Hause.

Simmance, Eliza (English, active 1873-1928) — often called Elise, she decorated and designed ceramics for Doulton, at Lambeth.

Smith, Jessie Wilcox (American, 1863-1935) — cover designer, illustrator; studied with Thomas Eakins and Howard Pyle; collaborated with friends Elizabeth Shippen Green and Violet Oakley.

Socard, Edmond (French, b. 1869) — painter of stained glass windows, active turn of the century.

Solon, Leon Victor (French, 1872-1957) — painter and posterist.

Somme, Theophile Francois (French (?)) — sculptor, active turn of the century.

Sonnier, Leon Julien Ernest (French) — painter and interior designer; decoration designer for Maxim's restaurant, Paris, with Louis Marnez.

Steinlen, Theophile Alexandre (Swiss-born, 1859-1923) — designer and graphic artist; textile designer before 1872, when he moved to Paris and concentrated on career as an illustrator and noted posterist; sometimes used pseudonyms "Petit Pierre" and "Jean Caillou."

Stratton, Mary Chase (American, 1867-1961) — founder of the Pewabic Pottery in Michigan; introduced her Losanti line in 1890s; name change after marriage to Porter.

Sturbelle, Camille Marc (Belgian, b. 1873) — sculptor, designer of vases, clocks, mirrors, etc.; active turn of the century.

Sumner, George Heywood (English, 1853-1940) — Pre-Raphaelite artist and illustrator, a major influence upon English Art Nouveau.

Szabo, A.G. (Hungarian-born) — metalworker and designer active in Paris at the turn of the century.

T

Teplitz-Turn — marking found on some ceramics, denoting a region of Bohemia noted for its art potteries, notably, the Amphora Porcelain Works and the Alexandra Works.

Testa, Carlo (Italian) — designer/craftsman, active early 20th century.

Thorn-Prikker, Johan (Dutch, 1868-1932) — painter, furniture and textile designer; his painting turned more toward Symbolism after contact with Peul Verlaine c. 1892; worked in textile design under influence of Javanese patterns c. 1898; moved to Germany c. 1904 and was friend of van de Velde; influenced development of Catholic church-related frescoes, mosaics, stained glass; in furniture, sought new forms for utilitarian pieces.

Tiffany, Louis Comfort (American, 1848-1933) — painter, designer in ceramics, textiles, metals, jewelry, lighting fixtures, and especially glass; established group known as "Associated Artists" in New York, early 1880s; Tiffany Glass Company created 1885 to market stained glass; Favrile glass (iridescent) created c. 1893; Tiffany Studios created to manufacture and market wide variety of decorative items, going bankrupt 1932; Tiffany died the following year; glass production had ended 1928; one method of dating numbered Tiffany glass which has been promoted in the past involves the use of the prefix or suffix letters (prefixes A-N indicate production 1896-1900; Prefixes P-Z indicate production 1901-1905; Suffixes A-N were for 1906-1912, while

Prefixes P-Z were for 1913-1920); this system doesn't explain the many anomalies of Tiffany glass numbering, nor does it explain glass produced in the 1920s.

Toorop, Jan (Dutch, 1858-1928) — painter and graphic artist; Java-born, studied in Amsterdam and Brussels; his mysticism was fed by his membership in the Rosicrucians, and in 1905 he converted to Roman Catholicism; posters and bookbindings occasionally reflect the mystical elements.

Toulouse-Lautrec, Henri de (French, 1864-1901) — painter, printmaker, posterist; did first posters 1891, first color lithographs 1892; illustrated the international element of Art Nouveau through visits with van ve Velde in Brussels, 1894, and with Wilde and Beardsley in London, 1895; considered a major figure in development of French Art Nouveau graphics.

Toussaint, Fernand (Belgian, 1873-1955) — painter who did a few posters.

Traquir, Phoebe (English) — jewelry maker and designer, active at the turn of the century, especially early 1900s.

Tuck, Alvin (American (?)) — designer of bronze objects attributed to him, manufactured by Tiffany Studios.

U

Union Glass Company — glass manufacturer located at Somerville, Massachusetts; established 1857 by Amory and Francis Houghton; art glass production begun c. 1893; factory ceased all production 1924; their iridescent glass, usually with an opaque or creamy translucent body, named "Kew Blas," after rearrangement of letters of factory superintendent William S. Blake's initials and last name.

Utrillo, Maurice (Spanish, 1883-1955) — posterist and painter.

V

Vallin, Eugene (French, 1856- c. 1923) — furniture designer, worked in naturalistic forms; associated with Louis Majorelle early 20th century, at Nancy.

Val-St.-Lambert — Belgian glassmaking firm established early 1800s; Art Nouveau designs appeared early 20th century, from designers such as van de Velde, Surrurier-Bovy, and Wolfers.

van de Velde, Henri (Belgian, 1863-1957) — theoretician, educator, designer of furniture, stoneware, porcelain, metal objects; published *Le Deblaiment d'Art* (The Cleansing of

Art), 1894, showing what he hoped the "new art" could accomplish; major factor in setting up the Libre Esthetique display, Brussels, 1894; headed the Weimar School for Arts and Crafts, 1906- c. 1914, the predecessor of the Bauhaus school under van de Velde's successor, Walter Gropius; among his major principles in design: linearity, unity of design, and functionality (as opposed to ornamentation); a major European design force in the Art Nouveau movement.

Van Rysselberghe, Theodore (Belgian (?), 1862-1926) — posterist and painter.

Verneuil, Maurice Pillard (French, b. 1869) — poster artist and craftsman; wrote design study on flowers and plants, from which he received many of his design inspirations; active at turn of the century.

Verre, Francais, Le — cameo glass made 1920-1933 by Scheider factory; mottled, usually decorated with floral designs.

Vever, Henri (1854-1942) — and Paul — Parisian jewelry designers; operated Maison Vever; took part in Paris Exhibitions of 1878 and 1889; international fame achieved by 1900; major jewelry designers, ranking with Lalique.

Villon, Jacques (pseudonym of Gaston Duchamp, French, b. 1875) — painter and printmaker; joined Atelier Cormon 1895, mainly concerned with illustration and lithography; a friend of Toulouse-Lautrec; turned to Cubism, 1911.

Voysey, Charles Francis Annesley (English, 1857-1941) — architect, theoretician, designer of furniture, carpets, wallpaper, household utensils; greatly influenced by Arthur Mackmurdo; major spokesman for English Arts and Crafts Movemvent; style was characterized by clean lines, simplicity, grace.

W

Wallander, Alf (Swedish (?)) — designed for Rorstrand porcelain factory, c. 1890, possibly until 20th century.

Walter, Almaric (French) — pate-de-verre glass maker and designer at Nancy; some of his glass made under contract to Daum, 1908-1914; started own firm 1919.

Walton, George (English, 1867-1939) — architect, decorative arts designer, interior designer; studied at Glasgow School of Art; active early 20th century.

Weiss, Emil Rudolf (German, b. 1875) — painter, graphic artist, designer; studied Paris and Germany; contributor to *Pan;* after 1897, active all types book design for publishers Eugen

Diederichs, die Insel, and S. Fischer; taught applied art Berlin, 1907-1933; husband of sculptor Renee Sintenis.

Weller Pottery — Zanesville, Ohio-based pottery founded by Samuel A. Weller in late 19th century; successor to both Lonhuda and Louwelsa potteries.

Wiener, Rene (French, 1856-1939) — decorator and book binder; active at turn of the century.

Willette, Adolphe Leon (French, 1857-1926) — posterist and graphic artist.

Wolfers, Philippe (Belgian, 1858-1929) — jeweler, jewelry designer, and sculptor; the family firm, Wolfers Freres, was Belgium's crown jewelers; later, he opened own shop; during 1890s used ivory extensively on naturalistically-influenced forms, receiving credit for introducing the use of Congo ivory on refined items of per-adornment; originally worked in France's typical neo-rococo style, turning to the Art Nouveau floral and insect motifs by the mid-1890s; by 1900 became more abstract and symmetrical in designs; after 1905, slowly abandoned jewelry and interior design in favor of sculpture; exhibited at Turin Exposition, 1902.

Wurttembergische Metallwarenfabrik (W.M.F.) — metalworking factory at Geislen, Southeast of Stuttgart, Germany; worked in copper, pewter, nickel, silver and plated wares; by 1900, they had 3,000 workers; Art Nouveau emphasis after 1900.

Z

Zsolnay, Vilmos (Hungarian) — founder of pottery at Pecs, Hungary, 1862; active at the turn of the century.

GLOSSARY

ACID-ETCHING — 1. on glass, a method of changing the appearance of the glass surface by exposing the surface to hydrofluoric acid, or a combination of hydrofluoric and sulphuric acids, permitting the acid to etch away a portion of the glass. This was used to produce some satin glasses, as well as in overlay glass, when the outer layer (or a portion of it) would be etched away. 2. on metal, a method of producing a surface design or pattern through the application of acid to the surface.

AURENE — Steuben Glass' name for their iridescent glass, produced 1904-1930.

BATIK — an originally Javanese cloth, decorated through dyeing, using a wax-resist method on portions of the cloth not intended to be dyed; imported into Holland and influential in some Art Nouveau work there. Batik-like designs were also incorporated into wallpapers and other textiles.

BISQUE — a form of ceramic fired only a single time to harden it; unglazed, the ceramic piece could then be painted.

BLANK — an often undecorated piece of ceramics or glass. Blanks were often shipped to decorating firms for whatever decoration was to be supplied. In ceramics, the blank might be used in decoration by amateur or professional studio painters.

BLOWN-OUT — a term applied to certain ceramics, describing a design or portion of a design in which a three-dimensional area forms part of the pattern, accomplished by press-moulding.

BRASS — a metallic alloy consisting of copper and zinc. A turn-of-the-century reference lists casting brass as containing 16 parts of copper and 8 parts of zinc.

BRONZE — a metallic alloy of copper and tin, sometimes with other metals added to vary its properties, used in casting and moulding; a turn-of-the-century reference lists its composition as 9 parts of copper plus 1 part of mixed tin and zinc.

BRITANNIA METAL — a metallic alloy of tin hardened with copper and antimony; it is similar to pewter, but it differs in having more tin, no lead, plus antimony. The resulting alloy produces a silvery-white metal which can take a very high shine. Other metals than those named may also be found in some variants of this alloy.

CABOCHON — an unfaceted, convex-cut stone; glass "jewels" with cabochon cuttings were often used in Art Nouveau jewelry, lighting and decorative pieces.

CALCITE — Steuben Glass' special name for a 2-layer glass introduced in 1910. The outer layer was Ivrene (q.v.), the inner plated layer either of blue or gold Aurene (q.v.).

CAMEO GLASS — a type of glass composed of multiple, separate layers of glass, usually of differing colors, which are cut or etched away to give depth and permit the creation of patterns and forms, also known as OVERLAY GLASS; this glass may be composed of two, three (DOUBLE OVERLAY), four (TRIPLE OVERLAY), or even more separate layers of glass. Care should be taken to differentiate between true cameo glass, in which the design portion is raised above the surrounding glass, and INTAGLIO cut glass, in which the design is below the level of surrounding glass.

CARAT — a unit of weight, used for measuring both cut and uncut diamonds, equal to .200 grams; **one** of the criteria for determining the value of diamonds. Compare with KARAT.

CHAMPLEVE — a method of enameling in which depressions are cut in metal, ground powdered glass or enamel is melted and poured in and permitted to harden and solidify, and the surface is then ground smooth (flush with the metal) and polished.

CHASED — indented, as in chased metal designs.

CLOISONNE — a method of enameling in which the frit (ground powdered glass) is melted into reservoirs formed by soldering wires to the surface of the metal.

CORALENE — an art glass made in Europe and the United States during the late 1800s, in which small colored beads of glass were fired onto the exterior of the glassware; among major recognized patterns: Coral, Seaweed, and Wheat. This, as with so many other types of glass, has been reproduced, but many of the reproductions are easy to detect; the glass beads fall off if rubbed.

CROWN DERBY — see ROYAL CROWN DERBY.

CROWN MILANO — a satin-finished glass made by the Mt. Washington Glass Company. It was often decorated with floral motifs and applied gold.

DEPOSE — a marking found on many objects of French manufacture, indicating that the design for the object in question had been registered (similar to a design patent).

DORE FINISH — gold appearance over bronze.

EMBOSSING — surface designs in which patterns are moulded above the level of the surface of surrounding glass/ceramics/metal, leaving the design higher than the remainder of the piece. The opposite process from INTAGLIO.

EMERALD CUT — a cutting for gemstones using faceted cuts in square or rectangular shapes.

ENGRAVING — the cutting of lines into a hard substance, such as metal or glass.

ETCHING — a method of producing surface decoration by controlled application of acid; see ACID-ETCHING.

EWER — a handled pitcher having a wide spout.

FAIENCE — an earthenware glazed with an opaque tin glaze.

FAVRILE — trade name for Louis Comfort Tiffany's iridescent glass, usually found in blue or gold, either decorated or undecorated; in production from the 1890s until the late 1920s.

FILIGREE — a fine metalwork, delicate and ornate, characterized by extensive openwork or the appearance of such.

FINIAL — in lamps, the terminal part, such as the screw atop the lamp, which may be simple or ornately figural.

FIRE POLISHING — in glass, the re-exposure of a moulded object to the heat of the furnace to smooth out irregularities, performed immediately after moulding and done very briefly to avoid destroying the moulded pattern.

FOUNDRY — an establishment in which metals are melted and subsequently poured into moulds (casting), as in the establishments which manufactured cast figures.

GILDING — the application of gold or simulated gold to the surface of an object.

GROUND — especially in ceramics, glass, and graphics (or any field utilizing multiple coloration), the color of the basic background.

GROUP — in figures (such as bronze figures), two or more persons, animals, birds, or some combination of these depicted together upon a single base.

INCISED DECORATION — one which is carved into the surface of a piece.

INTAGLIO — a carving in a hard object to produce a design below the surface; used in the decoration of ceramics, glass, metals, gems; also used in some printing processes.

IVRENE — Steuben Glass' pearly iridescent opaque white glass.

JUGENDSTIL — the German version of Art Nouveau, as popularized by the German arts publication, *Jugend.* Although other magazines in Germany (such as *Dekorative Vorbilder*] also showcased Art Nouveau, the term "Jugendstil" caught on with the public.

KEW BLAS — an Art Nouveau-styled glass made by the Union Glass Company, Somerville, Massachusetts, from the 1890s until 1924; it was primarily opalescent.

LINEN BACKING — term used when speaking of posters which have been attached to a fabric, giving the poster added strength and resistance to wear and tear.

LITHOGRAPH — an image created by the process of lithography, an indirect printing method in which the non-image areas are treated with a resistant medium (oil) before the printing ink is applied to a plate, from which the image is printed. More properly, the color lithographs which abounded late in the 19th and early in the 20th centuries (including those in the Art Nouveau styles) were examples of CHROMOLITHOGRAPHY, lithographic printing in multiple colors.

LUSTER or LUSTRE — ceramics decorated by the addition of metallic compounds to the glaze which, after firing in a kiln, create an iridescent metallic film on the surface of the object.

MARQUETRY — the fitting together of small pieces of vari-colored veneers or other substances (horn, gold or other metals, ivory) into patterns depicting such objects as birds, animals, trees, etc., for use in decorating furniture.

MUSEUM MOUNTING — in posters, the placement of the paper poster sheet or sheets against a firm plastic mount for display purposes.

NATURALISM — a term denoting the accurate representation of individual objects without necessarily taking into consideration the lighting or the objects' relations to other objects. This is different from REALISM (q.v.).

ORMULU — 1. brass made to look like gold; 2. ground gold leaf used as gilt pigment.

PARCEL-GILT — term applied to metal objects (such as bronze figures or other decorative items) which are only partially covered with gilding.

PATE DE VERRE — literally, "paste of glass," in which ground powdered glass is moistened and pressed into shape in molds, then fired in kilns; the process is attributed to Henry Cros, who rediscovered the technique c. 1884. Once a molded piece is fired in the kiln, it can be carved and sculpted.

PATE SUR PATE — literally, "paste on paste," a pottery type made by placing layer upon layer of tin pottery paste to form a design.

PATINA — 1. a rather indefineable luster that accompanies daily use and the passage of time upon objects of wood and metal, caused by minute surface scratches and chemical changes such as oxidation; the process is often hastened by burial of the object, exposure to elements, normal weathering, etc. 2. an artificial process of "pickling" the surface of bronze to give it an old appearance, producing any of several colors; referred to as "patination."

PEWTER — one of several alloys containing tin as the main compenent; earlier forms often used lead as a major ingredient. Other metals present may include copper, bismuth, and antimony. In general, pewter with a higher tin content will have more of a silvery appearance than a dull, greyish finish.

PLATING — the process of bonding a metal (such as silver, bronze, or gold) to a metal of lesser value. Beginning in the 19th century this was accomplished using electricity (ELECTROPLATING), permitting the middle classes to enjoy having items with an appearance which previously only the upper classes could afford. In silverplating, notes author Marc Hudgeons, the average piece has only about two per cent by weight of silver.

PLINTH — a squared block usually serving as a base, as the plinth of a bronze figure. The composition may differ from the rest of the object.

PLIQUE-A-JOUR — a translucent enameling contained within wire metal frames without backings, resembling leaded stained glass.

PRECIOUS METAL — a term referring to three main metals: gold, silver, and platinum. All other metals are considered BASE METALS.

PRUNT — a button of glass with an impressed design.

QUATREFOIL — a conventional four-petal flower form.

REALISM — art depicting often commonplace subjects within their environments. Compare with NATURALISM (q.v.).

REPOUSSE — shaped or decorated with relief patterns made by hammering or pressing from the reverse side, used of metal items.

RESERVE — in auctions, a private, secret price agreed to by the consignor and auctioneer; should the bidding not reach the reserve price, the item returns to the consignor.

REVERSE PAINTING — a method of glass decoration in which the design is painted on the interior surface (as in lamps) so it will appear correctly to the viewer.

SCRAFFITO — technique of ceramics decoration in which the body of the vessel is covered with liquid clay (slip) and the decoration scratched through it to reveal the clay beneath.

SEZESSION — a group of artists, craftspeople, and designers at various places who seceded from academic styles of the day, identifying themselves variously with Impressionist painting or Art Nouveau design. Among the most important movements: that of Munich, 1892; Vienna, 1897; Berlin, 1899. The various Sezession styles in turn became increasingly academic, prompting further secessions from them and in reaction to them.

SIGNATURE — a means of identifying and attributing a work of art or design by some mark on the object. Some signatures were actual holographic signatures or reproductions of such; others might be etched in block or other lettering, or molded into the piece. A peculiar decorative device during the Art Nouveau periods was the incorporation of a signature into the design of the piece, seen especially in the glass and furniture of Galle. One maker or company might have many — even dozens — of different signatures.

SILVER DEPOSIT — in glass, a decoration upon the surface of glass accomplished by depositing a layer of metallic silver on the surface in an often floral design.

SLAG GLASS — a marbled glass produced in America and England, often used for small decorative objects and in some lamp shades, especially the paneled shades from firms such as Bradley & Hubbard. American versions were often tan or brownish, streaked with cream or white; other styles might include purple, red, blue or other colors.

SOCLE — a projecting piece at the foot of a figure.

STERLING SILVER — an assured standard of silver, being 92.5 percent pure, or fine; usually expressed as 925/1000 fine, or .925. Copper is the metal usually added to give the silver extra hardness and durability.

SYMBOLIST MOVEMENT — an interesting example in which a French literary movement gave its name to associated painters and designers. The adherents to this movement believed that all art should reflect deep meanings through the use of symbols having significance other than what they appeared to have. The movement was influential in the lives of many French designers.

TAZZA — a shallow cup, plate, or vase on a raised pedestal, often used as a centerpiece; may be made of ceramic, glass, or metal.

TERME — a bust on an elongated vertical self-stand.

TILE — a generally flat individual block of clay, thin in proportion to its length and width. The term is usually reserved for a single piece of relatively small size, the maximum generally thought of as 12" x 6"; larger single pieces are referred to as PLAQUES. A group of such tiles placed together to form a design or picture is called a PANEL.

TRIPTYCH — a folding tableau made up of three sections, depicting a religious or religiously-referential symbolic painting or other art form, often used as an altar piece.

UNDERPLATE — a plate meant to be used under another piece, such as the underplate beneath a sherbet.

VERMEIL — a type of gold-plating.

VERRE-DE-SOIE — silky iridescent glass pieces created by spraying a crystal piece with stannous chloride solution, making the piece translucent. The process was used by Steuben Glass as well as by other companies.

WHITE GOLD — gold alloyed with nickel, palladium, or a combination of the two to produce a silvery apearance; usually used in jewelry.

WHITE METAL — an inexpensive alloy which may contain tin, lead, copper, bismuth, antimony; the color depends upon the degree of tin or lead. That containing higher amounts of tin is whiter in color. Often used as a base for plating.

BIBLIOGRAPHY

To attempt to amass a collection of books on Art Nouveau is to attempt to build a small library. The diverse subject matter, the specialized books which may have a chapter or a few paragraphs devoted to the period, the rapidly-growing onslaught of books dealing specifically with the subject, the original primary source material which has been reprinted — all go to make up the well-rounded library.

This is not a guide to building such a library. Instead, it is an idea of the works consulted in the preparation of this book. As such, it does not include some of the "standard" works on the Art Nouveau designs. Included are both the esoteric and the commonplace.

Don't overlook or bypass magazine and trade paper articles about the Art Nouveau stylings. Some of the best, most concise writings on the subject have been published in the pages of periodicals. Obtaining copies of some of them may prove a bit of a problem, however.

Arwas, Victor. *Belle Epoque Posters & Graphics.* New York: Rizzoli, 1978.

— *The Liberty Style.* New York: Rizzoli, 1979.

Austwick J., and Austwick, B. *The Decorated Tile.* New York: Scribners, 1981. (See especially Chapter Six.)

Baker, Lillian. "Art Nouveau and Art Deco Jewelry," in *The Antique Trader Weekly,* January 21, 1981; pp. 66-69.

— "Hatpin Vanities," in *The Antiques Journal,* January, 1979, p. 64.

Bennett-Lynch, Bobbie. "Art Nouveau Leaders Staged Revolt in Lamp Design," in *Southern Antiques,* May 1978, pp. 8-9.

Bishop, Robert, and Coblentz, Patricia. *The World of Antiques, Art and Architecture in Victorian America.* New York: Dutton, 1979.

Bount, Henry, and Blount, Berniece. *French Cameo Glass.* Des Moines, IA: Wallace-Homestead, 1968. (Highly recommended!)

Bowers, Q. David, and Martin, Mary L. *The Postcards of Alphonse Mucha.* no place (Glen Burnie, MD): private, 1980.

Bracegirdle, Cyril. "The Bronze Busts of Barye," in *Spinning Wheel,* September/October, 1981, pp. 53-55.

Joan Campbell. *The German Werkbund: The Politics of Reform in the Applied Arts.* Princeton, New Jersey: Princeton University Press, 1978.

Callen, Anthea. *Women Artists of the Arts and Crafts Movement 1870-1914.* New York; Pantheon, 1979.

Carlisle, Dwight, W. "Unveiling An Allegory," in *Spinning Wheel,* July, 1955, pp. 14-15.

Clark, Garth, and Hughto, Margie. *A Century of Ceramics in the United States, 1878-1978.* New York: Dutton, 1979.

Cox, Claude V. *Ludwig Moser, 1833-1916, "Royal Glass Artisan."* Decatur, IL: Coxes Collectibles, 1978.

Cummins, Virginia Raymond. *Rookwood Pottery Potpourri.* Silver Spring, MD: Nothing New, 1980.

Davis, Frank. *Antique Glass and Glass Collecting.* London: Hamlyn, 1973.

Dreppard, Carl W. *ABC's of Old Glass.* New York: Award Books, 1970.

Duncan, Alastair. *Art Nouveau Sculpture.* New York: Rizzoli, 1978. (Recommended)

Fitzpatrick, Paul J. "The Cincinnati Pottery Club," in *The Antiques Journal,* September, 1981, pp. 20-23, 43.

Grafton, Carol Belanger, editor. *Treasury of Art Nouveau Design & Ornament.* New York: Dover, 1980.

Grover, Ray, and Grover, Lee. *Art Glass Nouveau.* Rutland, VT: Charles E. Tuttle Co., 1967. (Recommended for its broad scope and coverage of the period's glass.)

— *Carved & Decorated European Art Glass.* Rutland, VT: Charles E. Tuttle Co., 1967. (Recommended)

Howard, Susan B. "Chelsea and Dedham Pottery," in *Spinning Wheel,* July, 1955, pp. 24-25.

Huxford, Sharon, and Huxford, Bob. *The Collectors Catalogue of Brush-McCoy Pottery.* Paducah, KY: Collector Books, 1978.

— *The Collectors Encyclopedia of Roseville Pottery,* Paducah, KY: Collector Books, 1976.

— *The Collectors Encyclopedia of Roseville Pottery, Second Series.* Paducah, KY: Collector Books, 1980.

— *The Collectors Encyclopedia of Weller Pottery.* Paducah, KY: Collector Books, 1979.

Jones, Vere. "The Fascinating World of Martinware," in *The Antiques Journal,* June, 1979, pp. 19-21.

Joseph, J. Jonathan. "The Art Glass of Louis Comfort Tiffany," in *Spinning Wheel,* January-February, 1966, pp. 8-10, 32.

Klamkin, Marian. *The Collector's Book of Art Nouveau.* New York: Dodd, Mead, 1971.

Lathan, Ian. *Olbrich.* New York: Rizzoli, 1980.

Leigh, James T. "Lalique: A Versatile Artist," in *Southern Antiques,* December, 1980, pp. 3, 8-9.

— "Sculptors Fell Victim To the Assembly Line," in *Southern Antiques*, January, 1981, pp. 1, 6-7.

— "Moorcroft Bridged Gap in Changing Pottery World," in *Southern Antiques*, May, 1979, pp. 1, 10-11.

— "European Pottery Rediscovered," in *Southern Antiques*, June, 1980, pp. 1, 12-13.

— "Steuben, a Hallmark in American Glass," in *Southern Antiques*, October, 1977, pp. 1, 10-11.

Lipson, Karen. "Art Nouveau," in *Diversion*, August, 1981, pp. 36-37, 77. (only about glass of the style)

McKean, Hugh F. *The "Lost" Treasures of Louis Comfort Tiffany*. Garden City, NY: Doubleday, 1980. (Recommended)

Madsen, Stephen Tscudi. (trans. Ragnar Christopherson). *Sources of Art Nouveau*. New York: Da Capo, 1975. (Highly recommended for students of the field!)

Manley, C.C. "English Glass for the Collector," in *The Antiques Journal*, April, 1979, pp. 28-31, 53.

Meyer, Florence E. *The Colorful World of Nippon*. Des Moines, IA: Wallace-Homestead, 1971.

Moody, C.W. *Gouda Ceramics: The Art Nouveau Era in Holland*. no place: private (?), 1970.

Mourey, Gabriel; Vallance, Aymer; et al. *Art Nouveau Jewelry & Fans*. New York: Dover, 1973. (Originally published in 1973 under the title, *Modern Design in Jewellery and Fans: by the Artist Craftsmen of Paris, London, Vienna, Berlin, Brussels, Etc.*]

Naeve, Milo M. *Identifying American Furniture*. Nashville, TN: American Assn. for State and Local History, 1981.

Ormond, Suzanne, and Irvine, Mary E. *Louisiana's Art Nouveau: The Crafts of the Newcomb Style*. Gretna, LA: Pelican, 1976.

Pear, Lillian Myers. *The Pewabic Pottery: A History of Its Products and Its People*. Des Moines, IA: Wallace-Homestead, 1976.

Pevsner, Nikolas. *Pioneers of Modern Design*. London: Penguin, 1960. (Chapter 4, "Art Nouveau," is recommended as a somewhat antagonistic European view of the movement; Pevsner sees design in the late 1800s at a fork in the road, one way leading to the Modernistic movement, the other "into the blind alley of Art Nouveau" (p. 89))

Revi, Albert Christian. *American Art Nouveau Glass*. Camden, NJ: Nelson, 1968.

— *Nineteenth Century Glass: Its Genesis and Development*. Revised Edition. New York: Galahad Books, 1967.

— "William T. Gillinder's American Cameo Glass," in *Spinning Wheel*, September, 1964, p. 11.

Rainwater, Dorothy T. *Encyclopedia of American Silver Manufacturers*. New York: Crown, 1975. (recommended)

Rheims, Maurice. *19th Century Sculpture*. New York: Harry N. Abrams, 1977. (See especially Chapter 7, "Pre-Raphaelites; Art Nouveau")

Schlegelmilch, Clifford J. *Handbook of Erdmann and Reinhold Schlegelmilch Prussia – Germany and Oscar Schlegelmilch Germany Porcelain Marks*, Third Edition. Flint, MI: private, 1973.

Schmutzler, Robert. *Art Nouveau*. New York: Harry N. Abrams, 1978. (highly recommended!)

Selz, Peter, and Constantine, Mildred. *Art Nouveau: Art and Design at the Turn of the Century*, Revised Edition. New York: The Museum of Modern Art, 1975. (highly recommended!)

Traub, Jules S. *The Glass of Desire Christian*. Chicago: The Art Glass Exchange, 1978. (Traub's well-reasoned argument, that Christian, working at Burgun, Schverer & Co., was actually responsible for much of the early "signed" Galle glass, is worth reading, whether one agrees or disagrees.)

Webber, Norman W. *Collecting Glass*. New York: Arco, 1972. (See especially Chapter VIII)

Wittlich, Petr. *Art Nouveau Drawings*. London: Octopus, 1974.

no author. *The Biloxi Art Pottery of George Ohr*. Exhibition catalog, Mississippi State Historical Museum (Jackson), April 21-May 21, 1978.

no author. *Highlights of Pewabic Pottery*. Ann Arbor, MI: Ars Ceramica, Ltd., 1977 (adapted from Fred Bleicher, William C. Hu, & Marjorie E. Uren, *Pewabic Pottery: An Official History*, also published 1977)

AUCTION CATALOGS

Some of the most interesting, informative, and colorful reading in the world of antiques literature can be found in the pages of auction catalogs. Some of the major houses, which hold specialized Art Nouveau (or Art Nouveau and Art Deco) auctions, offer a combination of scholarship and intensive descriptions for the items in their attractive catalogs.

The general auction catalogs from most major houses include Art Nouveau items, too. Depending upon the number of lots and the general focus of the particular auction, one may find only a few Art Nouveau pieces or a few dozen.

So it's the specialized catalogs which provide the best look at the Art Nouveau field. Time and again I turned to two catalogs in particular; neither, though, was limited to the Art Nouveau styles, although both were heavily salted with Art Nouveau designs. Both were products of Phillips New York, and each had a wholly satisfactory text written by Jack Rennert.

The World of Posters was the catalog for Phillips' auction #326, held November 15, 1980; the catalog is now generally known as *"Phillips III"* and remains a useful reference work. Of the 617 lots of posters contained, more than one-third of them are in the Art Nouveau styles.

Easily the most attractive auction catalog one could hope for is *100 Poster Masterpieces*, the catalog for Phillips' auction #373, held May 2, 1981. Each lot is reproduced on a page of its own, faced with descriptive text about the artist, the subject, or the particular poster. Almost half the posters contained — and they are beauties, each in full color! — are in Art Nouveau styles.

Other fine specialized catalogs, from Sotheby Parke Bernet, Christie's, and Phillips were also consulted. Such catalogs are good references for the collector who wants to get serious about his/her collection. You just may find something or other in them you wish to bid on, and if you get the catalogs before the auctions, bid you may! Just don't forget that at each major auction house in this country there is now a 10% buyer's premium tacked on to the "hammer" price.

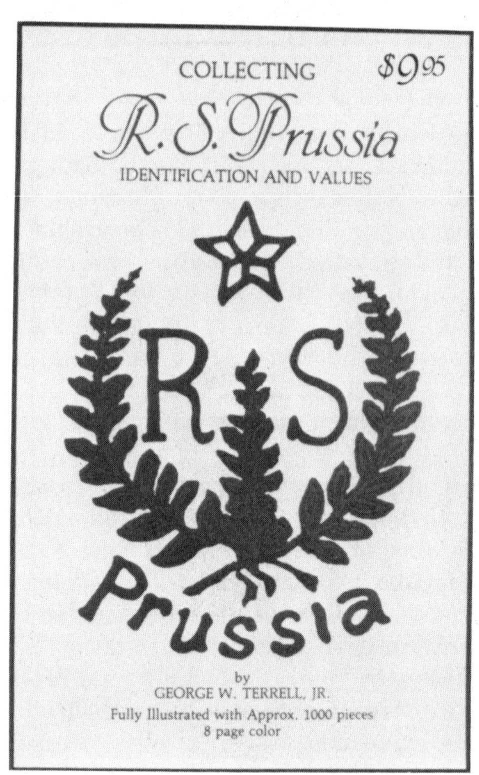

IDENTIFICATION AND VALUES

COLLECTING R.S. PRUSSIA

by George W. Terrell, Jr.

The author, a collector himself, has called on numerous experts, nationwide, to help in compiling this most comprehensive, illustrated value guide for the collectors of R.S. PRUSSIA. Approximately 1200 pieces shown in black & white plus approx. 100 pieces in full color. Introductory information includes: brief history of manufacturer, how to detect forgeries, definition of molds, identification of marks (including rare marks, "GERMANY", "VIENNA" etc.) plus much more information needed by both the novice & expert collector. Each piece is identified: "Ex: Chocolate Pot, 10½", nut mold, Assorted flowers, Green shading, Red Mark, plus value.
A Glossary is included.

240 pages, including 12 pages in color, 5¼ x 8¼, $9.95
ISBN 0-89689-027-9

Other Identification & Value Guides

from

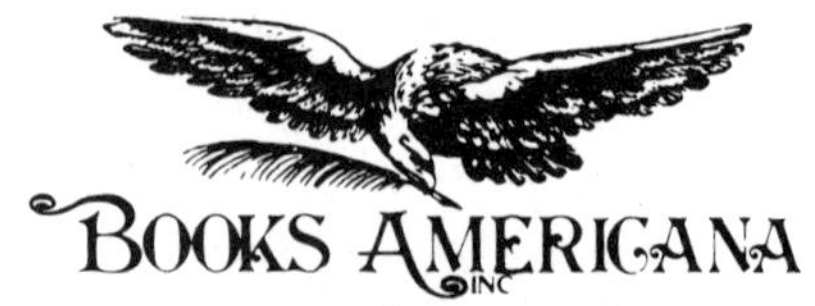